11th International Conference on Axiomatic Design (ICAD 2017)

MATEC Web of Conferences Volume 127 (2017)

Iasi, Romania
13 - 15 September 2017

Editor:

Laurentiu Slatineanu

ISBN: 978-1-5108-4970-9

Printed from e-media with permission by:

Curran Associates, Inc.
57 Morehouse Lane
Red Hook, NY 12571

Some format issues inherent in the e-media version may also appear in this print version.

Printed by Curran Associates, Inc. (2017)

For additional information, please contact EDP Sciences – Web of Conferences at the address below.

EDP Sciences – Web of Conferences
17, Avenue du Hoggar
Parc d'Activité de Courtabœuf
BP 112
F-91944 Les Ulis Cedex A
France

Phone: +33 (0) 1 69 18 75 75
Fax: +33 (0) 1 69 28 84 91

contact-edps@webofconferences.org

Additional copies of this publication are available from:

Curran Associates, Inc.
57 Morehouse Lane
Red Hook, NY 12571 USA
Phone: 845-758-0400
Fax: 845-758-2633
Email: curran@proceedings.com
Web: www.proceedings.com

TABLE OF CONTENTS

The 11th International Conference on Axiomatic Design

September13-15, 2017

Iaşi, România

Honorary Chair

Nam P. **Suh**, MIT, USA

Conference Chair

Laurenţiu **Slătineanu**, TU of Iaşi, România

Conference Co-chair

Petru **Duşa**, TU of Iaşi, România

Local Organising Committee

Antonio M. **Gonçalves-Coelho**, *FCT/Universidade Nova de Lisboa, Portugal*

Cătălin **Dumitraş**, *TU of Iaşi, România*

Christopher A. **Brown**, *Worcester Polytechnic Institute – USA*

Eugen **Axinte**, *TU of Iaşi, România*

Felicia **Banciu**, *Politechnic U of Timişoara, România*

Gheorghe **Nagîţ**, *TU of Iaşi, România*

Laurenţiu **Slătineanu**, *TU of Iaşi, România*

Margareta **Coteaţă**, *TU of Iaşi, România*

Mary Kathryn **Thompson**, *Danmarks Tekniske Universitet, Denmark*

Miguel **Cavique Santos**, *Escola Naval, Portugal*

Nicolae **Seghedin**, *TU of Iaşi, România*

Oana **Dodun**, *TU of Iaşi, România*

Petru **Duşa**, *TU of Iaşi, România*

Vasile **Merticaru,** *TU of Iaşi, România*

Junior Members: Andrei **Mihalache**, Marius **Rîpanu**, Mihai **Boca** *TU of Iaşi, România*

The International Advisory Committee

KEYNOTES:

Prof. Masayuki NAKAO, University of Tokyo, Japan
"Applying Axiomatic Design to Engineer's Job Search Defining DP of abduction skills for FR of new product development"

Masayuki Nakao received bachelor and master degrees from the University of Tokyo in 1981 and 1983. He entered the Hitachi Metals Co. Ltd. as a researcher of magnetic recording, and worked HMT Technology Corp. its subsidiary company in California, as a production manager of hard disk from 1989 to 1992. In 1991, he took the doctor degree of the University of Tokyo on tribology between magnetic heal and disk. In 1992, he returned to the University of Tokyo as an associate professor, and has been a professor of Dept. of Engineering Synthesis from 2001 to the present. He is making researches on production technologies: precise/micro/nano manufacturing, instruments design for nano/bio/medical sciences and conventional technologies of molding, pressing, cutting and so on. Especially, He likes teaching and publishing on creative design and lessons from failure. He is a vice-chairperson of the NPO, Association for the Study of Failure.

Prof. Inas KHAYAL, Dartmouth College, USA
"Assessing, Designing and Analyzing Healthcare Systems"

Dr. Inas Khayal is an Assistant Professor at the Dartmouth Institute of Health Policy & Clinical Practice at the Geisel School of Medicine and Adjunct Assistant Professor at the Department of Computer Science at Dartmouth College. She earned her PhD in Bioengineering from both the University of California, Berkeley and San Francisco. Dr. Khayal is a highly interdisciplinary translational researcher focused on improving chronic disease health outcomes. Her work began in biomedical research using technology within the clinic. It expanded to Internet-of-Things enabled social and environmental sensing outside the clinic and within 'real-world' living labs. She currently addresses the reality of the multi-level interconnected systems we live in. Her work acts at the intersection of engineering, medicine and innovation seeking to develop systems solutions that curb the growth of chronic disease. She was awarded as a 2017: Systems Science Scholar by AcademyHealth and Robert Wood Johnson Foundation New Connections Scholar.

Prof. Christopher A. BROWN, Worcester Polytechnic Institute, USA
"Axiomatic Design of Athletic Equipment for Reducing Injuries without Limiting Performance - case studies in new product development"

In 1983 Brown earned his PhD at the University of Vermont where he learned about Axiomatic Design from Nam Suh. He then spent four years as a scientific collaborator in the Materials Department at the Swiss Federal Institute of Technology. For two years he was a senior research engineer designing product and processes at Atlas Copco's European research center.
Since the fall of 1989 Chris has been on the faculty at WPI. Chris has published over a hundred articles on axiomatic design, sports engineering, manufacturing processes, and surface metrology. He has patents on characterizing surface roughness, devices for friction testing, and on sports equipment for reducing injuries. He teaches grad courses on axiomatic design of manufacturing processes, and on surface metrology, and an undergraduate course on the technology of alpine skiing. He also consults, and teaches courses, for industry on axiomatic design and on surface metrology.

Rajesh JUGULUM, CIGNA, USA
"Use of Decomposition Principles in Data Management"

Rajesh Jugulum, Ph.D., is the Director of global data strategies at Cigna. Prior to joining Cigna, he held executive positions in these areas at Citi Group and Bank of America. Rajesh completed his Ph.D. under the guidance of Dr. Genichi Taguchi. Before joining financial industry, Rajesh was with Massachusetts Institute of Technology, where he was involved in research and teaching. He taught Axiomatic design course with Prof. Nam Suh at MIT. Currently, he also teaches at Northeastern University, Boston. Rajesh is the author/co-author of several papers and four books including books on data quality and design for lean six sigma. He is also working on another book that focuses on combining data and process disciplines. Rajesh is an ASQ fellow and his other honors include American Society for Quality's Feigenbaum medal and International Technology Institute's Rockwell medal.

Tutorial Session 1

Prof. Christopher A. Brown, PhD, FASME
Director, Surface Metrology Laboratory
Mechanical Engineering Department
Worcester Polytechnic Institute
100 Institute Rd., 235 Washburn Bldg.
Worcester, MA 01609-2280
Phone: 508 831-5627 cell: 508 560-6986
brown@wpi.edu
https://www.wpi.edu/people/faculty/brown

An Introduction to Axiomatic Design

The fundamental principles of Axiomatic Design (AD) and its application are reviewed. The main goals are to help attendees to begin using axiomatic design and perhaps better appreciate many aspects of the conference. Insights and perspectives of over 30 years of teaching and practice will be included.

Nam Suh at MIT started AD in the late 1970s. The underlying supposition is that all good designs comply with just two axioms: 1) they maintain the independence of the functional elements and 2) they minimize the information content.

AD can help with innovation, add value, and reduce cost in the design process and in the design solution, as well as in its use. In the tutorial emphasis will be placed on techniques for decomposing design problems so that the axioms can be applied systematically, with corresponding functional and physical domain hierarchies. The use of metrics will also be covered.

This tutorial is intended design engineers and engineering students, who might have never used AD, or who would like to see my perspective on using and teaching it for over 25 years.

Please read professor's Christopher Brown short biography in the keynote section.

Tutorial Session 2

Prof. Joseph Timothy Foley, PhD
School of Science and Engineering,
Reykjavik University, Iceland
Venus 3, +354-599-6569
foley@ru.is
http://www.ru.is/starfsfolk/foley

Axiomatic Design for Everyone!

Axiomatic Design~(AD) was originally conceived for and continues to focus on highly technical subjects, particularly the design of mechanical systems. Recent publications have explored deploying AD in new disciplines, implying its universality. This tutorial begins with examining the philosophy of AD to understand how it can be generalized for deployment in new fields. We continue our exploration of the worlds of creatives, hackers, and troublemakers to see what design issues they need addressed. Through their eyes, we gain a deeper understanding of how the core of Axiomatic Design can be applied by anyone!

Dr. Joseph Timothy Foley (MIT BSc '99, MEng, '99, PhD '07) has worked as a researcher and designer in a large variety of fields with a heavy emphasis on infrastructure and mechatronics. His graduate research at MIT focused on integrating RFID into smart devices in a scalable and secure way. He worked as a postgraduate researcher in the Environmentally Benign Manufacturing group at MIT in partnership with SKF, investigating methods of reducing the impact and energy usage of manufacturing processes. At iRobot's Government and Industrial division, he developed shape-changing robots as the technical lead for the Harvard-MIT-iRobot DARPA ChemBots team. This research resulted in a US patent on the manufacture of enhanced Shape Memory Alloy springs, a topic he still is researching.

He is now an assistant professor at Reykjavik University and teaches topics in mechatronics and mechanical design. He has integrated Axiomatic Design into the courses he currently teaches to provide students with a common framework for the heavily multi-disciplinary nature of modern computer-controlled manufacturing and smart devices.

His research interests include aircraft maintenance automation, product design, embedded smart devices, wireless communication, physical security, and engineering-artist collaborations. His most recent developments in Axiomatic Design research include Creative Axiomatic Design (CIRP DC 2016), Desirable Complexity (ICAD 2017), and Axiomatic Design as an Ontology (CIRP DC 2017).

Tutorial Session 3

Prof. Miguel Cavique, PhD
Sciences and Technology Department
Escola Naval, Base Naval de Lisboa
Alfeite, 2810-001 Almada, Portugal
Phone: +351 210 902 094 cell: +351 964 025 006
cavique.santos@marinha.pt

Redundant Design

Redundant designs belong to a special kind of designs, in which the number of design parameters is larger than the number of functional requirements. Such designs can also be uncoupled, decoupled or coupled, and this tutorial presents seven theorems that help identifying and generating good redundant designs. Different forms of redundancy are considered, specifically the functionality-related alternative and augmentative kinds.

Miguel Cavique is Professor at the Naval Academy in Naval Engineering, field of Mechanics. He received the diplomat Engineer from the IST (now part of the Lisbon University) in 1983, the Master from the IST in 1991 and the PhD from the New University of Lisbon in 2011.
During his lifelong, he always maintained a parallel academic career and industrial jobs or activities. In the 80s, he worked at the gas network of Lisbon, a department of the Electricity of Portugal (EDP), running the department of network design. Thus, changed to IBM as system engineering where he gave support to bank customers on relational databases. In a similar period, was Assistant at the Faculty of Sciences of Lisbon and Auxiliary Professor at the Lusiada University until 1996 in the fields of Mathematics and Statistics. In the Polytechnic of Setubal (1991-2015), he dedicated his work to the areas of gas networks and air conditioning, making consultancy on air conditioning design and energy auditing of buildings. Moreover, he owned and industrial enterprise and further a commercial one on air conditioning systems, which maintains until now. Is specialist on air conditioning by the chartered association of engineers in Portugal, life member of the commission of the air conditioning specialization of the same association, and President (2016-17) of the Portugal Chapter of ASHRAE (American Society of Heating, Refrigeration and Air-Conditioning Engineers). Prof. Miguel Cavique devoted the last ten years to the development and application of Axiomatic Design (AD), in particular in what concerns to the design of air conditioning systems, and most recently to the application of AD to the naval industry.

Poster Session

1. ***Vlad Cazacu***: Application of Axiomatic Design Principles in the Case of a Device for Automated Testing of Phones and Tablets Touchscreen.

2. ***Madalina Popa***: Deposition Technology of Thin and Hard Films on Cutting Tools

3. ***Marius Boca***: Axiomatic Design used in Developing a CNC Micro Machine Tool

4. ***Marian Maniga, Costel Amariucai***: Hydrogen Generator

5. ***Adriana Stratan, Ana Ciumeica***: Equipment for Abrasive Jet Cutting

6. ***Sergiu Olaru, Alina Olaru***: Approach of Die Conception by Axiomatic Design \

7. ***Ionut Madalin Pista***: Axiomatic Design Process in Developing a Technological Device for Automated Assembly

8. ***Florina Cadar, Alexandru Enachi***: Equipment for Roto-molding

9. ***Bogdan Pralea***: Study of an Algorithm regarding Production Scheduling for Injection Mould Manufacturing"

10. ***Vasile Ermolai, Alexandru Pohonțu***: Automated Naval Photo-Electricity Collector

11. ***Gheorghe Bosoancă***: Device for Wire Electrical Discharge Machining

12. ***Cosmin Ionuț Iluc***: Street Art

13. ***Mihaela Ețcu***: Device for Studying the Effect of Singular Electrical Pulses

edp sciences

MATEC Web of Conferences

Statement of Peer review

In submitting conference proceedings to MATEC Web of Conferences, I certify to the Publisher that I adhere to the **Policy on Publishing Integrity** of the journal in order to safeguard good scientific practice in publishing.

1. All articles have been subjected to peer review administered by the proceedings editors.
2. Reviews have been conducted by expert referees, who have been requested to provide unbiased and constructive comments aimed, whenever possible, at improving the work.
3. Proceedings editors have taken all reasonable steps to ensure the quality of the materials they publish and their decision to accept or reject a paper for publication has been based only on the merits of the work and the relevance to the journal.

Title, date and place of the conference

The 11th International Conference on Axiomatic Design - ICAD 2017
September 13-15, 2017
Iasi, Romania

Proceedings editor(s):

Laurentiu Slatineanu

Date and editor's signature

22.09.2017

17, avenue du Hoggar - PA de Courtabœuf – BP 112 - 91944 Les Ulis Cedex A (France)
Tél. : 33 (0)1 69 18 75 75 - Fax : 33(0)1 69 07 45 17 – www.edpsciences.org

Applying Axiomatic Design to Engineer's Job Search Defining DP of abduction skills for FR of new product development

Masayuki Nakao[1,*], and *Kenji* Iino[2]

[1] The University of Tokyo, Department of Engineering Synthesis, School of Engineering, Hongo7-3-1, Bunkyo-ku, Tokyo 113-8656, JAPAN
[2] SYDROSE LP, 475 N. 1st St., San Jose, CA95112, USA

Abstract. Japan completed its acquisition of western technologies in 1990, however, industries that emerged through the process are facing zero growth now. The industries now need FR_1: Develop new products, in addition to FR_2: Maintain conventional products. On the other hand, in hiring new graduates from universities, such skills of DP_1: Expertise knowledge in engineering, and DP_2: Basic academic and management skills (leadership, loyalty, communication skills, and so on) have been valued. Students, on the other hand, are judged by ambiguous variables like PV_1: School reputation and PV_2: Interview, and receive job offers a year before graduation. This process, when viewed as a design process, is clearly coupled with both DP_1 and DP_2 required for both FR_1 and FR_2. The two DPs are effective for FR_2 and have been proved successful, however, DP_1 alone sometimes fails to meet FR_1. The situation led to requiring DP_1': Abduction and demonstration skills to be judged by PV_1': Joint research or internship, a hiring system close to the western style. FRs are then uncoupled and DP_1' may allow finding a student suited for FR_1, however, the universities are not ready to teach DP_1' to the students.

1 Introduction

This paper shows the results of our experiment of applying Axiomatic Design to recruiting of engineering graduates from universities. The subjects were students in the Mechanical Engineering (ME) Department in the School of Engineering at the University of Tokyo, where the authors teach. The paper identifies Functional Requirements (FRs) for manufacturing businesses, sets the competencies looked for in engineers as Design Parameters (DPs), then the Process Variables (PVs) are the methods of selecting students with such competencies. With the design equation set so, Axiomatic Design allows us to evaluate the independence axiom [1].

Chapter 1 reviews the histories of Japanese manufacturing industries and the above ME department, and Chapter 2 explains the design equation of past

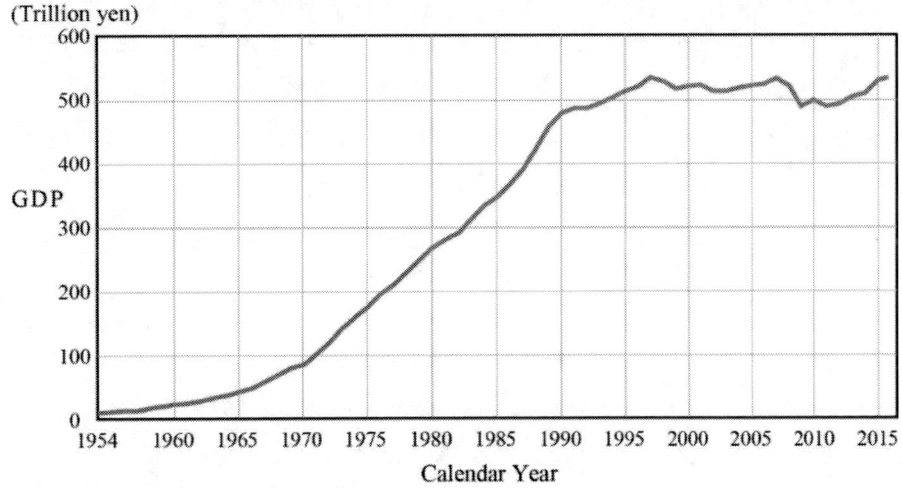

Fig. 1. Transition of Japan nominal GPD [http://www.esri.cao.go.jp/jp/sna/menu.html].

* Corresponding author: nakao@hnl.t.u-tokyo.ac.jp

recruitment and their problems. Chapter 3 proposes a new design equation for recruiting graduating students in the future, and Chapter 4 discusses ideal education to meet the design equation and the problems. Chapter 5 summaries our work.

The University of Tokyo was established in 1877 when the Meiji Restoration that ended the Shogun era was complete and it is the leading University in Japan with 140 years of history to 2017. When it was established, the University educated its students to introduce western technology and domesticate the skills following the national slogan of "Enrich the state, strengthen the military." This driving force turned around and lost its effect in 1990.

Figure 1 shows the transition of Japan's Gross Domestic Product (GDP) in the post-World War II years since 1954 [2]. In 1945, immediately after the War, the Japanese GDP had tumbled down to about 1.5 trillion Japanese Yen (JPY), i.e., about US$0.1 trillion at the current exchange rate. After the War, Japan entered its "economic miracle" years and its GDP kept growing to reach JPY500 trillion (US$5 trillion). Just before 1990, however, the Japanese economy faced the "bubble burst" in real estate and stock markets. It was the beginning of Japan's zero-growth economy which has been around for 27 years still in this year 2017.

Manufacturers like Sony, Toyota, Hitachi and so on had grown large at the time of 1990 and to alleviate the effects of higher JPY value and trade friction, they built factories and entered the market overseas. These corporations globalized and as of 2017, their domestic factories and employees consist only about 30% of their overall resources. In other words, they kept growing because their overseas markets grew, however, their domestic markets have been saturated and so are the Japanese businessmen.

Figure 2 shows where graduates from the ME Department have started working for during the 40 years of 1976 to 2016. The number of graduates have been about 100 to 150 annually summing Bachelor of Arts (BA) and Master of Science (MS) graduates. The vertical axis shows the graduate student counts with the upper positive half being those in manufacturing and the lower negative half non-manufacturing. The trend shows a turning point around 1990.

During the 110 years before 1990, 80% of the graduates started working in the manufacturing industry and the remaining 20% in non-manufacturing like, electric power, railway service, the central government and so on. Around 1984, the ratio of students starting in manufacturing started to drop to reach only 44 (42%) in 1990. At the time, the drop in manufacturing recruits raised the number in non-manufacturing like finance (banking and security), trading, investment, and consulting.

The trend, however, did not last long with the burst of bubble economy and the recruits starting with manufacturing rose back to 70 (65%). Around this time, however, favored industries shifted from material (steel and mining) and heavy industry (nuclear, electrical, automobile, train building) to IT machinery of computers, magnetic discs, liquid crystal displays, semi-conductors, optical fibers, and so on.

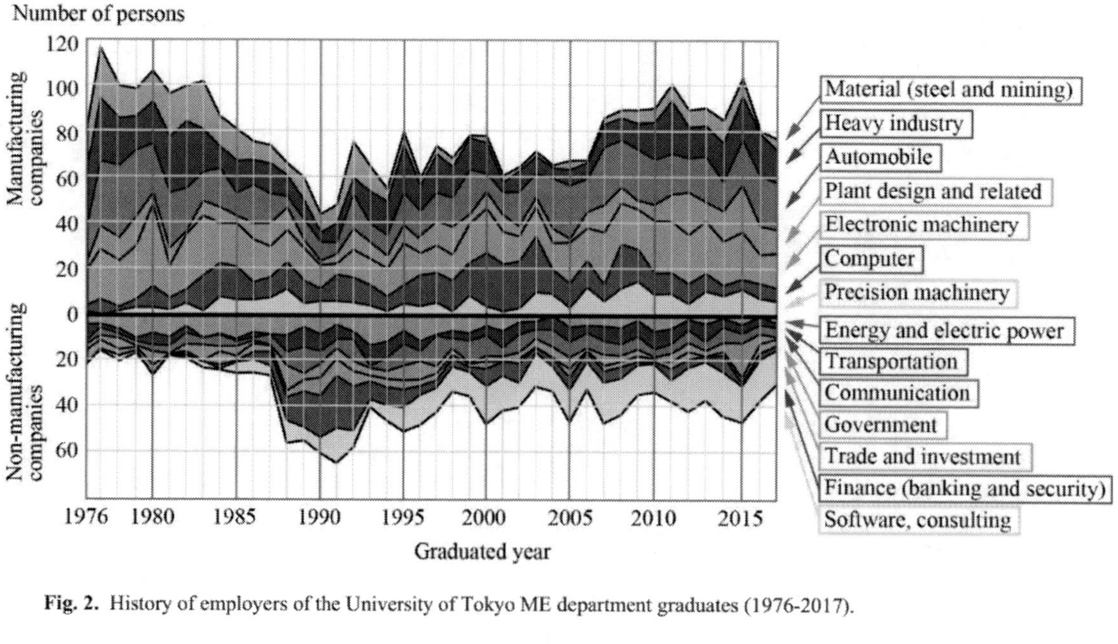

Fig. 2. History of employers of the University of Tokyo ME department graduates (1976-2017).

DOI: 10.1051/matecconf/201712701001

$$\begin{Bmatrix} FR_1\text{: Develop new products} \\ FR_2\text{: Maintain conventional products} \end{Bmatrix} = \begin{bmatrix} X_{11} & x_{12} \\ -x_{21} & X_{22} \end{bmatrix} \begin{Bmatrix} DP_1\text{: Expertise knowledge in engineering} \\ DP_2\text{: Basic academic and management skills} \end{Bmatrix}$$

$$\begin{Bmatrix} DP_1 \\ DP_2 \end{Bmatrix} = \begin{bmatrix} y_{11} & y_{21} \\ y_{21} & y_{22} \end{bmatrix} \begin{Bmatrix} PV_1\text{: School reputation} \\ PV_2\text{: Interview} \end{Bmatrix}$$

$$\{ C_1\text{: Minimize cost and time for recruiting} \} = \begin{bmatrix} Z_1 & Z_2 \end{bmatrix} \begin{Bmatrix} PV_1 \\ PV_2 \end{Bmatrix}$$

Fig. 3. Conventional design equation for recruiting engineering graduates.

Later in 2002, at the time of the so-called IT bubble burst, IT machinery industries sharply lost their popularity and the heavy industries and transportation equipment building regained their attractions. Further, the 2011 Great East Japan Earthquake caused industries like nuclear, semi-conductor, and cellular phones to drop almost to zero and in turn, automobile, batteries, and power electronics enjoyed increase of new hires.

The university faced its turning point in 2004, when it changed from a national institute to a national university corporation with the same faculty and administrative staff. The employees were freed from the detailed national institute rules, however, it was the starting point of having to earn their own operational funds. The Graduate School of Engineering, up to 2004, annually received JPY10 billion from the national budget to cover its administrative cost (labor and education), and additional JPY3 billion from the government and private companies for research. After the reformation, however, with no increase in the administration budget, its research expense skyrocketed to about JPY15 billion, i.e., 5 times. The research fund hired young researchers and the number of papers increased. The QS world ranking ranks our department at number 8 in Mechanical, Aeronautical & Manufacturing Engineering [3].

The education program, on the other hand, hardly has made any changes in the basic mechanics lectures since the school hired Charles West in 1877 who introduced the western style mechanical engineering curriculum. The hands-on courses, on the other hand as we will introduce in Section 4, gradually made some changes since 2000, from projects that follow design cases in the west to projects that have the students produce something new on their own.

2 Conventional design equation for recruitment

Companies in the manufacturing business are always after growth and maintaining selling existing products are insufficient for survival. They have to continuously develop future products as an FR. Figure 3 shows the requirements for these businesses; FR_1: Develop new products, and FR_2: Maintain conventional products.

FR and DP in the figure relate as follows:

For FR_1 of new product development, companies acquire technology from western countries or develop their own new ones. For such development, DP_1: Expertise knowledge in engineering is required. On the other hand, conventional products in FR_2 have already won the trust from the customers, thus, engineers are required to keep implementing small improvements without making any large leaps and only DP_2: Basic academic and management skills (leadership, loyalty, communication, and so on) in sales and maintenance are sufficient.

Next about the interfering components in the design matrix. First, x_{12} is the effect of DP_2 on FR_1. The basic skills of DP_2 alone cannot develop new products, however, it can support the development team to shorten the development time, thus, is has small contribution x_{12} with the small x. The component x_{21} is the effect of DP_1 on FR_2, that the distinguished skills of DP_1 may venture to make big modifications on stable products FR_2 and cause a major drawback that can threaten the entire company, thus it has a negative sign with a small x, $-x_{21}$. The interferences are non-zeros, i.e., the design is coupled.

Also, as Figure 1 showed, Japan has made zero growth throughout these 27 years, and the sole reason is because there were not enough new products of FR_1. The expertise knowledge of DP1 cannot produce new innovative products and the X_{11} component in the design matrix was small. In general knowledge of mechanics and physics in DP_1 are effective for analysis, however, is not effective for synthesis. A different set of skills specialized for design were in need.

Next are the relations among DPs and PVs.

The human resources (HR) departments at major corporations in Japan make once a year recruitment of large numbers of engineers needed for the next fiscal year (starting in April in Japan) from universities. The system is quite different from western companies where managers hire the necessary number of people in their groups when necessary. Japanese companies like Sony, Toyota, and Hitachi start their search in March of 2017 to hire engineers to start working in April of 2018 and conduct interviews by June to narrow down the candidates to about 200 to 400 to employ.

$$\begin{Bmatrix} FR_1\text{: Develop new products} \\ FR_2\text{: Maintain conventional products} \end{Bmatrix} = \begin{bmatrix} X_{11} & 0 \\ 0 & X_{22} \end{bmatrix} \begin{Bmatrix} DP_1'\text{ : Abduction and demonstration skills} \\ DP_2\text{ : Basic academic and management skills} \end{Bmatrix}$$

$$\begin{Bmatrix} DP_1' \\ DP_2 \end{Bmatrix} = \begin{bmatrix} Y_{11} & 0 \\ 0 & Y_{22} \end{bmatrix} \begin{Bmatrix} PV_1'\text{ : Joint research or internship} \\ PV_2\text{ : Interview} \end{Bmatrix}$$

$$\{ C_1'\text{ : Minimize cost and time for development} \} = \begin{bmatrix} Z_1 & 0 \end{bmatrix} \begin{Bmatrix} DP_1' \\ DP_2 \end{Bmatrix}$$

Figure 4. New design equation for recruiting engineering graduates.

Since the HR departments have to complete the search in such a short period, they do not carry out written examinations and base their judgement on PV_1: School reputation, to evaluate DP_1: Expertise knowledge in engineering. In other words, they preliminarily hire the planned number of students based on recommendations from professors. DP_2: Basic academic and management skills are also evaluated with impressions gained through short 30 minute to 1 hour interviews (PV_2). The HR departments adopted PVs in Figure 3 because they satisfied the constraint C_1: Minimize cost and time for recruiting.

Such recruitment proceeds in ambiguous reputations and impressions, thus the components y_{11}, y_{12}, y_{21}, and y_{22} all make unclear effects on the DPs. Sociologist Hattori proved this fuzziness and his book [4] was a best seller in 2017. Substituting DP in the lower equation into the upper equation shows that the design equation that relates PV to FR gives a coupled design. In other words, hiring students from well-known universities after interviews does not necessarily heighten the odds for accomplishing the FRs.

3 Design equation for future recruitment

As the earlier sections explained, the design equation for recruitment in Figure 3 is not a good strategy for developing new products or markets. Both the industries and universities had such suspicions. Figure 4 shows our new proposal as the design equation for recruitment. Differences with Figure 3 are in DP_1, PV_1, and C_1.

First, the skills needed for developing new products are changed to DP_1': Abduction and demonstration skills. They are the same as efforts in validating a hypothesis which is the basic concept of science. Abduction is the skills in identifying a set of FRs and DPs for a new product in a short time without induction or deduction. Engineers in general, however, dislike illogical and reckless abduction. In actual design, copying someone else's design is accepted in the business world as long as the royalty is paid, thus the designers do not go after new inventions. When designs are worked into products, the reliability is a large factor, therefore, designers tend to use parts with proven track of trouble free uses instead of trying newly invented parts.

A good abduction is, of course, backed by expertise knowledge (DP_1) and that by a skilled engineer is not unscientific. Abduction, however, does not automatically come out from the brain by pouring expert knowledge into it. Producing abduction takes a separate education explained in the following section.

Next, our proposed design equation changes PV_1 to evaluate the skills for the new DP_1'. The PV is PV_1': Joint research and internship. A joint research lasts for a long period of a year or longer whereas an internship is a month or more of work experience for a student. This variable is not suited for the above C_1 of minimizing the cost and time for recruitment. Needless to say, however, working together with the employment candidate for an extended time is more effective in evaluating the skills compared to an hour of interview. This method is in practice for candidates of senior engineers in the western world and Japanese trading companies and consulting industries have started experimenting with the method for executive candidates that make about 20% of the entire recruits.

Lastly about constraints, the above C_1 is replaced with our proposed C_1': Minimize cost and time for development. Of course, the cost covers the recruiting cost, however, some expense in recruiting would be tolerable because hiring an unfit engineer can lead to failure and business loss.

For the design equation, DP_1': Abduction and demonstration corresponds to FR_1: New products and DP_2: Basic academic and management skills to FR_2: Conventional products; both relations are independent. Also the long but accurate PV_1': Internship would correspond to DP_1', and the short but inexpensive PV_2: Interview to DP_2; also independent correspondences. The design equation shows an uncoupled design and FR_1' will succeed with high probability.

Developing human resources in 2 groups may pose a concern that members of the two teams can turn uniform and lack energy, however, a company that adopted this method of recruitment have identified a resource with both DP_1' and DP_2 qualifications who has been promoted as an executive candidate.

DOI: 10.1051/matecconf/201712701001

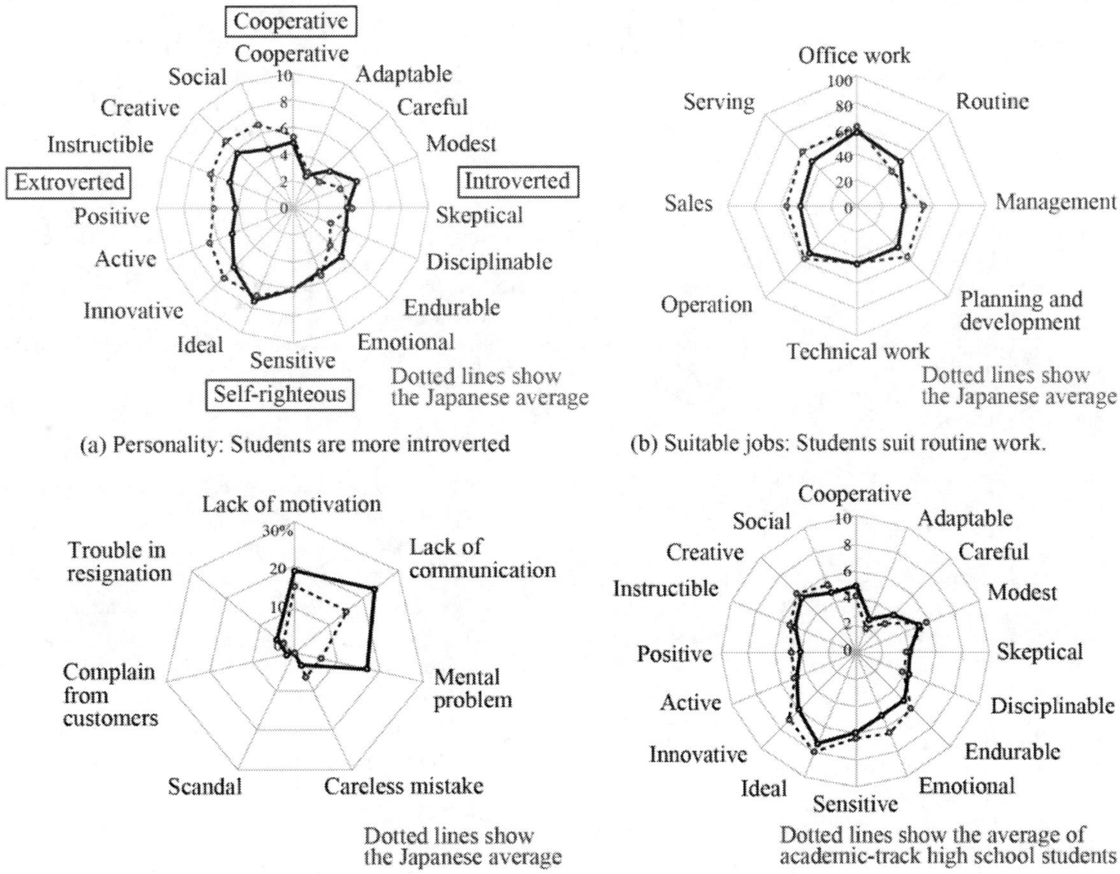

(a) Personality: Students are more introverted

(b) Suitable jobs: Students suit routine work.

(c) Risk to employer: Students pose large risk to employment.

(d) Personality is similar with high school students

Fig. 5. Personality radar chart of the University of Tokyo ME students (solid line)

4 Education to realize the new design equation for recruitment and its issues

The authors started joint research projects at JPY40 million (about US$0.4 million) a year per company since 2006 after our university turned into a corporation. Part of the purpose was to select students suited for DP_1' in the above design equation for recruitment in Figure 4. Our research lab carries out research in manufacturing technology with Komatsu, Toyota, Asahi Glass, Mitsubishi Heavy Industry, Sony, and so on. Bill Gates have also made a donation to conduct research in Internet of Things (IoT). When students participating in these joint research projects are identified with high skills of abduction, they often join the company after graduation.

Also, educational courses to actively train such resources started since about the year 2000. They are exercises to find their own design solutions from abduction. Junior students go through exercises every afternoon; In the spring/summer semester, groups of 4 design and fabricate free-style Stirling engines; In the fall/winter semester the students design and produce their own ideas of robots or games using mechatronics in duos. In the first year of graduate studies, a Project-based learning class has corporate sponsors set FRs and the students find DPs on their own. In this course, the students put their DP_1': Abduction and demonstration skills in practice and for their Bachelor's or Master's degrees, the students have to challenge research projects with novelty and innovation.

There have been no design methodology that explain how to gain skills in abduction. Axiomatic Design is no exception. The general trend, however, is if one, even with limitations in basic knowledge, tries out with courage, abduction skills start to come to life.

Personal observation, on the other hand, finds some students that totally lack that courage to venture and that is the biggest problem. Figure 5 shows the results of a personality questionnaire (by Net & ASKs), with 144 Yes/No type questions, we conduct each year with the above ME department students [5]. As (a) shows, the students were more introverted than the average 3 million Japanese. The results also showed that these students better suit routine work compared to the Japanese average (b). Without any mistakes, they can repeat the routine work consistently. Our ideal expectation is that they would suit technical, planning, or management work to lead manufacturing companies, however, their introversion lacked the power to lead people.

(c) shows risks to the employers. Some of the students are so introverted that they lack communication skills and their possibility of facing mental problems was twice the national average. Among the job hunting students to start working in April 2017, there were 10 that had not yet received official job offers by September 2016, i.e., 6 months into their job hunting. That is very rare for students at the University of Tokyo. Six of the 10 students (60%) had received strong warnings of possible mental problems, a warning that is only given to 3% of the average Japanese. (d) compares the university students' personality distribution with that of academic-track high schools. The striking resemblance is clear. To put it in a clear way, the Japanese educational system that determines who enters universities based only on entrance examinations, that tests the students' skills in memory, gather introverted students that are good at routine work as elites to the University of Tokyo.

Forming teams of introverted students and having them polish up their abduction skills, unrelated to power of memory, are hard work for the faculty. The instructors have to challenge projects not found in textbooks nor google. Ever since they were at grade schools the students have taken the strategy of starting from easy to solve problems and developing their skills in tackling problems that are more complex but with known solutions. They have a hard time selecting DPs that they are not sure if they can be realized.

The questionnaire results after the above exercise courses told us that students point to encouragement from instructors and teaching assistants during consultation as keys to successful completion. Once they are given the courage, students with lots of specialized technical knowledge can make abductions. The authors instruct young instructors when they are approached by puzzled students, not to teach them the solutions but to provide coaching to guide their thinking. It may be the slow way in terms of efficiency, however, for design education in Japan, it is important to have the students learn to think for themselves without knowing the solutions.

5 Summary

This paper expressed the system of recruiting fresh engineers in Japan with a design equation in Axiomatic Design. The formulation set corporate goals to FR_1: Develop new products, and FR_2: Maintain conventional products. In the past, human resource skills to accomplish them had been set to DP_1: Expertise knowledge in engineering, and DP_2: Basic academic and management skills. Furthermore, the selection of students were based on PV_1: School reputation, and PV_2: Interview. Japan in the zero-growth period after 1990 can no longer just copy western technology and has to start developing its own new products, thus, these DP_1 and FR_1 turned no longer effective in meeting the goals. The FRs and DPs were both coupled designs with low probability of success, and furthermore, the fuzzy PV_1 was ineffective in hiring human resources with the capability of developing new products DP_1.

The authors proposed setting DP_1': Abduction and demonstration skills in place of DP_1, and PV_1': Joint research or internship in place of PV_1. These replacements turn the design equation an uncoupled one to increase the probability of meeting FRs and DPs. The authors carried out PV_1': Joint researches to identify students with DP_1': Adduction. In addition since about 2000, we have developed exercise courses to enhance the students' abduction skills that have the student come up with their own DPs. The largest problem found was that some students are satisfied with their studies of passive written tests and lack the courage to actively challenge new abductions.

References

1. N.P. Suh, *Axiomatic Design: Advanced Application*, Oxford University Press (2001)
2. Cabinet Office, Government of Japan, Gross Domestic Product Statistics, http://www.esri.cao.go.jp/jp/sna/menu.html
3. QS Quacquarelli Symonds Limited, QS World University Rankings by Subject, https://www.topuniversities.com/subject-rankings/2017
4. Y. Hattori, *Study of selecting*, Shinchosha (2016)
5. M. Nakao et al., *Mind wandering, brain training to acquire values from cobwebs*, Nikkan Kogyo Shimbun (2017)

ADjustadesk — An Adjustable Height Desk

Joseph Timothy Foley[1,⋆], *Arnór Freyr* Símonarson[1], *Hilmar Þór* Símonarson[1], *Lúðvík Friðrik* Ægisson[1], and *Andri Þór* Goethe[1]

[1] *Reykjavik University, Engineering Department, Menntavegur 1, 101 Reykjavik, Iceland*

Abstract. It is no wonder that demand of adjustable desks is increasing in the world. People are dealing with long hours sitting down and many have musculoskeletal system problems due to this. Our idea started with this concept but then we applied it for the Reykjavík University workshop which really needs better facilities to keep your laptop and other equipment out of harm's way while working on projects. Our idea is to make an affordable adjustable desk that is suitable for a workshop environment. It will only be mechanical, unlike most desks which are driven by electrical motors. To reduce the gravitational force of the desk we will use gas struts, this will give the desk more flowing motion. The desk met all our requirements. After building the desk we tested it and can withstand 200 kg on the top and can be pushed from all sides with 50 kg without flexing. It slides up and down with smoothly and locks in position without any problems.

1 Introduction

With so many advances in technology, our lifestyles are changing, and as a result, we are spending a lot more time sitting down, which is also called "being sedentary". We sit while driving to school, all day in school, doing homework after school, and in front of the TV at home [1]. Research on physical activity has mainly focused on time adults do intensive exercise, 30 minutes a day is normally the target. However recent studies highlight the importance of focusing on the balance of light intensity exercises and sedentary. One of the concern after this new research was how to reduce or break up prolonged sitting time. This can help to reduce your risk of developing heart disease, diabetes cardiovascular disease, and other prevalent chronic health problems. This will also increase your metabolism which will help to stay in shape [2].

With this in mind, we wanted to design a robust adjustable desk for the Reykjavik University workshop. The height of the desk will be adjusted by man power with the help of a gas strut which will make it feel like it's floating. The problem is that the workshop does not have many places to work at and not much money to improve it, so we wanted to make that improvement possible. Our desk will be a step toward a better workshop and that is our goal. Another thing to consider is the effect sitting has on our musculoskeletal system and adjustable desk will counteract the long hours a student spends sitting down. The prototype will cost around 40000 ISK (379 USD) when it's ready and that is considerably lower price than other manufacturers offer, as can be seen in Section 1.1. When the desk will go in production the aim is to sell it for around 45000 ISK (425 USD) since then the manufacturing labor will not be volunteer work anymore.

Axiomatic design was used to develop the design for the AdjustaDesk from customer needs to functional requirements and then design parameters. Axiomatic design is a good method to use in designing since it helps in keeping things simpler and making the design work every time.

1.1 Background

During the 18th and 19th centuries standing while working was desired because it thought that it would increase productivity. It was extremely popular and was a sign of prestige and wealth [3]. Indeed many great minds worked at standing desks, such as Stan Lee the famous comic-book author and creator of the Marvel-Universe. A much-circulated photo of him writing in his back yard bears this caption: "Always wrote standing up — good for the Figure — and always faced the sun— good for the suntan!" [4]. We grouped adjustable height desks (AHD) into categories, each with advantages and disadvantages:

Set-up AHD: usually has a set of pins or an adjustable screw to change the height when the desk is being put together.

Crank AHD: uses a crank handle attached to a power-screw to adjust the height.

Counterbalanced AHD: uses levers or pulleys and weights to change the heights.

Spring-loaded and Pneumatic AHD: use a compressed spring (or gas-spring) to reduce the effort needed by the user to change the height to preset values. A gas-spring may have a valve to allow the user to set the force or displacement value.

⋆e-mail: foley@ru.is

Fig. 1. Electric adjustable desk from Ergolift [6]. Notice the AC mains access module on the top.

Electric AHD: have a motor that engages the desk height mechanism, often a power-screw.

The Set-up AHD wouldn't be changed after setup, its low cost and easy to assemble but not adjustable in everyday use. A Crank AHD is easy to use and cost efficient but can be hard to raise if there is heavy equipment on it. Counter-balanced, spring loaded or pneumatic AHD can be quickly adjusted but can only handle low weights, usually up to 50 kg. Electric AHDs are the easiest to use but the main drawback is the high cost.

Alternatively, there are adjustable height accessories i.e. Miscellaneous AHD for existing desks, often for the keyboard, mouse, and monitor. They are relatively cheap but their usage is limited [5]. Similar products have been made by various companies like Ergolift and Prima but they both use an electric motor to do the lifting. We will be using gas struts to do the main lifting so that the part that moves up/down should be almost weightless when not loaded. The idea is when you put stuff on the desk and lift/lower it, you should only be lifting the extra weight on the desk since the desk itself is "weightless" because of the gas struts. This is a one of a kind desk as we could not find the same concept for sale on-line. Our goal is to make this desk cheaper with the same functionality for the customer. Similar Ergolift desk costs 84900 ISK (802 USD) [6] with no accessories and the Prima desk costs 62900 ISK (594 USD) [7] with no accessories. A desk that is already in Reykjavik University but not suitable for the workshop can be seen in Figure 3.

2 Design

The concept came from members of the designer's group because they had been having back pain and they had been thinking of a practical solution and wanted to make their own desk for a low cost because they are poor students.

Fig. 2. Electric adjustable desk from Prima [7].

Fig. 3. Existing electric adjustable desk used at Reykjavik University.

The back pain is due to excessive sitting which is common for students and people working in office jobs.

2.1 Design process

The Axiomatic design theory is a system of using matrix methods to analyze the transformation of Customer Needs into Functional Requirements and to find a Design parameter to satisfy these conditions. Axiomatic design focuses on Functional Requirements and Design Parameters (FRs and DPs) and the connections between them, through a process of mapping between the functional domain to the physical domain [8].

There are two design axioms that distinguish a great design. Axiom 1 involves the relationship between functions and physical variables and Axiom 2 involves with the complexity of the design, what parts to use and etc. These axioms can be stated in a variety of semantically equivalent forms. The declarative form of the axioms is the following [9]:

- Axiom 1 *The independence Axiom* Maintain the independence of FRs
- Axiom 2 *The information Axiom* Minimize the information content of the design

Axiom 1 states that during any design process, we go from the FRs in the functional domain with the DPs in the physical domain. The mapping must be conducted so that a particular Design parameter Functional requirement must affect only its referent Functional requirement [9]. When this objective is achieved, the design matrix will be diagonal as each DP relates to only one FR with no coupling, this is called uncoupled matrix. When the matrix is not uncoupled it can be either decoupled or coupled. Decoupled matrix is path dependent, meaning that the sequence of implementation of the DPs is critical and starts with the DP that affects most FRs, followed by the DP that affects the second most number of FRs and so on. When off-diagonal elements exist the matrix cannot be organized to a triangular form, this is called coupled [8]. Axiom 2 states that the design with the least information content is the finest design. When multiple options of DPs have been developed these axioms can be used to choose the finest set of DPs. You want to choose DPs to provide the least coupling preferably no coupling while preserving minimum information content [8].

The Axiomatic Design process of the adjustable desk started by analyzing the customer's needs then processing them into functional requirements. Proposed concepts were worked out, followed by further research analysis of the proposed solutions. The final step was to compare the design to the customer needs and make sure every single need was met.

2.2 Customer attributes

At the beginning of the design, we discussed what we as students wanted for this desk. After some discussion and research, we assumed the target customer to be workshop owners and created our list of customer needs accordingly.

Customer needs regarding the desk: CN_1: Adjustable desk that suits people in common sizes.
CN_2: The desk has to be steady so you can lean on it while working.
CN_3: It should be affordable
CN_4: It should have electrical sockets
CN_5: The top panel should endure hammer beatings and fluids without deteriorating.

2.3 Constraints

Constraints affect the design though they are not functional requirements. Constraint number one was set by the University as our budget and constraint number two was set by us to keep within the budget.

Constraints regarding the desk:
C_1: Total cost can not exceed 40000 ISK (378 USD).
C_2: Can be manufactured in the RU workshop.

2.4 Functional requirements

Functional Requirements must begin with an action verb. FR's must be able to be validated so when the construction is done some experiments will be done to confirm if the FR's are met [9].

Functional Requirements regarding the desk:
FR_1: Positions a work surface vertically
FR_2: Stays stable when worked on
FR_3: Locks in position
FR_4: Powers appliances
FR_5: Endures hammer strikes and fluid spills on surface

2.5 Design parameters

Once we know our FR's for the desk we can find our DP's to satisfy our FR's. DP's are in the physical domain so they start with a noun [9].

Design parameters regarding the desk:
DP_1: Man power with help of gas strut
DP_2: Stiff materials and wide base
DP_3: Pull pin locks the desk
DP_4: Sockets mounted on desk
DP_5: Steel sheet metal to cover the top panel

2.6 Design matrix

Now with the FR-DP mapping completed the next step is to build the design matrix. The design matrix shows how the DPs satisfy the corresponding FRs. It is a visual representation of how much each FR is affected by each DP. An uncoupled matrix is purely diagonal and that is what you should aim for because then each DP only affects one FR. Our matrix is decoupled because both DP_1 and DP_3 affect FR_1 because to lift (DP_1) the desk the pull pins (DP_3) have to be pulled out. We could not conceive of a less coupled solution [9].

$$\begin{Bmatrix} FR_1 \\ FR_2 \\ FR_3 \\ FR_4 \\ FR_5 \end{Bmatrix} = \begin{bmatrix} X & 0 & X & 0 & 0 \\ 0 & X & 0 & 0 & 0 \\ 0 & 0 & X & 0 & 0 \\ 0 & 0 & 0 & X & 0 \\ 0 & 0 & 0 & 0 & X \end{bmatrix} \begin{Bmatrix} DP_1 \\ DP_2 \\ DP_3 \\ DP_4 \\ DP_5 \end{Bmatrix} \tag{1}$$

2.7 Description of the design

Throughout the design, we had the principle of symmetry in mind which is closely related to stability. Stability of one of our FR's so it is important to keep in mind. Moments are not created and the system only expands but does not bend. According to Abbe's principle bending creates angular deformations which are amplified with distance, and hence are generally to be avoided [10]. This relates directly to Nam P. Suh's corollary 5 which implies the use of symmetry when it's consistent with the FRs and constraints [9]. For the sliding guidance, we used Saint-Venant's Principle for jamming. It says that the length of the sliding interface should be 3-5 times the diameter in our case [10].

The final frame is assembled out of 2 separate frames connected by hydraulic gas struts. The gas struts are there to counter the weight of the part of the desk that moves

Fig. 4. Pull pin in unlocked position.

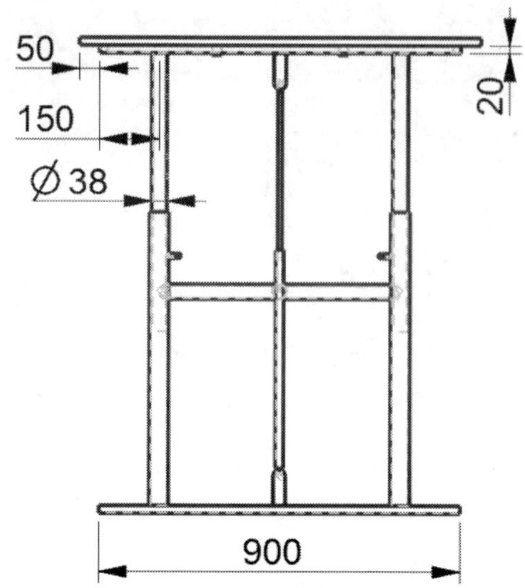

Fig. 5. Front view of the desk from Creo, all dimensions in mm.

up/down. To find the type that we chose we had to calculate how much force would be needed to make the top panel "weightless". To lock the desk in the right position there are indexing plungers (pull pins) on each leg see Figure 4. And to unlock it you simply pull them out and twist them 90 so it stays out while you are adjusting the height, they will be mounted onto of the outer leg pipe. To keep the desk on track the upper frame slides into the bottom frame. The outer pipe will have the indexing plunger mounted at the top and the inner pipe will have holes in it so it can be locked in various positions. The smaller one will go into the larger one with a 1mm clearance at all sides. They will work as guides and support. The square tubings used to connect the pipes are $80 \times 20 \times 2$ mm, that will be stiff enough. And $20 \times 30 \times 2$ mm profiles to strengthen the frame goes under the desk to connect the legs. To strengthen the overall desk a stiffening bracket was built and welded between the two legs of the bottom frame, this was made from the same pipe as the inner pipes of the legs, can be seen in Figure 7 and 8. The top panel is 2×1 m and build out of 21 mm thick plywood board. It will be bolted to the upper frame. To strengthen and protect the surface from wear and tear a panel a 1 mm steel sheet will be glued to the plywood. The design can be seen in Figure 8 and all relevant dimensions in Figures 5, 6 and 7 Under the desk, located in the middle of the long side, at both sided, there will be double electrical sockets connected together. A cable coming from one of the sockets with a length of 5 m will be used to connect the desk to a wall socket.

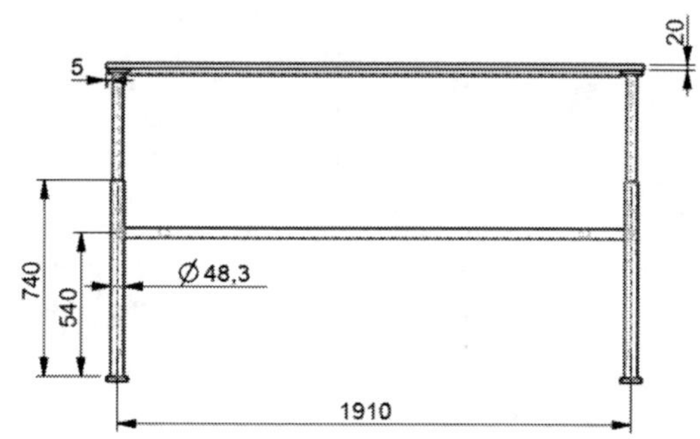

Fig. 6. Side view of the desk from Creo, all dimensions in mm.

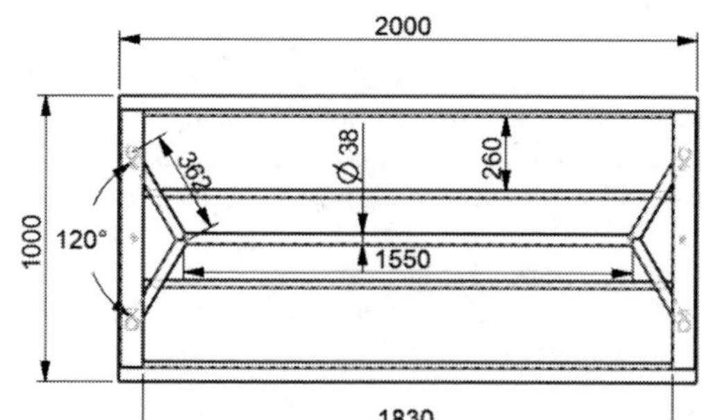

Fig. 7. Top view of the desk from Creo, all dimensions in mm.

2.8 Assumptions

We assume that the density of the plywood to be $600\,\mathrm{kg\,m^{-2}}$, and of the steel to be $7800\,\mathrm{kg\,m^{-2}}$. The desk will be located inside, so rusting and corrosion will not oc-

Table 1. Information on flat materials used in construction for calculating the mass.

Material	Density [$kg\,m^{-2}$]	Volume [m^3]	Mass [kg]
Plywood	600	0.040	24.0
Sheet metal	7800	0.002	15.6

Table 2. Beam specifications for calculating the mass.

Beam	[$kg\,m^{-1}$]	Length [m]	Mass [kg]
80×mm20 profile	3.00	2	6.0
20×mm20 profile	1.13	4	4.5
38×mm2.6 tubing	2.23	3	6.6

cur. The floor should be fairly level. Placing objects on the desk should be done with common sense and not dropped on it with the sharp corner down [11].

2.9 Calculations

We estimated the amount of material that will be used and calculate the weight from the density and volume of the material to choose the correct gas struts. Mass per length-meter is given in the catalog for the steel beams. Since the gas struts only lift the top part of the desk the calculations only take the top part of the desk into consideration.

$$m = \mu l \tag{2}$$

Equation 2 [12] is to calculate the mass of the beams in the top part of the desk where m=mass [kg], l=total length [m] and μ=mass per unit length [$kg\,m^{-1}$]

$$m = \rho V = \rho lwh \tag{3}$$

Equation 3 [12] is to calculate the mass of the plywood and steel sheet metal where m=mass [kg], ρ=density [kg/m^3], V=volume [m^3], l=length [m], w=width [m] and h=height [m].

The total mass of the top part of the desk is estimated to be 56.7kg or around 550N thus gas struts were chosen for 600N.

3 Experiments

Now that the design was complete, it was time to test if the prototype would meet the specified requirements. Due to the large range of possible uses, the focus was on qualitative usage tests:

- basic structural tests
- stability tests
- impact tests
- ease-of-adjustment tests
- surface compatibility tests

Table 3. Tests performed on the adjustable desk prototype.

Test	Load [kg]
Structural Strength	200
Sideways Load	50
Frontal Load	50

The structural test applied 200 kg on top of the desk without significant deflection. Then a force of 50 kg was applied on the ends when in highest position to test for stability, on every side. Thirdly there was a test to see if the gas struts worked like they were supposed to, by making it easier to lift and lower the height of the desk. There was also a test to see if the desk was able to withstand heavy blows on top of it e.g. from a hammer. The first test was performed by Arnór and Andri, combined weight of about 200 kg, walking around on top of the desk without it permanently deforming. In the second test, they leaned on the desk applying 50 kg combined. We know the forces by using a scale to measure their weight, both standing up straight and leaning on the scale with the same angle as they did on the desk. There was not an opportunity to test if the gas strut system worked due to significant delays in shipping. Although we couldn't test the gas struts, we tested the movement of the desk by hand and it slid smoothly up and down. The test for heavy blows was performed by hitting a steel beam on the desk with a 2 kg sledgehammer. The results are that the desk is strong enough to withstand 200 kg workload and is also robust enough not to wobble when sideway force is applied. The sheet metal on top of the desk makes it able to withstand a hammering and fluid spills which are easy to clean. From these tests, we make that assertion that this desk is robust enough to be used in the workshop at Reykjavik University.

4 Result and discussion

The desk met all FRs in Section 2.4: it slid easily enough up and down and was extremely stable. The tests listed in Section 3 were performed and the desk met all the requirements except for the assisted lift test due to the omission of the gas springs. That said, the desk moved up and down the way it should by hand and when the springs arrive, we are confident that they will be sufficient. The loads for the tests can be seen in table 3. The desk held up well with 200 kg on it and was stable when leaned on from the side it didn't wobble or move around. The top panel came out great with the sheet metal on top of the plywood, robust enough with a tough durable surface.

This design could be developed further by adding more customizations such as the electrical sockets. For serious workshop usage it would be better to have an adjustable force gas strut to adjust the force needed to lift or lower the desk. This design allocated 3000 ISK for the fixed

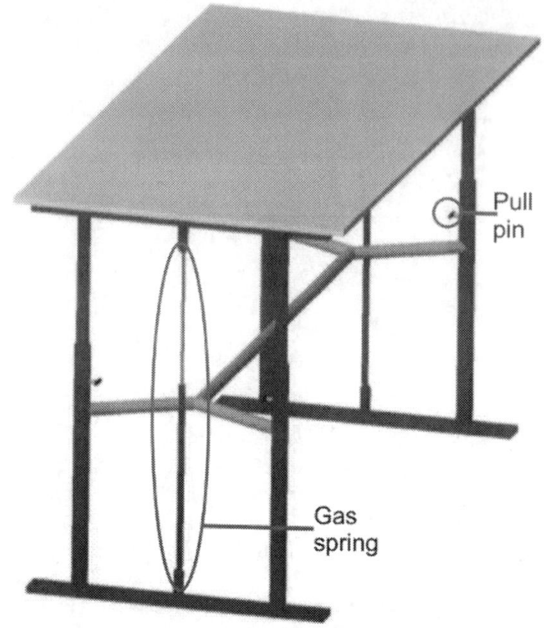

Fig. 8. Final design view of the desk from Creo.

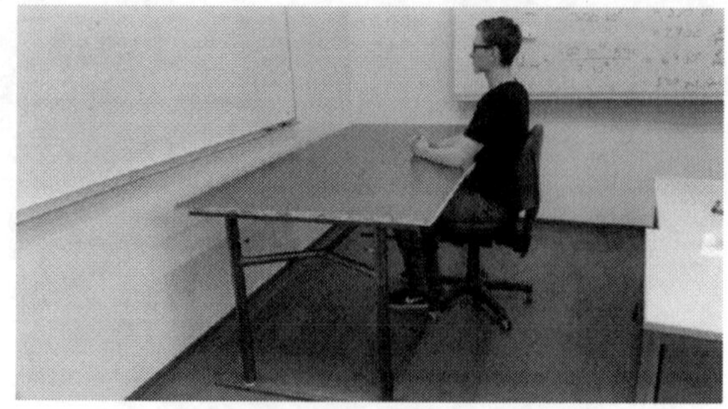

Fig. 9. Test subject sitting at the desk.

Fig. 10. Test subject standing at the desk.

gas struts instead of more than double that cost for the adjustable struts. If the adjustable gas strut were to be added to the desk, the range of working weights would be increased.

There were some difficulties in the manufacture of the desk prototype. When the steel parts were welded together, there was unexpected amounts of warping, so some parts had to be cut loose and re-welded. Future designs would employ square profiles with fasteners to join together the frame. To fit the three pipes together in the inner frame they had to be notched: square profile would not require this operation.

5 Conclusion

The ADjustadesk prototype was a success: as can be seen in Section 3 the desk did pass all the relevant tests. We tested if it is possible to adjust the height of the desk [FR_1] and that works very well considering that the gas struts are missing, because of reasons listed in Section 3. We tested for stability [FR_2] by applying force on the sides of the desk the result was that we did not experience an excessive displacement in any direction. The locking of the desk in a specific height FR_3 was tested simultaneously as tests for [FR_2] by locking the desk in place while we performed the structural tested. The ability to power appliances [FR_4] is two electrical sockets fasten under the desk with a 5-meter electrical cable which makes it possible to have the desk centrally located in the room. The desk height intervals turned out great for both sitting and standing at the desk as can be seen in Figure 9 and Figure 10 This adjustable desk highlights the strengths of Axiomatic Design: we gained an understanding of the interaction between each of the elements and worked hard to keep them from interfering from each other. Ultimately, this and clear Functional Requirements are what made this project successful.

References

[1] SA Health, *The risk of sitting too much*, `http://www.sahealth.sa.gov.au/wps/wcm/connect/public+content/sa+health+internet/healthy+living/is+your+health+at+risk/the+risk+of+sitting+too+much`
[2] N. Owen, A. Bauman, W. Brown, *Too much sitting: a novel and important predictor of chronic disease risk?*, BMJ Journal **43** (2009)
[3] J. Kelly, *History of standing desks* (2012), `https://notsitting.com/standing-desks/general-info/history/`
[4] L. Swanson, *The definitive guid to actual famous standing desk users* (2016), `http://well9to5.com/famous-standing-desk-users/`
[5] Height Adjustable Desk Advise, *What are the different types of heigth adustable desks* ((n.d.)), `http://www.heightadjustabledeskadvice.com/types-of-height-adjustable-desks/`
[6] skrifstofa.is, *Ergolift rafmagnsbord* ((n.d.)), `https://www.skrifstofa.is/bord/rafmagnsskrifbord/ergolift-idt-rafmagnsbord`

[7] egskrifstofuhúsgögn.is, *Prima rafmagnsbord* ((n.d.)), http://www.xn--egskrifstofuhsggn-e0b7e.is/bord/skrifbord/prima-rafmagnsbord
[8] D.S. Cochran, J.T. Foley, Z. Bi, *Use of the Manufacturing System Design Decomposition for Comparative Analysis and Effective Design of Production Systems*, International Journal of Production Research p. 24 (2016)
[9] N.P. Suh, *The Principles of Design* (Oxford University Press, 1990)
[10] A.H. Slocum, *FUNdaMENTALS of Design* (Massachusetts Institute of Technology, 2007), http://pergatory.mit.edu/resources/FUNdaMENTALS.html
[11] The Engineering Toolbox, *Density of solids* (2017), http://www.engineeringtoolbox.com/density-solids-d_1265.html
[12] H.D. Young, R.A. Freedman, *Sears & Zemansky's University Physics with Modern Physics 13th edition* (Jim Smith, 2012)

DOI: 10.1051/matecconf/201712701003

Axiomatic Design Aspect of a Braking System Redesign

Kenji Iino[1,*], *Aitor* Arruti[2], and *Masayuki* Nakao[3]

[1]SYDROSE LP, San Jose, California, 95112, USA
[2]Technical University of Denmark, 2800 Kgs. Lyngby, Denmark
[3]The University of Tokyo, Hongo. Tokyo 113-0033, Japan

Abstract. A rollator is a commercial product on the market for aiding people with difficulty in walking by themselves. Users are typically strong enough to walk without aid, but will easily feel exhausted within short distances. The product is popular in advanced countries with fairly good walkway conditions with their simple structure and ease of use without any driving power. The product's simple design led to a great number of companies developing their design and putting them quickly in the market. Rushed design, however, sometimes can cause subtle issues with the product. One particular product was found with a drawback in its operability that engaging the hand activated brake can make the following forward movement difficult. This paper discusses the design issue with Axiomatic Design and proposes a remedy that removes the drawback.

1 Introduction

Our world has a problem of growing population and particularly a higher ratio of elderlies in the coming years. WHO predicts [1] that the ratio of people at age 75 or above, currently at 3.3%, will reach 8.1% in the year 2055 (Figure 1). Japan, in particular, has a more serious prediction [2] with the same 2055 ratio reaching a stunning 19.7% from the current 9.1% (Figure 2).

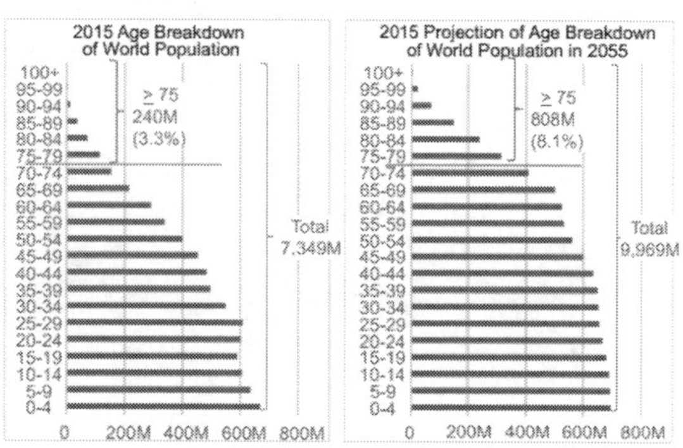

Fig. 1. Age breakdown of world population in 2015 and 2055.

As people age, a number of bodily functions degrade and losing the ability to walk without any support is one of such functions. To help those affected with walking difficulty and disability, tools in the market start from a cane, crutches, a wheel-less walker, a walker with wheels, a rollator, a wheelchair, an electric wheelchair, and a mobility scooter, in the order of increasing level of support and complexity. In the same order, the power of mobilization shifts from human to tool.

Fig. 2. Age breakdown of Japanese population in 2015 and 2055.

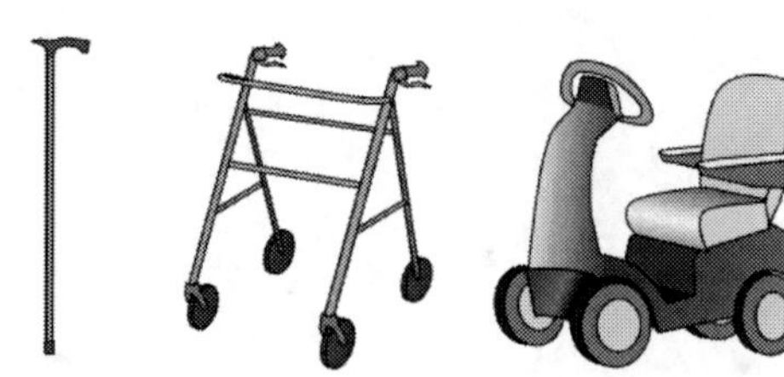

Fig. 3. Walking (mobility) aids with different levels of support.

A specific rollator model caught the attention of the authors and it turned into the topic of our study. Our attention started with Axiomatic Design [3] Analysis of the model's braking system. It worked fine in stopping the rollator, however, the user had difficulty moving forward again from the stopped position. Our analysis

* Corresponding author: kiino@sydrose.com

pinpointed the specific part that was causing the problem. It was a part for stopping the moving rollator that interfered with the functional requirement (FR) of moving the rollator forward.

Our work followed the analysis with redesign of the braking system with a different configuration. The new design removed the interference and freed the forward moving functional requirement from the braking system. In other words, the new design reduced the interfering component in the design matrix negligibly small.

This paper is a report of the results of a 3-month assignment by a visiting student from Denmark.

2 Original design

2.1 High level FR analysis

The FR for a rollator is to "aid user in walking." Instead of a wheelchair, the user is not fully off the feet, thus, this highest level FR is further broken down to: "partially support body weight," the main FR of "aid forward motion," and the FR in case the user wants to avoid colliding into objects or other people, "stop the motion." Figure 4 is the Design Record Graph [4] for the high level conceptual design of a rollator. The left side of the figure shows the first level decomposition of the highest level FR into the next level FRs.

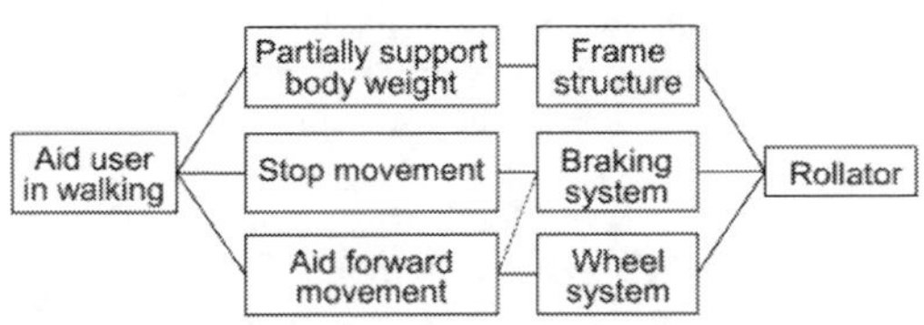

Fig. 4. High level Design Record Graph of rollator.

Our earlier paper [4] pointed out how refining the design into detail can hide interferences among design components because a detail single part tends to have only one functional requirement. Similarly, design interference is hard to identify in early stages of conceptual design because rough sketches of the design concepts without detail still do not have interfering components.

The designer of the rollator probably did not recognize the design interference by the braking system to the FR of "Aid forward movement" which was not intended. It was only after detail design was carried out that a part in the braking system was shaped in a way to interfere with the forward movement. Eq. (1) is the design equation of the high level decomposition. The designer did not intend to have the italic *x* in the design matrix with the early conceptual design.

$$\begin{Bmatrix} \text{Partially support body weight} \\ \text{Stop movement} \\ \text{Aid forward movement} \end{Bmatrix} = \begin{bmatrix} X & 0 & 0 \\ 0 & X & 0 \\ 0 & x & X \end{bmatrix} \begin{Bmatrix} \text{Frame structure} \\ \text{Braking system} \\ \text{Wheel system} \end{Bmatrix} \quad (1)$$

2.2 Detail of the braking system

Disassembling the braking system revealed how it transferred the user's grasping force to the braking system to stop the wheel rotation.

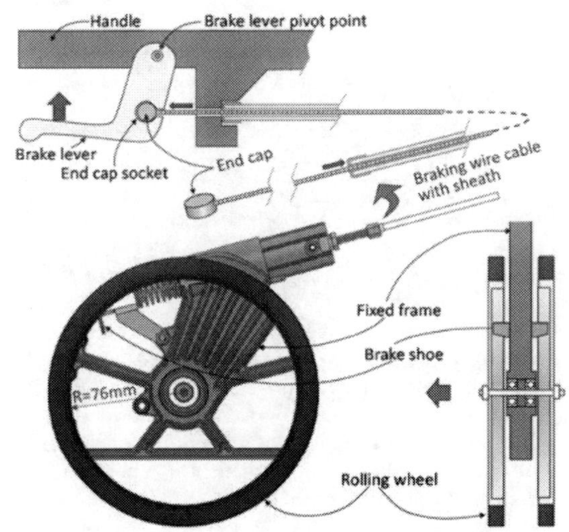

Fig. 5. Original braking system design of our subject rollator.

Figure 5 sketches the wide view of the user engaging the brake. When the user grasps the brake lever with the handle, the brake lever rotates clockwise around its pivot point and the end cap socket pulls the braking wire out from the sheath. At the other end at the wheel, the braking wire is pulled into the sheath. The end cap on the wheel side thus pulls the brake shoe to turn it clockwise around the brake shoe pivot point (Figure 6). The brake shoe then pushes against inside of the wheel rim to apply friction against the wheel to stop its rotation.

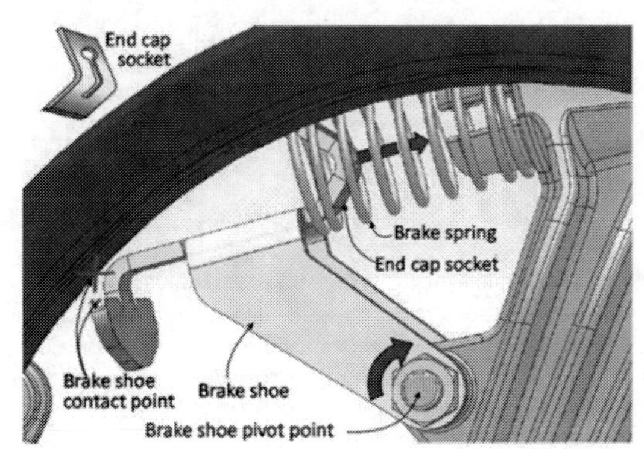

Fig. 6. Engaging the brake to the wheel (Brake shoe at rest).

The upper left corner of Figure 6 shows the slit in the brake shoe that allows placing the end cap in the socket for exerting pulling force on the brake shoe.

The designer placed the brake spring in Figure 6 so that when the user releases the brake lever, it exerts spring force to push the brake shoe back into its rest position, that is, to disengage the shoe from the wheel.

Figure 7 shows the detail Design Record Graph for this braking system.

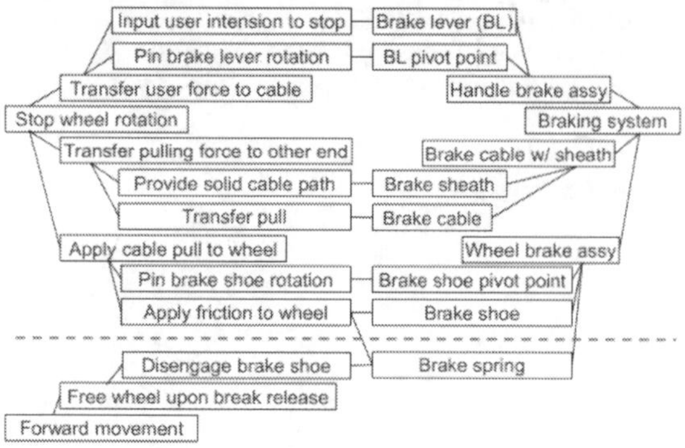

Fig. 7. Design Record Graph of braking system.

Although the brake spring is part of the braking system, its function is to allow forward movement for the rollator from its rest position. Eq. (2) is the design equation for this braking system at a level with more detail than Eq. (1). Note that without the movement FR, the equation shows a completely independent design from an Axiomatic Design aspect.

$$\begin{Bmatrix} \text{Transfer user force to cable} \\ \text{Transfer pulling force to other end} \\ \text{Apply cable pull to wheel} \end{Bmatrix} = \begin{bmatrix} X & 0 & 0 \\ 0 & X & 0 \\ 0 & 0 & X \end{bmatrix} \begin{Bmatrix} \text{Handle brake assy} \\ \text{Brake cable w/ sheath} \\ \text{Wheel brake assy} \end{Bmatrix} \quad (2)$$

Eq. (3) is the design equation at the fine detail level. When applying braking friction to the wheel, the force has to overcome the brake spring force to push the brake shoe away from the wheel rim. The italic *x* in Eq. (3) shows that the "Friction to wheel" function is affected by the "Brake spring."

$$\begin{Bmatrix} \text{Input user int. to stop} \\ \text{Pin BL rotation} \\ \text{Provide cable path} \\ \text{Transfer pull} \\ \text{Friction to wheel} \\ \text{Pin B shoe rotation} \\ \text{Disengage B shoe} \end{Bmatrix} = \begin{bmatrix} X & 0 & 0 & 0 & 0 & 0 & 0 \\ 0 & X & 0 & 0 & 0 & 0 & 0 \\ 0 & 0 & X & 0 & 0 & 0 & 0 \\ 0 & 0 & 0 & X & 0 & 0 & 0 \\ 0 & 0 & 0 & 0 & X & 0 & x \\ 0 & 0 & 0 & 0 & 0 & X & 0 \\ 0 & 0 & 0 & 0 & 0 & 0 & X \end{bmatrix} \begin{Bmatrix} \text{Brake lever (BL)} \\ \text{BL pivot point} \\ \text{B sheath} \\ \text{B cable} \\ \text{B shoe} \\ \text{B shoe pivot point} \\ \text{B spring} \end{Bmatrix} \quad (3)$$

This brake spring is an odd part because physically it belongs to the braking system, however, its function is a sub-function of the function of aiding forward movement. The broken blue lines in Figure 7 and Eq. (3) indicate the functional split of braking and moving forward.

2.3 Problem with the original design

Figure 8 shows the brake shoe when the brake is engaged to stop the wheel from rotating. The red curve is the inner surface of the wheel rim where the brake shoe makes contact for braking.

As the figure shows, when the brake cable is pulled to the right, the brake shoe, with wings extending towards the two wheels that sandwich the frame, contacts the inner surfaces of the wheel rims. People, however, tend to exert more than just enough force in braking a moving object. The readers can recall their grasp on bicycle brake levers when they are stopped at an intersection. It is a natural action for a human rider who does not want the bicycle to start moving unintentionally when waiting for the cross traffic to stop.

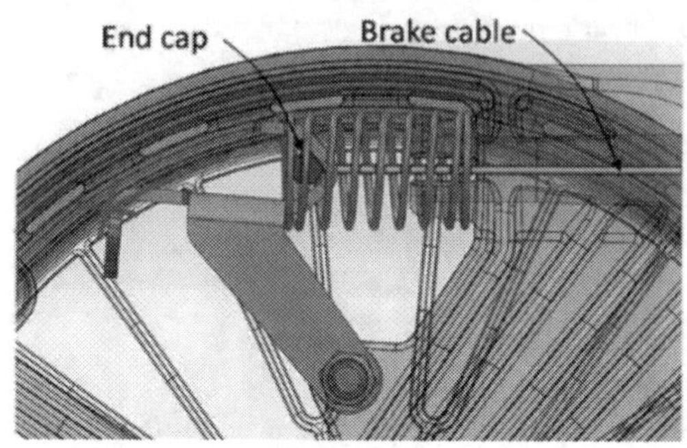

Fig. 8. Brake shoe when engaged.

This extra force on the brake cable ends up forcing the brake shoe to jam into the gap between its pivot point and the inner surface of the wheel rim. The action is equivalent to forcing a self-locking shim between the brake shoe pivot point and the wheel.

Figure 9 shows the nature of the problem. The red circle is drawn concentric to the brake shoe pivot point and to intersect the point of contact between the brake shoe and inner surface of the wheel rim. The tangent directions of the two circles are close, meaning the brake shoe (shim) can easily force its way into the gap between its pivot point (fixed to the frame) and the wheel.

Fig. 9. Original brake shoe pivot point.

As a result, when the user tries to move forward from the rest position, the wheels are locked into position with a shim jammed between the brake shoe pivot point, fixed to the rollator frame, and a wheel. In fact, once the original rollator was stopped by braking, it had to be pulled backwards before making a forward motion. The backwards motion forced the shim out of position and the brake spring then pushed the brake shoe all the way back to its rest position. The spring force of the brake spring was not strong enough to brake the shimming force on the brake shoe when it was jammed.

2.4 Modifying the design

Axiomatic Design analysis showed us that the problem with the design was an unintended interference of the brake shoe with the FR of moving the rollator forward. It was caused by a poor geometric configuration of the brake shoe, its pivot point, and the point of braking force application.

A modification that quickly comes to the mind is to move the pivot point so that the brake shoe engages the inner surface of the wheel rim at a right angle, instead of an angle close to being tangential to the wheel motion.

In doing so, however, to keep the braking force by the user on the braking lever about the same or smaller, the pivot point has to stay on the lower side of the solid blue line in Figure 9. The lever arm between the line of action of the braking cable and the pivot point has to equal or be larger than the original arm length L (31.6mm) in the figure.

Moving the red circle in Figure 9 around with its center on the solid blue line until the circle intersects with wheel at a right angle gives us the pivot point in Figure 10. Although not impossible to use this configuration, the brake shoe will be considerably larger and it will have to shape itself to work around the fixed frame rib at the 10 o'clock position. This design modification would have violated a geometric constraint in the physical world.

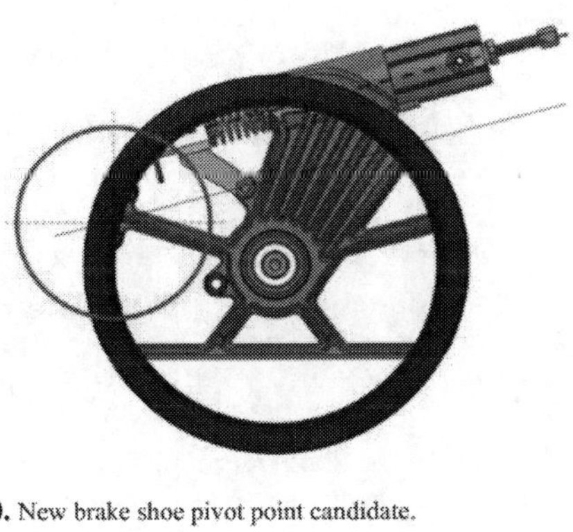

Fig. 10. New brake shoe pivot point candidate.

Figure 11 shows our new design. It has two additional links, and thus, three additional pivot points. In fact, it is a four-bar linkage design that keeps all parts within the area of the original design. Three moving links are clear in the figure, and the fourth is the fixed frame. The original brake shoe pivot point is kept as one of the pivot points on the fixed link. The link that pivots around this pivot point is pulled by the braking cable. The other pivot point on the fixed frame used an already open bolt hole on the frame.

This linkage design kept about the same amount of cable travel necessary to engage the brake and braking force. Figure 12 shows the brake shoe linkage when the brake is engaged. The geometric relation of the new pivot point for the contacting link and point of contact makes the braking force apply normal to the wheel rotation.

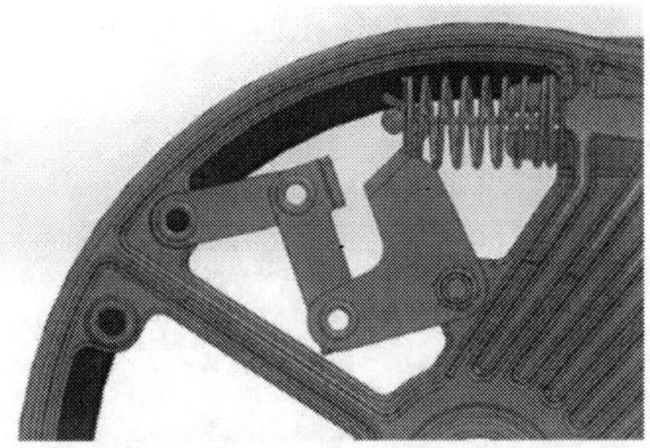

Fig. 11. New four-bar linkage design at rest position.

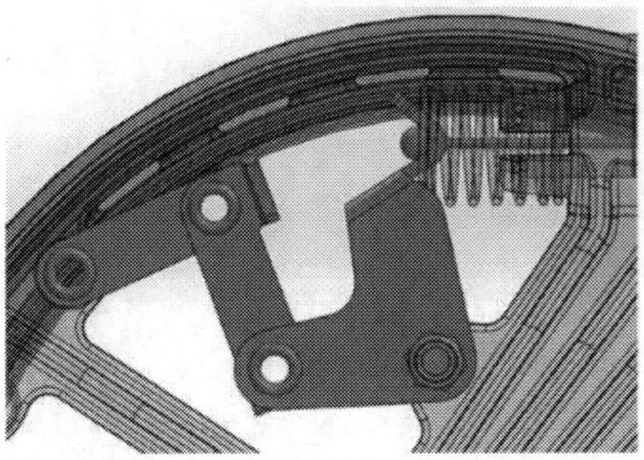

Fig. 12. New four-bar linkage design when brake engaged.

Using an existing wheel, a prototype was built with two dummy wheels and a brake lever to apply braking force to the real wheel. Figure 13 shows the prototype on the left. The right photo in the figure is the details of the three-link brake shoe design when engaged.

Fig. 13. Prototype (left) and detail of new four-bar linkage brake shoe.

The force the user had to apply to stop the prototype from moving was the same with the new design, when compared to the case with the original braking system mounted on the prototype. The prototype rollator was easy to move forward again from positions stopped by engaging the new brake. Even when the user applied somewhat excessive force to the brake lever, the rollator started to move forward again with ease when the break lever was released.

3 Discussion

3.1 Axiomatic design analysis of the new design

Axiomatic Design calls designs with diagonal design equations uncoupled, and those with triangular design equations decoupled. Decoupled designs are also proper except the design parameters (DPs) have to be arranged in a specific order to satisfy FRs [5].

In our case, the original design was decoupled (Eqs. (1) and (3)), however, in our attempt to find the brake shoe to satisfy FRs, the DP was not feasible against a spatial constraint (Figure 10). This attempt was not for satisfying the set of FRs, however, it was aiming to reduce the magnitude of the problematic interference x, i.e., the influence of the brake shoe configuration on the FR of making forward movement.

The new four-bar linkage design for the brake shoe also was in efforts of reducing the interfering component x to zero.

The question raised after completing the redesign was if the original design was really proper. If it was decoupled, the product would have satisfied the users but it did not.

What was overlooked in our original analysis was the passive influence of the brake shoe on the function of disengaging the brake shoe from the wheel rim when making a forward movement. This influence comes from the geometric configuration that Figure 9 shows. When the user releases the braking lever, the brake spring failed to disengage the brake shoe. The brake shoe was jammed between the frame and the wheel. This is shown with the red link in Figure 14. The design equation would have been as shown in Eq. (4), i.e., a coupled design.

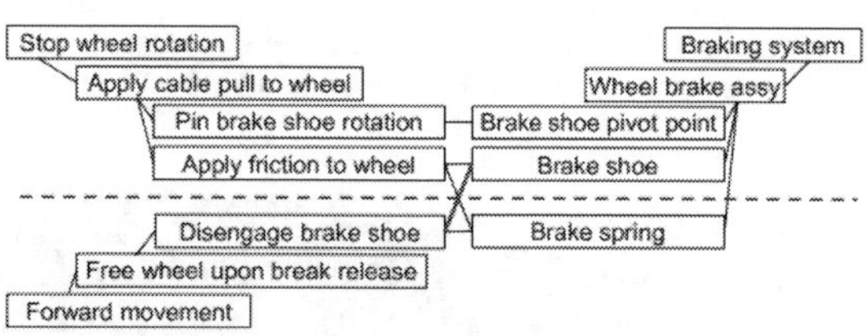

Fig. 14. New four-bar linkage design at rest position.

$$\begin{Bmatrix} \text{Input user int. to stop} \\ \text{Pin BL rotation} \\ \text{Provide cable path} \\ \text{Transfer pull} \\ \text{Friction to wheel} \\ \text{Pin B shoe rotation} \\ \text{Disengage B shoe} \end{Bmatrix} = \begin{bmatrix} X & 0 & 0 & 0 & 0 & 0 & 0 \\ 0 & X & 0 & 0 & 0 & 0 & 0 \\ 0 & 0 & X & 0 & 0 & 0 & 0 \\ 0 & 0 & 0 & X & 0 & 0 & 0 \\ 0 & 0 & 0 & 0 & X & 0 & x \\ 0 & 0 & 0 & 0 & 0 & X & 0 \\ 0 & 0 & 0 & 0 & x & 0 & X \end{bmatrix} \begin{Bmatrix} \text{Brake lever (BL)} \\ \text{BL pivot point} \\ \text{B sheath} \\ \text{B cable} \\ \text{B shoe} \\ \text{B shoe pivot point} \\ \text{B spring} \end{Bmatrix} \quad (4)$$

This type of passive interference identified, here in this case, meaning "a DP failing to perform its FR causes a different FR to persist" is difficult to identify.

The redesign with a four-bar linkage brake shoe eliminated the interference and turned the design matrix into a triangular one, back to Eq. (3), i.e., the originally coupled design was made decoupled.

4 Conclusions

An existing rollator design was investigated for a graduate student's 3-month project.

The student applied Axiomatic Design in identifying and explaining the problem with the existing design. The rollator, once stopped by engaging its brake, had to be pulled backwards before moving forward again.

The problem was the brake shoe configuration that jammed the wheel rotation upon engagement of the brake.

An attempt of modifying the DP to remove the interference was unacceptable due to spatial constraints.

Redesigning the brake shoe configuration nullified the unintended interference and the design turned into an decoupled design.

The prototype built demonstrated that the new four-bar linkage brake shoe performed equally well in terms of stopping the rollator motion and completely removed the problem of difficulty in restarting the rollator forward from a brake engaged stopped position.

It is difficult to identify passive interference of a DP on FRs. The passive interference we found was a DP failing to meet its FR causing persistence of another FR which would have stopped its function if the DP had succeeded.

References

1. United Nations, Department of Economic and Social Affairs, Population Division, *World Population Prospects: The 2015 Revision, Population by Age Groups - Both Sexes* (2015)
2. Cabinet Office, Government of Japan, *2016 Whitepaper: Aged Society* (2016)
3. N.P. Suh, *Axiomatic Design: Advances and Applications*, Oxford University Press (2001)
4. K. Iino and M. Nakao, Design Record Graph and Axiomatic Design for creative design education, *Proceedings of ICAD 2016*, PROCIR-D-16-00377 (2016)
5. G.S. Shin and G.J. Park, Decoupling process of a coupled design using the TRIZ module, *Proceedings of ICAD 2006*, ICAD-2006-04 (2006)

How to Compute the Information Content of 3-FR, 3-DP Decoupled Designs with Uniform Probability Density Functions for Their FRs

João Fradinho[1,*], *Miguel* Cavique[2], *António* Gabriel-Santos[1], *António* Mourão[1] and *António* Gonçalves-Coelho[1]

[1]UNIDEMI & DEMI, Faculdade de Ciências e Tecnologia, Universidade Nova de Lisboa, Campus de Caparica, 2829-516 Caparica, Portugal
[2]UNIDEMI, CINAV & Escola Naval, Base Naval de Lisboa – Alfeite, 2810-001 Almada, Portugal

Abstract. The computation of the information content of decoupled designs implies the use of conditional probability, because the existing design parameters must be adjusted in a certain order, as to fulfil all the existing functional requirements at the first trial. Nevertheless, the computation of the information content is hard to perform when the system range of the functional requirements is denoted by probability density functions. In their works, Suh and Park proposed a graphical method to compute the information content of 2-FR, 2-DP decoupled designs when the probability density functions of the FRs are uniform. This paper introduces an extension to the Suh and Park's previous findings. It presents a method that uses analytical and descriptive geometry techniques to compute the information content of 3-FR, 3-DP decoupled designs with uniform probability density distributions of their FRs, and an illustrative example is presented as well.

1 Introduction

Most of the current engineering design methodologies follow the costly and time-consuming trial-and-error pattern, as for example the ones proposed by Pahl & Beitz [1] and by Hubka [2]. Yet, cost and speed of the engineering design processes became critical by the end of the last century due to the increasing demand of better, faster, cheaper or more capable new products with a short time-to-market prerequisite.

In the late 1970s, N. P. Suh *et al.* [3] introduced a new design theory that was made widely known under the name of Axiomatic Design (AD) [4]. Suh's motivation was to provide scholars and engineers with a sound theoretical foundation for design that conforms to the criteria of modern science, as to foster significant advances in teaching and in practicing design. As a result, AD can be used to teach engineering design in a manner that is similar to mathematics or physics, and allows engineers to consistently avoid the trial-and-error design development cycle, which lets it easier to do it right at the first time, timely and at an affordable cost.

In AD, design is seen as a decision-making process, which success depends on the formal awareness on the functional objectives and constraints, as well as on understanding the engineering sciences and the technologies associated to the likely alternative design solutions.

The design decisions correspond to the mapping between each pair of adjacent design domains, namely the Customer Domain, the Functional Domain, the Physical Domain, and the Process Domain, as depicted in Figure 1.

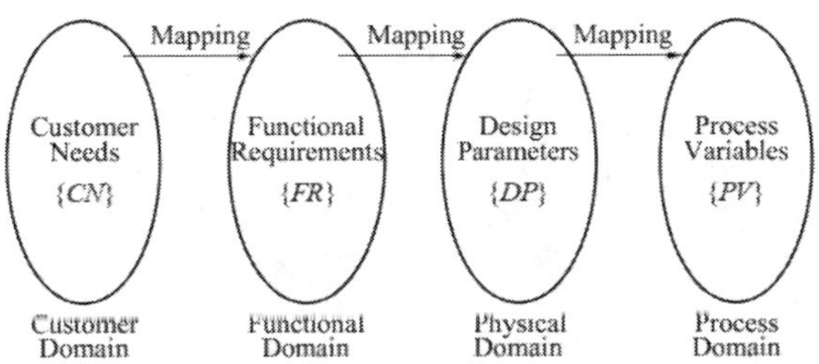

Fig. 1. The design domains.

Each design solution is represented by a design equation. For example, the mapping between the functional and the physical domains is of the form

$$\{FR\} = [A]\{DP\} \qquad (1)$$

where $\{FR\}$ is the vector of the functional requirements, $\{DP\}$ is the vector of the design parameters, and $[A]$ is the design matrix, for which

$$A_{ij} = \frac{\partial FR_i}{\partial DP_j},\ i = 1,..\ m,\ j = 1,..\ n \qquad (2)$$

The AD fundamental decision criteria are based on the independence axiom and on the minimum information axiom [4].

For the cases where $m = n$, two kinds of design solutions fulfil the independence axiom: the uncoupled designs, in which the values of the design parameters

* Corresponding author: jmf@fct.unl.pt

(DPs) can be adjusted in an arbitrary order as to attain the prescribed values for the FRs; and the decoupled designs, in which the values of the DPs can be set in a certain order, so that setting the value of each DP only impacts one FR. Therefore, the uncoupled designs have diagonal design matrices, while decoupled designs have triangular design matrices. A third kind of designs with $m = n$ — the coupled designs — does not conform to the independence axiom and should be avoided [4].

According to AD's theorem 1, designs with $m > n$ are coupled, while designs with $m < n$ are redundant. Redundant designs can be reduced to uncoupled designs or to decoupled designs, or even to coupled designs, as per AD's theorem 3 [5], depending on the manner their design matrices are populated [6].

The Minimum Information Axiom is used to compare multiple design solutions *i.e.*, when multiple sets of different DPs can be used to fulfil the same set of FRs in an independent manner.

The concept of information content is the same that was adopted in the Shannon's theory of communication [7].

The computation of the information content of a 1-FR, 1-DP design can be explained as follows.

Figure 2 depicts the probability density function (pdf) of fulfilling the system's FR. In the same figure, the system range represents the whole ability range of the system, while the design range is the working range that the designer is looking for [4]. The greyed area represents the so-called common range of the design.

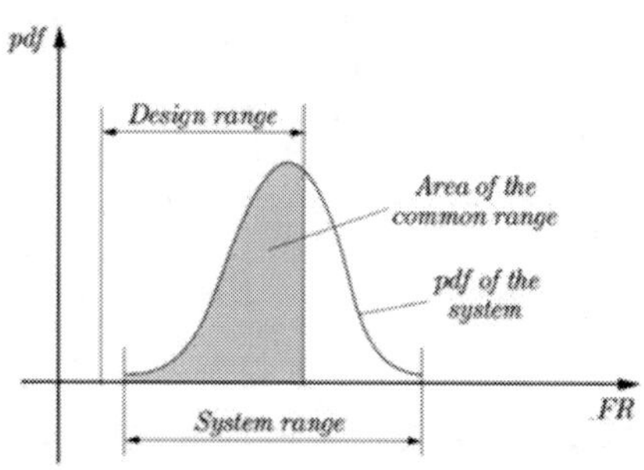

Fig. 2. The system range, the design range and the common range of a 1-FR design.

The probability density function relates to the probability of success of the system, so that the whole area of the system range is such that

$$\int_{-\infty}^{+\infty} pdf(FR)dFR = 1 \tag{3}$$

The probability of the design fulfilling the FR within the design range is given by

$$p = \frac{\text{Area of the common range}}{\text{Area of the system range}} \tag{4}$$

The information content of the design, I, expressed in bit, is computed trough

$$I = \log_2 \frac{1}{p} = -\log_2 p \tag{5}$$

For the case of an m-FR design, the total probability of success, p_T, is

$$p_T = \prod_{i=1}^{m} p_i \tag{6}$$

where p_i is the probability of success of FR_i.

Thus, the information content of the design is

$$I_T = \sum_{i=1}^{m} I_i \tag{7}$$

Suh [8, pp 179-185] and Park [9, pp 38-51] showed that a graphical method could be used to compute the information content of 2-FR, 2-DP decoupled designs when the probability density functions of both FRs have a uniform distribution. The present work contains an extension to the aforesaid method applied to 3-FR, 3-DP decoupled designs with uniform probability density functions of their FRs.

2 The information content of 3-FR, 3-DP decoupled designs

The computation of the information content of multiple-FR designs is simple for uncoupled designs because the probability of fulfilling each FR does not depend on the remaining FRs. However, this is not the case of the decoupled designs, for which the probability is conditional.

According to Equation (1), the design equation of a 2-FR, 2-DP decoupled design is

$$\begin{Bmatrix} FR_1 \\ FR_2 \end{Bmatrix} = \begin{bmatrix} A_{11} & 0 \\ A_{21} & A_{22} \end{bmatrix} \begin{Bmatrix} DP_1 \\ DP_2 \end{Bmatrix} \tag{8}$$

Hence, the random variations of the FRs due to the random variations of the DPs are given by

$$\begin{Bmatrix} \delta FR_1 \\ \delta FR_2 \end{Bmatrix} = \begin{bmatrix} A_{11} & 0 \\ A_{21} & A_{22} \end{bmatrix} \begin{Bmatrix} \delta DP_1 \\ \delta DP_2 \end{Bmatrix} \tag{9}$$

Equation (9) shows that δFR_1 is statistically independent, while δFR_2 is statistically dependent with respect to δFR_1.

In short, Park [9, p. 40] showed that the problem stated by Equation (9) can be depicted in the physical domain by Figure 3, for the case of $A_{ij} \geq 0$ and

$$-\Delta FR_i \leq \delta FR_i \leq \Delta FR_i,\ \Delta FR_i \geq 0 \tag{10}$$

$$-\Delta DP_i \leq \delta DP_i \leq \Delta DP_i,\ \Delta DP_i \geq 0 \tag{11}$$

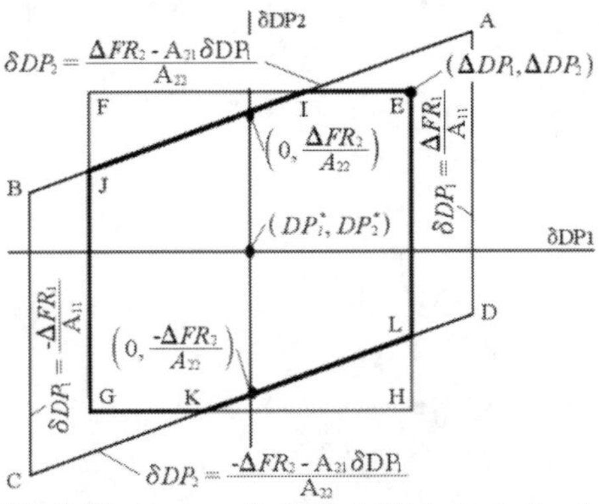

Fig. 3. The isogram of a 2-FR, 2-DP design in the physical domain [9].

The parallelogram ABCD of Figure 3 is the system range of the design, while the quadrilateral EFGH is the design range and the hexagon IJGKLE is the common range. Thus, for the case of uniform probability density functions, the information content is given by

$$I_u = \log_2 \frac{1}{p} = \log_2 \left(\frac{\text{Area of quadrilateral EFGH}}{\text{Area of hexagon IJGKLE}} \right) \quad (12)$$

The areas of the quadrilateral EFGH and of the hexagon IJGKLE can be computed by integration, using the equations that were found by Park [9] and that are included in Figure 3. Yet, those areas can be much more easily evaluated using a 2-D CAD system capable of measuring areas of closed polygons.

This method can be extended to 3-FR, 3-DP decoupled designs with uniform pdfs. The random variation of the functional requirement, δFR_i, due to the random variation in a design parameter, δDP_j, is expressed as

$$\begin{bmatrix} \delta FR_1 \\ \delta FR_2 \\ \delta FR_3 \end{bmatrix} = \begin{bmatrix} \frac{\partial FR_1}{\partial DP_1} & 0 & 0 \\ \frac{\partial FR_2}{\partial DP_1} & \frac{\partial FR_2}{\partial DP_2} & 0 \\ \frac{\partial FR_3}{\partial DP_1} & \frac{\partial FR_3}{\partial DP_2} & \frac{\partial FR_3}{\partial DP_3} \end{bmatrix} \begin{bmatrix} \delta DP_1 \\ \delta DP_2 \\ \delta DP_3 \end{bmatrix} \quad (13)$$

Denoting the elements of the design matrix by A_{ij}, we have

$$\begin{bmatrix} \delta FR_1 \\ \delta FR_2 \\ \delta FR_3 \end{bmatrix} = \begin{bmatrix} A_{11} & 0 & 0 \\ A_{21} & A_{22} & 0 \\ A_{31} & A_{32} & A_{33} \end{bmatrix} \begin{bmatrix} \delta DP_1 \\ \delta DP_2 \\ \delta DP_3 \end{bmatrix} \quad (14)$$

Now, let us suppose the following unbiased tolerance ranges:

$$-\Delta FR_i \leq \delta FR_i \leq \Delta FR_i \quad (15)$$

$$-\Delta DP_j \leq \delta DP_j \leq \Delta DP_j \quad (16)$$

Let us also suppose that

$$\Delta FR_i \geq 0; \ \Delta DP_j \geq 0; \ A_{ij} \geq 0$$

and that

δDP_j are statistically independent;

δFR_2 is statistically dependent to δFR_1;

δFR_3 is statistically dependent to δFR_1 and δFR_2.

Under these conditions, we have

$$\begin{aligned} \delta FR_1 &= A_{11}\delta DP_1 \\ \delta FR_2 &= A_{21}\delta DP_1 + A_{22}\delta DP_2 \\ \delta FR_3 &= A_{31}\delta DP_1 + A_{32}\delta DP_2 + A_{33}\delta DP_3 \end{aligned} \quad (17)$$

so that

$$\begin{aligned} \delta DP_1 &= \frac{\delta FR_1}{A_{11}} \\ \delta DP_2 &= \frac{\delta FR_2}{A_{22}} - \frac{A_{21}}{A_{22}}\delta DP_1 \\ \delta DP_3 &= \frac{\delta FR_3}{A_{33}} - \frac{A_{32}}{A_{33}}\delta DP_2 - \frac{A_{31}}{A_{33}}\delta DP_1 \end{aligned} \quad (18)$$

The combination of Equations (15), (16) and (18) gives

$$\begin{aligned} &-\Delta FR_1 \leq A_{11}\delta DP_1 \leq \Delta FR_1 \\ &-\Delta FR_2 \leq A_{21}\delta DP_1 + A_{22}\delta DP_2 \leq \Delta FR_2 \\ &-\Delta FR_3 \leq A_{31}\delta DP_1 + A_{32}\delta DP_2 + A_{33}\delta DP_3 \leq \Delta FR_3 \\ &-\Delta DP_1 \leq \delta DP_1 \leq \Delta DP_1 \\ &-\Delta DP_2 \leq \delta DP_2 \leq \Delta DP_2 \\ &-\Delta DP_3 \leq \delta DP_3 \leq \Delta DP_3 \end{aligned} \quad (19)$$

Equation (19) represents the limits of the design in the physical domain. The first three conditions characterize the system range and the last three denote the design range.

The system range is the intersection of three pairs of semi-spaces. The first condition represents two profile planes that are parallel to the projection plane ($\delta DP_2 O \delta DP_3$); the second one represents two vertical planes that are parallel to δDP_3 axis; and the third condition represents two planes that are oblique to the three projection planes.

Figure 4 shows the intersections of the six planes with the orthogonal projection planes. The values of A_{ij}, ΔFR_i and ΔDP_j were considered as positive in the graphic representation. Thus, the vertical and the oblique planes open to the right.

The design range is a quadrangular prism that is also centred in the origin.

The bold line solid of Figure 5 is the 10-face polyhedron [AA'''II'JJ'KL'C''C'MM'NN'PQ'] that represents the common range of the problem under study. It is obtained through the intersection of the solids that represent the system and the design ranges.

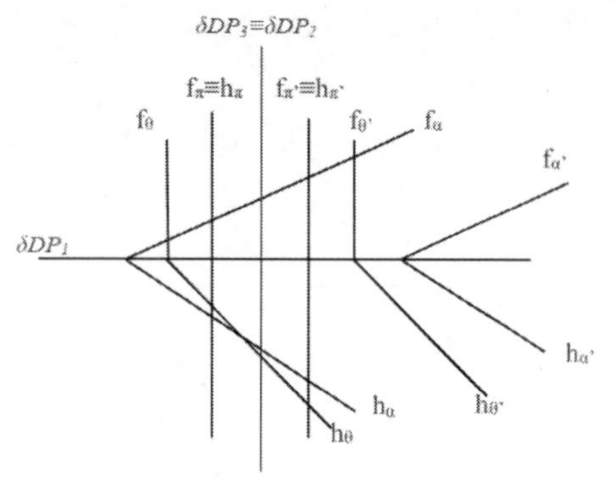

Fig. 4. The six planes that determine the system range in the DP domain.

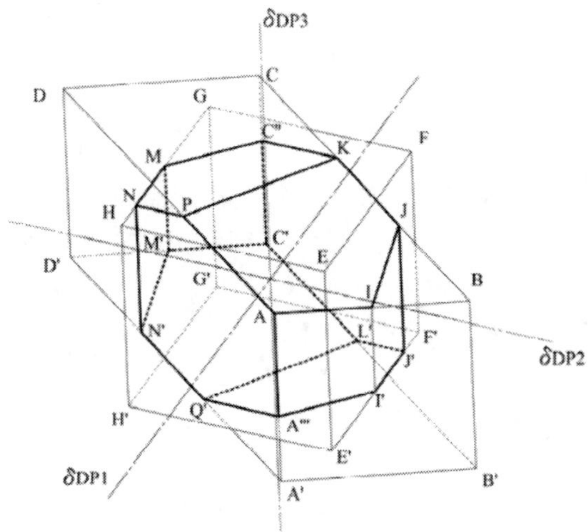

Fig. 5. The system, the design and the common ranges.

The system range is the 6-face polyhedron [ABCDA'B'C'D'] with two profile faces ([ADA'D'] and [BCB'C']), which belong to planes π and π'; two vertical faces ([ABA'B'] and [CDC'D']), belonging to planes θ and θ'; and two oblique faces ([ABCD] and [A'B'C'D']) that belong to planes α and α'.

The design range is the quadrangular prism [EFGHE'F'G'H'] with faces parallel to the projection planes.

The coordinates of the vertices of the system and of the design ranges of Figure 5 are:

$$A\left(\begin{array}{l}\dfrac{\Delta FR_1}{A_{11}};\\ \dfrac{\Delta FR_2}{A_{22}}-\dfrac{A_{21}}{A_{22}}\dfrac{\Delta FR_1}{A_{11}};\\ \dfrac{\Delta FR_3}{A_{33}}-\dfrac{A_{32}}{A_{33}}\dfrac{\Delta FR_2}{A_{22}}-\left(\dfrac{A_{31}}{A_{33}}-\dfrac{A_{32}}{A_{33}}\dfrac{A_{21}}{A_{22}}\right)\dfrac{\Delta FR_1}{A_{11}}\end{array}\right)$$

$$A'\left(\begin{array}{l}\dfrac{\Delta FR_1}{A_{11}};\\ \dfrac{\Delta FR_2}{A_{22}}-\dfrac{A_{21}}{A_{22}}\dfrac{\Delta FR_1}{A_{11}};\\ -\dfrac{\Delta FR_3}{A_{33}}-\dfrac{A_{32}}{A_{33}}\dfrac{\Delta FR_2}{A_{22}}-\left(\dfrac{A_{31}}{A_{33}}-\dfrac{A_{32}}{A_{33}}\dfrac{A_{21}}{A_{22}}\right)\dfrac{\Delta FR_1}{A_{11}}\end{array}\right)$$

$$B\left(\begin{array}{l}-\dfrac{\Delta FR_1}{A_{11}};\\ \dfrac{\Delta FR_2}{A_{22}}+\dfrac{A_{21}}{A_{22}}\dfrac{\Delta FR_1}{A_{11}};\\ \dfrac{\Delta FR_3}{A_{33}}-\dfrac{A_{32}}{A_{33}}\dfrac{\Delta FR_2}{A_{22}}-\left(-\dfrac{A_{31}}{A_{33}}+\dfrac{A_{32}}{A_{33}}\dfrac{A_{21}}{A_{22}}\right)\dfrac{\Delta FR_1}{A_{11}}\end{array}\right)$$

$$B'\left(\begin{array}{l}-\dfrac{\Delta FR_1}{A_{11}};\\ \dfrac{\Delta FR_2}{A_{22}}+\dfrac{A_{21}}{A_{22}}\dfrac{\Delta FR_1}{A_{11}};\\ -\dfrac{\Delta FR_3}{A_{33}}-\dfrac{A_{32}}{A_{33}}\dfrac{\Delta FR_2}{A_{22}}-\left(-\dfrac{A_{31}}{A_{33}}+\dfrac{A_{32}}{A_{33}}\dfrac{A_{21}}{A_{22}}\right)\dfrac{\Delta FR_1}{A_{11}}\end{array}\right)$$

$$C\left(\begin{array}{l}-\dfrac{\Delta FR_1}{A_{11}};\\ -\dfrac{\Delta FR_2}{A_{22}}+\dfrac{A_{21}}{A_{22}}\dfrac{\Delta FR_1}{A_{11}};\\ \dfrac{\Delta FR_3}{A_{33}}+\dfrac{A_{32}}{A_{33}}\dfrac{\Delta FR_2}{A_{22}}-\left(-\dfrac{A_{31}}{A_{33}}+\dfrac{A_{32}}{A_{33}}\dfrac{A_{21}}{A_{22}}\right)\dfrac{\Delta FR_1}{A_{11}}\end{array}\right)$$

$$C'\left(\begin{array}{l}-\dfrac{\Delta FR_1}{A_{11}};\\ -\dfrac{\Delta FR_2}{A_{22}}+\dfrac{A_{21}}{A_{22}}\dfrac{\Delta FR_1}{A_{11}};\\ -\dfrac{\Delta FR_3}{A_{33}}+\dfrac{A_{32}}{A_{33}}\dfrac{\Delta FR_2}{A_{22}}-\left(-\dfrac{A_{31}}{A_{33}}+\dfrac{A_{32}}{A_{33}}\dfrac{A_{21}}{A_{22}}\right)\dfrac{\Delta FR_1}{A_{11}}\end{array}\right)$$

$$D\left(\begin{array}{l}\dfrac{\Delta FR_1}{A_{11}};\\ -\dfrac{\Delta FR_2}{A_{22}}-\dfrac{A_{21}}{A_{22}}\dfrac{\Delta FR_1}{A_{11}};\\ \dfrac{\Delta FR_3}{A_{33}}+\dfrac{A_{32}}{A_{33}}\dfrac{\Delta FR_2}{A_{22}}-\left(\dfrac{A_{31}}{A_{33}}-\dfrac{A_{32}}{A_{33}}\dfrac{A_{21}}{A_{22}}\right)\dfrac{\Delta FR_1}{A_{11}}\end{array}\right)$$

$$D'\left(\begin{array}{l}\dfrac{\Delta FR_1}{A_{11}};\\ -\dfrac{\Delta FR_2}{A_{22}}-\dfrac{A_{21}}{A_{22}}\dfrac{\Delta FR_1}{A_{11}};\\ -\dfrac{\Delta FR_3}{A_{33}}+\dfrac{A_{32}}{A_{33}}\dfrac{\Delta FR_2}{A_{22}}-\left(\dfrac{A_{31}}{A_{33}}-\dfrac{A_{32}}{A_{33}}\dfrac{A_{21}}{A_{22}}\right)\dfrac{\Delta FR_1}{A_{11}}\end{array}\right)$$

$$\mathrm{E}\left(\Delta DP_1;\Delta DP_2;\Delta DP_3\right)$$
$$\mathrm{E'}\left(\Delta DP_1;\Delta DP_2;-\Delta DP_3\right)$$
$$\mathrm{F}\left(-\Delta DP_1;\Delta DP_2;\Delta DP_3\right)$$
$$\mathrm{F'}\left(-\Delta DP_1;\Delta DP_2;-\Delta DP_3\right)$$
$$\mathrm{G}\left(-\Delta DP_1;-\Delta DP_2;\Delta DP_3\right)$$
$$\mathrm{G'}\left(-\Delta DP_1;-\Delta DP_2;-\Delta DP_3\right)$$
$$\mathrm{H}\left(\Delta DP_1;-\Delta DP_2;\Delta DP_3\right)$$
$$\mathrm{H'}\left(\Delta DP_1;-\Delta DP_2;-\Delta DP_3\right)$$

The coordinates of the vertices of the common range depend on the six planes $\left(\pi,\pi',\theta,\theta',\alpha,\alpha'\right)$ that define the system range, as well as on the six planes parallel to the axes that define the design range, herewith named by their own coordinates:

$$\left(\Delta DP_1,\Delta DP_2,\Delta DP_3,-\Delta DP_1,-\Delta DP_2,-\Delta DP_3\right).$$

Each vertex is the intersection of three of these 12 planes, as follows

$$\mathrm{A}(\pi\cap\theta\cap\alpha)$$
$$\mathrm{A'''}\left(\pi\cap\theta\cap-\Delta DP_3\right)$$
$$\mathrm{I}\left(\theta\cap\Delta DP_2\cap\alpha\right)$$
$$\mathrm{I'}\left(\theta\cap\Delta DP_2\cap-\Delta DP_3\right)$$
$$\mathrm{J}\left(\pi'\cap\Delta DP_2\cap\alpha\right)$$
$$\mathrm{J'}\left(\pi'\cap\Delta DP_2\cap-\Delta DP_3\right)$$
$$\mathrm{K}\left(\pi'\cap\alpha\cap\Delta DP_3\right)$$
$$\mathrm{L'}\left(\pi'\cap\alpha'\cap-\Delta DP_3\right)$$
$$\mathrm{C''}\left(\pi'\cap\theta'\cap\Delta DP_3\right)$$
$$\mathrm{C'}\left(\pi'\cap\theta'\cap\alpha'\right)$$
$$\mathrm{M}\left(\theta'\cap-\Delta DP_2\cap\Delta DP_3\right)$$
$$\mathrm{M'}\left(\theta'\cap-\Delta DP_2\cap\alpha'\right)$$
$$\mathrm{N}\left(\pi\cap-\Delta DP_2\cap\Delta DP_3\right)$$
$$\mathrm{N'}\left(\pi\cap-\Delta DP_2\cap\alpha'\right)$$
$$\mathrm{P}\left(\pi\cap\alpha\cap\Delta DP_3\right)$$
$$\mathrm{Q'}\left(\pi\cap\alpha'\cap-\Delta DP_3\right)$$

The common range is a 10-face, 16-vertex, 22-edge polyhedron, which confirms the Euler's formula.

The coordinates of the vertices are:

$$\mathrm{A}\begin{pmatrix}\dfrac{\Delta FR_1}{A_{11}};\\ \dfrac{\Delta FR_2}{A_{22}}-\dfrac{A_{21}}{A_{22}}\dfrac{\Delta FR_1}{A_{11}};\\ \dfrac{\Delta FR_3}{A_{33}}-\dfrac{A_{32}}{A_{33}}\dfrac{\Delta FR_2}{A_{22}}-\left(\dfrac{A_{31}}{A_{33}}-\dfrac{A_{32}}{A_{33}}\dfrac{A_{21}}{A_{22}}\right)\dfrac{\Delta FR_1}{A_{11}}\end{pmatrix}$$

$$\mathrm{A'''}\left(\frac{\Delta FR_1}{A_{11}};\frac{\Delta FR_2}{A_{22}}-\frac{A_{21}}{A_{22}}\frac{\Delta FR_1}{A_{11}};-\Delta DP_3\right)$$

$$\mathrm{I}\begin{pmatrix}\dfrac{\Delta FR_2}{A_{21}}-\dfrac{A_{22}}{A_{21}}\Delta DP_2;\\ \Delta DP_2;\\ \dfrac{\Delta FR_3}{A_{33}}-\dfrac{A_{31}}{A_{33}}\dfrac{\Delta FR_2}{A_{21}}+\left(\dfrac{A_{31}}{A_{33}}\dfrac{A_{22}}{A_{21}}-\dfrac{A_{32}}{A_{33}}\right)\Delta DP_2\end{pmatrix}$$

$$\mathrm{I'}\left(\frac{\Delta FR_2}{A_{21}}-\frac{A_{22}}{A_{21}}\Delta DP_2;\Delta DP_2;-\Delta DP_3\right)$$

$$\mathrm{J}\left(-\frac{\Delta FR_1}{A_{11}};\Delta DP_2;\frac{\Delta FR_3}{A_{33}}+\frac{A_{31}}{A_{33}}\frac{\Delta FR_1}{A_{11}}-\frac{A_{32}}{A_{33}}\Delta DP_2\right)$$

$$\mathrm{J'}\left(-\frac{\Delta FR_1}{A_{11}};\Delta DP_2;-\Delta DP_3\right)$$

$$\mathrm{K}\left(-\frac{\Delta FR_1}{A_{11}};\frac{\Delta FR_3}{A_{32}}+\frac{A_{31}}{A_{32}}\frac{\Delta FR_1}{A_{11}}-\frac{A_{33}}{A_{32}}\Delta DP_3;\Delta DP_3\right)$$

$$\mathrm{L'}\left(-\frac{\Delta FR_1}{A_{11}};-\frac{\Delta FR_3}{A_{32}}+\frac{A_{31}}{A_{32}}\frac{\Delta FR_1}{A_{11}}+\frac{A_{33}}{A_{32}}\Delta DP_3;-\Delta DP_3\right)$$

$$\mathrm{C''}\left(-\frac{\Delta FR_1}{A_{11}};-\frac{\Delta FR_2}{A_{22}}+\frac{A_{21}}{A_{22}}\frac{\Delta FR_1}{A_{11}};\Delta DP_3\right)$$

$$\mathrm{C'}\begin{pmatrix}-\dfrac{\Delta FR_1}{A_{11}};\\ -\dfrac{\Delta FR_2}{A_{22}}+\dfrac{A_{21}}{A_{22}}\dfrac{\Delta FR_1}{A_{11}};\\ -\dfrac{\Delta FR_3}{A_{33}}+\dfrac{A_{32}}{A_{33}}\dfrac{\Delta FR_2}{A_{22}}-\left(-\dfrac{A_{31}}{A_{33}}+\dfrac{A_{32}}{A_{33}}\dfrac{A_{21}}{A_{22}}\right)\dfrac{\Delta FR_1}{A_{11}}\end{pmatrix}$$

$$\mathrm{M}\left(-\frac{\Delta FR_2}{A_{21}}+\frac{A_{22}}{A_{21}}\Delta DP_2;-\Delta DP_2;\Delta DP_3\right)$$

$$\mathrm{M'}\begin{pmatrix}-\dfrac{\Delta FR_2}{A_{21}}+\dfrac{A_{22}}{A_{21}}\Delta DP_2;\\ -\Delta DP_2;\\ -\dfrac{\Delta FR_3}{A_{33}}+\dfrac{A_{31}}{A_{33}}\dfrac{\Delta FR_2}{A_{21}}-\left(\dfrac{A_{31}}{A_{33}}\dfrac{A_{22}}{A_{21}}-\dfrac{A_{32}}{A_{33}}\right)\Delta DP_2\end{pmatrix}$$

$$\mathrm{N}\left(\frac{\Delta FR_1}{A_{11}};-\Delta DP_2;\Delta DP_3\right)$$

$$N'\left(\frac{\Delta FR_1}{A_{11}};-\Delta DP_2;-\frac{\Delta FR_3}{A_{33}}-\frac{A_{31}}{A_{33}}\frac{\Delta FR_1}{A_{11}}+\frac{A_{32}}{A_{33}}\Delta DP_2\right)$$

$$P\left(\frac{\Delta FR_1}{A_{11}};\frac{\Delta FR_3}{A_{32}}-\frac{A_{31}}{A_{32}}\frac{\Delta FR_1}{A_{11}}-\frac{A_{33}}{A_{32}}\Delta DP_3;\Delta DP_3\right)$$

$$Q'\left(\frac{\Delta FR_1}{A_{11}};-\frac{\Delta FR_3}{A_{32}}-\frac{A_{31}}{A_{32}}\frac{\Delta FR_1}{A_{11}}+\frac{A_{33}}{A_{32}}\Delta DP_3;-\Delta DP_3\right)$$

3 An illustrative example

The probability of success of a design, p_s, as well as of its information content, I, are given by

$$p_s = \frac{V_c}{V_{dp}} \tag{20}$$

$$I = -\log_2 p_s \tag{21}$$

where V_c is the volume of the common range and V_{dp} is the tolerance volume for the design parameters, which is the design range.

The design depicted in Figure 5 will be used as an illustrative example, where it was assumed that

$$\Delta FR_1 = 2 \text{ length units} \tag{22}$$

$$\Delta FR_2 = 3 \text{ length units} \tag{23}$$

$$\Delta FR_3 = 4\tan 35^\circ \text{ length units} \tag{24}$$

$$A_{11} = A_{22} = A_{33} = 1 \tag{25}$$

$$\Delta DP_1 = \Delta DP_2 = \Delta DP_3 = 3 \text{ length units} \tag{26}$$

As a result, the design equation of this decoupled deign is

$$\begin{bmatrix} FR_1 \\ FR_2 \\ FR_3 \end{bmatrix} = \begin{bmatrix} 1 & 0 & 0 \\ 1 & 1 & 0 \\ \tan 35^\circ & 1 & 1 \end{bmatrix} \begin{bmatrix} DP_1 \\ DP_2 \\ DP_3 \end{bmatrix} \tag{27}$$

This means that the intersection of the profile planes (π and π') crosses the dDP_1 axis at points 2 and -2, the vertical planes (θ and θ') at 3 and -3, and the oblique planes (α and α') at 4 and -4. In addition, the vertical planes open 45° to the right and the oblique planes open 35° to the right, horizontally and frontally.

Thus, the volume of the common range, V_c, is the volume of the polyhedron [AA'''II'JJ'KL'C''C'MM'NN'PQ']. This volume can be computed, although very hard to attain.

Therefore, a 3D solid modeller software was used to evaluate V_c.

$$V_c = 90{,}31 \text{ volume units} \tag{28}$$

The volume of the tolerance region for the design parameters, V_{dp}, is

$$V_{dp} = 8\times\Delta DP_1\times\Delta DP_2\times\Delta DP_3 = 216{,}00 \text{ vol. units} \tag{29}$$

Thus, the probability of success and the information content are given by

$$p_s = \frac{90{,}31}{216{,}00} = 0{,}42 \tag{30}$$

$$I = -\log_2 p_s = 1{,}26 \text{ bit} \tag{31}$$

4 Discussion

As one can see, Figure 5 is the extension for the case of a design with 3-FR, 3-DP of the 2-FR, 2-DP problem that is depicted in Figure 3.

Section 4 of this paper shows how difficult can be the computation of the information content of a 3-FR, 3-DP design, even for designs with uniform pdfs, as is the case of Figure 5. In the same section, one can also see how easy can be the computation of the information content using an advanced 3D solid modeller.

It would be easy to prove that if ΔDP_1, ΔDP_2 and ΔDP_3 were sufficiently small, then the whole design range would be contained in the system range and the information content would be null.

5 Conclusions

The computation of the information content of uncoupled designs is easy, independently of the number of FRs, because the involved probabilities are always independent. However, the most arduous issue of Axiomatic Design is the computation of the information content in all the other cases.

In the case of 2-FR, 2-DP decoupled designs with uniform pdfs, where conditional probability is present, Suh and Park showed that the computation is relatively easy through numerical or graphical computation.

The present paper deals with 3-FR, 3-DP decoupled designs with uniform pdfs. This is a much more difficult problem to solve than the solution presented by the two aforesaid authors. In fact, Figure 3 shows that the common range of the 2-FR, 2-DP designs is a 6-vertex polygon, while the common range of a 3-FR, 3-DP design is a 16-vertix polyhedron, as is can be ascertained through Figure 5.

Given that it is still possible to represent the last problem in a 3D space, than one can overtake the hard to implement the numerical computation of the information content through the use of an advanced solid modeller, as it was done in Figure 5.

Although it seems a very small advance in the state-of-art, the possibility to easily solve 3-FR, 3-DP designs with uniform pdfs by using solid modelling software is a significant advance in what concerns to design practise.

The authors gratefully thank the sponsorship of Fundação para a Ciência e Tecnologia through the Strategic Project UID/EMS/00667/2013 – UNIDEMI.

References

1. G. Pahl, W. Beitz, *Engineering Design: A Systematic Approach* (London: The Design Council, 1988).
2. V. Hubka, *Principles of engineering design*, (England: Butterworth & Co, 1982).
3. N.P. Suh, A. Bell, D. Gossard, On an axiomatic approach to manufacturing and the Design Axioms, *J Eng Power-T ASME*, **100**: 127-130, (1978).
4. N.P. Suh, *The principles of design* (N.Y.: Oxford University. Press, 1990).
5. N.P. Suh, *Complexity: Theory and Applications*, (N.Y.: Oxford University Press, 2005).
6. A.M. Gonçalves-Coelho, G. Neştian, M. Cavique, A. Mourão, *Tackling with Redundant Design Solutions Through Axiomatic Design*, Int J Precis Eng Man, **13**: 1837-1843, (2012).
7. C. Shannon, *The mathematical theory of communication*, The Bell System Technical Journal, **27**: 379-423, 623-656, (1948).
8. N.P. Suh, *Axiomatic Design: Advances and Applications* (N.Y.: Oxford University Press, 2001).
9. G.-J. Park, *Analytic Methods for Design Practice* (London: Springer-Verlag, 2007).

MATEC Web of Conferences 127, 01005 (2017) DOI: 10.1051/matecconf/201712701005
ICAD 2017

Functional Case Test Design to Optimize the Software Development in Italian Tax Processes (Part I): Methodology Definition

Fernando Rolli*, *Chiara* Parretti, *Paolo* Citti, and *Massimo* Rinaldi

Department of Innovation and Information Engineering, Guglielmo Marconi University, Via Plinio 44 - 00193 Rome, Italy

Abstract. In Europe's general context of economic integration, the National States have preserved a few competences. Among them, the most important competence is taxation management, which has now become an important lever to stabilize the State's budget and to meet the economic parameters set by the European Agreements. From this perspective, it is crucial to identify a software development mode to reduce the time spent for the implementation/adjustment of the tax payment software application and, at the same time, to minimize the overall risk level. In software development, approximately 40% of time is spent in a series of testing activities: this stage of the development process is mostly placed at the end of the implementation activities. Consequently, since many testing activities have to be waived in order to meet the deadlines for software delivery, applications that are not entirely in compliance with the user's needs and/or entailing non-compliance are more likely to be introduced. This paper focuses on improving the testing process in tax procedures. The proposed method aims to improve the process, by introducing an integrated procedure based on Axiomatic Design. The approach developed will facilitate a reduction both in the testing preparation time and in performing the test cases. In this scenario, it will be possible to optimize the data compilation process, to verify the compliance within the technical specifications as provided by the Italian Revenue Agency, to identify possible critical scenarios with a proactive approach, and to avoid classes of non-conformities.

1 Introduction

The applications used for the management of tax obligations must comply with the regulations introduced by the budgetary laws and their implicit regulatory mechanisms, and have, therefore, an annual feature. In Europe's general context of economic integration, the National States have preserved a few competences, and the management of taxation the most important of them. The Revenue Agencies have become an important lever to stabilize the budget and meet the economic parameters set by the European Agreements. It is crucial, in this scenario, to identify a software development mode that can effectively reduce the time spent for implementations/adjustments to be applied to the tax payment software applications, as well as minimize the overall risk level. In the software development's life-cycle, around 40% of the time is spent for a various number of testing activities [1]. This phase of the development process is mostly placed at the end of the implementation activities, thus implying that, in order to meet the software delivery deadlines, many testing activities are being neglected. This situation can lead to consequences such as the release of applications that do not correspond exactly to the customer attributes and/or with a high level of non-compliance. The use of the selection system of the functional tests with an AD approach can, instead, reduce the testing time -because many activities can be anticipated- and, at the same time, ensure the coverage of the functional requirements. As of literature, there are indeed several procedures based on AD that have successfully applied AD to optimize processes in several fields [2-4].

2 Building an integrated testing process

The current scientific literature has widely shown that it is impossible to produce a completely error-free software. Nonetheless, this issue should not prevent programmers from seeking new ways of improving the testing process, to increase software's quality level and to optimize both the time and the resources used. The aim of this article is to define an integrated process in the test case preparation for verifications of a functional-type on the applications used to manage the fiscal deadlines. Each test case (CT) consists of a set of required instructions to run a test on a defined object: it is formalized by the input data for the test, by the expected result and by the conditions of test application. This article focuses on optimizing the process of selection and execution of functional tests. In particular, this paper proposes an integrated methodology for the

* Corresponding author: f.rolli@unimarconi.it

selection of test cases, starting from the most abstract logical levels of functional requirements decomposition and proceeding to test the elementary code objects produced. The final objective of this integrated process is to build a complete test case matrix, which will allow to associate a specific test case to each decomposed functional requisite. This mechanism guarantees the coverage of each functional requirement with a specifically selected test case. From this perspective, the choice of test cases is no longer merely tied to the experience of designers –or, even worse, to chance - rather it follows a logically consistent path.

3 Testing process architecture

3.1 Testing process

The testing phase has the task of verifying the adherence to the functional and performance requirements and the correctness of design and coding. Unfortunately, a major part of this phase is placed at the end of the software implementation process. Therefore, it is affected by any problem related to the urgency of its release. Moreover, software companies are often unequipped in terms of cross-reference teams that could help identify the test cases and allow the implementation, which should be performed by highly trained personnel – and which, above all, should not be directly involved in the design and coding phases [5, 6]. First of all, it is part of a good practice to run a thorough estimate of the time and resources devoted to testing. Secondly, considering these estimates, a plan must be defined for the quality of testing. This plan has to include the resources to be used, the time needed, the levels of accuracy required to produce the software, and the functional coverage of the test cases (test case matrix) [7].

3.2 V model testing process

In scientific literature, there are various testing models, each with their own significance in specific contexts. In the present article, we will refer to the so-called V Model, which better adapts to the axiomatic decomposition process of the functional requisites. The figure below illustrates the operating methods of the testing process, according to the V-model [6-8]. On the left, Figure 1 shows the test preparation activities, which are built starting from the customer attributes up to the coding phase of software objects. At each logic level, the test cases deemed necessary to verify the implementation phase are created. The problem that arises at this stage of the process is to verify the adequacy and the functional coverage of the various test cases. The problem is solved with the so-called 'software static testings' – in other words, with checks that do not involve the execution of a program or parts of it [7]. The present article focuses in particular on this side of the testing process, proposing an AD approach to test case designing. The second part of the process, instead, concerns the execution of test cases on the software produced. In this case, we speak of dynamic testing. The process starts with tests on the single software components and continues with integration testings and a system testing, to finally reach testing for the procedure acceptance performed by the client. This process may involve recycling. At each stage, testing results must be recorded and any updated documents related to the project must be saved in special repositories and made available online at any time. A corporate Database can be possible for this purpose: it should be accessed by staff involved in the project.

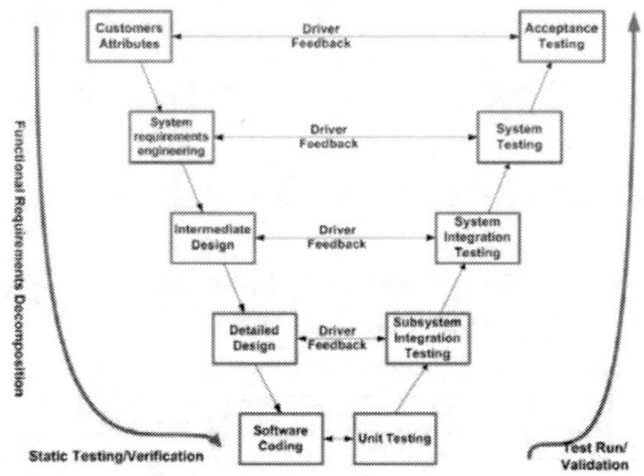

Fig. 1. V model testing process.

3.3 Non-conformity management

In case of more complex projects, it is useful to keep a record of the detected and corrected malfunctions encountered during testing, as well as any non-conformities occurred after the release of the application. A specific supporting service can analyse and categorize all non-conformities (NC) using a multi-level database with a HNCR approach (Holistic Non-Conformity Reduction) [9-11]. A Database of this type allows recording any malfunctioning through the assignment of unique and structured elementary data. This process triggers a proactive intervention, performing an analytical insight carrying an impact on several NCs at a time. In this way, we avoid an unnecessary and time-consuming activity of addressing them one by one. In this context, value is given to the experience gained over the years, on a more general level, with a 'lesson-learned' approach that can be used to solve problems, starting to troubleshoot from their deepest roots. The adoption of the HNCR approach mentioned above, allows to define, starting from every single non-conformity, the clusters of problems occurring at a major level of abstraction. This abstraction allows to solve more non-conformities at the same time, and to implement any additional preventive policies [11-13]. Similarly, appropriate test cases on specific issues can be set. In this way, we can avoid solving problems one by one, as soon as they occur. In addition, the recording and cataloguing of the problems arisen at any stage of the software's life cycle allows producing valuable statistics that will be useful in future projects.

4 Design of an integrated testing system for fiscal procedures

The AD design methodology can be used to optimize the design process [14, 15] and the execution of functional tests both in case of a custom implementation of a fiscal procedure and in case of an annual adjustment of the tax management software. The final objective of this integrated process is the construction of a complete test case matrix. The matrix must allow the coverage of all functional requisites. In this way, we can avoid duplicating the activities or, considering a worse scenario, skipping the verification of the important functionalities of the software produced. The whole testing process is described in Figure 2.

4.1 Fiscal requirements decomposition

4.1.1 Functional requirements decomposition

The documentary management described in subsection 3.3 allows to predefine the possible areas for intervention quite in advance, thus improving the method application's procedures. In article [11], Rolli et al. proposed a specific AD methodology to detect the robust decomposition of the functional requirements. In the present article, the same decomposition methodology is used to associate each identified functional requirement to its own specific test case. This strategy will allow us to define the minimum test-case set needed to guarantee the coverage of the functional requirements to be tested, and the logical consistency of the configuration that will be obtained. The whole process of decomposition will be now described, as per Figure 2 below.

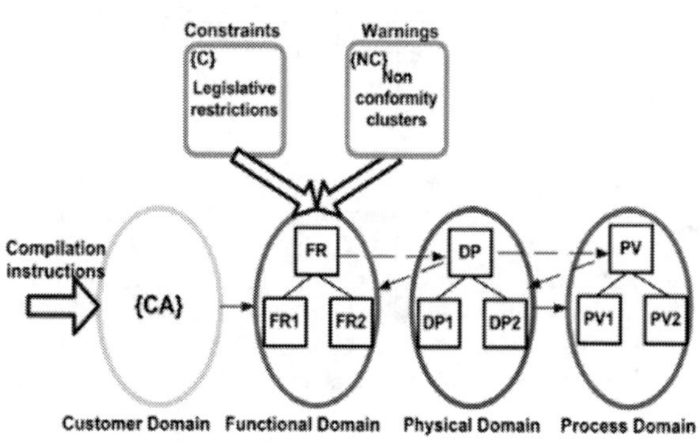

Fig. 2. Testing process architecture. Source [11].

4.1.2 Definitions and correspondences

As far as the taxation management processes are concerned, the customer attributes (CA) consist in the technical specifications and the compiling instructions provided extensively by the Revenue Agency. Likewise, the design constraints (C) are the restrictions imposed by the regulations, such as tax deadlines and the modalities of electronic transmission of tax statements. (NC) are the non-conformity clusters defined in the process of cataloguing and reclassification of historical non-conformities detected by the supporting service. They have a proactive value and represent warnings for specific areas of concern, and must be taken into account during the annual preparation of test cases. The system's functional requirements (FR) are the design formalization of the fiscal procedures to be implemented or adjusted, under the conditions imposed by the design constraints and in respect to the indications given by the analysis of non-conformity clusters. Design parameters (DP) are the personal data, the income data and the fiscal data to be processed and compiled. Nonetheless, we consider as process variables (PV) the software components that implement the objects defined at the designing stage.

4.1.3 Correspondence between functional decomposition and software testing levels

The decomposition of the functional requirements follows a zigzagging process in the set of data, producing the logical design of the system at its greatest level of detail [11, 16, 17]. At each level, it is possible to define a particular type of test. For example, at a logic design level, the coverage matrix of functional tests corresponds to the single tests execution plan (Unit Test). At an intermediate level of abstraction, the testing coverage matrix corresponds to the system tests execution plan (Integration Test). Consequently, at the highest level of abstraction we have the definition of the acceptance test plan. This correspondence is made possible by using the correlation matrix between functional requirements and data sets. For each level of abstraction, this matrix indicates the relationship between decomposed functional requirements and the set of reference data (DPij), in respect to the implemented methods (Aij ()). This means that the decomposition of the system's functional requirements (FR) does not only lead to the identification of the data files (DP) –which are the object of a logical treatment-, but also of the test cases to be performed in order to detect any malfunctions.

	DP_1	DP_2	DP_3
FR_1	$A_{11}()$		
FR_2		$A_{22}()$	
FR_3			$A_{33}()$

Fig. 3. Correlation matrix between functional requirements and data sets.

4.1.4 Compatibility between Object-oriented Design and Axiomatic Design

The proposed decomposition approach is particularly effective when combined with object-oriented software implementation techniques. These techniques allow using simplifications and correspondences, which are extremely useful during the setting of test cases. In particular, we used the Axiomatic design of object-oriented Software Systems (ADO-OSS) methodology to optimize the entire software's life cycle [16, 17]. To illustrate this approach, the following correspondence is introduced. Considering the mapping between Functional domain and Physical domain, the zigzagging process allows to decompose the functional requirements in parallel with the datasets for which such requirements have meaning. The zigzagging process has produced the decomposition of functional requirements, as represented in the figure below:

Level 0	DP
FR	A

Level 1	DP_1	DP_2	DP_3
FR_1	A_{11}		
FR_2		A_{22}	
FR_3			A_{33}

Level 2		DP_1			DP_2	DP_3
		DP_{11}	DP_{12}	DP_{13}	DP_{21}	DP_{31}
FR_1	FR_{11}	$A_{11,11}$	$A_{11,12}$	$A_{11,13}$		
	FR_{12}		$A_{12,12}$			
	FR_{13}			$A_{13,13}$		
FR_2	FR_{21}				$A_{21,21}$	
FR_3	FR_{31}					$A_{31,31}$

Fig.4. Decomposition process.

The requirements' decomposition moves to a level of detail deemed sufficient to define all the elements necessary for the design. Then, the ADo-oSS methodology allows to translate this decomposition into UML (Unified Modeling Language) diagrams, which are the essential tool to design and implement a software system [16-19]. This new representation is a consequence of the properties of "legacy", "polymorphism" and "encapsulation" of the object-oriented programming techniques. In this case, the FRi functional requirement is defined as the object that is implementable by the methods on the i-th row in the decomposition table (Aij) that have access to the DPij data files, according to the mapping in the corresponding table. At the most detailed level of decomposition, objects it will be represented by elementary methods and data files [11, 16].

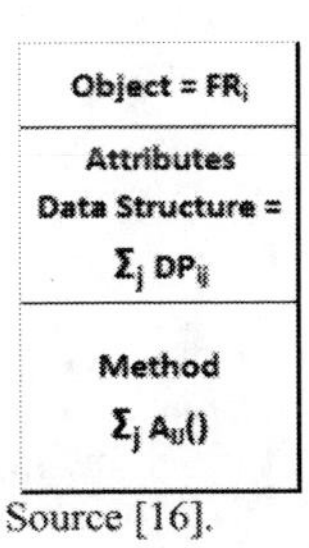

Fig. 5. Class diagram. Source [16].

Therefore, the decomposition of functional requirements can be represented by the following simplified UML diagram:

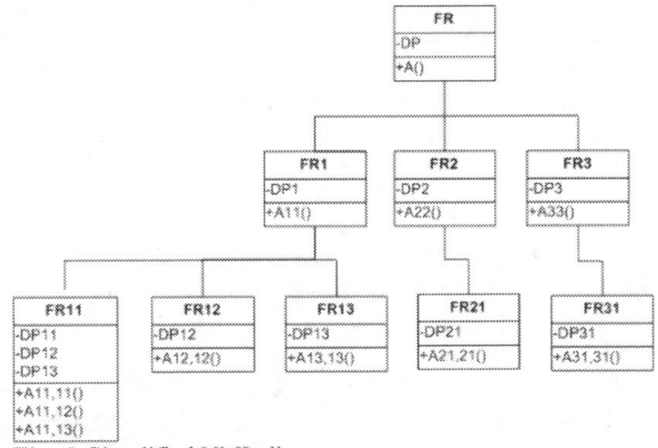

Fig. 6. Simplified UML diagram.

4.2 Selecting the minimum set of test cases

4.2.1 Model selection based on the Function point analysis

The present article proposes an integrated system for the arrangement of functional test cases, using a decomposition approach based on the verification of the axioms of independence and information [11, 16]. The axiom of independence ensures consistency in the coverage of the functional requirements - for which, at least one test case will be performed. The axiom of information allows to select the minor requirement in case of more functional requirement configurations. Function Points [11] are a tool to estimate the information content of the system. Therefore, a robust configuration of the functional requirements is the one that has a lower number of function points, considering the same level of functionalities provided. This is the solution that carries the minor effort, in terms of timing and design costs, but also -and especially- in terms of preparing and executing the tests. In fact, there is an empirical relationship between the capacity of the software to be tested, and the effort needed to test the software expressed in man/days. Capers Jones [20] estimates that the number of test cases can be determined by the function-point estimate for the corresponding effort. The formula is Number of Test Cases = (Function Point Effort)$^{1.2}$. The actual effort in person/days is then calculated with a conversion factor obtained from previous project data. In this case, cataloging and archiving project data in a structured multi-level database, as described in paragraph 3.3, also allows obtaining data on productivity. This information can be obtained from the overall implementation data from the previous software versions of the tax management program to be adapted, or, in their absence, from similar previous developing experiences. In addition, the use of function point analysis (FPA) allows to define a testing plan from an end-user perspective, simplifying many steps and taking advantage of many correspondences, as we will discuss in the following paragraphs.

4.2.2 Effort estimation

The relationship between decomposed functional requirements and data files can be represented in equivalent form with UML diagrams. UML diagrams allow an estimate of the software development project's effort, by using the Function Point measurement technique [21-24]. In this case, the data structures (DPij) represent data files (ILF and EIF); while the methods (Aij) represent the transactional functions (EI, EO, EQ) [11, 22, 23]. By counting the function points of the project, it is possible to estimate the cost in terms of man/days. Indeed, techniques such as COCOMO II allow to determine an estimate of the time required to complete the project [25, 26]. Then, the knowledge of a particular type of project allows to categorize the estimated man/resources by their professional profile, and match them to the various phases of the software's life cycle. In testing, we often refer to the golden rule of Frederick P. Brooks [1], according to which 40% of the estimated time for a software project should be used for the testing stages. This rule is still valid. However, in the case of projects to be developed in familiar contexts, experience helps to obtain a lower percentage of commitment. In this case, the background series of similar projects can provide useful information.

4.2.3 Alternative effort-estimation methodologies

Several authors criticize the use of FPA to calculate the effort of the various testing activities, on the grounds that, it is difficult to make an estimate in the absence of detailed functional requirements, [27]. Therefore, various alternative effort-estimation methodologies of the test cases were set, such as the Use Case Point (UCP) and the Test Case Point (TCP). These are measuring techniques borrowed from the FPA, of which they keep some simplified elements. However, in this article we must stress the importance of the FPA, since it is generally considered as an accepted standard for software estimations. Other methodologies are not standard, yet their diffusion is very limited. Instead, the context of study of this article concerns the software systems for fiscal management, for which the technical and regulatory specifics are well known. In addition, the transition from any present software version to one related to the following year can be easily managed by using the FPA technique.

4.3 Test Case Attribution by level of functional decomposition

The proposed methodology consists in associating, to each functional decomposition level, the minimum set of test cases in order to verify each decomposed functional requirement. Thus, the logical design of the system not only does follow its corresponding functional test plan, but the same selection of the tests can affect the implementation phase, directing designers towards easier testable solutions - in other words, with a lower risk level. In fact, this organic approach to the selection of test cases allows to match the functional architecture of the system with a network of test cases already defined in the system designing phase. In this way, we can avoid neglecting parts of the system, especially during the integration process of elementary modules and sub-systems. For the small and medium enterprises and organizations, this method constitutes a major advantage: in fact, it allows to define the complete organization of functional tests to be performed already during the software designing phase. In the present article, for simplicity's sake, we set three decomposition levels of the functional requirements. In this case, each level of decomposition corresponds to a specific type of test. The highest abstract logic level corresponds to the system test: this type of test has, as its objective, the verification of the application in its entirety, in an environment that is similar to production. The second level concerns, instead, an integration test among self-contained program modules. At this stage, the interface among the various parts of the system is verified. Finally, the third level concerns the verification of self-consistent elementary objects. As shown in Figure 8, the test configuration is performed starting from the most abstract logic level to the most basic level, following the decomposition of the functional requirements with an axiomatic approach. Alternately, the testing execution starts with a verification of the individual elementary components. Then, the execution of the integration between the various elementary modules and\or sub-systems is verified. This testing phase can be anticipated: it is not necessary for all the sub-systems to be available, some can be simulated by specially developed software applications [5-7]. This allows to split the development activities among different teams that can work in parallel. Finally, a system test execution is performed, and it is carried out in an environment similar to production. Instead, the acceptance test is carried out by the software client, and it is performed in order to verify the compliance of the product developed by the supplier in terms of technical specifics. Basically, the acceptance test is identical to the system test.

4.4 Building the Test Case Coverage Matrix

The decomposition of the functional requirements with an AD approach allows building a correlation matrix with some important features. It represents the robust decomposition of the functional requirements [11, 24]. For example, for each A_{ij} element of the matrix of Figure 4, we need to build a specific test case (CT_{ij}). A set of d data input is defined, where $d \in DP_{ij}$ so that A_{ij} (d) is correct when it meets the specifications of Fr_{ij}, or it is incorrect if it is different from the result expected from the functional requirement [28, 29]. For example, the $A_{11,11}$ () method is verified with the execution of the $CT_{11,11}$ functional case test. Therefore, $CT_{11,11}$ includes the input data to be used for the test and for the application rules provided by the program. For this reason, the $A_{11,11}$ (d) result obtained by performing $A_{11,11}$ () on the d data input with $d \in DP_{11}$, is correct if it meets the specifications of FR_{11}. It is incorrect if it is different from the expected result from the functional requirement. The correctness of the $A_{11,11}$ () method in respect to a d data input is indicated with "ok" ($A_{11,11}$, d). The $A_{11,11}$ () function is correct, i.e., $ok(A_{11,11}) \Leftrightarrow \forall\, d \in DP_{11}, ok(A_{11,11}, d)$ [28]. Therefore, the test case $CT_{11,11}$ may be considered ideal, if the absence of malfunctions detected implies the absence of a total malfunction, i.e. $ok(A_{11,11}, CT_{11,11}) \Rightarrow ok(A_{11,11})$. In other words, this occurs if further testings do not detect any malfunctions that have not already been discovered by $CT_{11,11}$. The aforementioned process determines the following test case coverage matrix:

		CT_{11}	CT_{12}	CT_{13}	CT_{21}	CT_{31}
FR_1	FR_{11}	$CT_{11,11}$	$CT_{11,12}$	$CT_{11,13}$		
	FR_{12}		$CT_{12,12}$			
	FR_{13}			$CT_{13,13}$		
FR_2	FR_{21}				$CT_{21,21}$	
FR_3	FR_{31}					$CT_{31,31}$

Fig. 7. Test case coverage matrix

This matrix ensures the complete coverage of the functional requirements. This is the minimum configuration that allows to verify that the A_{ij} () methods comply with the functional specifications required by the Revenue Agency instructions.

5 Conclusions

The methodology proposed in this article helps setting functional tests already at a software designing stage, reducing the overall time required for software development. In addition, the axiomatic decomposition of functional requirements allows to identify the suite of test cases that have a full functional coverage. At least one test case is set for every single software object. It is acknowledged that it is impossible to build tests that can demonstrate the absence of malfunctions in a software program, but we can arrange a detect & debug dynamic mechanism for software errors that results in a 'lesson learned' approach for any following version of the program. Such mechanism, based on a methodical cataloguing of the non-conformities detected both during the development phase and during the application's execution phase, allows to define a specific test case for each class of non-conformity. Moreover, the reuse of test cases related to any previous software versions allows to focus on the effort of the system components affected by the annual regulatory changes that are intrinsically typical of the taxation management systems.

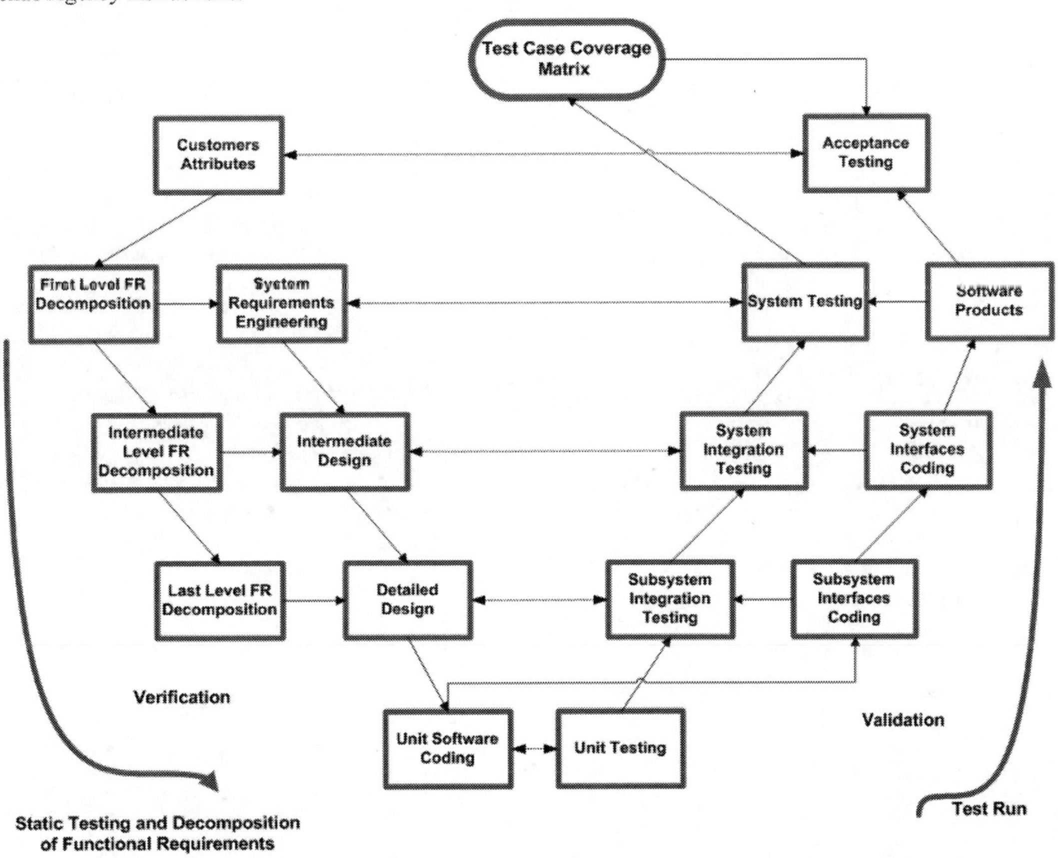

Fig. 8. Test Case Design Process.

This paper is dedicated to the memory of our wonderful colleague and co-author of this work, Dr. Massimo Rinaldi, who recently passed away.

References

1. F. P. Brooks Jr, *The Mythical Man-Month: Essays on Software Engineering* (Addison-Wesley, 1995);
2. G. Arcidiacono, K. Yang, J. Trewn, L. Bucciarelli, *Application of Axiomatic Design for Project-Based Learning Methodology*, Proc. CIRP, **53**, 166-172 (2016);
3. G. Arcidiacono, A. Giorgetti, M. Pugliese, *Axiomatic Design to improve PRM airport assistance*, Proc. CIRP, **34**, 106-111 (2015);
4. G. Arcidiacono, D. T. Matt, E. Rauch, *Axiomatic Design of a Framework for the Comprehensive Optimization of Patient Flows in Hospitals*, JHE, vol. **2017** (2017);
5. I. Sommerville, *Software Engineering* (Addison-Wesley, 2009);
6. G. J. Myers, *The Art of Software Testing*, (John Wiley & Sons,, 2004);
7. A. Avellone, M, Cislaghi, E. Colonese, *Collaudo e qualità del Software*, (AICQ-CI, Uni Service, 2010);
8. D. G. Firesmith, *Common System and Software Testing Pitfalls: How to Prevent and Mitigate Them: Descriptions, Symptoms, Consequences, Causes, and Recommendations*, (SEI Series in Software Engineering, 2013);
9. C. Cavallini, A. Giorgetti, P. Citti, A. Meneghin, *Sviluppo di un approccio olistico per l'analisi e la risoluzione delle non conformità,* AISS, **3,** 1 (2012);
10. F. Rolli, A. Giorgetti, P. Citti, *Integration of Holistic Non-Conformities Management and Axiomatic Design: a case study in Italian Income Tax Returns Management,* Proc. CIRP **34**, 256-262 (2015);
11. F. Rolli, A. Giorgetti, P. Citti, M. Rinaldi, *Improvement of the compilation process of the Italian income certifications: a methodology based on the evaluation of the information content (Part 1),* Proc. CIRP **53,** 56-62 (2016);
12. A. Giorgetti, C. Cavallini, A. Ciappi, G. Arcidiacono and P. Citti, *A holistic model for the proactive reduction of non-conformities within new industrial technologies,* IJMERR, **6**, 4 (2017);
13. A. Giorgetti, G. Arcidiacono, A. Ciappi, R. Barbieri, and P. Citti, *HNCR model following robust approach*, QREI (forthcoming);
14. G. Arcidiacono, P. Placidoli, *Reality and illusion in Virtual Studios: Axiomatic Design applied to television recording*, Proc. CIRP, **34**, 137-142 (2015);
15. G. Arcidiacono, A. Giorgetti, A. Ciappi, *An Axiomatic Design framework for reliability improvement*, ACM International Conference Proceeding Series, pp. 214-217;
16. NP Suh, *Axiomatic Design - Advances and Applications*, (Oxford University Press, 2001);
17. SH Do, NP Suh, *Object-oriented software design with axiomatic design*, Proc. CIRP **49**, 278-84, (2000);
18. C Togay, AH Dogru, JU Tanik, *Systematic component-oriented development with axiomatic design*, JSS, **81**, 115 (2008);
19. P.J. Clapis PJ, J.D. Hinterstiener, *Enhancing object-oriented software development through axiomatic design*, Proc. ICAD **1**, 271-77 (2000);
20. C. Jones, *Applied software measurement*, (McGraw-Hill, 2008);
21. A.J. Albrecht, *Measuring Application Development Productivity*, Proc. SHARE/GUIDE IBM Appl. Development Symposium 83-92 (1979);
22. IFPUG, *Function Point Counting Practices Manual*, (IFPUG, 1999);
23. R. Meli, L. Santillo, *"Function Point Estimation Methods: a Comparative Overview,* Proc. FESMA'99, 271-286 (1999);
24. F. Rolli, A. Giorgetti, P. Citti, M. Rinaldi, *Information content evaluation to obtain robustness of the management in Italian fiscal process (Part 2): optimization of Italian income certification process of the year 2016,* Proc. CIRP **53**, 63-69 (2016);
25. A.L. Rollo, *Functional Size measurement and COCOMO – A synergistic Approach*, Proc. SMEF 259–67 (2006);
26. L. De Rore, M. Snoeck, G. Poels, and G. Dedene, *Cocomo II as productivity measurement: a case study at KBC*, (SSRN Electronic Journal, 2008);
27. S. Nageswaran, *Test Effort Estimation Using Use Case Points,* QW2001 (2001);
28. J.B. Goodenough, S.L. Gerhart, *Toward a theory of test data selection,* SIGPLAN Notices, **6**, 10 (1975);
29. L. Bougè, *A contribution to the theory of program testing*, TCS **37**, 151-181, (1985).

MATEC Web of Conferences **127**, 01006 (2017) DOI: 10.1051/matecconf/201712701006
ICAD 2017

Applying Axiomatic Design and Conceptual Independence in the Domain of IT Systems

Debbie Tarenskeen* and *René* Bakker

HAN University of Applied Sciences, Arnhem and Nijmegen, The Netherlands

Abstract. In this paper we explain why Axiomatic design has not been applied in large system of systems information technology architectures in health care organizations in the Netherlands. We have found in extensive case studies of IT systems that the Independence axiom could not be found in the existing Information systems. This causes great concern for the adaptability of systems. Although best practices in system engineering advice decoupling of system functionality, findings show that the Independence Axiom has not been applied to functional requirements. A number of difficulties was exposed to the researcher and IT architects, when they tried to identify and to demarcate functional requirements in existing systems. In IT systems a distinction is made between business and system functions and software engineers emphasize decoupling of system functions. That has resulted in a strong coupling of business information and technical application logic. This means Conceptual dependencies are often at the heart of the difficulties. Decoupling these dependencies in applications seems a candidate for ordering requirements in a way that keeps the functional requirements independent from each other. Conceptual independence signifies a complete decoupling of the concepts and relations of the Business domain from the technical functionality. The paper describes the difficulties when applying the Independence Axiom in the Information systems domain and argues that a combination of Conceptual independence and Axiomatic design is achievable. The authors adapt the Design matrix with Conceptual independence. We conclude that applying Conceptual independence is crucial when constructing IT systems based on Axiomatic design.

1 Introduction

In this paper we will argue that Axiomatic design cannot be applied in IT systems consisting of many subsystems, because of Conceptual dependencies. In a paper of Suh in 1998, he argues that Axiomatic design can be applied in system design for different kinds of systems, including systems for Information technology [1]. The authors found in three case studies that IT systems were hard to change. They examined the IT systems and detected that Axiomatic design had not been applied. In the next chapter we will outline the three case studies in health care. In chapter 3 we will explain that Axiomatic design was applicable in the cases according to Suh [2], but could not be found in system architecture diagrams. We even encountered difficulties when trying to restructure the systems according to the Independence axiom.

Next in chapter 4 we will extend on the aspects that hindered direct application of Axiomatic design. The aspects show an interdependence between technical functionality and business terms. We call this interdependence Conceptual dependence conform McGinnes' definition [3]. The principle of Conceptual independence is explained in chapter 5. We propose a model for system architecture of IT systems with independent components in Chapter 5.

In chapter 6 Conceptual independence is positioned in the Design matrix of Axiomatic design. We conclude with stressing the importance of applying Conceptual independence when constructing IT systems based on Axiomatic design.

2 Description of case studies

The authors have studied three cases in health care in the Netherlands in the period 2012-2015 where existing systems needed to adapt to new health care requirements and processes. In the organizations a complex IT infrastructure functioned sufficiently and reliably for the current care organization. The board of directors in all three cases wanted to re-evaluate the IT systems in the light of new requirements. In all case studies we developed models of the IT architectures in collaboration with the IT architects in case 1, 2 and 3 or with the IT department in case 2. When compared to de facto IT architecture methodologies for change, the end goal of the IT architects was a Roadmap for adapting the existing IT system architecture to an IT architecture suitable for new requirements. This way of working resembles the TOGAF method in IT architecture practice [4].

2.1 Cases in health care

Two case studies were performed in hospitals, one hospital was still in the design phase and was planned to be a central node (with a physical building in Utrecht) in a network of care centers. The latter were departments in already existing hospitals. The other hospital was a regional medium sized hospital. The remaining case study was performed in a Home care institute that also provided facilities for intern patients and the elderly [5, 6].

The first case study took place from November 2012 until April 2013, the second from March 2013 to November 2014, the last from February 2015 until June 2015.

Examples of new requirements were:

• In all processes patients and their family are primary,

• Care processes and information must be organized around the patient and its family and not around medical specializations,

• All Information that is involved in the invoicing process must be integrated within the invoicing process as a whole,

• Achieve an increase in efficiency in planning of diagnosis and treatment with IT,

• Supporting IT for workflows of persons involved in planning of the ordering process of diagnosis and treatment.

2.2 Case study 1 National hospital for child oncology

The reason for developing a new system architecture was the establishment of a new national hospital for child oncology, that would integrate laboratory functions and treatment, integrate knowledge from research in this area and treatment and coordinate care centers across regions in the Netherlands. Information technology that existed in an academic hospital nearby would be reused where possible [7]. The IT architecture model, that was eventually selected by the IT architects can be seen as a simplified version of an enterprise architecture in which strategic goals were detailed in requirements for applications. In the Requirements analysis stage all strategic goals were specified into Services and those were specified in requirements for every one of the 90 applications.

2.3 Case study 2 Home care organization

The organization in this case functioned mainly as a care organization and provided home care and care for the elderly. It had 5000 employees and about 3000 volunteers at the time of study [8]. The IT architect and IT expert started with formulating strategic goals, because the organization was in the process of changing its health care vision and strategy. The ultimate goal however, was to judge if the current system was up to the required changes and could be maintained in its current form. The Board of directors was planning to update and replace parts of the system that were not functioning according to state of the art requirements.

2.4 Case study 3 Medium sized regional Hospital

In the third case study a regional hospital in the Netherlands is being studied [9]. The hospital is in the last stage of changing its paper-based operations to digital operations in the health care processes. The goal of the IT architects is to deliver a consistent vision of the changes in health care services as foreseen and the specified supporting IT functionality.

In the case studies the methods for changing existing systems were examined and notated. Practice showed that systems were difficult to change. We examined if in the existing systems the principles of Axiomatic design were applied.

3 Application of the Independence Axiom

Since in all three cases IT architects needed to adapt systems to new requirements, the lines of demarcation in the Information system architecture are crucial knowledge.

Our scope of Information system architecture is not confined to one Information system only. We have found that the IT systems in health care include Electronic Health records, in the Netherlands called Electronic Patient Dossier, systems for financial administration, systems for management, systems for special equipment such as MRI scan, systems for Enterprise resource management, systems for procurement.

3.1 Functional Requirements

In Information technology a distinction can be made between system functions and business functions. System functions are necessary in all organizations that need information for the working process such as storage of data, searching in collections of records, exchanging data between servers, exchanging data between servers and applications.

Business functions are functions that are useful in a specific organizations or industry, such as accessing a Patient Dossier, accessing and analyzing medical diagnosis, registration of a new patient, planning medical treatment in health care. In these functions specific health care terms are included in the system functions. Often the system functions can only be valuable for health care if information in information systems can be accessed with health care terms.

In papers of Suh regarding system design, he emphasizes the zigzagging over different domains when designing the definitive system [10]. In this paragraph I will explain how zigzagging over domains is applied in IT Requirements analysis. The Customer domain in IT consists of needs of the board of directors, but also of the medical specialists and other care professionals, such as nurses, and the information needs of patients. The iterations of Customer domain to the Functional domain in the ideal case will lead to independent Functional requirements. Then it will be possible to link the FRs to the Physical domain. The preconditions for zigzagging from the Customer Domain to the Functional domain in Information system design are fulfilled. In case 1 the Requirements analysis was performed with 11 working groups of stakeholders. It resulted in 133 requirements with 793 Relations to Applications.

3.2 Decoupling Design parameters in IT

We have found that the Independence Axiom could have been applied in Information systems design in the same way as Axiomatic design prescribes. This is possible, because in realizing and programming of IT systems decoupling modules and functions by way of interfaces between different components in a system is good practice in software engineering. Patterns of decoupling system components are seen as qualitative high standards of software and are described in standard IT publications, such as in Larman [11], Buschman [12] and Bass [13]. Therefore we have concluded that Axiomatic design can be applied for defining independent or decoupled elements as Design parameters in IT systems in health care.

3.3 Conclusion of applicability of Axiomatic design

If we take the statements of IT engineering at face value, we can conclude that Axiomatic design can be achieved in designing and realizing IT systems. In the next chapter we will explain that demarcation lines in IT systems do not follow functional requirements.

4 Demarcation lines in IT systems in case studies

4.1 Case study 1 and 3: National hospital for child oncology and Regional hospital

Because we wanted to find the FRs of the existing systems in IT system architecture, first we have examined the most important FRs.

In case 1 in the hospital new requirements were formed because the vision of care as care for a patient and its family led to a changed vision of IT support. The IT support should adapt to organizing the systems around the patient and its family, instead of organizing the applications around medical specializations, its administration and registration needs. In case 3 strategic goals were specified in changing certain work flows for care processes. The new work flows should include communication and exchange of data with medical professionals from outside the hospital.

We have sought demarcation lines in IT systems for these FRs, and distinguished independent Runtime components in IT systems. The demarcation lines in existing systems in the hospitals were based on "applications" provided by suppliers for Information technology for health care.

We conform to the definition of application in this case study used by the IT architects in the study. An application can be defined in two ways:

1. A computer program that can be installed and run independently of other computer programs, and that delivers functionality defined by the supplier. The application can sometimes be coupled to medical equipment or can use open standards for communication. Features for network connections and communication over the network in proprietary standards and protocols are usually present.
2. A loosely coupled component in a computer program can also be an independent component, e.g. a module or functionality that can be turned off or on, depending on the possibilities that the supplier offers.

We have found in the cases that most of the functional requirements have been implemented in the applications in a way that is historically grown, and based on the knowledge that the suppliers had of the business processes of their customers, the health care organizations in the past.

Remarkably in both Hospitals was that a central position in the IT systems was reserved for the Electronic Patient Dossier. However the data belonging to the EPD was distributed among multiple sub applications that each have access to a part of the data of patients.

In both hospitals the IT system architecture consisted of applications that did not follow the distinctions between FRs.

4.2 Case study 2: Home care and cure

In the second case study we were interested in the divisions that IT technical experts were making when viewing the IT system architecture. We researched methods of change in IT system architecture in collaboration with technical IT architects.

An example of part of the IT system can be seen in Figure 1. In this figure the components in the system, do consist of applications (A, E and F), however these and the other systems are executing system technical functions, such as: storage of employee data and scheduling data, and exchange of data between one component and the other.

We can point out the following elements from part of the IT system architecture:

- A: The mobile application for input of employee data,
- A-B: A connection from the mobile device to the first proprietary database,
- B: The first database that communicates with the mobile device and stores the data in the IT systems,
- B-D: A connection from the first proprietary database to a second more general database,
- C: System that couples data to dashboards,
- D: The second database that collects all data from the first data storage database,
- D-E: Data output to combine data from data storage database to general information,

• E: The database that collects all general information, about history of illnesses, diseases, base tables. Also administration of invoices and finances. Indications for care in relation to insurances,
• E-F: Output of data from E to database F,
• F: The database that stores financial data for yearly reports.

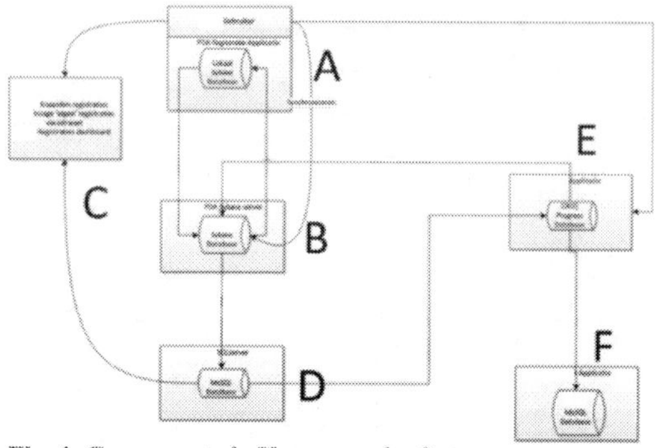

Fig. 1. Components in Home care institute.

The components are partly delivered by suppliers, partly these are custom made components. We add a third definition for an independent element in IT system architecture:

3. A computer program that can be installed and run independently of other computer programs, and that delivers more general system functionality. Examples are: data bases, input systems, file systems, hardware drivers, software components that enable network communication.

In this case the diagram focuses on system functions [14]. Applications are only named applications in this context when interaction with users is performed.

4.3 IT Actions for adapting systems

We will list the different IT actions in Table 1 that can change business and system functionality: Add a component, delete a component, change a component. However there is a fourth way of changing the IT systems, that is well known in software engineering as configuring systems with configuration files or in registry systems on the machine. Configuration are based on a structure that can be simple or more complex, they can even take the form of a conceptual model, with concepts that are structured and related. With changes in the content of the configurations (file) the behaviour of the Runtime component is changed without changing the component itself. Runtimes like these are called "computer language interpreters" or interpreters for scripting languages.

In all cases in Table 1, described above the changes must be foreseen. A component can only be added to a system when collaboration with other components is built in, in all system components that are concerned. A component can only be deleted when it does not contain functionality expected or needed by other components (dependencies). A component can only be changed, when changes do not affect communication with other components, or influence configurations of other components.

Table 1. Changing system by changing components and connections.

Behavior change	Structural change
Add component	Add communication line
Delete component	Delete communication line
Change component	Change communication line
Change configurations	Change structure of communication

A configuration of a component or a model based configuration file can only be changed in predefined ways, as the component "expects" configurations, and cannot cause unexpected or new behavior [15, 16], unless something goes wrong.

When the behaviour change concerns more than one component, communication between components must be changed. Connections can be added or deleted, thereby influencing the flow of information through the system. With the Independence axiom adding, replacing and deleting components or connections based on changing FRs will be feasible. We propose in the next chapters that also the option of "changing configurations" must be taken into account when designing Information systems.

4.4 Difficulties encountered when changing systems

In the cases that were studied we have found that the IT architects in comparison to experts from IT departments used different conceptual models for looking at the IT systems. IT (Enterprise) architects started with the strategic goals and vision on health care in mind and proceeded from there with defining business processes, such as in health care: Diagnose, Provide medical results, Propose treatment, Care plan, Medicine plan, Monitor and measure. These processes will be supported by IT services, and Functional requirements can be formulated as Functional requirements for these IT services [5]. The technical IT architects however, were looking at systems of system components and were interested in system failure and system functionality.

Despite the different views on the system, all cases showed that interdependency of conceptual data and system functionality obstructed required changes.

4.4.1 Patient data distributed and structure unknown

In the first case study, the changes required reorganization of applications, because the data for patients and their family was needed in a central place. IT architects found that data was distributed over different applications, and that the overall structure of patient data did not reside in one place, so to have access to the patient data structure from each application as needed. The data was structured in such a way as to accommodate the work flow and processes of medical specialists. Functional requirements were coupled to applications in a many to many relational structure. Therefore we conclude that the Independence axiom was not applied.

4.4.2 General system components adaptable

In the second case study the system consisted of system components and general system functions such as: storage, exchange of data and software for input devices. All components were dedicated to one system function, in which "business data and business information" were encapsulated.

The Functional requirements were not easy to locate in a system were information structures were hidden from view. Therefore we conclude that the Independence axiom had not been applied.

4.4.3 Work flow data distributed and work flow steps in applications are fixed

In the third case study in the Regional Hospital the IT architects sought to reorder the processes in which patients visited different departments in hospitals for medical examinations, medical results and diagnosis. The planning of these visits to different locations, the order in which the visits were planned was subject of study.

It was found, that although the application platform had been recommended as flexible, especially where workflows were concerned, the reorganization of workflows was not easy. The main cause of this, was the fact that documentation of the workflow formalization was difficult to understand. IT architects wanted to try out alternative workflows, but there were no tools supporting this. Functional requirements were not traceable in the previous workflows and we concluded that the Independence Axiom had not been applied. A clear distinction between Business concepts and technical implementation of workflows had not been made.

The problem of interdependencies of Conceptual models and technical logic in applications has been remarked and described as Conceptual dependence by McGinnes, we explain this in Chapter 5.

5 Conceptual independence

5.1 Conceptual dependencies

McGinnes describes how conceptual dependence can limit the changes one can make in independent elements in a system [3]. He describes Conceptual dependence as interdependency between the terms in the Business domain and the technical implementation of the application. In the previous paragraph we have shown that difficulties in adaptabilities in systems are the result of conceptual dependencies. We argue that a decomposition of functionality without separating the Business data from the system is insufficient.

Conceptual independence is based on separating the conceptual model from the technical application logic. A Conceptual model includes: all concepts, terms and instantiations from the business domain and their relations to each other, in a formalized model, it does not include behavior.

Conceptual independence is based on a meta model, in which the Conceptual model is filled in as data. For instance, the meta model consists of: Concepts, Relations, Attributes and Instances of concepts.

The characteristic of Conceptual independence is that the Conceptual model can change, without having to change the technical system that runs with the Concepts.

Because the Conceptual model is an instance of a meta model, it can be treated as data, we call it a soft model [3].

In a previous paper describing the pattern of Conceptual independence, we propose a complete division between the conceptual model where all business terms are collected in an Entity relationship-model (ER Model), as is customary in database design [14]. We then make a distinction in functions that are totally determined by the business and system functions that are general functions that can be applied also in other organizations. The latter need to be configured to this context/business. We propose the configuration of general functions instead of building functions anew for each organization, see model in Chapter 5.3. In 5.2 we give a recognizable example of Conceptual independence.

5.2 A Relational database management system as example of Conceptual independence

A well-known example of a Conceptual independent "application" can be found in a Relational Database Management System (RDBMS). This system can be deployed in any organization and filled with tables and table names specific to this organization. It can also store specific Business requirements in stored procedures and triggers that are fully determined by the business as concerned. These are functions that are programmed in a specific Data base language, dedicated for this purpose.

The DDL scripts in RDBMS can be seen as the Soft conceptual model, the database system as the Runtime conceptual model.

However, when applications are coded that access the database, the tables and names of tables are usually hard coded, and "expected" by the application, and therefore these applications do not conform to the principle of Conceptual independence.

5.3 A model for a complex IT system with Conceptual independence and Axiomatic design

If we combine Axiomatic design and Conceptual independence in an IT system we strive for replaceable components, for which each has the possibility to be adaptable to a specific Conceptual model. We outline this model in Figure 2 with Runtime components, each with its own functionality, such as: storage, exchange of data, access management, a rule engine. For specific functions, see Figure 3. These Runtime components all are based on the same meta model for conceptual models and can be configured with specific configuration languages.

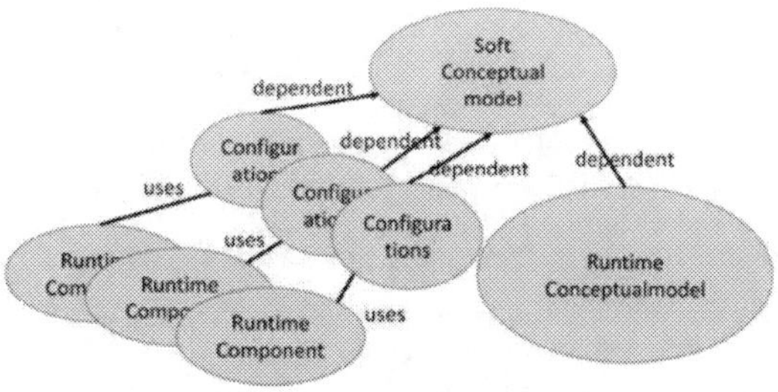

Fig. 2. Adaptable information system.

The Runtime components need a runtime Conceptual model such as a database system. A database system can be generated with a parser and generator system (not in diagram) without violating the Conceptual independence, see Figure 3.

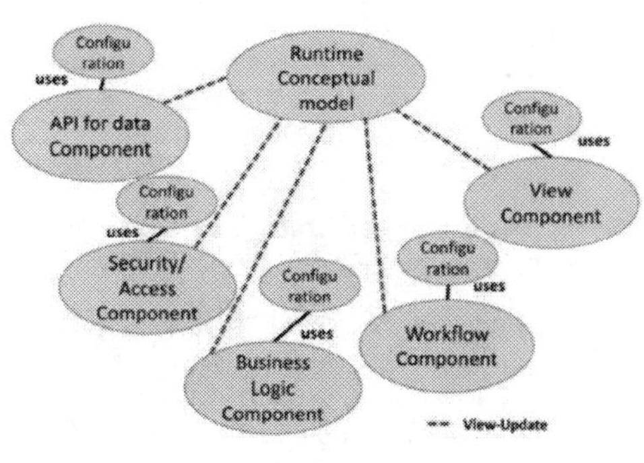

Fig. 3. Adaptable information system with system and business functions.

When the meta model, Soft conceptual model, the Runtime conceptual model and two Runtime components from Figure 3 are translated to a position in a Design matrix, we can map each independent Functional requirement to "one configuration" that adapts behaviour of the Runtime component. The configuration is then seen as a Design parameter. We will explain this in Chapter 6.

6. Adding Conceptual independence to the Design matrix of Axiomatic design

6.1 Soft Conceptual model and Runtime conceptual model added

We will describe an example of one general system function: "Show user interface for a specific Conceptual model" and one business function "Check consistency of data of one Conceptual model for an organization".

In Table 2 the Design matrix is represented. For each general functional requirement the Independence axiom is applied, which is dependent on the metamodel. The Runtime is "generated code" that means it will give access to information in the Soft conceptual model. The parser and generator system has been left out of the Design matrix for simplicity.

Table 2. Design matrix, example.

	Functional requirement	Design parameter										
		Meta-model	DP1	DP2	DP3	DP4	DP5	DP6	DP7	DP8	DP9	DP10
	Base meta model	x										
FR1	Store conceptual model	x	x									
FR2	Give runtime access to conceptual model	x	x	x								
FR3	Run rules	x			x							
FR4	Check Business Rule 1	x	x		x	x						
FR5	Check Business Rule 2	x	x		x		x					
FR6	Check Business Rule 3	x	x		x			x				
FR7	Present user interface at Runtime	x							x			
FR8	Present GUI specification 1	x	x						x	x		
FR9	Present GUI specification 2	x	x						x		x	
FR10	Present GUI specification 3	x	x						x			x

We could add a third Runtime component in the Design matrix for other services for the business, that can be decoupled from the system, but not from the Conceptual model. This component can be easily added in the same manner as the other Runtime components. One can check that Runtimes are reusable in other systems based on the same metamodel.

Table 3. Descriptions of DPs.

DP	Description
DP1	Conceptual Model in text
DP2	Runtime Conceptual model
DP3	Rule engine
DP4	Configuration 1 of Rule engine
DP5	Configuration 2 of Rule engine
DP6	Configuration 3 of Rule engine
DP7	user interface Runtime component
DP8	Configuration of user interface1
DP9	Configuration of user interface1
DP10	Configuration of user interface1

Descriptions of the DPs are represented in Table 3. Here every DP is described and the mapping of FRs to DPs can be traced forward and backwards.

Adding Conceptual independence to system design with Axiomatic design solves the interdependence of the technical application on business information and hard coded names and terms.

6.2 Design parameters and Process variables

In Axiomatic design another Design matrix can be constructed in which dependencies of Design parameters and Process variables are represented. Process variables refer to the way DPs are generated and therefore concern choices of resources. In IT we thus observe the choices of programming languages, human resources such as IT developers and specific tooling needed to deploy the system in a technical way [1]. In our example we have used a Metamodel for decoupling the Business terms from the technical implementation. It is disputable if this metamodel belongs to Design parameter or the Process variables. But, since it is essential for decoupling FRs we decide to explicitly include it in the first Design matrix in Table 2.

Table 4. Design matrix2, example.

DP	Description	Process Variable									
		PV1	PV2	PV3	PV4	PV5	PV6	PV7	PV8	PV9	PV10
DP1	Model in text	x									
DP2	Runtime Conceptual model		x								
DP3	Rule engine			x							
DP4	Configuration 1 of Rule engine				x	x					
DP5	Configuration 2 of Rule engine				x		x				
DP6	Configuration 3 of Rule engine				x			x			
DP7	User interface Runtime component								x		
DP8	Configuration of User interface1									x	x

Table 5. Design matrix2, example

PV	Description
PV1	Storage medium for Conceptual model
PV2	Database or Object base or other
PV3	Compiler 1
PV4	Syntax definition Rules
PV5	Rule1 in syntax
PV6	Rule2 in syntax
PV7	Rule3 in syntax
PV8	Compiler 2
PV9	Syntax definition UI
PV10	UI1 in syntax
PV11	UI2 in syntax
PV12	UI3 in syntax

However more can be said about the relation of DPs to PVs. In our example, we would need a medium for storage of the Conceptual model, compilers to generate Runtime components, a Runtime component that would provide access to the Conceptual model at runtime. For running the Rule engine and for presentation of the user interface, we need configurations in a syntax that is machine readable. Because we work with rules and screens that are independent of each other, independency of the configurations can be achieved. In Table 4 we show the PVs for the DPs in our example. The list of PVs is added in Table 5.

For readability, we have left out DP9 and DP 10.

In Table 5 we find different systems for storage, that are independent of each other, different syntaxes for the Runtime components and configurations in specific syntax for rules or UI screens.

7. Conclusion

Researchers have found in case studies that interdependence of Business terms and technical application logic is an important factor that made IT systems hard to change. We argue that FRs are independent, but that dependencies are implemented in systems in DPs by coupling Business terms and application behavior. Separating the business terms from the system components by means of a Metamodel, a Business data model and using configurations, gives designers the ability to define independent DPs. The PVs that have been described in this paper, demonstrate that the IT developers already have access to the tooling and resources to construct a system based on Axiomatic design.

8. Discussion

The ideas stated in this paper are difficult to accept by the IT architecture research community because in technical papers in software engineering the problem does not exist. We have demonstrated that the problem does exist in the case studies, where business functionality is primary.

In IT architecture research a separation of the Conceptual model from application logic is often seen as a theoretical construct that is not applicable in practice. In practice however, it can be observed that commercial companies are developing systems that generate conceptual independent applications. Three commercial businesses in the Netherlands present themselves as software developers for adaptable systems [17-19]. A first analysis of these platforms demonstrates that Conceptual independence has been applied, without the explicit reference to this principle. We are currently studying the extent to which they have also implemented the Independence axiom, and the Information axiom. Research with regard to these aspects is in progress. Another case study is in preparation in which a real-life system in health care will be developed based on these principles.

References

1. N.P. Suh, *Axiomatic design theory for systems.* Research in engineering design **10**, 4, 189-209 (1998)
2. N.P. Suh, S.H. Do, *Axiomatic design of software systems*, CIRP Annals-Manufacturing Technology. **49**, 1, 95-100 (2000)
3. S. McGinnes, E. Kapros, *Conceptual independence: A design principle for the construction of adaptive information systems*, Information Systems **47**, 33-50 (2015)
4. TheOpenGroup 2011. TOGAF Version 9.1 Evaluation copy. 9087536798, The Open Group.
5. D. Tarenskeen, S. Joosten, R. Bakker, *Using Ampersand in IT architecture,* in Proceedings of the CONFENIS-2013 : 7th International Conference on Research and Practical Issues of Enterprise

Information Systems, Prague, Czech Republic (TRAUNER Verlag, 201-209, 2013)

6. D. Tarenskeen, R. Bakker, Joosten, 2015. *Applying the V Model and Axiomatic design in the Domain of IT Architecture Practice.* Procedia CIRP. 34, 262-267 (2015)
7. UMCUtrecht 2012. Directieverslag 2012. http://www.umcutrecht.nl/nl/Over-Ons/Wat-we-doen/Jaarverslag-UMC-Utrecht, Accessed: 12-04-2017.
8. Carintreggeland 2014. Bestuursverslag 2013 Stichting Carint Reggeland Groep http://www.carintreggeland.nl/dbimages/Bijlagen/Bestuursverslag%202013%20Carintreggeland.pdf, Accessed: 4 -04-2017.
9. Interconfessionele_Stichting_Gezondheidszorg_Rivierenland, Culemborg', B.p.t. and Rivierenland', p.D.W.i.B.L.E.v.z. 2013. Jaardocument 2013. https://www.zrt.nl/upload/File/jaarverslagen/JAARDOCUMENT2013.pdf, Accessed: 4-4-2017.
10. N.P. Suh, *Axiomatic design: Advances and Applications* (Oxford University Press, New York Oxford, 2001)
11. C. Larman, *Applying UML and Patterns: An Introduction to Object Oriented Analysis and Design and Interative Development* (Pearson Education India, 2012)
12. F. Buschmann, K. Henney, D.C. Schmidt, *Pattern-Oriented Software Architecture, Volume 4: A Pattern Language for Distributed Computing* (Wiley, Chichester, UK, 2007)
13. L. Bass, P. Clements, R. Kazman, R. *Software architecture in practice.* (Addison-Wesley Professional, Upper Saddle River, NJ, 2012)
14. D. Tarenskeen, *Conceptual Independence as an Architecture Pattern for Adaptable Systems,* in Proceedings of the VikingPLoP '16 (Leerdam, AA, Netherlands, 2016)
15. D. Garlan, R. Allen, J. Ockerbloom, *Architectural mismatch: Why reuse is so hard.* Ieee Software **12**, 6, 17-26 (1995)
16. D. Garlan, R. Allen, J. Ockerbloom, *Architectural mismatch: Why reuse is still so hard.* Ieee Software **26**, 4, 66-69 (2009)
17. Mendix 2016. Drive digital transformation & innovation with Mendix aPaaS, https://docs.mendix.com/, Accessed: 13-1-2017
18. Thinkwise 2016. Bedrijfssoftware - Thinkwise. https://www.thinkwisesoftware.com/nl/, Accessed: 13-1-2017
19. CGI-Group 2016. SMART Process Acceleration Development Environment. https://en.wikipedia.org/wiki/SMART_Process_Acceleration_Development_Environment, Accessed: 13-1-2017

The Iterative Nature of the "Zig" and How to Define the "Hows"

Miguel Cavique[1,*], *João* Fradinho[2], *António* Gabriel-Santos[2], *António* Gonçalves-Coelho[2] and *António* Mourão[2]

[1]UNIDEMI, CINAV & Escola Naval, Base Naval de Lisboa – Alfeite, 2810-001 Almada, Portugal
[2]UNIDEMI & DEMI, Universidade NOVA de Lisboa, Campus de Caparica, 2829-516 Caparica, Portugal

Abstract. The AD's design equation depicts the relationship between the functional requirements (FR) and the design parameters (DP) by the design matrix (DM), through a unique zigzag decomposition path. At the "zig part" of each level of the zigzag decomposition, the designer needs to find out the DPs that can fulfil the given FRs. This paper proposes that the designer has to perform three main actions in a zig process in order to define the design equation: to define the DPs at a nominal condition and its magnitude; to evaluate the interactions of the DP with the system at actual conditions; and to check back the set of FRs verifying if they fit inside the design range. The purpose of this paper is to illustrate the actions performed on a zig, emphasising the changes that may occur in the arrangement of the design during the synthesis of the DM at any level of the decomposition. At each level of decomposition, the estimation of the DPs that fulfil the FRs allows the designer to define a subset of the DM, making it possible to evaluate afterwards the DM with all the interactions of the system. Moreover, in what concerns to the information content, it is possible to evaluate the probability of success of the system taking into account the interactions of the system and the tolerances of the DPs. This paper presents an example regarding the evaluation of the DM using the equations of the design for a variable air volume (VAV) air conditioning system.

1 Introduction

Nam P. Suh described in his book, "The Principles of Design" [1], the Axiomatic Design (AD) theory, stating that there are rules to do a good design.

AD defines the design in four domains, the Customer, the Functional, the Physical and the Process Domain, as depicted in Figure 1. Moreover, a design is subjected to Constrains (CS) not depicted in the figure. A mapping process allows reaching the image of a domain in the next adjacent domain in a sequence of decisions. Reaching the last domain, the process flows to a lower level, decomposing the elements already defined. Therefore, the hierarchical decomposition of the elements of a domain interconnects with the previous level of the adjacent domains. This is the so-called zigzag process: zig when going from one domain to the adjacent domain at the same level of decomposition; zag when returning back to the previous domain reaching a lower level of decomposition.

The middle relationship is the turning point of the engineering work on design, as it connects the Functional Domain to the Physical Domain.

The Functional Domain contains the functional requirements (FR), that expresses "what we want to achieve?", and the Physical Domain the design parameters (DP), or "how we will achieve it?".

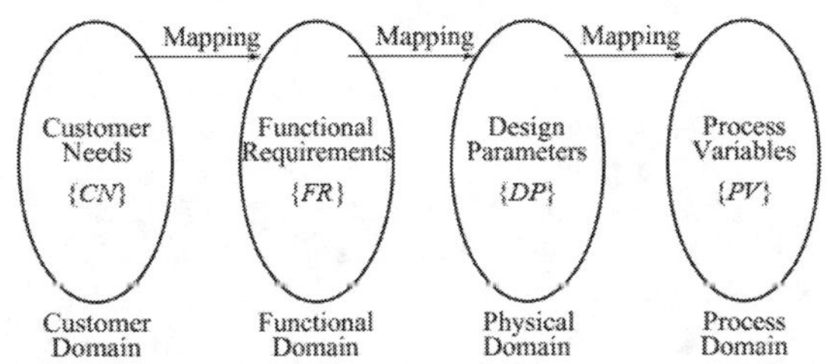

Fig. 1. The design domains.

Equation 1 expresses the result of the mapping between the FR and the DP domains, where $[A]$ is the design matrix (DM), and FRs and DPs are vectors expressed in the design equation by curly brackets.

$$\{FR\} = [A] \cdot \{DP\} \quad (1)$$

According to AD, a good design has to follow two axioms, the "independence axiom" and the "information axiom". The first axiom states that a good design is uncoupled or decoupled, the former having a diagonal design matrix and the latter a triangular DM. The information axiom allows to choose the design with the higher probability of success between a set of possible solutions.

The design equation may cause to a beginner a first feel of easiness of the AD theory, which in turn may jeopardise the result of his design.

The aim of this paper is to help performing the zig process between the Functional Domain and the Physical

* Corresponding author: cavique.santos@marinha.pt

Domain, highlighting a way to help achieving the Equation 1.

The apparent simplicity of AD has a meaning. Karl Popper said that the simplest theories have a great advantage: "Simple propositions should be more appreciated than the less simple ones because they tell us more, because their empirical content is greater; and because they are better testable" [2, p. 155]. Accordingly, it is likely that a large number of authors developed, articulated and interrelated AD to other theories.

Next subsection briefly describes some major contributions on the development of AD, starting by emphasizing the way the tasks that a zig needs.

1.1 Literature review

The zig is a synthesis process that involves "reasoning operations, decision process, and selection methods" [3]. On the other hand, the hierarchical decomposition in each domain is an analytical process. The zig process corresponds to the process that flows from "what" to "how". The hierarchical decomposition includes a reverse process, the zag that flows from "what I achieved" to "why" [4].

D. Tate proposed a "roadmap of activities in decomposition" concerning the process of the zig [5, p. 42] and the process of zag [5, p. 40]. Figure 2 depicts the diagram proposed by D. Tate for the zig process, showing two main tasks: "defining and selecting sub-DP", and "setting DP parameter values".

This diagram shows that failing to achieve the appropriate definitions for the DPs during the decoupling, or failing the optimization process, one has to go back in the design.

The theoretical developments on AD of the last years mainly focus on the following subjects:

- AD principles and the market;
- Mapping between the Customer Needs (CN) and the Functional Requirements (FR);
- Nature of FRs;
- Design equation and the design matrix;
- Nature of information and the computation of the information content of a design.

Regarding the market Masayuki Nakao presented a surprising conclusion. In AD a good design is uncoupled or decoupled, which is a "superb effort of innovation", leading to simple artefacts that work correctly [6]. Anyway, there is a weakness in good designs: they are easy to copy by the competition [6]. He argues that to stay in the market, the design should hide some FRs, while concealing in unopened areas the matching DPs. Furthermore, some effective applications might be coupled in order to avoid antagonistic entities to replicate the solution of a design [7].

To do a design accepted by the market the design team must start by defining the customer needs. Theory of Practices is a theory of the social sciences that allows identifying the components of a practice, namely the materials, meanings and competences. The elements of Theory of Practices have a close relation to the CNs and the FRs, helping to define the mapping between the Customer Domain and the Functional Domain [8].

The Customer Domain includes the needs of all stakeholders that interact with the product under design during its lifecycle. After identifying the needs of the stakeholders, it is possible to define the requirements of the product, respecting the constrains of the design [9].

The success of a product in the market depends mostly on the mapping between the CNs and the FRs. As stated by Suh [1, p. 29] "... the final design cannot be better than the set of FRs that it was created to satisfy". As a matter of fact, in a survey during the period of 2008 to 2009, to 475 everyday products with a ward of good design in Japan, it was found that "20% of all the products" creating "excitement beyond imagination" had special FRs or DPs [10].

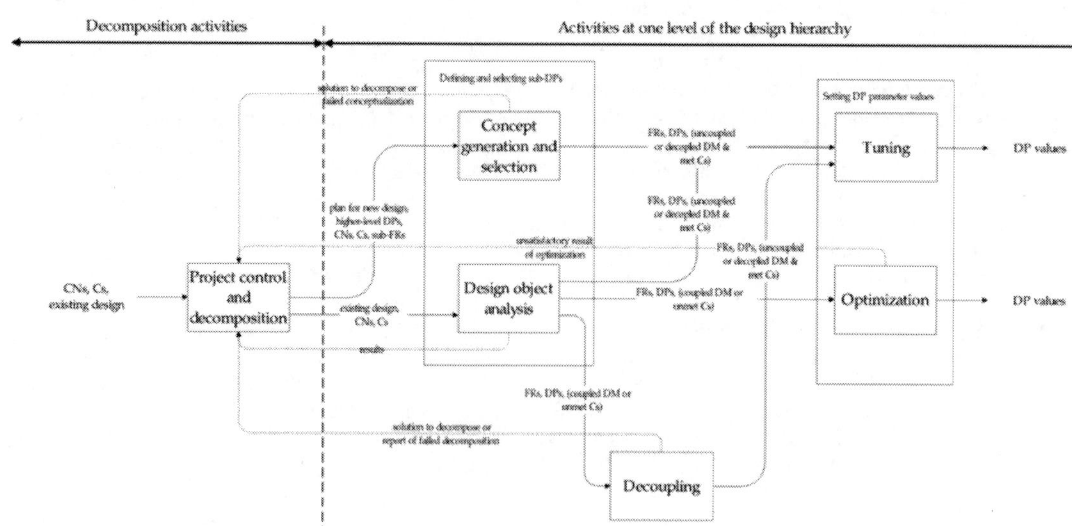

Fig. 2. The zig according to Derick Tate [5].

Therefore, defining the FRs is a major step in design. FRs are commonly verbalized actions. M.K. Thompson gave an important contribution regarding what an FR is [11], by assuming that some design requirements are non-FR. Moreover, she shows that there are a selection criterion and an optimization criterion that are often confused with FRs. Non-FR are many times defined as "to be", as it happens in FRs defined as "to be aesthetic", or to "taste like", therefore expressing characteristics of the entity, not an action. This concept proposed by Thompson is similar to the subjective functions in Value Analysis (VA).

Value Analysis is a design theory raised by Lawrence D. Milles during the World War II that defines primary and secondary functions. Primary functions are objective functions associated to an action, and secondary functions may be subjective [12].

Christopher Brown proposed the need of metrics to guide the definition of FRs, and to select the corresponding DPs, in order to prove that at each stage of decomposition the FRs are "collectively exhaustive and mutually exclusive (CEME)" [13].

In this sense, many actions in engineering are transformations of physical quantities into other physical quantities, like the transformation of electric current into a displacement. Aibin Zhu proposed a definition of FRs by composing "a set of carefully selected physical quantities", and the FR is the transformation of a physical quantity into another one [14].

In a different way, Éfren Benavides [15, 16] associated the FRs to physical variables. The set of physical equations that governs the phenomenon allows defining the design equation. As physical equations usually depend on many variables, typically the set of equations describes a redundant design. Benavides proposes whenever possible to freeze some of the DPs and choose the ones that define a linear design equation.

D. Matt uses the set of physical equations to design a "flexible assembly operation focused on consumer demand". Evaluating the effects on variations on demand and annual evolution of an enterprise, he proposes a re-initialization loop to allow a functional periodicity in the management design of an enterprise [17].

Anyway, defining good FRs is not a warranty of attaining a good design. The fulfilment of FRs can be disrupted by the interdependency between FRs and "variability" [18]. Hilario Oh "develop a mathematical understanding for the two types of failures". The solution of the inverse of Equation 1 helps to achieve the DPs in an iterative process [18]. The formulation shows that the determinant of the design matrix cannot be zero, a generalized statement of Axiom 1 of AD. Moreover, this condition is necessary to attain a zero bias in the functional domain, relating therefore the mathematical formulation to the 2nd Axiom.

A common source of variance of the FRs is the influence of the tolerances of the DPs calculated by the design equation. In mechanical engineering, the variance of FRs may arise from the synthesis of tolerances. Synthesis of tolerances can be seen as a redundant decoupled design, due to the fact that generally there are more parts than interfaces. Such synthesis "should be integrated in the design structure, instead of being done in the final steps of the design" [19]. Tolerances define the range of acceptance of FRs and therefore the information according to the AD theory. For coupled designs with 2 DPs and 2 FRs it is possible to calculate the minimum information for an uniform probability distribution [20].

The decomposition process allows defining any design, starting at the high level requirement and ending in the leaves of the decomposition tree. This procedure applies in the evaluation of any design, for a passenger movement inside a large airport [21] or for the design of a faucet. In the development of AD theory it is necessary to reach the "how to apply the theory", making it possible to spread AD in the engineering field.

2 The proposal

In the AD theory the zig process is a synthesis process that expresses the "what" to "how" and the zag process that goes from "what" to "why" in the next level of decomposition [4]. In the end of the zag, the design process achieves the children FRs that have to be CEME. The problem on applying AD during the zig process is to answer to "how can we achieve suitable DPs?".

It is important to notice that the zig process follows the reverse direction stated on Equation 1: FRs are known and the designer needs to find the DPs in the Physical Domain. Therefore, at each level of decomposition it is necessary to test a set of DPs in order to know if they fulfil the corresponding FRs.

The theorems of AD give a great benefit in performing this task, helping to formulate the problem, as well as to evaluate and to select a concept.

This paper proposes a way to help defining the DPs, therefore highlighting the box of Fig. 2 named "defining and selecting sub-DP".

The FRs' metrics are defined trough equations, making their values possible to vary over time or change according to the stage of the system.

This paper proposes two conditions at which a system can operate: the "nominal condition" (NC) and "actual condition" (AC). FRs may have different nominal conditions which occur when FRs reach their engineering maxima. In engineering, a maximum is usually defined in probabilistic terms, regarding to the conditions the system will work. Examples of these maximums are the cooling load of a building that depends on the weather, the strength of a ship that depend on the sea conditions, or the forces in a metallic structure that are a combination of loads, wind and seismic actions. Actual conditions are all the conditions at which a system needs to perform during the working period, which includes the nominal conditions.

To reach the design equation it is necessary:

- Define or calculate the DPs that fulfil the FRs at the defined engineering "nominal condition";
- Evaluate the interdependencies between the FRs and the proposed DPs in the actual conditions;

DOI: 10.1051/matecconf/201712701007

- Check the influence of the tolerances of the DPs, and noise effects on the functional domain, and evaluate the probability of success of the design;
- Evaluate back at the same level of decomposition if the FRs are CEME.

Therefore at one level of decomposition, the designer first raises a design equation at nominal conditions and only after obtains the design equation at actual conditions, the so called DE. Thus, the design equation might have the elements defined during the study of the design at nominal conditions.

Hilario Oh [18] expressed the design Equation 1 by the following Equation 2, equal to a set of non-linear equations, where $\{DP\}$ is the root vector of the equation

$$f\{DP\}-\{FR\}=0 \quad (2)$$

The solution of a set of non-linear equations can be achieved by the Newton-Raphson iterative process, starting at any proposed $\{DP_k\}$, according to Equation 3.

$$\{DP_{k+1}\}=\{DP_k\}-[J]^{-1}\cdot\{f\{DP\}-\{FR\}\}=0 \quad (3)$$

Where $[J]$ is the Jacobian matrix of the transformation of $\{DP\}$ into $\{FR\}$, therefore being the design matrix $[A]$. This equation is strictly valid if the Jacobian matrix exists and if this matrix is invertible [18]. The formulation of Equation 3 has the advantage of showing the need of a sequence of DPs to achieve the root of the equation.

Using the formulation of Hilario Oh it is possible to show the evolution of the design from the nominal conditions to the actual conditions. The design team usually starts to define what the nominal conditions are. Thus, it allows defining and computing the DPs, the design equation and the corresponding DM at nominal conditions [A_{NC}]. Equation 4 shows the corresponding design equation:

$$\{FR_{NC}\}=f_{NC}\{DP_{NC}\} \quad (4)$$

At actual condition, the DPs need to change by ΔDPs, performing FR by adding a f_I equation.

$$\{FR_{AC}\}=f_{NC}\{DP_{NC}\}+f_I\{DP_{NC}+\Delta DP\} \quad (5)$$

Expressing the second term of Equation 5 as a first order Taylor series, Equation 5 becomes:

$$\{FR_{AC}\}=f_{NC}\{DP_{NC}\}+f_I\{DP_{NC}\}+[J]\{\Delta DP\} \quad (6)$$

Or:

$$\{FR_{AC}\}=f_{AC}\{DP_{NC}\}+[J]\cdot\{\Delta DP\}=A_{AC}\cdot\{DP_{AC}\} \quad (7)$$

Equation 7 is the so-called design equation, which shows that the DM may be obtained by the sum of two DMs.

The design team may use the DM [A_{NC}] mainly for evaluation purposes and the [A_{AC}] for evaluation of performance and control purposes.

Achieving the DPs is not as straightforward as Equation 2 might show, but is a sequence of conceptual trial-and-error experiments. Therefore, the zig representation is not a process, but the final representation of a sequence of processes.

Figure 3 depicts the "defining and selecting the DPs" at a level of decomposition, explaining the way to perform the process represented in Figure 2. The inputs of the process IN_1 come from the previous zag, bringing the DPs, CNs, CS of the higher level and the FRs at nominal conditions (FR_{NC}). Then, the design team proposes a set of DPs to perform the FR_{NC}, evaluates the DM (A_{NC}) and comes back to the functional domain in order to check if the FR_{NC} are fulfilled. During this process, DPs and DE may change, being possible the need to modify the set of FRs and evaluate if they are CEME. The process of checking if the FRs are CEME is not shown in Figure 3, as it would be required to relate the FRs with the parent FRs. The design team may conclude that the design has no solution (No Sol.), so that they have to go back to the previous level of decomposition.

During this first stage, the design team looks for the main important relations between each FR and the DPs, by estimating the value of the elements of the design matrix. In other words, all the $\left|\frac{\partial FR}{\partial DP}\right|$ which values are lower than a certain threshold are discarded.

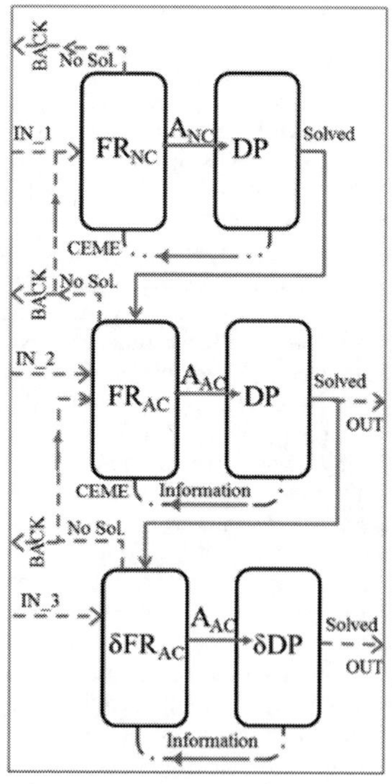

Fig. 3. Defining and selecting the DPs at a specific level of decomposition.

If there is a solution, the process needs a new input (IN_2), regarding the metrics of the FRs when the system works at the actual conditions. In addition, the new input brings the range of acceptance of the FRs, making possible to evaluate the information of the system. In many engineering applications the range of the FRs is defined as the "higher the better".

The information is accounted by the probability of the system to fulfil the FRs, when undergoing all possible situations in time, taking into account all interactions defined by the DM and the DPs at typical values. This is a first approach to the information that may be acceptable for existing designs, or similar.

At this stage of definition of DPs, the design team once more raises a new design matrix, the A_{AC}, check the fulfilment of the FRs and evaluate back if the FRs are CEME, trying at the same time to reduce the couplings between the FRs. If the FRs cannot be fulfilled, the design team may need to revaluate the nominal conditions, or to decide to go back to the previous level of decomposition. According to the diagram depicted in the previous Figure 2 of section 1.1, if the solution is accepted, the design may need to be tuned, or if the design is coupled it may need to undergo a decoupling process or an optimization process.

The design team may want to check the performance of the accepted solution, needing the input of the variation of the FRs (input IN_3 at Fig. 3). This allows the design team to check the tolerances of the DPs and to evaluate the information of the system at any situation in time. The design team also checks the system behaviour, taking into account the interactions defined by the DM and the effects of tolerances in the DPs.

Once more, the process may go back to redefine the FRs and DPs at the actual condition stage, or go back to the previous level of decomposition. Otherwise, it follows the aforementioned process for an accepted solution.

3 Example of the zig process

The following example helps us to show the existence of the two design equations during the zig process at the second level of decomposition of a design.

The example is about an air conditioning system, the variable air volume system, which is working in cooling mode. In the air conditioning industry it is common to use the acronym HVAC that stands for heat, ventilation and air conditioning, and VAV for the variable air volume system. In working conditions, the VAV system may lack to deliver steadily the minimum amount of outside air (OA) into some spaces, while delivering more OA than necessary to other spaces [22].

To satisfy the CNs of any HVAC system, the design team needs to fulfil the first order FRs: "Remove the heat" and "Provide the indoor air quality (IAQ)" at each space. VAV systems are a class of HVAC systems that remove the heat by convection, making a stream of air to be supplied into the space at a lower temperature than the room set-point temperature. To accomplish this requirement, the sensible power to remove Q varies according to the $\dot{m}$, the mass airflow, and ΔT, the difference between the indoor comfort temperature and the supply air temperature into the room. Equation 8 shows the above mentioned relationship being cp the specific heat for air.

$$Q = \dot{m} \cdot cp \cdot \Delta T \tag{8}$$

According to Equation 8, removing the heat load can be accomplished by maintaining the supply airflow and varying the temperature, or by maintaining the ΔT and varying the airflow. VAV systems use the second alternative.

In what concerns to the IAQ, it can be defined for any system according to the OA flow and computed tacking into account the number of persons and the floor area. Therefore, being q_p the OA per person, and q_s the OA to remove the contaminants of a space of floor area S, and np the number of persons, the needs of OA flow, q, may be expressed by Equation 9, an expression that sum both effects.

$$q = np \cdot q_p + S \cdot q_s \tag{9}$$

Figure 4 depicts a sketch of a VAV serving two spaces, space 1 and any other space n, allowing one to see the differences of behaviour of the system between spaces without having to show all spaces. The Figure shows a single duct (item 1) VAV that supplies a variable amount of air through the VAV boxes (item 2), according to the temperature T of each room. The cooled air at a supply temperature (Ts) comes from the air-handling unit (AHU), which also intakes the building's needs of outside air (OA) and exhausts a similar amount of airflow extracted from the spaces. A part of the return air (RA) mixes with the OA, making the supply air to include a certain amount of stale air coming from the inside. Moreover, the amount of OA delivered at each room depends on the load of the room, as increasing the load increases the supply airflow and therefore the OA delivered in the room.

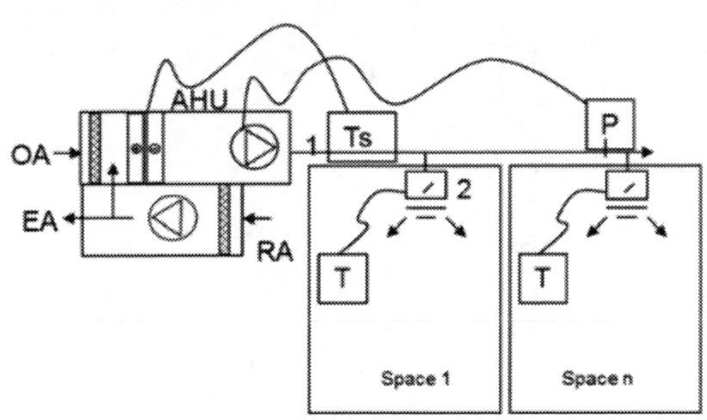

Fig. 4. VAV single duct system (box heaters and AHU dampers not shown).

The decomposition of FRs to DPs can help to define the major equipment of the VAV system at the design level of maximum load and maximum OA flow condition. The maximum load of the building allows the designer to define the cooling system of the AHU, and the maximum load at each space, the terminal equipment. Moreover, the total needs of OA of the building allow to define the OA of the AHU, and the OA needs of each space may be taken into consideration when defining the minimum position of the damper in the VAV box.

Equation 8 makes it possible to choose the VAV boxes, which size is determined by the airflow that is required to remove the maximum load at a certain supply temperature.

Table 1 shows the FRs and the DPs of the design decomposition until the second level of the design of a single duct VAV system [23]. Notice that there are no specific DPs for providing OA to each space, because the OA is mixed in the airflow supplied by the AHU.

Table 1. FRs and DPS of the VAV single duct in cooling mode.

FRs	DPs
FR1- Achieve indoor thermal comfort	DP1- Temperature control system
FR2- Provide IAQ	DP2- Outdoor air control system
FR1.1- Remove heat from space 1	DP1.1- 1's VAV box airflow
FR1.2- Remove heat from space n	DP1.2- n's VAV box airflow
FR1.3- Provide total airflow supply	DP1.3- AHU flow system
FR1.4- Adjust Ts of the AHU	DP1.4- AHU cooling coil system
FR2.1- Provide OA to space 1	
FR2.2- Provide OA to space *n*	
FR2.3- Provide building total OA flow	DP2.3- AHU OA system

Table 2 shows the design, at the aforementioned design level. Therefore "Remove the heat load", FR1.1 and FR1.2 depend on the airflow (DP1.1 and DP1.2) and on the air temperature difference, achieved at this level by the cooling system of the AHU (DP1.4).

Table 2. Design matrix at nominal conditions.

	DP1	DP2	DP1.1	DP1.2	DP1.3	DP1.4	DP2.3
FR1	X						
FR2	X	X					
FR1.1			X			X	
FR1.2				X		X	
FR1.3					X	X	
FR1.4						X	
FR2.3							X
FR2.1			X				X
FR2.2				X			X

Regarding the IAQ, DP2.3 fulfils FR2.3, computed the needs of OA for the all building according to Equation 9, which corresponds to the maximum amount of air that the building needs at nominal conditions. The position of the FR2.3 line was changed as to improve the readability of the design matrix.

The IAQ at each space (FR2.1 and FR2.2) varies according to the OA fraction in the supplied air, depending on the VAV box and on the OA delivered by the AHU. A common solution to this problem is to set a minimum position for the damper of the VAV box, in order to allow delivering at any time a minimum amount of air into the space [23].

Using the DM of Table 2 one can define the VAV box for each space and total OA of the AHU, as well as the airflow supply and the total cooling power. Some couplings arise in the design due to the fact that all VAV boxes are interconnected through a single duct, and because the airflow is a mix of OA and stale air.

At this time, all DPs are selected for maximum loads or OA needs, which occur at different times for all the building and for each space.

Table 3 shows the design matrix at the actual working conditions. Concerning to "removing the heat" (FR1.1 and FR1.2), anytime a dumper of a VAV box changes its angle, the pressure in the duct changes, forcing the adjustment of the other ones. Moreover, when a space has no load, then the minimum amount of air delivered by the VAV box may cause the space to overcool. There are two possible solutions for this problem: to adjust DP1.4 to another temperature on a trade-off between temperature and airflow; or to introduce a reheat coil in the VAV box that allows heating the airflow if necessary.

Regarding the IAQ, anytime the cooling load decreases at any space, then the airflow supply must be reduced and therefore the amount of OA also reduces. Moreover, the amount of OA in the supply air varies according to the airflow required by each VAV box, coupling the OA at each space to all the other spaces. This issue is represented by the squared block of "X" in the lines corresponding to FR2.1 and FR2.2 of Table 3.

Table 3. Design matrix at actual working conditions.

	DP1	DP2	DP1.1	DP1.2	DP1.3	DP1.4	DP2.3
FR1	X						
FR2	X	X					
FR1.1			X	X		X	
FR1.2			X	X		X	
FR1.3					X	X	
FR1.4						X	
FR2.3							X
FR2.1			X	X			X
FR2.2			X	X			X

To avoid a shortening of OA the VAV damper is set to a 30% minimum and the amount of OA for the building might increase by about 30% [23].

4 Discussion

In engineering design it is typical to define a solution at a certain level of decomposition and after simulate the behaviour of the design. Based on the experience of the authors, examples of this procedure happen when defining a fluid network, a metal structure, or a HVAC system.

In the higher-level representation of these designs, designers raise a sketch of the solution and discuss it. During this discussion, the design team often identifies the need for new DPs that may enforce them to go back and identify some forgotten FRs. After accepting a sketch, a similar process occurs during the calculation procedure.

Therefore the zig process at each decomposition level uses interdependent trial-and-error loops. Highlighting this concept supports linking the procedures of common good design in engineering to the approach of designing in the AD framework. In other words, the concept helps any expert designer to see the AD theory as a strong tool, instead of putting it aside because it seems difficult to apply.

The main benefits of AD to a design expert are the guidance to reach a solution, the evaluation of the design concept and the help in selecting the best solution.

5 Conclusions

The contributions of the AD community during last years mainly highlights the need of a more precise formulation of the functional requirements (FRs); the use of metrics and equations to express the design equation; and the epistemic classification of the decomposition process of zigzag between adjacent domains.

There was a previous work of Derick Tate regarding the zigzag process that explains how to interrelate the functional requirements (FR) of the design with the design parameters (DP). In what concerns to the zig process he proposed a roadmap depicted in Figure 2, with two main boxes: "define and select the DPs" and "setting the DPs values".

The current paper is an attempt to explain the procedures needed to "define and select the DPs" at a certain level of the decomposition of the design. This procedure is a sequence of conceptual trial-and-error manoeuvres in order to solve the design equation.

There are two main proposals in this paper regarding the way to implement the box "define and select the DPs": the definition of the design matrix (DM) performed in two stages; and the calculation of the information content of the design considering first the interactions of the system and thus the tolerances of the DPs.

Regarding the former, to achieve the DM the designer may define the "nominal conditions" when a maximum value for each FR occur in the sense of an engineering probabilistic value. The mapping from the functional domain to the physical domain allows the designer to define the design matrix at nominal conditions. Afterwards, the system is evaluated considering all interactions at different time conditions allowing to attain the DM. During this procedure the design team uses the concept of metrics for the FRs, variable with time or according to the different situations the system might perform. At each mentioned stage, FRs are checked for being "cumulatively exhaustive and mutually exclusive" regarding their parent FRs.

Attaining the DM makes it possible to define the tolerances of the DPs, and to check if the tolerances of the DPs fulfil the tolerances of the FRs.

Regarding the information content, it is possible to obtain the information of the system after defining the DM, by computing the probability of the system to perform within the ranges defined for the FRs. During this stage the designer worries at the time step about the behaviour of the system, considering the values for the typical value of the DPs. Afterwards, using the tolerances of the DPs it is possible to check the probability of success of the system at each situation or time step.

The authors gratefully thank the sponsorship of Fundação para a Ciência e Tecnologia through the Strategic Project UID/EMS/00667/2013 – UNIDEMI.

References

1. N.P. Suh, *The principles of design* (Oxford University Press, 1990)
2. K. Popper, *A Lógica da Pesquisa Científica* (Cultrix, 17th Portuguese Edition, 1972)
3. S. Lu, A. Liu, *A Logic-based Foundation of Axiomatic Design*, Proceedings of ICAD 2011, Daejeon, March 30-31 (2011).
4. M. Thompson, *Where is the why in Axiomatic Design?*, Proceedings of ICAD2014, Campus de Caparica, September 24-26 (2014)
5. D. Tate, *A roadmap for decomposition: activities, theories, and tools for system design*, Doctoral Thesis (Massachusetts Institute of Technology, 1999)
6. M. Nakao, *Surprising disadvantage of uncoupled design in staying competitive in the global market*, *Procedia CIRP*, **53**, 136–141 (2016)
7. J. Foley, E. Puik, D. Cochran, *Desirable complexity*, *Procedia CIRP*, **53**, 101–106 (2016)
8. J. Flores, A. Gonçalves-Coelho, A. Mourão, M. Cavique, *Theory of practices as a means to uncover the customer needs*, Procedia CIRP, **34**, 25–30 (2015)
9. M. Thompson, *Improving the requirements process in Axiomatic Design Theory*, CIRP Annals – Manuf, Tech., **62**, 115–118 (2013)
10. M. Nakao, S. Nakagawa, *A superb Industrial Design has special FRs or DPs that go beyond the customer's imagination*, Proceedings of ICAD 2011, Daejeon, March 30-31 (2011)
11. M. Thompson, *A Classification of Procedural errors in the definition of functional requirements in axiomatic design in Axiomatic Design Theory*, Proceedings of ICAD 2013, Worcester, June 27-28 (2013)

12. L. Slătineanu, O. Dodun, M. Coteaţă, I. Coman, V Manole, C. Gika, *Requirements statement in product design*, IOP Conf. Series: Materials Science and Engineering, **161**, no. 012042 (2016)
13. C. Brown, R. Henley, *Metrics for Developing Functional Requirements and Selecting Design Parameters in Axiomatic Design*, Procedia CIRP, **53**, 113–118 (2016)
14. A. Zhu, A. Liu, W. Chen, S. Lu, Physical Quantity Vocabulary for Functional Representation, Procedia CIRP, **34**, 13–18 (2015)
15. J. Rodríguez, E. Benavides, *The vacuum cleaner as a case study for teaching conceptual design*, Proceedings of ICAD 2013, Worcester, June 27-28 (2013).
16. E. Benavides, J. Rodríguez, *Methodological Contradictions Solved by the Linearity Theorem: the vacuum cleaner as a case study*, Proceedings of ICAD 2014, Campus de Caparica, September 24-26 (2014)
17. D. Matt, *Application of Axiomatic Design principles to control complexity dynamics in a mixed-model assembly system: a case analysis*, Int. J. of Prod. Res., Taylor & Francis, **50**, 1850-1861 (2012)
18. H. Oh, "Mathematical Underpinnings for Achieving Design Functional Requirements", *Procedia CIRP*, **50**, 228–233, (2016)
19. J. Fradinho, A. Mourão, A. Gabriel-Santos, A. Gonçalves-Coelho, *An Axiomatic Design interpretation for the synthesis of dimensional tolerances*, Procedia CIRP, **53**, 89–94 (2016)
20. J. Fradinho, A. Mourão, A. Gabriel-Santos, A. Gonçalves-Coelho, *Finding the minimum information content in 2-FR, 2-DP coupled designs*, Procedia CIRP, **53**, 78–82 (2016)
21. G. Arcidiacono, A. Giorgetti, M. Pugliese, *Axiomatic Design to improve PRM airport assistance*, Procedia CIRP, **34**, 106–111 (2015)
22. M. Cavique, A. Gonçalves-Coelho, *Axiomatic design and HVAC systems: An efficient design decision-making criterion*, En. and Build., **41**, 146-153 (2009)
23. M. Cavique, J. Fradinho, A. Mourão, A. Gonçalves-Coelho, *Decoupling the Design of Variable Air Volume Systems by Tuning the Tolerances of the DPs*, Procedia CIRP, **53**, 83–88 (2016)

Mobile Motorcycle Lift for the Common Man

Joseph Timothy Foley[1,*], *Guðmundur Þórir* Sigurðsson[1], *Jóhann Smári* Gunnarsson[1], *Jón* Gautason[1], and *Ólafur Jósef* Ólafsson[1]

[1] *Reykjavik University, Menntavegur 1, Reykjavik 101, Iceland*

Abstract. Motorcycle enthusiasts often need to spend significant amounts of time tuning and improving their bikes. Traditionally this is done by hobbyists by using the bike's own stand which can be dangerous due to its instability. For those with a little more money, a dedicated free-standing bike stand is the fixture of choice. Unfortunately, many of the bike stands are too expensive, too big, or have very weak ergonomics. In this paper, we present a motorcycle lift designed using Axiomatic Design that has a small footprint, is adjustable for a large range of different bikes and users, and can be mounted without the user lifting the bike. Though this prototype design is more expensive than the simple bike stands, we believe its functionality makes it well worth the extra cost.

1 Introduction

The goal of this project was to design a motorcycle lift focused on the practical maintenance needs of a motorcycle owner that are lacking in affordable lifts. The most common complaint is that the bike can't be moved around when you have removed the wheels. This is often discovered when using the most common low-cost lifts that are commonly employed: milk crates and other milk storage devices. Amateur motorcyclists often cannot afford a space devoted to just one ongoing project, so there is a need for mobility while minimizing the footprint of the lift. In addition, the lift should take up very little space when not in use to free up space for other projects in your garage or other work-spaces.

Like the name implies, the Mobile Motorcycle Lift is designed to lift up a motorcycle both to do maintenance on it and for safety inspections before each ride. Every motorcycle rider that rides on dirt bikes or road bikes needs a lift with these features to perform safety inspections and regular maintenance. Motorcycle owners dream of having a fully-featured motorcycle lift as found at the professional mechanic, but such lifts are far out of the financial means of most owners. Our goal was to make the perfect motorcycle lift as a careful balance of features and cost.

2 Prior art

The majority of low-cost lifts use a scissor configuration to convert an actuator that is very high force into sufficient displacement while keeping the entire mechanism compact. A motorcycle is positioned such that the engine or the wheel engages a locking device; often a retaining strap is used to fixture the bike to the top surface. Once the motorcycle is secured, either a crank is turned or a hydraulic mechanism is engaged.

Our survey of existing lifts showed that some of the common complaints from our user base were not addressed by the existing lifts. People wanted to a way to change the oil quicker and without spilling it all over the garage. Others were irritated that there was never enough space to put down their tools. All wanted a lift that was mobile so that different areas were easier to access and the bike could be put temporarily in storage while it was being worked on.

There is also one design flaw found in many of the lifts: when the front of the motorcycle is being taken apart, the lifts may tilt back uncontrollably until the back wheel of the motorcycle hits the ground. Many lifts take up too much space when not being used as well as not lifting high enough.

On the lower price range of the lifts, a common complaint was that the motorcycle itself had to be lifted onto the mechanism. When dealing with the heavy load of a motorcycle, this can easily translate into pulled muscles and a strained back. Everyone surveyed was excited for a lift that the motorcycle could be rolled onto or could slide underneath the bike.

The Black Widow lift (Figure 1) is small and compact and mobile. Unfortunately, the wheels can't easily be disengaged while in use since the wheels are attached to a separate dolly (Figure 1-c) that can be put under the lift [1]. Disengaging the wheels would require the user to remove the dolly from under the lift while the bike is on top: this would require lifting the entire weight of the motorcycle and the lift. The lift can also be used without the wheels but then it can't be moved around: Figure 1-b shows the lift configuration without wheels. This design only has a

*e-mail: foley@ru.is

DOI: 10.1051/matecconf/201712701008

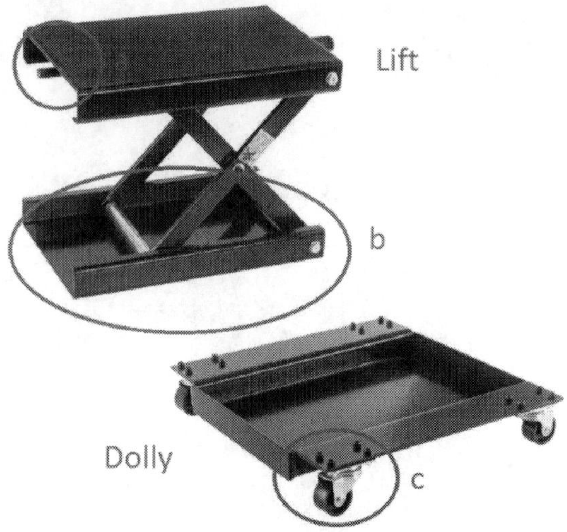

Fig. 1. Black widow lift [1]

Fig. 2. Pennsylvania Motorcycles lift [2]

manual screw jack system, not a hydraulic jack (Figure 1-a). Without a hydraulic jack, the lifting process is a lot slower and takes more effort to lift. In addition, no provision is made in this jack design for securing the bike to the lift.

A lift from Harbor Freight made by Pittsburgh Motorcycle is shown in Figure 2. This device lifts the motorcycle to a good work height using a hydraulic piston and has wheels that can be disengaged before the motorcycle is put on top (see Figure 2-b) [2]. The motorcycle is rolled up the ramp and screw-clamp is tightened to hold the front wheel. This process is slow for securing the wheels making it not convenient if the lift is often moved around. However, the main drawback of this design is the fact that it takes up a lot of space while it's not being used. There are also concerns that the clamp on the front wheel (Figure 2a) is not secure, resulting in an unstable mount. Even if the clamp is sufficient, this lift is incompatible with work being performed with the front wheel removed. The large footprint of the lift provides good stability but at a cost of large weight and inconvenient storage.

3 Design

We began the process of designing our "perfect" amateur motorcycle lift based upon a survey of complaints from motorcycle enthusiasts we knew in Iceland. We applied the Axiomatic Design methodology to structure and focus the complaints into a coherent set of needs (Section 3.2) from which requirements (Section 3.3) could be drawn up.

3.1 Design Methodology

Axiomatic design provides the theoretical foundation to generate and evaluate design solutions of complex systems [3]. It is a systems design methodology using matrix methods to systematically analyze the transformation of customer needs into functional requirements, design parameters, and process variables. Axiomatic Design as a mechanical design process focuses on the definitions of Functional Requirements (FRs), Design Parameters (DPs) and their interrelationship through a process of mapping between the functional domain and the physical domain.

The design process is to select the best set of DPs to satisfy the given FRs following certain criteria [4]. One goal of Axiomatic Design is to minimize the number of DPs, which can achieve FRs independently [3]. Specifically, functional requirements (FRs) are affected to design parameters (DPs) in a manner of "coupling". FRs and DPs coupling is communicated in a design matrix as shown in Equation 1. In this design matrix, coupling is represented as non-zero coefficients.

There are two axioms used in this method: Axiom 1 states that the independence of the FRs must be maintained, and Axiom 2 states that the information content should be kept at minimum [3]. In short, designers must minimize the coupling on non-diagonal elements of the design matrix and choose implementations (DPs) that meet their coupled requirements with the highest probability. After analyzing the customer's needs, we were able to set functional requirements and then design parameters. An example of an "uncoupled" Design matrix can be seen in Equation 1. For two requirements (FRs) and two implementations of those requirements (DPs), this is considered an optimal design with respect to coupling (Axiom 1).

$$\begin{bmatrix} FR_1 \\ FR_2 \end{bmatrix} = \begin{bmatrix} A_{11} & 0 \\ 0 & A_{22} \end{bmatrix} \begin{Bmatrix} DP_1 \\ DP_2 \end{Bmatrix} \qquad (1)$$

3.2 Customer needs

The focus group (customer) for this product would be regular motorcycle owners, particularly off-road riders who have to do a lot of maintenance to their bike, e.g. tire and oil change, suspension, and clutch work. The goal of any motorcycle lift is to make maintenance on the motorcycle easier. This top-level goal is described as CN_0. From this top-level goal, the rest of the needs are decomposed.

- CN_0: Better motorcycle maintenance working conditions
  - CN_1: Easy storage
  - CN_2: Compact when stored
  - CN_3: Motorcycle secure and stable on lift to prevent any possible danger due to it falling.
  - CN_4: Fit under the motorcycle so it doesn't require being lifted on to the lift
  - CN_5: Can be moved around

3.3 Functional requirements

Functional requirements (FRs) are a minimum set of independent requirements that completely characterize the functional needs of the design solution in the functional domain.[3] The functional requirements below are decomposed from a top-level FR_0. As per best practices [4], each FR must start with an action or transformational verb and be verifiable.

- FR_0: Make maintenance easier than with existing lifts for the average person.
  - FR_1: Lift motorcycle to comfortable working height.
  - FR_2: Keep work-space organized.
  - FR_3: Move the motorcycle around the shop.
  - FR_4: Stays stable when parts are removed.
  - FR_5: Take maximum 1 m^2 of floor space when not in use.

3.4 Design parameters

Design parameters (DPs) are the elements of the design solution in the physical domain that are chosen to satisfy the specified FRs [3]. As in the previous domains, the DPs are decomposed from a top-level DP0. [4] suggests that DPs should start with a noun or quantity and be something that can be compared or quantified.

- DP_0: Scissor lift mechanism with extended legs, tool/part tray/magnet and oil catch pan
  - DP_1: Hydraulic cylinder and a scissor mechanism
  - DP_2: Tool tray/magnet and a oil catch pan
  - DP_3: Wheels on undercarriage
  - DP_4: Spring-loaded hold-down mechanism
  - DP_5: Folding undercarriage/extension legs with wheels

3.5 Design matrix

The design matrix (see Equation 2) is then constructed to see how the FR's are related i.e. how one FR affects the other. The goal here is to have a diagonal design matrix, which means no FR affects another FR, which we were able to accomplish. We are therefore not worried about the order of elements in the design and are not afraid of disabling other parts by changing the size and shape of each individual part.

$$\begin{Bmatrix} FR_1 \\ FR_2 \\ FR_3 \\ FR_4 \\ FR_5 \end{Bmatrix} = \begin{bmatrix} X & 0 & 0 & 0 & 0 \\ 0 & X & 0 & 0 & 0 \\ 0 & 0 & X & 0 & 0 \\ 0 & 0 & 0 & X & 0 \\ 0 & 0 & 0 & 0 & x \end{bmatrix} \begin{Bmatrix} DP_1 \\ DP_2 \\ DP_3 \\ DP_4 \\ DP_5 \end{Bmatrix} \quad (2)$$

3.6 Our Design

All the group members are motorcycle owners or former motorcycle owners, so all had an opinion what would make the perfect lift. Our assumption was that the most common service operations were on tires and the suspension which requires that the front and/or back part of the motorcycle be disassembled. That creates a large moment on the base of the lift which must be taken into account. In our concept, the gap between the front and back leg is more than the width of the lift to account for the moment. A spring-loaded mechanism is used to ensure the bike is fixtured to the lift and doesn't tip over.

They are an oil catch pan underneath the top plate and magnets on the side to hold the tools in one place while working on the motorcycle. The weight of motorcycles can vary between different brands and sizes so it can be very hard to lift the motorcycle up on the stand. Therefore, our lift slides right under the motorcycle when in its lowest position, eliminating the need to lift the motorcycle up on the lift. A lift without wheels can't be moved around very easily. If the wheels are permanently engaged the risk of accidentally moving the lift while applying force to the motorcycle increases rapidly. Our lift would have wheels that can be engaged and disengaged by simply locking or unlocking them. A lift with this feature set could not be found on the Internet.

Our lift can be seen in early stage of design Figure 3 and in last stage of design in Figure 4.

3.7 Description of the design

One of our goals was to be able to slide the lift under the motorcycle. To accomplish this, the oil catch pan had to be mounted on the lift after the lift was raised to highest position (Figure 4). The oil catch pan (Figure 5) is mounted with hooks that are hooked to the oil catch pan: the holes that the hooks go into can be seen in Figure 5. The average amount of engine oil in a motorcycle is 1.5 L. The volume of the oil catch pan is 4 L so the oil catch pan wouldn't be full when the engine would be drained, making it easier to remove the oil catch pan without spilling the oil. A 3/8" threaded hole is on the bottom of the oil catch pan for draining with a mini valve.

Fig. 3. Lift in first stage of design

Fig. 4. Lift in highest position with oil catch pan

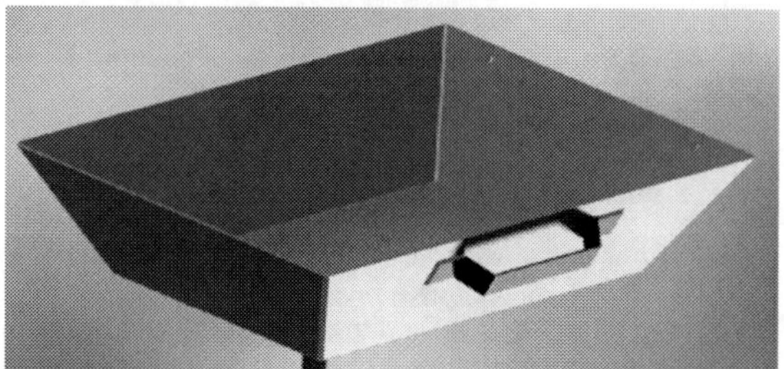

Fig. 5. Oil catch pan

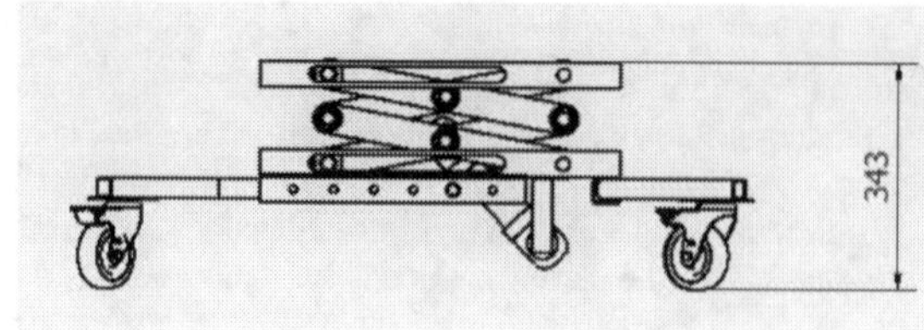

Fig. 6. Height of the lift in lowest position, dimensions in mm

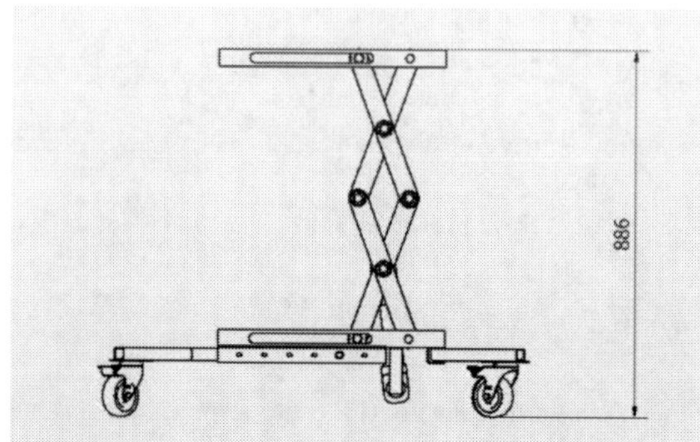

Fig. 7. Height of the lift in highest position, dimensions in mm

When the lift is in lowest position the height is 343 mm, seen in Figure 6, and in the highest position, the height is 886 mm, as can be seen in Figure 7.

One of our goals was to have a securing mechanism that would engage automatically when the motorcycle was being worked on. To accomplish this, the hold-down spring mechanism connects the motorcycle foot-pegs to the highest scissor axle. When the lift is raised to highest position, it applies tension on the spring mechanism because the length has increased. You can observe the difference in length from the top plate of lift and highest scissor axle in Figure 6 and Figure 7.

3.8 Materials

The scissor lift is made primarily of regular steel profiles. Other parts needed to build motorcycle lift are two springs to hold motorcycle stuck on the lift, four strong swivel wheels so it can be easily moved around, oil catch pan made from sheet metal to make oil change easier, a magnetic bar for tools, a hydraulic cylinder, fasteners, and paint.

The total cost of the building the prototype (not including the hydraulic cylinder) is approximately 25000 ISK. The first idea was to use hydraulic cylinder found from StarHydraulics [5] which costs 299 USD and shipping cost would be about 80 USD. Price and shipping including the VAT (24 %) the total cost of the hydraulic cylinder would be around 53570 ISK. Due to the high price and lead time, we found more practical to use standard hydraulic bottle jack instead of the hydraulic cylinder they are listed

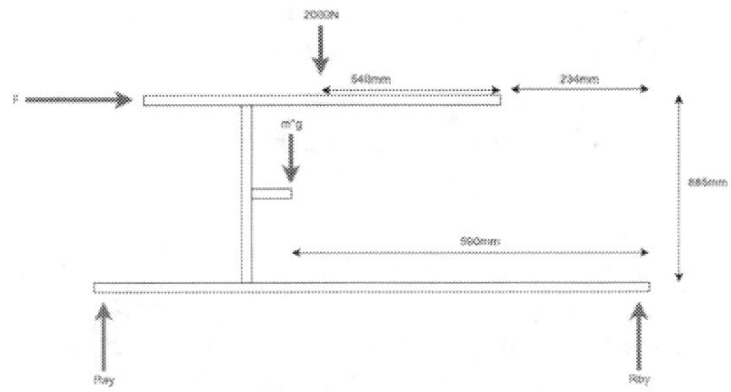

Fig. 8. Force diagram for our lift

for around $20 on eBay and are easily available in many places. The total material cost would end up to be around 30000 ISK.

4 Analysis

4.1 Comparison

The stability of the lift is a major aspect of the design. An unstable lift is both dangerous to the user and the stability affects the usability of the mechanism (Section 3.3). To calculate the stability of the lift, we looked at the maximum force that might be applied horizontally on the motorcycle without the lift tilting over. We set up a free body diagram as seen in Figure 8, and use Equation 3 to calculate moment around point B. We assume the lift to be simply supported and the reaction force at point A to be equal to zero (reaction force at point A becomes a negative when the moment due to the horizontal force becomes larger than the moments from the masses of the lift and the motorcycle). We look only at the case when the lift is almost tilting over (sign of the reaction force is flipping) and we assume the force due to the mass of the motorcycle to be 2000 N (200 kg). Maximum allowable force (without the lift tilting over), when the lift is in the position of maximum height and the wheel legs are in the shortest mode, is $F = 1492$ N. The maximum force when legs are fully extended is $F = 2098$ N.

However, using the same method to calculate theoretical maximum vertical force before tipping over will give us a statically indeterminate problem because the force never reaches out of the bottom frame (no negative torque), and therefore the vertical stability ratio is infinite. To compare this to other designs we calculated the same maximum horizontal force for another lift on the market. The result of this analysis is that the maximum force before tilting over was $F = 1118$ N, which shows the huge advantage of our design because the maximum lifting height is significantly lower in the design of this lift.

$$\tau = Fl \tag{3}$$

Equation 3 is used to calculate the moment, where τ is moment in N m, F is force in N and l is distance from the force applied to the point where the moment is calculated in m.

Table 1. Loads and boundary conditions.

Placement	Load [N] / boundary cond.
Top	4×500
Center of mass	Gravity
Outside edges of legs	Fixed

Fig. 9. Result of stress analysis.

Fig. 10. Displacement under maximum load.

4.2 Structural analysis

It is important to analyze if the lift can withstand the load required by the Functional Requirements (Section 3.3). The loads and the boundary conditions for the structural analysis can be seen in Table 1.

As seen in Figures 9, 10, and 11, the stresses never exceed the yield strength of the materials used (the safety factor is acceptable) and the maximum displacement under the maximum load is about 4.5 mm.

5 Conclusion

This motorcycle lift will help make motorcycle maintenance easier than ever. The tool tray will help people using the lift to remember where they put their tools and bolts since there is a convenient place to store them on the motorcycle lift, all in one place. The lift will be lower than a regular motorcycle lift which avoids having to lift the motorcycle on top of the lift first. It will lift the motorcycle high enough to reach an ergonomic working height

Fig. 11. Safety factor of the design under maximum load.

so the user can stand upright while working on the bike. The design has wheels on the bottom, which can be engaged and disengaged at will, to make it easier to move the lift around a garage even if the motorcycle is on the lift in full working height. The lift has a robust fixturing mechanism to hold the bike on the lift and prevent the bike from falling off the lift. The design is compact, occupying so little space that it can placed almost anywhere while storing it between maintenance sessions. All functional requirements of the design are fully satisfied, as listed:

- FR_1 is satisfied with a height of 886 mm when in top position: a comfortable working height while standing up.
- FR_2 is satisfied with an attached magnetic bar so the user can keep all his tools in one place. The oil catch pan will keep the lift and working area clean from oil spilling when changing engine oil.
- FR_3 is satisfied with locking swivel wheels so it is easy to roll it around the garage floor.
- FR_4 is satisfied because the self-locking spring fixture keeps the bike from falling off the lift when parts are removed.
- FR_5 is satisfied with extension legs to add stability for the swivel wheels so the lift only takes $0.76\,m^2$ of space when fully compact.

We can say that our motorcycle lift design is a successful design and all requirements are satisfied. Axiomatic Design greatly helped make our design process systematic and sure that we had clear goals for the project and guidance to how they should integrated.

References

[1] Discount Ramp, *Black widow steel motorcycle jack — 1,100 lb capacity*, accessed 2017-03-22, `http://www.discountramps.com/motorcycle-scissor-jack/p/BW-1604/`

[2] Harbor Freight Tools, *Pittsburgh motorcycle 1000 lb. capacity motorcycle lift*, accessed 2017-03-22, `http://www.harborfreight.com/automotive-motorcycle/lifts-stands/1000-lb-capacity-motorcycle-lift-69904.html`

[3] N.P. Suh, *The Principles Of Design* (Oxford University Press, Inc., 1990)

[4] D.S. Cochran, J.T. Foley, Z. Bi, *Use of the Manufacturing System Design Decomposition for Comparative Analysis and Effective Design of Production Systems*, International Journal of Production Research p. 24 (2016)

[5] StarHydraulics, *Item hf500-7in (stock), 1 ton (t) foot — operated hydraulic jacks* (2017), accessed 2017-03-22, `http://hydraulic-pumps.starhyd.com/item/lift-jacks/1-ton-t-foot-operated-hydraulic-jacks/hf500-7in-stock`

MATEC Web of Conferences **127**, 01009 (2017) DOI: 10.1051/matecconf/201712701009
ICAD 2017

The Faucet Reloaded: Improving Axiomatic Design by Example

Joseph T. Foley[1,*], *Erik* Puik[2], and *David S.* Cochran[3]

[1] *Reykjavik University, Menntavegur 1, Reykjavik 101, Iceland*
[2] *HU University of Applied Science Utrecht, Oudenoord 700, 3500 AD Utrecht, Netherlands*
[3] *Purdue University - Fort Wayne 2101 E. Coliseum Blvd., ETCS 229B, Fort Wayne, IN USA*

Abstract. Axiomatic Design Theory and Complexity Theory have made large impacts in the research of design methodologies, but a major obstacle to widespread use is the challenge of teaching it. A standard example used for educating students on the importance of coupling in Functional Requirements involves the difference between a two-valve and a lever-type faucet. Unfortunately, this simplistic example has its limitations in implementation due to imbalances in pressure and temperature variation. Strangely enough, these limitations turn out to be inspirations for expanding the example to make it better for teaching Axiomatic Design and Complexity Theory. In this work, we update the faucet example to map it to real-world application. Secondly, the concepts of 'Information in Design' and 'Complexity in Axiomatic Design' are explained from a perspective that increases understanding and acceptation by students and learning professionals. Lastly, we highlight other illustrative examples in manufacturing including the Manufacturing System Design Decomposition.

1 Introduction

Teaching by example is such a common practice in the modern education system that we don't think bout it.

In the case of Axiomatic Design, the traditional example for learning about the possible coupling between functional requirements (FR) is the problem of designing a proper faucet [1][2, p7,50–55]. Oddly enough, this example does not show up in Suh's first book on the subject "Principles of Design" [3]; instead, an similar example discussing the design of a Reaction Injection Molding (RIM) system is discussed. The first reference to Axiomatic Design of a faucet is by Swenson and Nordlund in 1996 in an unpublished report which is not available on the Internet [4]. This example was developed by Gunnar Sohlenius in the early 1990's during a visit with Nam Suh at MIT to make the newly-developed independence axiom easier to explain. This example was first published in 2001 [1]. In particular, he wanted to make it very clear what the difference between a coupled and uncoupled design was [5].

In the standard example, we consider two FRs that must be fulfilled:

FR$_1$ control the flow (Q) of water

FR$_2$ control water temperature (T)

The traditional faucet design has these DPs: [2, p.7].

DP$_1$ Opening angle of hot water valve, ϕ_1

DP$_2$ Opening angle of cold water valve, ϕ_2

*e-mail: foley@ru.is

and results in a coupled design matrix (Eq 1):

$$\begin{Bmatrix} \mathrm{FR}_1 \\ \mathrm{FR}_2 \end{Bmatrix} = \begin{bmatrix} X & X \\ X & X \end{bmatrix} \begin{Bmatrix} \mathrm{DP}_1 \\ \mathrm{DP}_2 \end{Bmatrix} \tag{1}$$

When instead a lever-type faucet is used which is able to separately match flow and temperature, these DPs are presented:

DP$_1$' Handle lifting

DP$_2$' Handle moving sideways

This new design has an uncoupled design matrix as shown in Equation 2.

$$\begin{Bmatrix} \mathrm{FR}_1 \\ \mathrm{FR}_2 \end{Bmatrix} = \begin{bmatrix} X & 0 \\ 0 & X \end{bmatrix} \begin{Bmatrix} \mathrm{DP}_1 \\ \mathrm{DP}_2 \end{Bmatrix} \tag{2}$$

For this purpose, the different kinds of faucets do a great job of simplifying the explanation of these two states. However, students who go home to test the concept on their lever-type faucets are quickly disappointed by the fact that it doesn't seem to be true.

2 Going deeper into the land of faucets

Joseph T. Foley, this paper's Icelandic author discovered these implementation problems with this example in his kitchen (Figure 1). The kitchen faucet has a pair of valves that are connected to a single valve stem. Pulling the valve stem out increases the flow, and rotating it up and down changes the temperature mix, at least in theory. From an outside inspection, this design has the same interface as the traditional "uncoupled" faucet design used in the example.

Fig. 1. IKEA Ringskär (201-764-37) kitchen faucet installed in the author's kitchen.

Table 1. Temperature and Flow rate independence test results of IKEA Ringskär faucet. The faucet was calibrated using shutoff valves beneath it to a temperature of 41 °C when at medium temperature and maximum flow. Low flow is defined as the minimum needed to conveniently wash one's hands. Medium flow is approximately halfway between off and on. Medium temperature is defined as the mark halfway between hot and cold on the faucet. SE is Standard Error [6, p21].

Setpoint		Measurement			
Temp.	Flow	Mean °C	n	σ °C	SE °C
Low	Low	7.3	36	0.05599	0.00933
Low	Med	7.1	31	0.04016	0.00721
Low	Max	7.1	36	0.13628	0.02271
Med	Low	30.5	22	0.22811	0.04863
Med	Med	37.4	27	0.16486	0.03173
Med	Max	41.0	29	0.34840	0.06470
Max	Low	74.2	28	0.11841	0.02238
Max	Med	74.9	29	0.13646	0.02534
Max	Max	75.0	31	0.09344	0.01678

The internal mechanism is not immediately obvious but one can expect it to be a linkage or cam adjusting the flow in the two valves. One would guess that this is the ideal configuration.

Unfortunately, this is not the case. From an interface standpoint, this design is clearly superior, but the implementation leaves a lot to be desired. As can be shown in the simple tests in Table 1, the two values are not independent[1,2]. The question is what is wrong with this faucet or perhaps what could be wrong with the ideal faucet design described? Foley attempted to balance the different hot and cold water pressures (more about that later) using the pressure regulation supply valves coming from the wall. This did not correct the problem, but at least found a consistent set point at one flow rate that gave consistently pleasant water temperature when the temperature was set to the middle.

Suh goes further with this exploration of the faucet design in [1, p120–124] focusing particularly on the design of the valve gates to ensure that the mixed proportion is independent of the total valve aperture. This goes a long way towards improving the practicality of teaching the faucet example, but it is often overlooked.

This type of faucet has an additional time-independent weakness that exposes a teaching moment in the faucet example. It is often assumed that the water pressure in both the hot and cold are very similar and that the hot temperature is not hot enough to give the user a significant burn. Having a similar pressure and temperature gives a wider range of aperture sizes that will provide the desired temperature and flow rate. Both of these assumptions are false in Iceland, where the hot water is 72 °C and comes out at approximately twice the pressure of the cold water. To make matters worse, the pressures and temperatures vary greatly from region to region depending upon how the geothermally heated water was extracted and regulated at the point of entry in the house. This means that a set of apertures as mentioned in [1] would need to be highly customized for Icelandic environments, otherwise the range of outputs would be very limited.

A time-dependent element is missing from the example that becomes apparent when something affects the pressure. We often assume that the hot water coming from a supply pipe is already at the maximum temperature; in reality it often takes significant time for the stagnent water in both pipes to reach the expected values. The flushing of a toilet or the filling of a dishwasher can cause the cold water pressure to suddenly drop and burn the user. In the case of the kitchen faucet in Figure 1, activation of the dishwasher caused the temperature to jump from 37 °C to 50.819 °C with $n = 23$, $\sigma = 0.30433$ °C, and SE = 0.06641 °C. Needless to say, this can cause a bit of a surprise to someone taking washing their hands or taking a shower, to the point of possibly jumping out at high speed and becoming quite injured. This is a significant enough problem that the US Massachusetts plumbing code 10.10.7.e states:

> "The water supply to a shower head shall be supplied through a Product-accepted individual thermostatic, pressure balancing or combination thermostatic/pressure balancing valve complying with ASSE 1016. The device shall conform to the following require-

[1] Foley's burned fingers were a strong motivation for this paper.

[2] All of the experiments in this paper were performed with a ThermoWorks Super-Fast Thermapen™, SN: E11401978. This instrument was last NIST certificate calibrated in 2011, but the author performed a calibration test with ice water and boiling water and found it within 0.3 °C accuracy and 0.1 °C repeatability.

Fig. 2. BOZZ YH 2101 Thermostatic Mixer installed in the author's bathroom.

Table 2. Temperature and Flow rate independence test results of BOZZ YH 2101. Medium flow is approximately halfway between off and on.

Setpoint Temp. °C	Flow	Measurement Mean °C	n	σ °C	SE °C
44	Low	44.8	28	7.86717	1.48675
44	Med	44.5	29	0.11425	0.02122
44	Max	44.4	23	0.12044	0.02511

ments: a. the device shall incorporate a design that limits the maximum deliverable temperature of hot water to 112°F (44.4 °C);" [7]

In Foley's bathroom, there is a faucet that is much closer to the Axiomatic Design idea (Figure 2): a thermostatic mixer. This valve has an active temperature-control element that biases the spring used for mixing the hot and cold water together. A similar mechanism was developed for temperature-sensitive commercial applications such as photographic developing as far back as 1933 [8]. This faucet was able to meet the Axiomatic Design ideal of decoupling the temperature and flow rate, at least from the perspective of the user as shown in Table 2. The temperature was maintained steadily at full flow even when the toilet was flushed with a mean of 44.0594 °C, $n = 32$, $\sigma = 0.766\,58$ °C, and SE = 0.135 51 °C.

2.1 What happened to the customer?

Interestingly enough, those who are familiar with traditional bathroom sink basins are witness to a different view of this coupling. In traditional English bathrooms, the hot and cold faucets are separate. This is because in the old times, the way to wash one's face was always by mixing water in a bowl, rather than a basin; in some cases, there wasn't any temperature control at all. This shows another element of the customer's need that is often forgotten in the faucet example. It is assumed that the customer desires a precise flow rate Q to be satisfied, or that there even is a flow during use. This is highly unlikely to be the case:

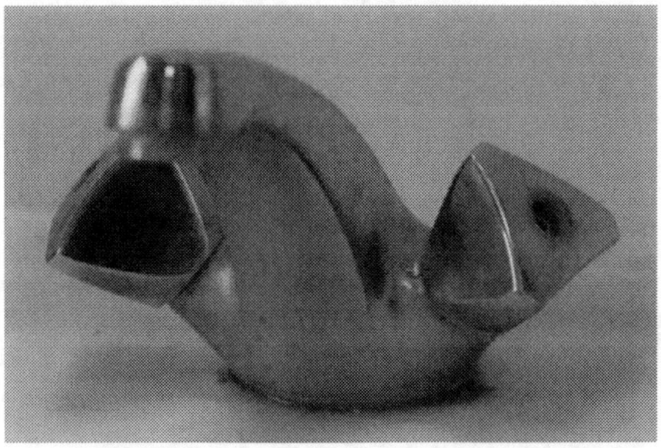

Fig. 3. Generic two-valve-stem faucet in the author's bathroom.

most of the time a flow rate just needs to be above a minimal amount. In Axiomatic Design terms, it means that we are misclassifying a Functional Requirement which should really be a Constraint [9, 10]. Once this transformation is complete, the two-FR example in Eq. 1 becomes a single-FR (Eq. 3) which can be easily solved by picking an initial value that meets the minimum flow requirement and increasing the other flow until the desired temperature is met. In practice, this is how people often solve the faucet problem, as inferior as a solution it may be.

$$\{FR_2\} = [X]\{DP_2\} \tag{3}$$

The other question is why are the clearly "inferior" two separate valve arrangement such as the one in Figure 3 still used? This is a question that is valuable for students to consider; the simple answers are cost and tradition.

What is missing from the way that the faucet is often taught is refocusing back on the customer. What does the customer actually want out of a faucet? El-haik emphasizes this as a critical step and suggests using Quality Function Deployment (QFD) to define Customer Attributes and FRs.[2, 5] Ulrich and Eppinger[11, p35] suggest a six-phase approach that starts by first describing the scope of the effort, then gathering raw data from the customer. We should be starting with the Customer Needs, then talking about the coupling in the FRs; otherwise, we might be solving the wrong problem! When teaching the faucet example, Foley starts by posing just such a question and examining the possible responses regarding how the faucet should be used:

1. "Warm water, but not too hot"
2. "38 °C water at 1.2 bar"
3. "I want to wash my hands"
4. "...just before performing open heart surgery in the heart of the Amazon"

Each of these customers has a hugely different desire out of their faucet. The majority of people are probably the first customer: someone who wants some warm water and doesn't actually care about the flow rate. This person may have trouble describing what "warm" means and may not have thought about how it will be used. Foley's comfortable temperature ranges for cleaning his hands were between 33–41 °C. The second customer who wants precise temperature and pressure probably wants a carefully calibrated temperature-controlled valve system; hopefully, they are ready for the large cost associated. For this customer, an information analysis is critical to ensure that the tolerances of the designed valve system meet their needs. The third customer is more specific than the first one and has a specific purpose in mind. The last customer is asking for an innovative sterilization system which a normal faucet will probably not fulfill.

These are each different design problems!

To summarize, to make the faucet example even better, we need to use it to:

1. teach students to evaluate the level of coupling through experiments,
2. work with customer needs and be confident that they are right before proceeding to functional requirements,
3. get a better understanding of the tolerances so that information can be evaluated.

The concepts of information and complexity are often a source of difficulty for students to understand; in the next section, we discuss some tactics to make the subject more approachable.

3 Information and Complexity in Design Reloaded

The concept of 'Information in Design' is probably even more difficult to explain by example than the concept of Independence; information in design is (i) an elusive understanding as it does not refer to the information about the design but about its behavior, and (ii) it seems to work in reverse with what you would expect, as being informed is usually a good thing and therefore information must be a positive quantity. To understand Information in Design it is good to go back to its origin.

3.1 Murphy's fame comes from ignorant designers

Information, as applied in Axiomatic Design, was initially proposed in Shannon's Information Theory [12] that in its turn was inspired by the concept of 'Entropy' as defined by Boltzmann [13]. Boltzmann proposed a scientific relation, the Boltzmann equation for ideal gases, that explains the relationship between the entropy of a certain quantity of gas and the number of ways the atoms or molecules of such a thermodynamic system can be arranged. Boltzmann's definition of entropy and Shannon's definition of information are very similar as was clarified by Weaver in the explanatory introduction of the book 'The Mathematical Theory of Communication' [14]. Weaver explains how information should be interpreted; as he states that 'the word information in communication theory relates not so much to what you *do* say as what you *could* say' meaning that information refers to the number of possible states of a particular situation. Applied on the problem of communication, as originally intended by Shannon, it explains the number of ways a transferred message could be interpreted, analog to the Boltzmann equation for the arrangement of molecules. More general, Weaver defines information as 'a measure of one's freedom of choice' and as such information is an indicator for the extent to which an incident or system is defined. This definition of information reduces its elusive character but the intuitively inverse effect remains; it is confusing that, in order to satisfy the Information Axiom, information in design is undesirable and it should be reduced. About this aspect, Weaver's statement; 'a measure of one's freedom of choice' must be viewed from the perspective of the system itself; in Axiomatic Design, that system is the product design.

It may seem inappropriate to think of a product design as something being associated with a stochastic characteristic but this is exactly what the information theory aims at; a good design is constrained to good behavior and there is no room left for any undesirable nature, simply because a well structured product design intrinsically eliminates all undesirable states of the design. Structure stimulates desired actions and excludes faulty behavior and therefore misperformance of a product design may be considered a consequence designers dispose of themselves because they do not have their business apart. Murphy's law is the result of underperformance of the designer by leaving a product design underconstrained. Because of this, the product design has options for behavior within a certain 'freedom of choice', and as a result, it will randomly select one of the available options. Some of these options may lead to unwanted behavior. *Summarized, freedom of choice within a product design, analog to information in design, will lead to the stochastic revelation of its behavioral options. As not all of these options show a positive outcome (usually there's only a single option with positive outcome), it means that the product design is not able to perform within expectations.*

3.2 Addressing the 'Lack of Regularities' in design

Further interpretation of information is made by Gell-Mann and Lloyd [15]. Gell-Mann and Lloyd relate information as defined by Shannon to 'Ignorance' or 'Uncertainty' and its cause is found in a 'Lack of Regularities' of the considered system (in our case a product or system design). Given the fact that designers are idealistic people that try to regulate their design as good as possible, and assumed they are provided with enough time and means to do so, the lack of regularities will be reduced as much as the knowledge of the designer permits. It means that acquisition of the right knowledge will lead to further reduction of regularities in design; this consideration makes information inversely related with 'knowledge of the designer'. In a situation where the designer has unlimited time and resources to acquire and implement the right knowledge, the product design will be fully regulated and therefore it will have no freedom of choice in its operation other than the envisioned way by the designer; as a result, information is eliminated from the system and all FRs of the product design will be satisfied. This leads to a more accessible way to deal with information in design. *Information in Axiomatic Design is a measure for the lack of regularities in a product design and it leads to uncontrollable behavior of the system; for this reason, the Information Axiom advises to reduce information and as a result, reduce the lack of regularities in the design.*

3.3 Bringing it together from the perspective of the Axioms

In line with this insight, a similar view may be applied on complexity in Axiomatic Design. Complexity in Axiomatic Design is defined as 'a measure of uncertainty in achieving the specified FRs', and as such, it is the result of a lack of regularities in the design. The four kinds of complexity in Axiomatic Design are (i) Real Complexity, (ii) Imaginary Complexity, (iii) Combinatorial Complexity, and (iv) Periodic Complexity. To understand these four kinds of complexity it is required to have a good overview of the basic role of the Axioms. Axiomatic Design facilitates the designer through two design phases [16, 17]:

- The 'Conceptual' design phase, by satisfaction of the Independence Axiom making sure that the designer is 'doing the right things';
- The phase of 'Robustness', by the satisfaction of the Information Axiom making sure that the designer 'does the things right'.

Now, things get a little tricky; though both Axioms apply regularities to the design, and as such, they both reduce the information in design according to the Shannon definition, however, only the contribution of the Information Axiom addresses 'information in Axiomatic Design'. This is an inheritance of the initial definition of information in Axiomatic design, where information is limited to the Information Axiom [3]. According to good practice in Axiomatic Design, independence in design is adequately addressed by the design matrix. As a result, application of information in design is not practically relevant for the Independence Axiom, and it was not applied for the theory behind it. For the Information Axiom, it indeed was a central theme and it was applied very effectively to address the many little things that address robustness of a product design. The result of these elementary choices is that the definition of information in Axiomatic Design is a subset of information in design according to Shannon and Weaver; in Axiomatic Design, it only addresses robustness, and according to the definition of Shannon, it addresses conceptual rigor and robustness. The same may be said for the definition of information according to Gell-Mann and Lloyd; 'a lack of regularities' is valid for both phases (conceptual and robustness). These different perspectives are inventoried in Figure 4. This concludes the tricky part.

Now, let's see how the different kinds of complexity are placed into this context. Imaginary Complexity deals

	Conceptual Stage of Design	Robustness Stage of Design
Practical Explanation	Doing the Right Things	Doing Things Right
Axiomatic Design	Indepence Axiom	Information Axiom
Shannon & Weaver	Information Theory	
Gell-Mann & Lloyd	Lack of Regularities	
Complexity Theory of Axiomatic Design	Imaginary Complexity	Real Complexity
		Periodic Complexity (time dependent)
		Combinatorial Complexity (time dependent)
Complexity Theory of Axiomatic Design Reloaded	Lack of Regularities in Design Matrix	Lack of Regularities in Matching Design Range
		Lack of Synchronisation of Processes
		Lack of organisation in (autonomous) processes that influence each other

Fig. 4. Overview of different perspectives on complexity.

with a lack of conceptual regularities that directly affects the Design Matrix (or vice versa). Real Complexity deals with a lack of regularities in design that affect robustness and this is equal to information in Axiomatic Design. The other kinds of complexity, Combinatorial Complexity, and Periodic Complexity, are specific versions of real complexity. These last two are 'Time-Dependent' kinds of complexity that, though they are basically the same, they may change as time passes, contrary to Imaginary and Real Complexity that are basically not affected by time. Figure 4 shows the complexity theory of Axiomatic Design and how it can be reloaded.

- Imaginary complexity can be considered as a lack of regularities in composing the design matrix;
- Real complexity is related to a lack of regularities in matching the design and system ranges;
- Periodic complexity is due to a lack of synchronization of processes;
- Combinatorial complexity is a lack of organization of processes that influence each other.

Finally, in theory it is possible to distinguish more forms of complexity, e.g. 'Time-Dependent Imaginary' kinds of complexity, where even the FRs may change, and though they are referred to in literature [18] they serve little practical use. Compare such a kind of complexity to 'performing open heart surgery without clean water in the heart of the Amazon, without first making a diagnosis', so all of a sudden it could turn out that the patient needs a kidney transplant instead.

Summarizing, both Axioms address information in design according to the definition of Shannon and Weaver, but Axiomatic Design only applies Information in Design for robustness, not for independence. The Complexity Theory of Axiomatic Design addresses this issue by defining Imaginary Complexity for issues related to the design matrix and Real Complexity for issues related to robustness. Real Complexity can be 'time-independent' or 'time-dependent'. In this last situation two kinds of complexity, combinatorial and periodic, have been defined. In all cases, complexity in design is a 'lack of regulations in the design'. Because of this, the design is not constrained to good behavior and may live a life of its own.

4 Manufacturing System Design Decomposition

Design relationships as represented by the axiomatic design equation using matrix notation is one way to communicate the relationships of a design. For large systems, with multiple levels of decomposition, an alternative to the matrix notation is a graphical illustration of the design in the form of a tree or decomposition. The Manufacturing System Design Decomposition (MSDD) uses axiomatic design to express the multiple FR and DP relationships that must be achieved simultaneously for a manufacturing system to become lean [19–21]. Lean is a name for the consequence of implementing a manufacturing system design. The MSDD communicates the manufacturing system design by relating high-level requirements to lower-level DPs [22]. This representation of a manufacturing system design provides a framework for innovation and further extension. Extension of the MSDD means the inclusion of additional FR-DP relationships; innovation may require new FRs and DPs.

Extension of the MSDD becomes apparent because of the knowledge of path dependency that is depicted in Figure 5. Path-dependent designs are also called partially coupled or decoupled designs [3]. The figure is arranged so that, at a given level of the decomposition, the DP that affects the most FRs is located on the left side, and then the DP that affects the next most FRs is next. The result of this arrangement of DPs is that the implementation sequence of DPs is identified. The benefit to the user is to understand the implementation priority and sequence of implementation of the DPs.

The structure of the MSDD illustrates the FRs that branch from a parent DP. With axiomatic design, a practical rule of thumb is to create a lower level of the design when there are two of more FRs that the parent DP, level above, must accomplish. For example, a DP0 will branch into multiple lower-level FRs. The parent-level DP is a noun that describes a physical solution that encapsulates and amalgamates the FRs defined in the next, lower-level of the design.

The graphical tree structure used to depict the axiomatic design of the MSDD provides a succinct and unambiguous understanding of the flow down of high-level requirements to lower-level requirements and rationale for the choice of the lowest-level DPs.

5 Conclusion

This paper has presented three different ways that Axiomatic Design teaching can be improved. The independence axiom focus on the standard faucet example has been expanded with a larger "product design" focus to include the customer. It also gives the opportunity to integrate time-dependent complexity as part of the analysis. Next, the challenging topic of "information" in the Shannon sense has been restated in terminology and concepts that are more approachable to students. Finally, we address the often discouraging appearance of the design matrix by restating it as a tree structure that maps design requirements and solutions as developed by the MSDD.

References

[1] N.P. Suh, *Axiomatic Design - Advances and Applications* (Oxford University Press, 2001)

[2] B.S. El-haik, *Axiomatic Quality: Integrating Axiomatic Design with Six-Sigma, Reliablity, and Quaity Engineering* (John Wiley & Sons, Hoboken, NJ, USA, 2005)

[3] N.P. Suh, *The Principles of Design* (Oxford University Press, 1990)

[4] A. Swenson, M. Nordlund, *Axiomatic Design of Water Faucet*, Saab Linkoping (Internal) (1996)

[5] N.P. Suh, *Keynote presentation*, in *Proceedings of CIRP Design Conference 2016* (KTH Sweden, 2016)

[6] C. Ireland, *Experimental statistics for agriculture and horticulture* (CAB International, Oxfordshire, UK, 2010)

[7] Massachusetts Office of Consumer Affairs, *248 CMR 10.00: Uniform State Plumbing Code*, Tech. rep., Massachusetts Government, Ten Park Plaza, Suite 5170, Boston, MA 02116, USA (2017), `http://www.mass.gov/ocabr/licensee/dpl-boards/pl/regulations/rules-and-regs/248-cmr-1000.html#10.10`

[8] J. Pym, *Temperature controlled valve* (1935), US Patent 2,004,636, `https://www.google.com/patents/US2004636`

[9] M.K. Thompson, *A classification of procedural errors in the definition of functional requirements in Axiomatic Design theory*, in *8th International Conference on Axiomatic Design (ICAD 2014)*, CIRP (Axiomatic Design Solutions, Inc., Worchester, MA, 2013), Vol. 32, pp. 1–6, jun. 27–28

[10] G. Bragason, S. Þorsteinsson, R.I. Karlsson, N. Grosse, J.T. Foley, *Heat-activated Parachute Release System*, in *Procedia CIRP, 9th International Conference on Axiomatic Design (ICAD)*, Procedia CIRP (Elsevier ScienceDirect, Florence, Italy, 2015), Vol. 34, pp. 131–136

[11] K.T. Ulrich, S.D. Eppinger, *Product Design and Development* (McGraw-Hill, 1995)

[12] C.E. Shannon, *A Mathematical Theory of Communication*, The Bell System Technical Journal **27**, 379 (1948)

DOI: 10.1051/matecconf/201712701009

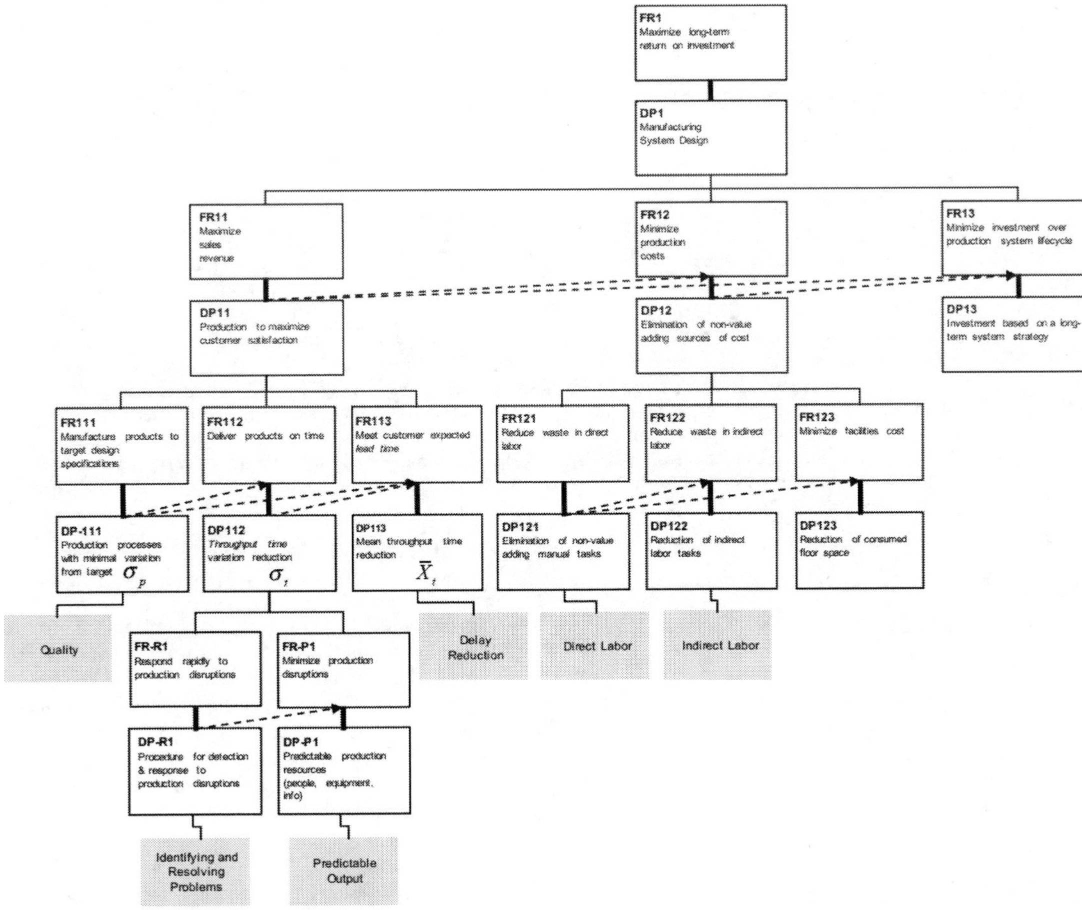

Fig. 5. Upper levels of the MSDD illustrating left to right implementation sequence of DPs [22].

[13] L. Boltzmann, *Vorlesungen Über Gastheorie, Vol. 1*, Theorie der Gase mit Einatomigen Molekülen, Deren Dimensionen Gegen die Mittlere Weglänge Verschwinden (Classic Reprint) (Forgotten Books, 2016)

[14] C.E. Shannon, W. Weaver, *The Mathematical Theory of Communication* (The University of Illinois Press, 1949)

[15] M. Gell-Mann, S. Lloyd, *Information measures, effective complexity, and total information*, Complexity **2**, 44 (1996)

[16] E.C.N. Puik, D. Ceglarek, *Axiomatic Product Design in Three Stages: A Constituent Roadmap That Visualises the Status of the Design Process by Tracking the Knowledge of the Designer*, ASME 2015 International Mechanical Engineering Congress and Exposition pp. V015T19A003–V015T19A003 (2015)

[17] E.C.N. Puik, D. Ceglarek, in *Axiomatic Design in Large Systems: Complex Products, Buildings Manufacturing Systems*, edited by N.P. Suh, A.M. Farid (Springer, 2016)

[18] T. Lee, *Complexity theory in axiomatic design*, Ph.d. dissertation, Massachusetts Institute of Technology (2003)

[19] D.S. Cochran, J.T. Foley, Z. Bi, *Use of the Manufacturing System Design Decomposition for Comparative Analysis and Effective Design of Production Systems*, International Journal of Production Research p. 24 (2016)

[20] D.S. Cochran, S. Hendricks, J. Barnes, Z. Bi, *Extension of Manufacturing System Design Decomposition to Implement Manufacturing Systems That are Sustainable*, Journal of Manufacturing Science and Engineering **138**, 101006 (2016)

[21] J.P. Womack, D.T. Jones, *Lean Thinking: Banish Waste And Create Wealth In Your Corporation*, new ed edition edn. (Simon & Schuster / Free Press, London, 2003)

[22] D.S. Cochran, J.F. Arinez, J.W. Duda, J. Linck, *A decomposition approach for manufacturing system design*, Journal of Manufacturing Systems **20**, 371 (2001)

Axiomatic Design for an Efficient Development of Optimized RPM Systems

Beniamino Pacifici, *Chiara* Parretti*, *Andrea* Girgenti, *and Paolo* Citti

Guglielmo Marconi University, Department of Innovation and Information Engineering, via Plinio 44, Rome, Italy

Abstract. New communication technologies and development of increasingly advanced systems for remote assistance create important opportunities related to the spread of e-health systems and devices for health monitoring and healthcare integration. Despite the increasingly widespread use of Remote Patient Monitoring (RPM) systems, especially in presence of chronic diseases, users' needs and requests are often disregarded due to poor customization of solutions. This is mainly due to the lack of truly interoperable tools allowing for horizontal integration between the various medical and specialized instruments. The proposed model works as a useful approach to ensure that the development of new solutions shall be partially guaranteed. The Axiomatic Design method is a suitable tool to identify the best solutions to meet users' needs.

1. Introduction

Long-term sustainability of health care provision raises serious concerns, due to increase in chronic diseases and gradual aging of population, which is making the provision of healthcare assistance more and more burdensome. To cope with this challenge, attention to healthcare management and efficiency of systems for therapies management have become a primary objective.

Developing a network, which provides the integration of health and social services with interoperable devices/systems, works as an optimized resource management tool. This network contributes not only to make the healthcare more tailored to the patient, but also to develop a more efficient and widespread prevention system. Moreover, these services allow remote treatment of chronic diseases and offer tools to healthcare providers to make clinical decisions faster and more reliable [1].

The progress of Remote Patient Monitoring solutions (RPM) is strongly stimulated by the simultaneous presence of socio-cultural factors that drive the market towards this direction:

- Users are progressively more willing to use wireless health monitoring systems,
- Governments push towards an optimization of healthcare costs,
- Average lifespan of people with chronic diseases to be treated is increasing, due to gradual aging of population,
- There are monitoring systems and sensors on the market, with an increasing diagnostic capacity for a growing number of chronic diseases and issues.

This article addresses the development of RPM solutions, clustered depending on users' needs, by means of a holistic approach. In this case, the AD methodology is an excellent help, especially in presence of a complex system, to analyze and transform Customer Needs (CNs) into Functional Requirements (FRs) and Design Parameters (DPs). Specifically, an application of the axiom of information is hereby proposed, using the Function Point Technique [2-7]. This methodology is used to measure the information content of FRs and DPs mutual relationships. Therefore, in this complex environment, it is possible to develop the most robust solution among the many ones that are possible thanks to AD methodology; moreover, among all of them, AD allows to choose the one that better meets the needs expressed by the users.

2. State of the art

There is a wide range of services and applications that are currently used with mobile devices to provide remote health care services. These systems can be categorized into two macro areas based on the type of service they provide: user services and systems meant to optimize the national health service. The first group includes services and applications which are used directly by individual patients and people interested in monitoring their health. The second group includes solutions that do not interact directly with patients, yet are implemented to improve the efficiency of health care (i.e.: services developed to support healthcare and/or administrative staff) [1, 8].

As of today, the most developed part of the first group is the remote monitoring of health conditions [9-10]. In Europe and the United States only, more than 200 million people are suffering of pathologies for which remote monitoring can be an optimal solution from a clinical standpoint [11-12]. These already identified users can add up new types of users, for whom solutions have not yet been implemented, such as patients who are

* Corresponding author: c.parretti@unimarconi.it

interested in fetal monitoring, healthy people groups who are interested in monitoring their health and people who are interested in preventive screening [11-12]. RPM systems have several advantages beyond healthcare costs reduction, which have been highlighted by several studies conducted on both patients and healthcare professionals:

- there is an increasingly patient satisfaction with health systems, as well as an improvement in the quality of life;
- there is an improvement in patients' better willingness to follow the treatments prescribed by the doctors;
- there is a simplification of work for healthcare staff;
- there is a reduction in emergency and hospitalization interventions.

Despite the development of many solutions, which offer several benefits, these are still sectoral and barely characterized for specific groups of users.

3. Challenges

The diffusion of RPM systems is slowed down by multiple factors that cause a lag in their large-scale adoption (Fig.1). The lack of interoperability and standards limits the possibility of integration between medical/specialist tools and those tools aimed at improving the quality of life of patients. ISO/IEEE 11073 Health Informatics-Medical/health device communication standards enable communication between medical, healthcare and wellness devices, as well as between external computer systems. However, these standards identify requirements related to small devices with limited resources of processor, memory and power [13, 14]. This leads to a slowdown in the development and spread of these services, compromising the quality of information and generating cost increases.

	Challenges			
Users	**Regulatory**	**Economic**	**Structural**	**Technological**
Health care provider	Lack of clarity on certification Lack of Interoperability Lack of compensation mechanism	Need for further evidence Conflicting incentives Change management	Low cohesion across levels and regions	Late involvement of doctors in solution design
Solutions vendor				Interoperability
Mobile service provider		Lack of clear reimbursement mechanism		Standardization Interoperability
Medical devices vendor				Standardization Interoperability
Doctors/ Patients		Lack of awareness of system benefits for the Doctors and patients		Significant training needs

Fig. 1. Summary of the main barriers to the development of mobile health systems.

Moreover, there are no unified rules for mobile application management in health and welfare industry, while from a legal perspective there is no adequate guarantee for the full protection of recorded data [15]. Additionally, there are other types of challenges such as:

- Political barriers: national and local health systems have different standards, while health policies often do not encourage the homogenization of systems,
- Definition barriers: healthcare and medicine are complex areas from a variety of perspectives, so both categories are difficult to define and categorize due to cultural, social, and contextual differences. In addition, medicine is a rapidly evolving field, thus mobile health standards shall adapt rapidly to contextual evolution with frequent revisions,
- User barriers: healthcare providers are often unsatisfied of devices currently available on the market because they are too sectoral and are not useful for patients' management; also end users often know that systems currently proposed are too complex.

4. Health systems functionality

The analysis of global context, regarding both users' needs and health systems requirements, suggests that the creation of a network for health and social services and integrated devices/interoperable systems, should focus on the following types of functionality [16]:

- health monitoring and comfort, such as systems related to patient monitoring, through direct employment of health professionals, when the complex/chronic patients have left the hospital. These systems should create a continuous supervision of the user's situation by means of various indicators, recorded and analyzed. Thus, these devices can greatly enhance the users' perception of their security, since they receive ongoing monitoring of their situation;
- Safety and speed of interventions in emergencies [17]: the systems enable the monitoring of early warning indicators related to critical situations (i.e. usage of bathroom and no long-term movement), through which it is possible to recognize false alarms thus avoiding unnecessary trips to the hospital,
- Knowledge of useful information: qualified support systems at home will help users in the resolution of everyday problems and concerns or to receive instructions and assistance from family,
- Support the performance of an activity: organization of daily activities that allow to smartly manage: time, nutrition, hydration, taking medication, etc. based on user specificity;
- Simplification of necessary actions, that being systems for automatic reordering of drugs with verification of stocks present together with the eating plan,
- Prevention tips and stimulus: systems can suggest how to perform normal daily activities to get a rehabilitative effect or make the necessary fun activities (i.e.: using a video games approach often used in rehabilitation contexts [18] for operations to be carried out by children). Self-testing systems monitor the current situation and its evolution through time,
- Compensation and assistance: systems can address/alleviate difficulties due to a certain disease related to environmental conditions. Programs designed for highly complex patients (for example, those with a functional or multiple disability) provide the

employment of installed devices that control their ability to live independently.

5. Axiomatic Design for RPM systems development

This article deals with the methodology of Object-Oriented Analysis and Design (OOAD) within the Axiomatic Design (AD) approach [19], applied to the design of a software that is able to find the best solution for customizing RPM systems starting from basic interoperable elements. This methodology simplifies the integration of AD approach into the software development through the Object-Oriented Programming (OOP) technique.

OOAD is a technical approach for analyzing and designing an application, system, or business by applying the object-oriented paradigm, as well as using visual modeling throughout the development life cycles to foster better stakeholder communication and product quality.

AD is a top-down design methodology (from general down to more detailed elements) starting from the Customer Needs (CNs), the Functional Requirements (FRs) can be defined after them, then the Design Parameters (DPs) as well. If the analysis is too abstract, a FR decomposition is performed and then corresponding DPs are identified. This process continues until the level of detail required for the project is reached [2, 20].

Axiomatic Design is based on the verification of axioms of independence and information. The axiom of independence guarantees design solutions in which the relationships between FRs and DPs are uncoupled or decoupled. This axiom states that when multiple FRs exist, the design solution should satisfy the condition with a diagonal design matrix. Thus, each DP will affect only its associated FR with no coupling occurring in the off-diagonal elements. This type of solution is said to be uncoupled. When independence is not achieved, there are two cases. In one case the design will be decoupled, meaning that the matrix can be rearranged to obtain a triangular state; in the other case, when off-diagonal elements exist and the matrix cannot be rearranged to a triangular state, the design is said to be coupled. An acceptable design is either uncoupled or decoupled [21].

The axiom of information allows to select the most robust solution, whenever there are multiple solutions, which corresponds to the project with the lowest information content. The concept is to find the system that satisfies FRs through DPs with the highest probability.

Thus, the designer may also select the solution, among the different functional substantial decompositions, requiring the least effort in terms of resources and development time. This approach is the same as choosing the functional decomposition with the lowest information content, meeting the same functional requirements at the same time [6].

However, in the software design field, Axiomatic Design is often applied through the verification of the independence axiom alone. Solutions identified this way are coherent from a design point of view but are not necessarily the most robust in a conceptual sense. Scientific literature on this subject often justifies the non-application of the information axiom, indicating difficulty of quantifying the content of software information [19]. In this article, an application of the axiom of information is proposed, using the Function Point Technique [2-7].

This methodology is useful to measure the information content of FRs and DPs relations. Therefore, in this complex system, the application of AD allows the development of the most robust solution among the many possible, and above all, the one that better meets the needs expressed by users.

A function point is a "unit of measurement" to express the amount of business functionality an information system (as a product) provides to users. Using a standardized set of basic criteria, each function is a numeric index according to its type and complexity. These indices are totaled to give an initial measure of size, which is then normalized by incorporating several factors relating to the software as a whole. The result is a single number called the Function Point index, which measures the size and complexity of the software product.

To sum up, the function point technique provides an objective, comparative measure that assists in the evaluation, planning, management and control of software production.

6. Holistic framework for the development of RPM systems based on user needs

The proposal of this article is the creation of a system able to align RPM systems and customers' needs (whether they are patients or healthcare professionals). The scheme, shown below in fig. 2, is a concept of the followed approach.

Customers need to be grouped in clusters to offer a different type of application related to same scope.

Requirements and characteristics of systems must be classified according to users' type (e.g. children, elderly, healthcare professionals, etc.). This is a key step during the procedure of customizing the service: having responses to demands expressed not only in terms of technology offered, but above all in usability of software or applications interface. This avoids reticence in system adoption and provides customer satisfaction.

In this phase, the clusters of customers can be identified with the aid of Lean Six Sigma (LSS) [22] instruments, based on the transformation from Voice Of Customer (VOC) to Functional Requirements and Design Parameters [23-28]. In this specific case, the Quality Function Deployment (QFD) tool helps transforming the users' needs into functional requirements, then subsequently applying the Axiomatic Design

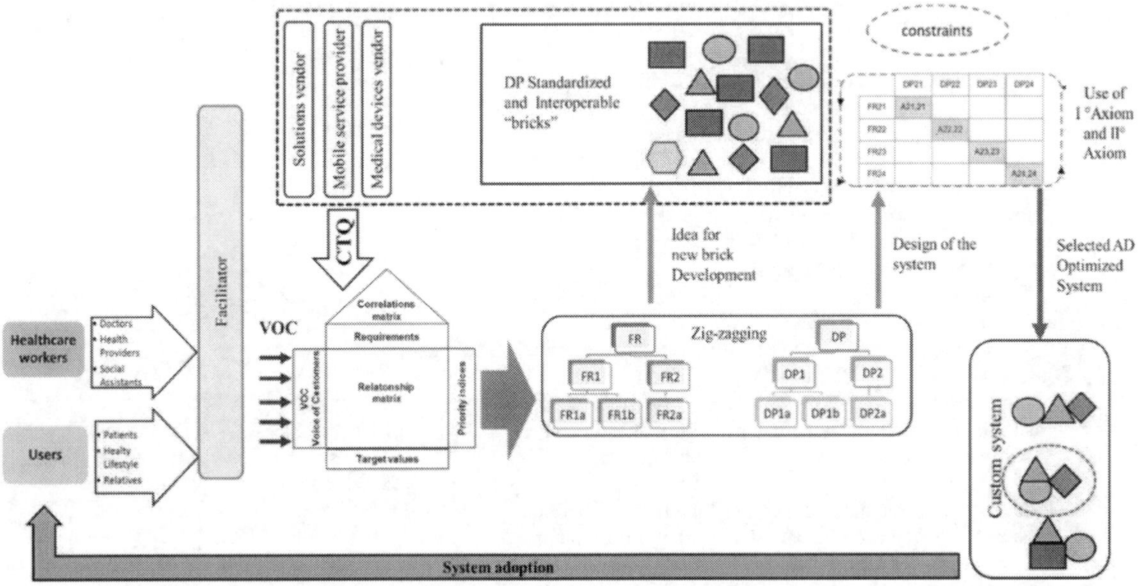

Fig. 2. Holistic Framework for the development of RPM systems based on user needs.

methodology. The effective versatility of AD has also been demonstrated by other specific applications not only in healthcare contexts but also in optimizing processes [29] and products [30].
According to the fig. 2, required FRs are also generated through continuous exchange of information that is collected by healthcare professionals. The involvement of healthcare professionals in this first phase reduces risks of inadequate construction of software features and avoids missing important information to be caught. Moreover, to make eHealth systems effective, coordination between various healthcare actors is crucial, starting from doctors among healthcare professionals, patients, informal caregivers until end users [31]. Health information provided by devices should be the one needed by healthcare operators to evaluate clinical situation, and must remain the same with no dependence from the user's cluster origin. For example, if a cardiovascular monitoring is required to monitor blood pressure, this value should be monitored whether it is an RPM system developed for the elderly users, or is developed for a pregnant woman.

All the users' and healthcare professionals' requirements are transformed through the aid of IT operators; using these specifications, they will develop elementary "bricks", which represent standardized and interoperable elements of RPM systems. The developers will assemble standardized bricks to organize their composition based on customer requests. In this phase, the QFD tool is also useful to identify the characteristics of the new bricks; in fact, it provides the weight of the technical performances needed by the specified cluster of users.

Now, the AD methodology is applied to ensure robustness of the RPM solution selected and assembled, more specifically by using methodology of Object-Oriented Programming applied to software design. The last phase of designing with AD is the identification of a decomposition between FRs and DPs, which corresponds to the conceptual process of system to be implemented in the software. Therefore, the output of AD design phase becomes the input for the software system programmers. Now, using OOP programming technique, which is a bottom-up system that starts from detail and goes to general, the best robust RPM solution can be obtained using the best single interoperable elements. The logic of system is the first phase of the software lifecycle.

To understand AD-OOAD, it is necessary to review the definitions of the words used in OOP and their equivalent words in Axiomatic Design. The fundamental construct for the object-oriented method is the "object", which is equivalent to FRs. Object-Oriented Programming decomposes a system into objects. Objects "encapsulate" both data (equivalent to DPs), and method (equivalent to relationship between FRi and DPi) in a single entity. Object retains certain information on how to perform certain operations, using the input provided by the data and the method embedded in the object. In terms of AD, this is equivalent to say that an object is [32]:

$$FRi = Aij \cdot DPj \tag{1}$$

The concept is to design a RPM system that meets the FRs through DPs, by measuring the information contents of relations between FRs and DPs through the Function Point technique. At each level of decomposition of the FRs, an estimate can be made in terms of function points. In general, there is a certain correspondence between FRs, DPs and the constituent elements of the calculation in the function point. For instance, let us consider the functional decomposition represented by the correlation matrix between FRs and DPs:

* Corresponding author: c.parretti@unimarconi.it

DOI: 10.1051/matecconf/201712701010

$$\begin{Bmatrix} FR1 \\ FR2 \\ FR3 \end{Bmatrix} = \begin{bmatrix} A_{11} & 0 & 0 \\ 0 & A_{22} & 0 \\ 0 & 0 & A_{33} \end{bmatrix} \cdot \begin{Bmatrix} DP1 \\ DP2 \\ DP3 \end{Bmatrix} \quad (2)$$

To illustrate the correspondence, we must consider that each functional decomposition can be represented with a module-junction structure diagram. Each module of the diagram includes property details and functionalities associated with them [19, 20, 31]. Therefore, a generic module (M) is defined as the row of design matrix that yields the FR of the row when it is multiplied by the corresponding DP [32].

Essentially, a module is an object that contains the data and the methods that allow to implement the functional requirement FR. Estimating the information content with Function Points (FP) provides an advantage for composing the best solution; in fact, a numeric value, which can be compared to other possible solutions, can be assigned to elementary interoperable elements or bricks.

Through this technique, elementary functions and data structures are identified, containing all the elements needed to develop a customized system. In this case, Axiomatic Design combined with OOP and FP selects the most appropriate RPM solution for the specific goal.

This standardization mechanism, together with the subsequent bricks construction, make it easy to keep up-to-date systems that will be able to follow technological evolution, continuous evolution of IT services and customer needs.

The development process of RPM solutions follows a flow, shown in Figure 3.

Starting from user clustering, a series of specific requests for each identified group is obtained. Through the QFD tool, such requests are translated into technical requirements by RPM developers in close connection with healthcare experts. The use of QFD also allows to understand the importance of technical features developed in customer optics [23-28].

Now, the functional requirements are identified and interoperable elements necessary for the development of RPM solutions (DPs) and their design constraints should be identified too.

Moreover, it is necessary to develop any needed interoperable elements if they are not available. Once all the needed elements are available, the system can be identified and optimized using AD axioms. In this case, the verification of the axiom of information is made by measuring the information content of system using the Function Point [2-3] technique. The assembly and the development of the selected best RPM solution can now be performed.

The presented framework might be a useful approach to ensure that development of new solutions shall already be partially guaranteed and will accompany the evolution of medicine and people's habits. Therefore, the application of QFD-AD and OOP is here performed in the healthcare environment, where "bricks" are customized and then assembled. The process becomes leaner and more robust in a context where the solutions developed are poorly declined into CNs.

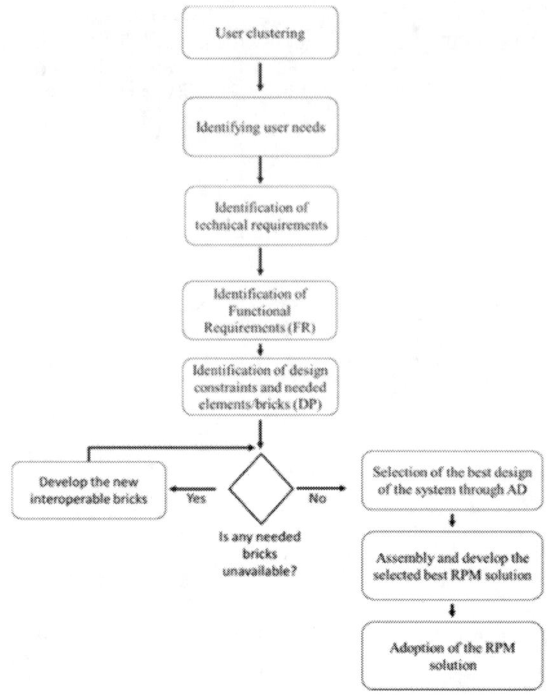

Fig. 3. Flow chart of the logical path.

7. Conclusions

Socio-economic convergence and development of reliable remote communications technology and devices make the prospect of massive introduction of RPM systems in healthcare sector very interesting. Despite the interest of many actors involved, most of the users' requests remain undone so far, as there is no system that cares about characterization of proposed solutions. In fact, most of the systems do not completely satisfy needs of either healthcare providers or users. The significant limit is certainly a lack of interoperable and standardized elements that allows a horizontal integration between different medical/specialized instruments and utilities aimed at improving quality of life. The proposed approach allows to overcome the aforementioned difficulties: it provides a method for selecting optimal RPM solutions, both for user satisfaction and simplification of the design process for the development of solutions, thanks to AD methodology. In fact, the presented process is useful to develop the minimal amount of software functionality and avoiding unnecessary implementations. Moreover, through the deployment of OOP and FP techniques, it is possible to realize an accurate planning of resources and costs, reducing the development time of RPM solutions. The holistic framework can be quickly refreshed, facilitating the exchange of technical information as well, thus following specialist medical and technological evolution.

In future works, this framework could be implemented, developed and tested, reaching full automation by providing software solutions capable of a mechanical selection of optimal bricks composition or a modification of the existing elementary bricks.

For this reason, the proposed model could be a useful approach to ensure that development of new solutions shall already be partially guaranteed and will accompany the evolution of medicine and people's habits.

References

1. A.A. Atienza., B.W. Hesse, D.H. Gustafson, R.T. Croyle, *E-health research and patient-centered care examining theory, methods, and application*, American Journal of Preventive Medicine **38**, 1, 85-88 (2010)
2. A.J. Albrecht, *Measuring Application Development Productivity*, Proc. of the Joint SHARE/GUIDE/IBM, 83-92, (1979)
3. D. Garmus, IFPUG Function Point Counting Practices Manual, Release 4.1, (1999)
4. R. Meli, L. Santillo, *Function point estimation methods: A comparative overview*, Proc of FESMA, **99**, 271-286, (1997)
5. F. Rolli, A. Giorgetti, P. Citti, *Integration of Holistic Non-Conformities Management and Axiomatic Design: a case study in Italian Income Tax Returns* Management, Proc CIRP **34**, 256-262, (2015)
6. F. Rolli, A. Giorgetti, P. Citti, M. Rinaldi, *Improvement of the compilation process of the Italian income certifications: a methodology based on the evaluation of the information content (Part 1)*, Proc CIRP **53**, 56-62, (2016)
7. F. Rolli, A. Giorgetti, P. Citti, M. Rinaldi, *Improvement of the compilation process of the Italian income certifications: an application on the tax model of the year 2016 (Part 2)*, Proc CIRP **53**, 63-69, (2016)
8. G. Arcidiacono, D. T. Matt, E. Rauch, *Axiomatic Design of a Framework for the Comprehensive Optimization of Patient Flows in Hospitals*, Journal of Healthcare Engineering **2017** (2017)
9. M. Kay, J. Santos, and M. Takane, *mHealth: New horizons for health through mobile technologies*, World Health Organization, vol. **64**, 7, 66-71 (2011).
10. mHealth and Home Monitoring, Berg Insight (2014).
11. Connecting patient with providers A Pan-Canadian Study on RPM, (2014)
12. Canada Health Infoway Benefits Evaluation Indicators Technical Report, Version 2.0 (2012)
13. J. Antonio, M.A. Zamora-Izquierdo, A.F. Skarmeta, *Interconnection framework for mHealth and remote monitoring based on the internet of things*, IEEE Journal on Selected Areas in Communications **31**, 9, 47-65, (2013)
14. M. Clarke, D. Bogia, K. Hassing, L. Steubesand, T. Chan, D. Ayyagari, *Developing a standard for personal health devices based on 11073*. EMBS 2007, 6174-6176, (2007)
15. M. Sandhya, R. M. Madhumitha, S. Sankar, *Analysis of Threats in Interoperability of Medical Devices*, International Journal of Medical, Health, Biomedical, Bioengineering and Pharmaceutical Engineering **11**, 5, 264-267, (2017)
16. B. Pacifici, C. Parretti, G. Arcidiacono, A. Giorgetti, A. Girgenti, *Conceptual framework for user based RPM*, Proc. International Conference on Industrial Engineering and Operations Management, (2017)
17. G. Arcidiacono, J. Wang, K. Yang, *Operating room adjusted utilization study*, International Journal of Lean Six Sigma **6**, 2, 111-137 (2015)
18. L. De Vito, O. Postolache, S. Rapuano, *Measurements and Sensors for Motion Tracking*, IEEE Instrumentation & Measurement Magazine **17**, 3, 30-38, (2014)
19. N.P. Suh, *Axiomatic design - advancements and applications* (Oxford University Press, 2001)
20. P.J. Clapis, J.D. Hinterstiener, *Enhancing object-oriented software development through axiomatic design*, Proc of ICAD (2000)
21. D.S. Cochran, J.T. Foley, B. Zhuming, *Use of the manufacturing system design decomposition for comparative analysis and effective design of production systems*, International Journal of Production Research **55**, 3, 870-890, (2017)
22. G. Arcidiacono, N. Costantino, K. Yang, *The AMSE Lean Six Sigma Governance Model*, International Journal of Lean Six Sigma **7**, 3, 233-266, (2016)
23. C. Cavallini,A. Giorgetti, P. Citti, F. Nicolaie, *Integral aided method for material selection based on quality function deployment and comprehensive VIKOR algorithm*, Materials and Design **47**, 27-34, (2013)
24. A. Giorgetti, C. Cavallini, A. Ciappi, G. Arcidiacono, P. Citti, *A holistic model for the proactive reduction of non-conformities within new industrial technologies*, International Journal of Mechanical Engineering and Robotics Research, **6**, 4, 313-317, (2017).
25. A. Giorgetti, C. Cavallini, G. Arcidiacono, P. Citti, *A mixed C-Vikor fuzzy approach for material selection during design phase: A case study in valve seats for high performance engine*, International Journal of Applied Engineering Research **12**, 12, 3117-3129, (2017).
26. A. Giorgetti, C. Cavallini, P. Citti, M, Delogu, *A Novel Approach for Axiomatic-Based Design for the Environment*, Axiomatic Design in Large Systems, 131-148 (2016)
27. A.M. Gonçalves Coelho, A.J. Mourão. Z.L. Pereira, *Improving the use of QFD with Axiomatic Design, Concurrent Engineering* **13**, 3, pp. 233-239, (2005)
28. A. Girgenti, B, Pacifici, A.Ciappi, A. Giorgetti, *An Axiomatic Design Approach for Customer Satisfaction through a Lean Start-up Framework*, Proc. CIRP **53**, 151-157, (2016)
29. G. Arcidiacono, A. Giorgetti, M. Pugliese, Axiomatic *Design to improve PRM airport assistance, Proceedings*, Proc CIRP **34**, 106-111 (2015)

30. G. Arcidiacono, P. Placidoli, *Reality and illusion in Virtual Studios: Axiomatic Design applied to television recording*, Proc CIRP **34**, 137-142 (2015)
31. K. Dansky, D. Thompson, T. Sanner, A framework for evaluating eHealth research. Evaluation and Program Planning **29**, 4, 397-404, (2006)
32. B.S EL-Haik, A. Shaout, *Software Design for Six Sigma: A Roadmap for Excellence*. (Wiley, 2010)

MATEC Web of Conferences 127, 01011 (2017) DOI: 10.1051/matecconf/201712701011
ICAD 2017

Construction of Patent Claims Using Axiomatic Design

Petru Dusa[1*], *Eugen* Purice[1], *Gheorghe* Nagit[1], *Oana* Dodun[1], *Marius* Ripanu[1] and *Laurentiu* Slatineanu[1]

[1]Technical University Gheorghe Asachi of Iasi, Bvd. D. Mangeron, Nr. 39A, Iasi, Romania

Abstract. Patent claims play an important role in every patent case and it is the core for evaluation of infringement, validity or originality. There are two main types of claims: the independent claims (stand on their own), and the dependent claims (depending on a single/several claim/claims). Axiomatic design is a design theory that is based on the axioms. The axiomatic design theory makes use of corollaries and theorems which guide/help designers mapping functional domain to physical domain. The relation between functional requirements and design parameters is assured by so called design matrix. In an ideal design the number of design parameters is equal to the number of functional requirements, and the functional requirements are always kept independent from each other. When there are more design parameters than functional requirements, the design is a redundant design. A coupled design can became decoupled by selecting different set of design parameters. The idea of construction of patent claims using Axiomatic Design is based on the assumption of independent claims as a part of an ideal design and dependent claims as a part of a decoupled design.

1 Introduction

Elaboration of the claims is a challenge when preparing the patenting documentation. In a patent, the claims define extension, the scope of the protection for which the patent is conferred. The claims are intended to define what is protected by the patent.

The Five IP Office (IP5) is a forum of five intellectual property offices. The members of IP5 are: European Patent Office (EPO), Japan Patent Office (JPO), Korean Intellectual Property Office (KIPO), State Intellectual Property Office of the People's Republic of China (SIPO) and United States Patent and Trademark Office (USPTO). "The IP5 Offices account for 90% of all patent applications filed worldwide and for 93% of all work carried out under the Patent Cooperation Treaty (PCT)."[1]

In all jurisdictions [2-15], the patent serves to exclude others from producing, using, importing, selling or offering for sale what the subject matter defines in the claims.

In order to exclude someone from the use of a patented invention, the claims must include a set of limitations that differentiate the invention from what has been done prior to the invention.

The claims are used to decide the area of protection offered by the patent, but the way of use may vary from one jurisdiction to another.

There are inherent difficulties in using language to define the boundaries of the right of use, and jurisprudence is criticized for the lack of a theoretical and practical coherence of building claims.

Claims can be a matter of concern at least from two perspectives: building claims and interpreting claims. Some theorists are working on structured framework for claims construction [16-18], others are more interested in ways of interpreting claims [19].

To reduce ambiguities in constructing and interpreting claims, consistent dictionaries of terms have been developed [20].

Patent Offices specialists use different tools to analyse claims, especially from the point of view of infringement of rights. Such an instrument is the claim chart.

A claim chart is a two-column table showing the main aspects of a patent claim in a column, and in the other column there are presented similarities with claims from other patents [21].

The purpose of this paper is to analyse and demonstrate the possibility of mapping concepts in the field of patents with the concepts of Axiomatic Design theory to develop an analytical tool useful in building / analysing patent claims.

2 The main concepts in the field of patents

2.1 Type of claims

Patents include multiple claims each of which represent a separate property right. Usually patents have independent claims and one or more dependent claims. Independent claims are written as standalone and dependent claims add some additional detail or limitation to that is claimed in the independent claim. There are possible for a dependent claim to depend from

* Corresponding author: pdusa@tcm.tuiasi.ro

another dependent claim which depends from an independent claim.

According with Rule 6 [4] claims shall contain:
(1) a statement indicating those technical features of the invention which are necessary for the definition of the claimed subject matter but which, in combination, are part of the prior art,
(2) a characterizing portion – preceded by the words "characterized in that," "characterized by," "wherein the improvement comprises," or any other words to the same effect – stating concisely the technical features which, in combination with the features stated under (1), it is desired to protect.

2.2 Disclosure of the invention

Patent application shall disclose the invention in a manner sufficiently clear and complete for it to be carried out by a person skilled in the art, without any inventive step [8, 15].

2.3 Unity of invention

Patent application shall relate to one invention only or to a group of invention so linked as to form a single general inventive concept [3, 4, 8, 15].

2.4 Novelty of invention

An invention shall be considered to be new if it does not form part of the state of the art. The state of the art shall be held to comprise everything made available to the public by means of a written or oral description, by use, or in any other way, before the date of filing of the Patent Office patent application [8, 15].

3 Axiomatic design theory (principles)

Axiomatic design [22, 23] is a design theory and methodology based on the Independence Axiom and the Information Axiom. The methodology contains corollaries and theorems which guide/help designers mapping functional and physical domains (see Figure 1).

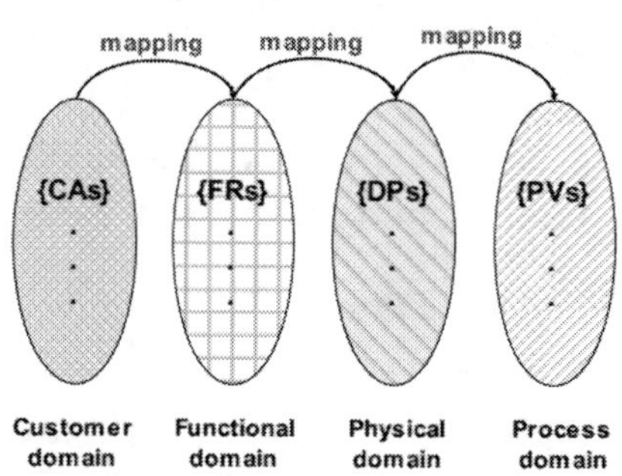

Fig. 1. Domains mapping [23, 24].

According with Axiomatic Design theory [22, 23] design involves a continuous interplay between what is wanted to achieve and how is wanted to achieve it. It must determine the design's objectives by defining it in terms of specific requirements called functional requirements (FRs). To satisfy functional requirements a physical embodiment characterized in terms of design parameters (DPs) must be created

The basic assumption of Axiomatic Design (AD) approach to design is that there exist two axioms that determine good design practice:

Axiom 1: The Independence Axiom (independence of FRs)

Axiom 2: The information Axiom (minimize the information content of the design)

Independence axiom may be mathematical expressed by the design equation (1):

$$\{FR\} = [A]\ \{DP\} \qquad (1)$$

Where:
$\{FR\}$ is the functional requirement vector;
$\{DP\}$ is the design parameters vector;
$[A]$ is the design matrix.

In particular case equation (1) can be written in the form shown in equation (2)

$$\begin{bmatrix} FR_1 \\ FR_2 \\ FR_3 \end{bmatrix} = \begin{bmatrix} A_{11} & A_{12} & A_{13} \\ A_{21} & A_{22} & A_{23} \\ A_{31} & A_{32} & A_{33} \end{bmatrix} * \begin{bmatrix} DP_1 \\ DP_2 \\ DP_3 \end{bmatrix} \qquad (2)$$

If all of the elements of the design matrix are nonzero axiom 1 cannot be respected and the design is called coupled design.

In the case when only the diagonal elements from design matrix are different from zero (see equation 3) the design satisfies the Axiom 1 and is defined as an uncoupled design.

$$\begin{bmatrix} FR_1 \\ FR_2 \\ FR_3 \end{bmatrix} = \begin{bmatrix} A_{11} & 0 & 0 \\ 0 & A_{22} & 0 \\ 0 & 0 & A_{33} \end{bmatrix} * \begin{bmatrix} DP_1 \\ DP_2 \\ DP_3 \end{bmatrix} \qquad (3)$$

A coupled design can be decupled. A case is presented by equation (4) where the design matrix is a triangular matrix. The independence of FRs can be assured by adjusting the design parameters in a particular order (DP1 first, DP2 second and third DP3).

$$\begin{bmatrix} FR_1 \\ FR_2 \\ FR_3 \end{bmatrix} = \begin{bmatrix} A_{11} & 0 & 0 \\ A_{21} & A_{22} & 0 \\ A_{31} & A_{32} & A_{33} \end{bmatrix} * \begin{bmatrix} DP_1 \\ DP_2 \\ DP_3 \end{bmatrix} \qquad (4)$$

This system is called decoupled design.

It was presented these fundamental elements of AD theory to serve the approach of the possible use of the theory for patent analysis and specifically for the construction of claims. The theory make use of many theorems and corollaries and in-depth knowledge can be obtained from de books written by the founder of the theory [22,23].

4 Mapping AD field concepts to the Patent field concepts

The analysis of several concepts used in the field of patents (see chapter 2) and the fundamentals of AD theory (see chapter 3) led to the hypothesis that AD theory could be used to build patent claims and to analyse the solutions claimed in existing patents.

On the one hand, the patent field calls for concepts such as independent claims, dependent claims, invention disclosure, novelty of the invention, and on the other hand AD uses concepts such as the axiom of independence, the axiom of minimizing information, redundant solution.

It was aimed to analyse how the concepts in the two fields could be mapped in order to use the methodology and scientific tools of the AD theory to solve some controversial problems in the patent field, especially in the construction and analysis of claims.

Table 1 shows how was mapped the concepts of Axiomatic Design field to concepts in the field of patents, especially the construction and analysis of claims. It can be seen that it was mapped the axiom of the independence of the factors with the independence / dependence of the claims. If the system had an uncoupled design, the claims should all be independent. In other words, if the number of functional requirements is equal to the number of design parameters and the design matrix is diagonal, the solution claims should be all independent.

Table 1. Mapping the Axiomatic Design field concepts with patent field concepts (claim construction and analyses)

Axiomatic Design Field		Patent Field
Axiom 1: The Independence Axiom (independence of FRs)	Ideal design (number of FR_s equal to number of DP_s (uncoupled design)	Independent claims
	decoupled design	Dependent claims
Axiom 2: The information Axiom (minimize the information content of the design)		Disclosure of the invention
When the original set of FRs is changed, a new solution must be found. The new solution may not be derived by simply modifying the previously obtained solution that was acceptable only for the original set of FRs [23].		Novelty of invention
Minimum number of FRs.		Unity of invention

If the design matrix is decoupled, then the solution also has dependent claims.

It was assumed that axiom 2 (minimizing the content of design information) from Axiomatic Design theory can be mapped with the rule contained in all patent jurisdictions relating to disclosure of the invention.

According with AD theory FRs are defined to be the minimum set of independent requirements that completely characterize the design objective for a specific need. Corresponding to a set of FRs there can be many design solutions. When the original set of FRs is changed, a new solution must be found. The new solution may not be derived by simply modifying the previously obtained solution that was acceptable only for the original set of FRs [22].

Some designers believe that if their products can perform more than specified, the products are better. The product is overdesigned. By consequence the product is more complex and less reliable than is necessary. A good designer must have the ability to choose a minimum number of FRs [22].

5 Case study

In the following, in accordance with the foregoing, an invention patent which has been granted by a patent office [24] will be subject to analysis. The patent relates to a flexible hose crimping machine. In the paper is presented the abstract of the patent, the relevant figures from the patent application (Figures 2-7) that allow the understanding of the solution and the claims.

The invention relates to an automatic crimping machine, used in particular for the assembly of flexible tubes, with or without insertion, on the nipples.

According to the invention's abstract , the automatic crimping machine is composed of a frame having a hydraulic block connected with an electronic equipment and a crimping head (A) assembled with a positioning block (B) and actuated by an oscillating hydraulic motor (2). The crimping head (A) consists of a stator (4) provided with some guides (5), in which they glide some gripping jaw (6), having assembled some crimping tools (7) around which are assembled the springs (8). The movement of the gripping jaw (6) resulting from the oscillating rotation, relative to the stator (4), on some bearings (9), of a rotor (10), which are joined with cams (11), in contact by some bearings (12) with some beams (13) which can slide on some ball guides (14) from the stator (4), turning the rotation movement of the rotor (10) into translation of the clamping dies (6). The positioning block (B) is constituted by a cylinder body (19) in which a piston (20) mounted in the middle of a tubular rod (21) having on its end a chuck collet (22) and a ruler on the other end with the limiter (23). Inside the tubular rod (21) there is moved a piston (24) mounted on a rod (25) carrying a conical element (26) which, together with the chuck collet (22), performs the gripping under the action of a fluid, which selected by a distributor (27), go through an orifice (j) into a cavity (k) in the cylinder (19), from where through an orifice (l) is introduced into a cavity (m) of the rod (21),producing first the pretension by first moving the piston (24) and then positioning by further displacement of the piston (20) by the discharge of the fluid from a cavity (n) by means of an orifice (o) associated with a hydraulic resistance (28), compared to the discharge of the fluid from a cavity (p) through an orifice (r) without hydraulic resistance.

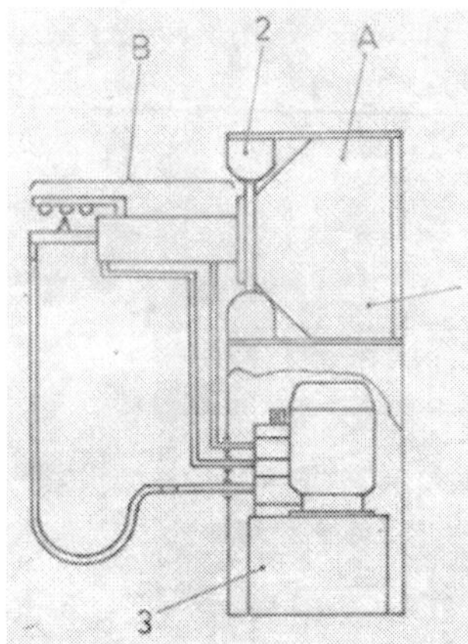

Fig. 2. Side view of the crimping machine [24].

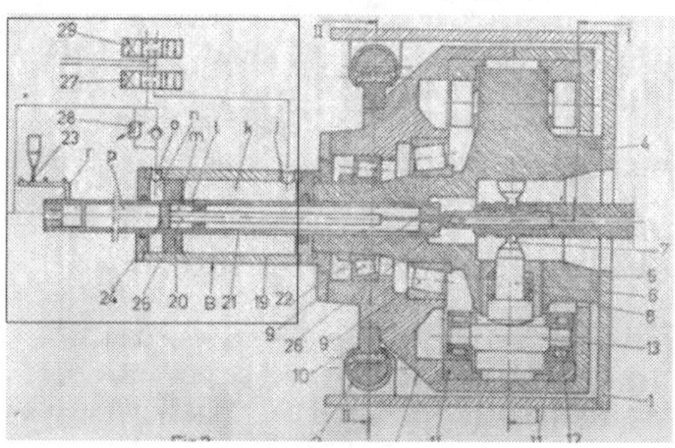

Fig. 3. Longitudinal section through crimp head and positioning cylinder [24].

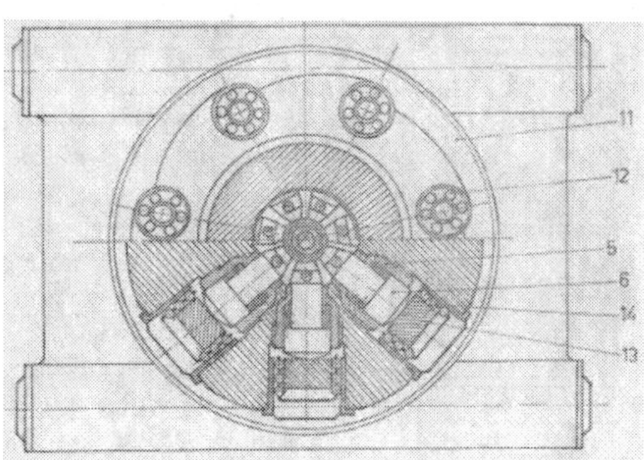

Fig. 4. Cross section through the crimping head [24].

The patent claims are presented below. In the text of each claim a reference was made to the figures containing elements specified in the text.

First claim (see Figures 2-5): An automatic crimping machine comprising a frame having in its interior a hydraulic block connected to an electronic equipment, *characterized in that*, in order to increase the productivity of the work, it includes a crimping head (A) assembled with a positioning block (B) and actuated by an oscillating hydraulic motor (2), the crimping head (A) consists of a stator (4) provided with some guides (5), in which they glide some gripping jaw (6), having assembled some crimping tools (7) around which are assembled the springs (8), the movement of the gripping jaw (6) resulting from the oscillating rotation, relative to the stator (4), on some bearings (9), of a rotor (10), which are joined with cams (11), in contact by some bearings (12) with some beams (13) which can slide on some ball guides (14) from the stator (4), turning the rotation movement of the rotor (10) into translation of the clamping dies (6).

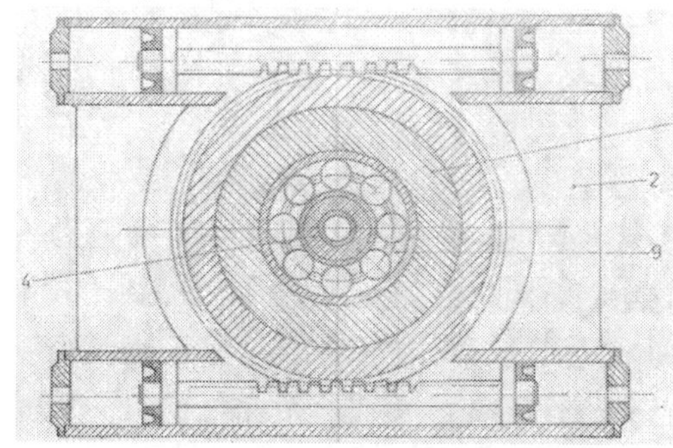

Fig. 5. Cross section through the crimping head presenting the oscillating hydraulic [24].

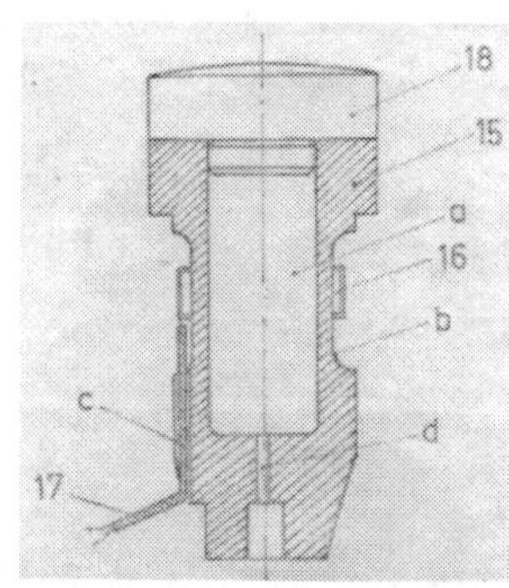

Fig. 6. Section through gripping jaw adapted for force measurement [24].

The second claim (see Figure 6): An automatic crimping machine as in claim 1, characterized in that, in a second constructive variant, one of the gripping jaw (6) is replaced with another gripping jaw (C) which is constructed of a body (15) , provided with a cylindrical bore (a) and a concentric throating (b), on which some strain marks (16) are attached, from which a conductor (17) which transmits the pressing information to the electronic control equipment, the body (15) being closed by a pressed cap (18) and provided with a hole (d) for eliminating the air.

The third claim (see Figure 7): an automatic crimping machine according to claim 1, **characterized in that** the crimping tool (7) has a conical area (e) in which two parallel planar surfaces (f) and a semitoidal surface (g) , the tool being provided with a cylindrical area (h) in which a flat surface (i) is machined.

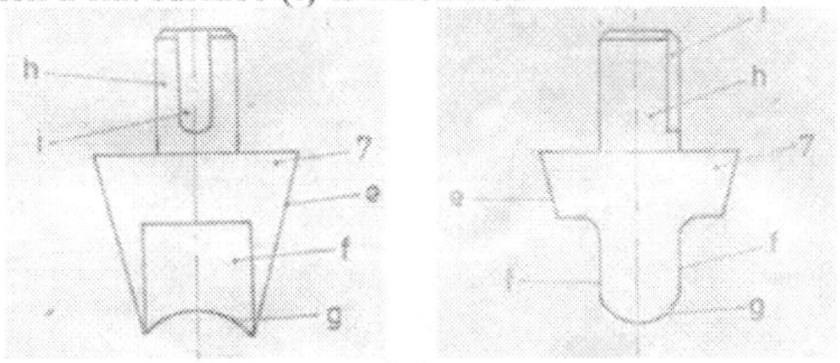

Fig. 7. Crimping tool [25].

The fourth claim (see Figure 3): an automatic crimping machine according to claim 1, characterized in that, the positioning block (B) is constituted by a cylinder body (19) in which a piston (20) mounted in the middle of a tubular rod (21) having on its end a chuck collet (22) and a ruler on the other end with the limiter (23). Inside the tubular rod (21) there is moved a piston (24) mounted on a rod (25) carrying a conical element (26) which, together with the chuck collet (22), performs the gripping under the action of a fluid, which selected by a distributor (27), go through an orifice (j) into a cavity (k) in the cylinder (19), from where through an orifice (l) is introduced into a cavity (m) of the rod (21),producing first the pretension by first moving the piston (24) and then positioning by further displacement of the piston (20) by the discharge of the fluid from a cavity (n) by means of an orifice (o) associated with a hydraulic resistance (28), compared to the discharge of the fluid from a cavity (p) through an orifice (r) without hydraulic resistance.

It is important to note, for the sake of understanding the context, that the product obtained by using the machine in the patent is a hose assembled by nipple crimping (as shown in Figure 8).

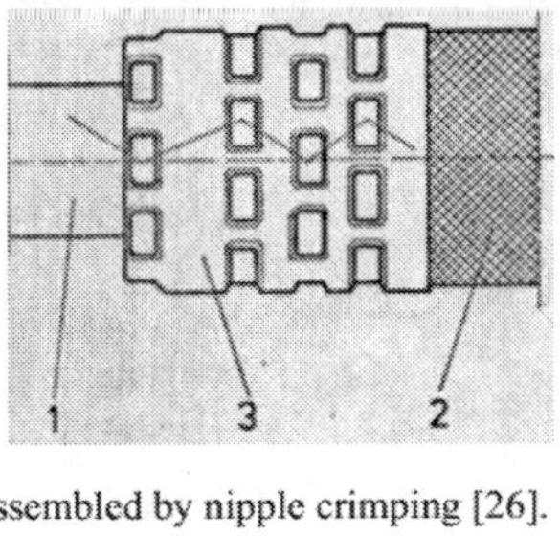

Fig. 8. Hose assembled by nipple crimping [26].

The analysis will be made from the perspective of applying the Axiomatic Design theory based on mapping concepts between the two fields. When analysing an existing system, we must determine the design matrix to see if the design violates the axiom 1 or not.

5.1 Identification of functional requirements

Analysis of the patent specification and claims as a whole reveals the following functional requirements:
FR_1 - Functional requirement crimping;
FR_2 - Functional requirement measurement;
FR_3 - Functional requirement positioning.

5.2 Identification of design parameters

Analysis of patent claims reveals the following design parameters:
DP_1 – Design parameter described in claim 1; assure functional requirements FR_1;
DP_2 - Design parameter described in claim 2; assure functional requirements FR_2 (measurement);
DP_3 – Design parameter described in claim 4, assure functional requirement FR_3 (positioning);
DP_4 – Design parameter described in claim 3;

According with Theorem 3, when there are more DPs then FRs the design is either a redundant design or a coupled design. When the design is redundant it may be possible to combine some of DPs that affect a given FR to form a ''dimensionless'' group [22].

The piece shown in Figure 8 and described in claim 3 is attached to each of the pieces 6 visible in Figures 3 and 4, thus providing the FR1 functional requirement. Thus, DP1 design parameter may combine with the DP4 design parameter to form a single parameter to meet the FR1 functional requirement. Thus, the number of functional requirements is equal to the number of design parameters (Ideal design according to Theorem 4).

5.3 Identification of design equation

According with Axiomatic Design when we analyse an existing design we must determine the design matrix to determine whether the design violate Axiom 1.Questions to be answered:
What kind of design does this matrix represent?
How the design should be modified to satisfy Axiom 1?

The equation of design, now, is what is shown in relation (5):

$$\begin{bmatrix} FR_1 \\ FR_2 \\ FR_3 \end{bmatrix} = \begin{bmatrix} A_{11} & 0 & 0 \\ A_{21} & A_{22} & 0 \\ 0 & 0 & A_{33} \end{bmatrix} * \begin{bmatrix} DP_1 \\ DP_2 \\ DP_3 \end{bmatrix} \quad (5)$$

Assuring the functional requirement FR2 (measurement) is made by adapting a piece 6 (see Figures 3 and 4) as shown in Figure 6 and described in claim 2. Under these conditions the independent functional requirements are assured but by a decoupled design matrix.

5.4 New structure for claim construction

In line with those presented in Table 1 on mapping concepts in axiomatic design with patent concepts, the following can be stated:
1. Claim 1 combines with claim 3 and forms a single independent claim;
2. Claim 2 remains an dependent claim;
3. Claim 4 becomes 3 and turns from an dependent claim to an independent claim.

Therefore, the initial claim structure consisting of an independent claim and three dependent claims should be replaced by a structure consisting of two independent claims and one dependent on all the legal consequences resulting therefrom.

6 Conclusions

The hypothesis made in chapter 4 according to which Axiomatic Design theory could be used to the construction of patent claims and to analyse the solutions claimed in existing patents appears to be confirmed.

The multitude of corollaries and theorems belonging to Axiomatic Design theory can be a powerful tool for scientifically solving a controversial issue in patenting: the claims.

Future work will be geared to different case studies to strengthen AD as a tool into patent field.

References

1. .Office of Policy and International Affairs: IP5, Available at: https://www.uspto.gov/patents-getting-started/international-protection/office-policy-and-international-affairs-ip5
2. United States Patent and Trademark Office, Office of Policy and International Affairs: IP5, Available at: https://www.uspto.gov/patents-getting-started/international-protection/office-policy-and-international-affairs-ip5
3. Patent Cooperation Treaty (PCT), Available at: http://www.wipo.int/export/sites/www/pct/en/texts/pdf/pct.pdf
4. Regulations under the Patent Cooperation Treaty, Available at: http://www.wipo.int/export/sites/www/pct/en/texts/pdf/pct_regs.pdf
5. Administrative Instructions Under The Patent Cooperation Treaty, Available at: http://www.wipo.int/export/sites/www/pct/en/texts/pdf/ai.pdf
6. Korean Patent Act, Available at: http://www.kipo.go.kr/upload/en/download/PATENT_ACT.pdf
7. Korean Enforcement decree of the patent act, Available at: http://www.kipo.go.kr/upload/en/download/ENFORCEMENT_DECREE_OF_THE_PATENT_ACT.pdf
8. The European Patent Convention and the Rules Available at: http://documents.epo.org/projects/babylon/eponet.nsf/0/F9FD0B02F9D1A6B4C1258003004DF610/$File/EPC_16th_edition_2016_en.pdf
9. Japan, Examination Guidelines for Patent and Utility Model, Available at: http://www.jpo.go.jp/tetuzuki_e/t_tokkyo_e/1312-002_e.htm
10. Japan, Examination Handbook for Patent and Utility Model, Available at: http://www.jpo.go.jp/tetuzuki_e/t_tokkyo_e/handbook_sinsa_e.htm
11. Japan, Handbook for PCT International Search and Preliminary Examination in the Japan Patent Office, Available at: http://www.jpo.go.jp/tetuzuki_e/t_tokkyo_e/pct_handbook_e.htm
12. Patent Law of the People's Republic of China Available at: http://english.sipo.gov.cn/laws/lawsregulations/201101/t20110119_566244.html
13. Rules for the Implementation of the Patent Law of the People's Republic of China, Available at: http://english.sipo.gov.cn/laws/lawsregulations/201403/t20140331_925757.html
14. Romanian Patent Law no. 64/1991 Available at: http://www.osim.ro/index3_files/laws/patents/Legea_nr64_1991_rep2014-en.pdf
15. Romanian implementing regulation to the Patent Law no. 64/1991, Available at: http://www.osim.ro/index3_files/laws/patents/implementingregmodif.pdf
16. Peter S. Menell, Matthew D. Powers, Steven C. Carlson, Patent Claim Construction: *A Modern Synthesis and Structured Framework*, Berkeley Technology Law Journal **25**, 2, 710-829 (2010)
17. Donald M. Cameron, *Claim Construction* available at: http://www.jurisdiction.com/patweb04.pdf
18. Ha Kung Wong and John P. Dillon, Fitzpatrick, Patent Claim Construction, Fitzpatrick, Cella, Harper & Scinto, with Intellectual Property & Technology, Available at: http://www.fitzpatrickcella.com/wp-content/uploads/Patent-Claim-Construction-Wong_Dillon.pdf
19. Christian E. Mammen, *Patent claim construction as a form of legal interpretation*, John Marshall Review of Intellectual Property Law 40 (2012), Available at: http://ssrn.com/abstract=2012571
20. Garrod Glossary of Judicial Claim Constructions in the Mechanical, Electro- Mechanical and Medical Devices Arts, Available at: http://www.pubpat.org/garrod-glossaries.htm
21. XLPAT's CLAIM MAPPER for Claim Chart Generation and Claim Mapping of Patents Available at: https://xlpatlabs.wordpress.com/tag/claim-chart-generator/
22. Suh N.P., The Principles of Design, New York : Oxford University Press, 1990.ISBN 0-19-504345-6
23. Suh N.P., *Complexity. Theory and Applications* (Oxford University Press, NY, 2005)
24. P. Dusa, St. Budacea, C. Tofan, C. Alexoaie, G. Bran, *Automatic crimping machine,* Patent RO no. 101886
25. P. Dusa, St. Budacea, F. Oproiu, I. Chiscop, *Crimping method,* Patent RO no. 106447

MATEC Web of Conferences **127**, 01012 (2017) DOI: 10.1051/matecconf/201712701012
ICAD 2017

Adapt!Evaluation - Evaluation for Design and Re-Design of Production Systems based on Axiomatic Design

Markus Stäbler[1,*], *Jakob* Weber[1], and *Kristin* Paetzold[2]

[1]Daimler AG, Process Development and Materials, 71059 Sindelfingen, Germany
[2]Universität der Bundeswehr, Institut für Technische Produktentwicklung, 85577 Neubiberg, Germany

Abstract. Since trends of our society are changing, the automotive industry has to handle new requirements within their production like vague quantities of production, fast integration of new technologies and an increasing variety of diversity. Therefore conventional life-cycles of production systems are broken up and re-design and changeability of complex systems have to be considered during their whole life time. Within this framework the paper proposes a novel approach to enable change during the life cycle of a production system and to enhance the usability of a re-design and change process by consistent interaction between the design and evaluation method. Thereby the focus is on the linkage of design and evaluation process to pursue a decrease of complexity and to point out the benefits which can be found by using Axiomatic Design Theory in this holistic context of the production system life-cycle. To validate the results of the paper and show up their benefits, a use case will describe and discuss the research.

1 Introduction

Due to shifting trends of our society, such as globalisation, individualisation and our fast moving nature, production systems are faced by huge challenges like vague quantities of production, fast integration of new technologies and an increasing variety of diversity. Since the conventional production system life-cycle is stretched to its limit, a new life-cycle with integrated phases of change or re-design is strived for (Fig. 1). To provide a good foundation the paper proposes a novel approach by combining the approach by Weber based on Axiomatic Design Theory (AD) with the evaluation approach for Changeability by Staebler. Therefor the holistic method *Adapt!* will be provided first to design a changeable production system and secondly, during its lifetime, to detect where and how much the production system has to be changed or to be re-designed to respond to new requirements. Thereby the focus of this paper is on the linkage of these two approaches and the benefit what may result.

In the first part of the paper the state of the art will be discussed and some basics will be named. Based on that, the new approach will be introduced. Moreover to explain the functionality of the method and validate the results, a use case of the automotive industry will be shown and discussed.

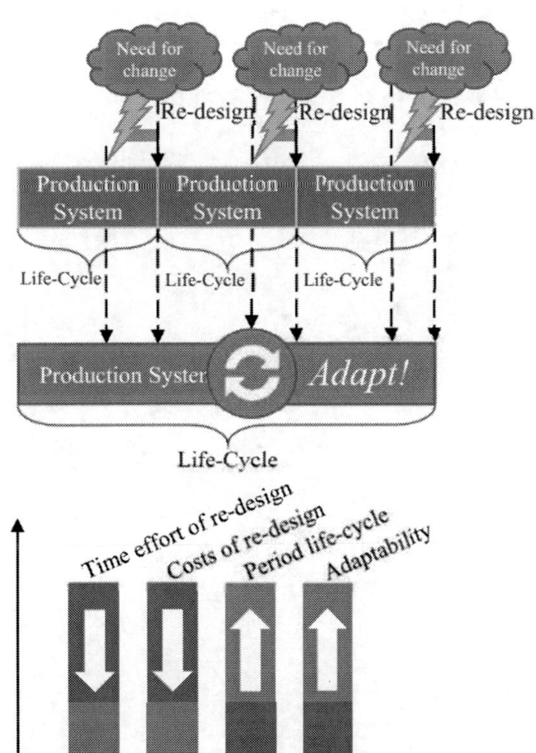

Fig. 1. Method Adapt! to ensure a long and adaptable life-cycle.

* Corresponding author: markus.m.staebler@daimler.com

Three key questions concerning the paper can be formulated:

- Is AD a suitable design method in a volatile environment?
- How can a holistic approach (Initial Design, Evaluation during life-cycle and Re-Design) in the context of changeability and based on AD look like?
- What are the benefits to build up an evaluation process upon a design process based on AD?

2 State of the art

To get a simultaneous knowledge base, in this chapter some basics, like changeability and life cycle in the context of production systems, will be explained. Further the principles of Axiomatic Design and related works dealing with re-design will be summarized.

2.1 Production system

According to Nyhuis a production system is a sociotechnical system which converts some kind of input through value-adding and associated processes into output values [1]. This paper focuses on production system as a mechanical system which can be consist of a single assembly station up to a complete assembly shop.

2.1.1 Life cycle of production systems

The term lifecycle can be defined as the "development of an organism in its various stages from initiation through maturity" [2]. This definition can be adopted to the topic product life-cycle or production life-cycle which are of interest for this approach (Fig. 2). A sizeable amount of literature exists on product lifecycle management.

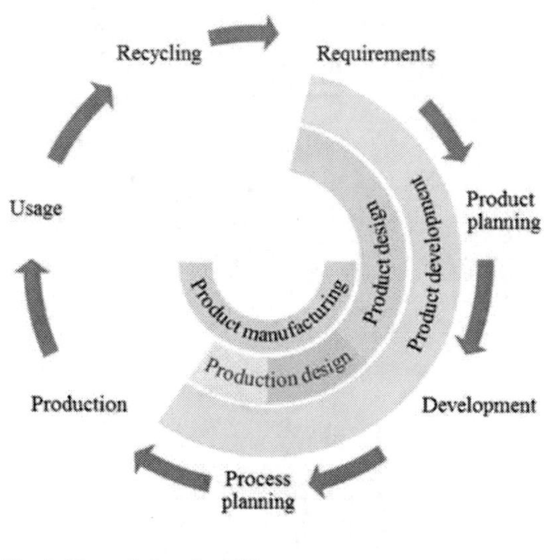

Fig. 2. life-cycle based on [3].

It is noticeable that the focus of previous research is not on change or re-design of production systems during one life-cycle [3,5,4].

2.1.2 Changeability

"Changeability has been proposed as an umbrella concept that encompasses many aspects of change on many levels within the manufacturing enterprise" [6, 7]. In this context, changeability of a production system is seen as a shift of an intrinsic flexibility corridor (Fig. 3) [1,8].

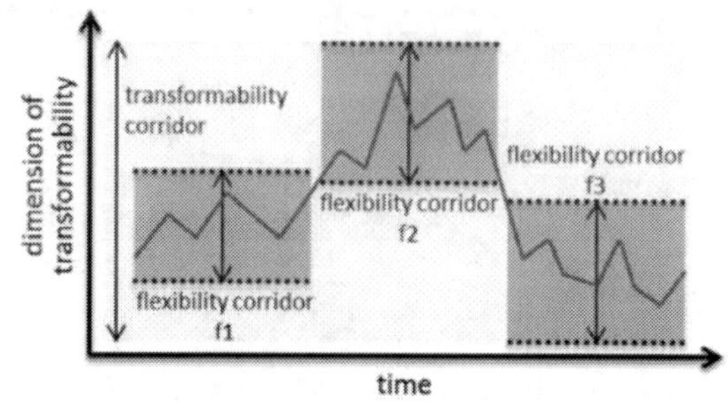

Fig. 3. Changeability as a shift of flexibility [9] based on [8].

To favour a production system to be changeable, several change enablers can be named [7]. Wiendahl et al. distinguish between three levels of a changeable physical system – First the Reconfigurable Manufacturing System, second the Reconfigurable Assembly System and third the Transformable Factory. Thereby the change enablers modularity and scalability serve as an intersection of the named physical system layers. [6]

2.2 Reducing complexity

Related to Pahl&Beitz, technical systems, like production systems, tend to be complex systems with a high grade of dependencies [10]. To cope well with complexity during the design process some kind of structure is needed [11]. One of the main characteristics of the Axiomatic Design Theory is structuring and reducing complexity [12, 13]. Several more design methods have their focus on structuring and reducing complexity [10, 11], but at this point it is not meaningful to mention them in-depth.

2.3 Axiomatic Design

Axiomatic Design, developed by Suh, is a design method based on two axioms: first the Independence Axiom which aims to avoid dependencies between design parameters and functional requirements and secondly the Information Axiom in order to choose the right solution with less complexity and as few information content as possible [12, 14]. The theory consists of four domains [12, 15]. First of all, Stakeholder Requirements (SR), has to be defined. Then Functional Requirements (FR) has its focus on "what" function should be realized and the Design Parameters (DP) contains the information "how" you want to achieve the corresponding FR. As a supporting design tool hierarchical tree and Design Structure Matrix are used. Within the hierarchical tree

 DOI: 10.1051/matecconf/201712701012

requirements and DP are fragmented for solution finding and, by using Design Structure Matrix (DSM), dependencies will be shown.

2.3.1 Axiomatic Design in context of changeability and re-design

Meanwhile there is a very extensive literature on Axiomatic Design in context of changeability and re-design. It would go beyond the constraints of this paper mentioning all of them. Hence, this paper makes a selection to give the reader a rough overview about the state of the art.

Farid developed a measurement possibility for re-configurability based on AD and widen the topic with some more change enablers like integrability or convertibility [16]. In the next step the author combined his results with a model based system engineering [15]. As a case study for re-design Gabriel-Santos et al. can be named. The focus of his approach is on Axiom 1 to increase productivity of the manufacturing system [17]. Holzner et al. combining FR with requirements for change to achieve a flexible and changeable manufacturing system, focusing on small and medium-sized enterprises.

2.3.2 Approach by Weber et al.

Weber et al. modified AD by focusing on Axiom 1. Thereby they want to achieve a simplification to increase the usability and acceptance in the industry (Fig. 4) [18].

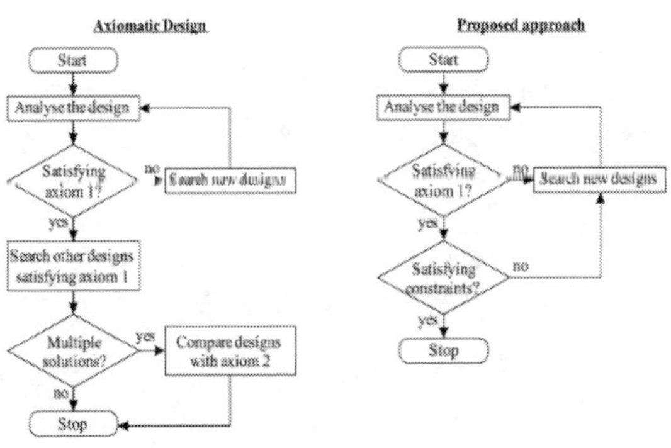

Fig. 4. Modification of AD to increase acceptance [18].

Aware of that, by neglecting Axiom 2, the optimum might not be determined, the results are good and robust enough by considering the dependencies of the system. As a second adaption colour-coding was established [19]. By colouring the Design Structure Matrix, it is possible to see the FRs' origins. So it can serve as a tool to enhance discussions with the company or the concerned division of the company.

3 Theoretical consideration

In order to achieve a changeable production system the procedure of Weber et al. is used which is based on AD Theory. Due to volatile circumstances the designed production system is exposed to a variety of change requirements during its lifecycle. Therefore, in this approach the method is extended with the evaluation approach by Staebler et al. to generate a holistic approach for Design and Re-Design (Fig. 5). The evaluation method answers the questions: "What subsystem should be changed first" and "What is the right degree of changeability" within the production system. However the focus of this paper is not about how the method works in general but if it has an added value by combining these two approaches and if AD is appropriate for this holistic approach.

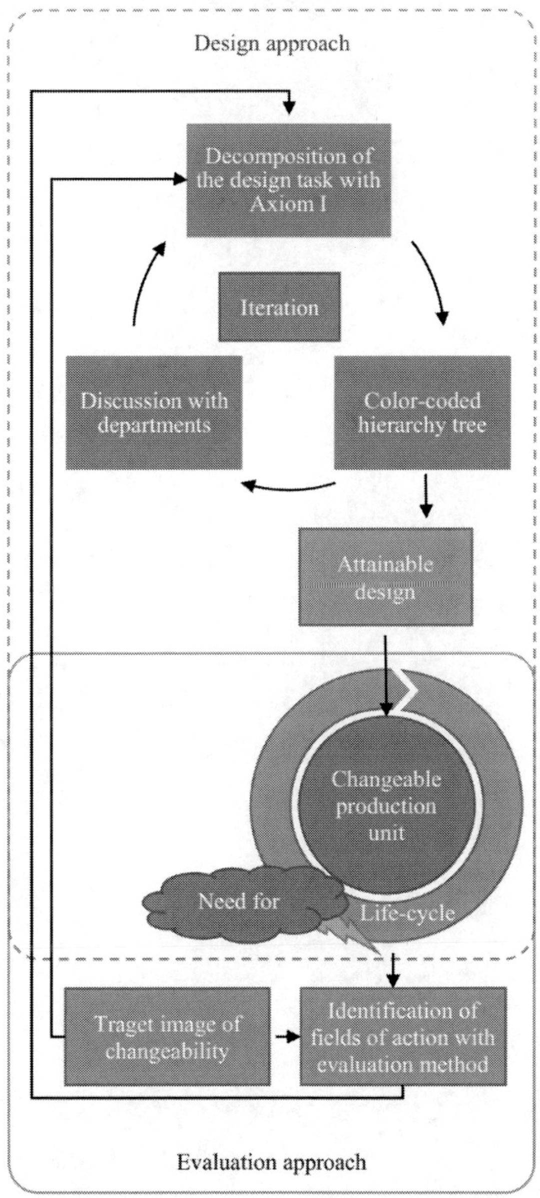

Fig. 5. Linkage between design and evaluation approaches.

So first the linkage between these two approaches will be discussed in the following subchapters.

 DOI: 10.1051/matecconf/201712701012

3.1 Evaluation process

The method has three cornerstones on which the evaluation is funded: the **effort** (when you want to implement change in a system), the **effectivity** (how positive is the effect of the entire system in context of changeability (when you change a part of it) and the **dependencies** within a system. As a first step subsystems have to be defined. Subsystems can be generated because of company structure, organisational reasons or by design parameters. To reduce complexity of the change process, subsystems should have as few dependencies as possible. Another reason can be named because neutrality favours changeability of a system. [1, 20]

3.1.2 Dependencies as a main evaluation parameter

One fundamental principle of the evaluation method is based on the Pareto Principle. That means that it might be possible to achieve 80% of the results with 20% effort. So under the assumption that independent subsystems are easier to change, the idea is to consider first subsystems which are as independent as possible. In reality a 100% independence of entire systems is of course not possible. That is why an evaluation of dependencies within a system has to be made.

3.1.3 Required input variables

To sum up, the evaluation method needs, in the context of dependencies, the information which subsystems are suitable for the evaluation and the following change process. Thereby the subsystems should have as few dependencies as possible and the degree of dependence should be determined.

3.2 Results of the design process

By using the AD theory in this case the primary goal is to achieve a changeable production system. During the design process a hierarchy tree and a Design Structure Matrix will be generated which enables to accomplish the primary goal. Sometimes it is seen as a means to an end, but in our case it implies a lot of information which can be used as required input variables of the following evaluation process.

3.2.1 Derived information from hierarchy tree

To avoid unnecessary work and complexity of the evaluation process, it is important to choose the right system layer. In practice it has been shown that the hierarchy tree is a good tool to get a fast overview over the complete production system and its degree of complexity. To get a first impression of the entire system it might be useful to enclose only the first layers of the hierarchy tree to generate subsystems. Then the results are getting more on an abstract level. Secondly, some branches of the tree can possibly be neglected. This leads to a reduction of evaluation time. Through its clear structure, the biggest benefit of the Hierarchy tree is the derivation of subsystems (Fig.6). To get a fast overview about defined subsystems each will be marked with a different colour. Subsystems can consist of one or more DPs on the same or different layers. By complex systems an iteration process with the DSM may be useful. By handling complex systems planning teams need a basis for their discussion and validation of decisions. So with this tool decisions get more transparent.

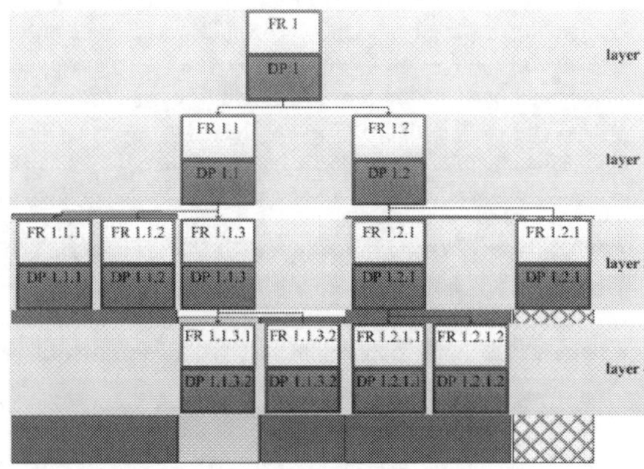

Fig. 6. Deriving subsystems based on hierarchy tree.

3.2.2 Derived information from DSM

As mentioned before, during the evaluation process the Design Structure Matrix is a tool to generate a changeable production system. In addition, it helps to quantify dependencies between subsystems. By deriving detected subsystems into the Matrix, dependencies can be seen very obviously (Fig. 7). Thereby FR i to DP i will be seen as independent and marked with green, dependencies within the same layer will be highlighted with yellow and dependencies to other layers with red. Intrinsic dependencies of a subsystem can be neglected and only relations between subsystems are of interest to an upcoming evaluation process.

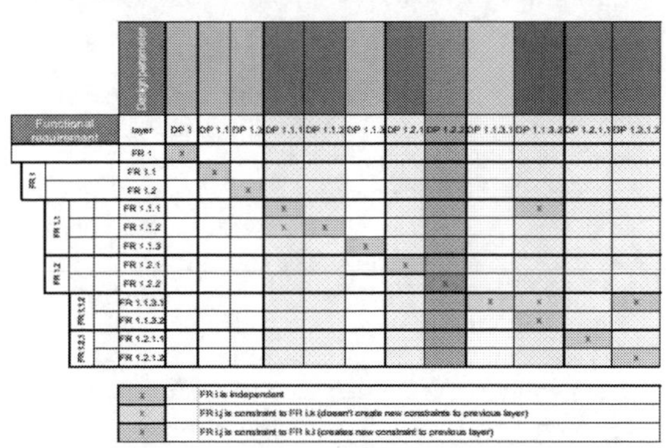

Fig. 7. Quantification of dependencies.

Because of searching for subsystems with as few dependencies as possible, it will not be distinguished between positive and negative dependencies. Indeed it will be differentiated between dependencies within the same layer or with other layers. According to the latest research, dependencies within a layer will be rated as one and dependencies to other layers as two. But this scale of assessment has to be confirmed by further use cases and research.

4 Use case

To improve changeability of the entire assembly production system in the automotive industry, a new concept of an entire assembly production system should be invented. Therefore the status quo of a conveyor system, three production units and the logistic system was recorded by means of Axiomatic Design. Optimally the design process was already realized by using Axiomatic Design. In this case the production system is a result of several decades of iteration. But to validate the research it is also sufficient to use AD afterwards. Derived from AD, the demand for action in the context of changeability was determined. Figure 8 shows the results of the status quo visualized by a hierarchical tree.

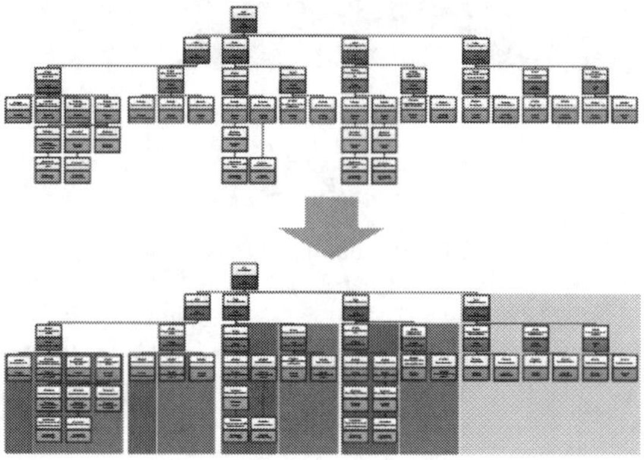

Fig. 8. Use case – building subsystems.

Based on this, three subsystems were built and visualized by colour. The yellow marked subsystem shows the conveyor system, blue all assembly operations and green all objects regarding logistic. Following subsystems were transferred to the dependency matrix (Fig. 9). Thereby all layers below the marked subsystems were considered too. After determining the dependencies, it can be stated that the conveyor system has less dependencies (1) followed by the subsystem assembly operations (11). The subsystem logistic has most dependencies (36). So by neglecting the other two cornerstones of the evaluation method, it can be deduced that we should first start to have the focus on the subsystem conveyor system because of its encapsulated structure.

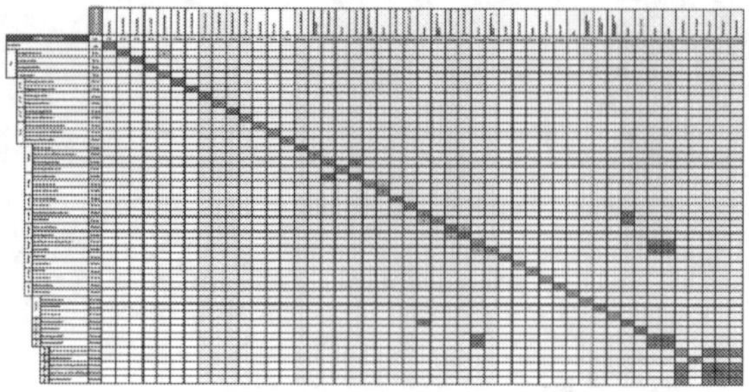

Fig. 9. Use case – quantification of dependencies.

5 Discussion

Regarding the introduced approach, results of the use case will be discussed and further key questions of the paper will be answered. The use case showed an improvement of the usability of the entire method compared to former development. Usability was measured by the effort of time during evaluation. Reduction of costs by implementing a continuous process of change and re-design in the life-cycle of a production unit can only be estimated and referred to existing literature about the benefit of intrinsic changeability of a system. Hence by increasing the user-friendliness the acceptance of using a method during the lifecycle becomes visible. Thus it can be stated that AD is a suitable design method in a volatile environment. As already mentioned there are numerous benefits to build up an evaluation process upon a design process with Axiomatic Design. Based on the independence, axiom suitable subsystems could be generated. It appears from the use cases that the complexity by determining dependencies is reduced immensely which leads to fast results.

6 Conclusion and outlook

This paper presented a novel approach by combining a modified axiomatic Design approach with a evaluation method for determining fields of action to increase the changeability of a production system and give answers to a continuously re-design process. It was shown that the method *Adapt!* improves the applicability of evaluation method based on axiomatic design by a lean linkage. After explaining the novel method the linkage of AD and the evaluation process will be demonstrated by an use case. In following research the method *Adapt!* has to be validated by more use cases. Furthermore it should be applied during a whole lifecycle of a product to manifest the benefits of it.

References

1. P. Nyhuis, Prod. Zent., *Changeable Production Systems: Shaping Today the Industry of Tomorrow (in German)*, 166, (2008)
2. H. Herrmann, H. Bucksch, Dict. Geotech. Engineering, 56 (2014)
3. M. Eigner, R. Stelzer, Springer, *Product Lifecycle Management: A Guideline for Product Development and Life Cycle Management (in German)*, **2**, 434 (2013)
4. A. Saaksvuori, A. Immonen, Springer, *Product Lifecycle Management*, **3**, 257 (2008)
5. J. Stark, Springer, *Product Lifecycle Management: 21st Century Paradigm for Product Realisation*, 573 (2011)
6. H.-P. Wiendahl, H.A. ElMaraghy, P. Nyhuis, M.F. Zäh, H.-H. Wiendahl, N. Duffie, M. Brieke, CIRP Manuf. Techn., Changeable Manufacturing - Classification, Design and Operation, **56** 783–809 (2007)
7. H.A. ElMaraghy, Springer, *Changeable and Reconfigurable Manufacturing Systems*, 414 (2009)
8. M.F. Zäh, N. Möller, W. Vogl., Proceed. Of CARV, *Symbiosis of Changeable and Virtual Production – TheEmperor's New Clothes or Key Factor for Future Success?* (2005)
9. M. Stäbler, J. Weber, K. Paetzold, Proceed. Of CIRP CATS, *Implementing Changeability in a System with Prioritization Indicators*, **44**, 50–54 (2016)
10. G. Pahl, W. Beitz, J. Feldhusen, K.-H. Grote, Springer, *Engineering Design: A Systematic Approach (in German)*, **6**, 780 (2005)
11. U. Lindemann, M. Maurer, T. Braun, Springer, Structural *Complexity Management: An Approach for the Field of Product Design*, 247 (2009)
12. N.P. Suh, Oxford Univ. Press, *Axiomatic design: Advances and applications*, (2001)
13. R. Fiege, Gabler, *Axiomatic Design: A Method for Service-Oriented Modeling (in German)*, **1**, 228 (2009)
14. N.P. Suh, Oxford Univ. Press, *The principles of design*, (1990)
15. A.M. Farid, N.P. Suh, Springer, *Axiomatic design in large systems: Complex products, buildings and manufacturing systems*, 322 (2016)
16. A.M. Farid, Proceed. of ICAD, *Axiomatic design and design structure matrix measures for reconfigurability & its key characteristics in automated manufacturing systems*, (2014)
17. A. Gabriel-Santos, A.M. Gonçalves-Coelho, P. Santos, J. Fradinho, A. Mourão, Proceed. of CIRP ICAD, *Redesigning a Manufacturing System Based on Functional Independence: The Case of a Tree Nursery*, **34**, 206–211 (2015)
18. J. Weber, J. Kößler, K. Paetzold, Proceed. of ICED, *An approach for industrial application of axiomatic design. International conference on engineering design* (2015)
19. J. Weber, D. Förster, J. Kößler, K. Paetzold, Proceed. of ICAD, *Design of Changeable Production Units within the Automotive Sector with Axiomatic Design*, **34**, 93–97 (2015)
20. C.L. Heger, Prod. Zent., *Evaluation of Changeability of Factory-Objects (in German)*, 224 (2007)

Guidelines for Application of the Constituent Roadmap of Product Design Based on Axiomatic Design

Erik Puik[1,*], *Joost* van Duijn[1], and *Darek* Ceglarek[2]

[1]HU University of Applied Sciences Utrecht, Padualaan 99, 3584 CH Utrecht, the Netherlands
[2]International Digital Laboratory, WMG, University of Warwick, Coventry, CV4 7AL, UK

Abstract. The 'Constituent Roadmap of Product Design' (CRPD) is a framework that is applied to track the designers' knowledge of a product design as it progresses during development. The Constituent Roadmap of Product Design was introduced in late 2015 and relies heavily on Axiomatic Design; it uses Axioms 1 and 2 to model understanding of the product- and manufacturing-design by the designer. A central theme when applying the Constituent Roadmap is a procedure of regularly updating the 'Check Matrix'. The Check Matrix is a table that continuously monitors the designer's knowledge position. Correct application of the check matrix is bound to a number of behavioural characteristics that need to be taken into consideration, e.g.: (i) in a decomposed system, it is not possible that a knowledge score at a certain hierarchical level exceeds that of one of its sublevels. A lack of knowledge is, similar to information in design, the sum of its subordinate knowledge deficits. (ii) on the other hand, the score in the check matrix indeed may exceed that of its lower levels during the process of zigzagging, as zigzagging is a process that advances top-down through the hierarchy of the product design.
This paper explains how to apply the check matrix under various circumstances without violating the hierarchical dependencies of good practice in design.

1 Introduction

The 'Constituent Roadmap of Product Design' (CRPD) is a systems-engineering tool (or an engineering design tool) to support the process of product development. The CRPD is applied to track a designer's knowledge, and understanding of a product design, as it evolves during the product design process. The CRPD was introduced in late 2015 and it is based on the complexity theory of AD [1]. It tries to combine ease of use while maintaining scientific substantiation. The CRPD is applicable by designers in the full range from 'novice' to 'experienced'. Because of this, the method is also suitable for educational purposes.
'Knowledge of the Designer' is the central theme of the CRPD. According to good AD-practice, satisfaction of Axioms 1 and 2 indicate that a designer has good understanding of his design. This is only possible if the designer is in possession of the necessary knowledge of that design, as the quality of a design will not exceed the knowledge of the designer [2]. The CRPD applies a number of four hierarchical levels to help the designer in the process of decomposition of the product design and its related production processes . It also distinguishes a number of three sequential development phases of the design. During the design process, the development status of the four hierarchical levels and three phases of the CRPD are tracked using a table that is called the 'Check Matrix'. The check matrix is a leading tool in the application process of the CRPD. This paper discusses a number of behavioural guidelines to enable simple and correct application of the check matrix.
The paper is organised as follows. Section 2 explains the background of the CRPD and how it is applied. Section 3 analyses the application of the CRPD and determines the issues that need to be well understood for proper application of the CRPD. Section 4 explains the methodology of investigation, and Section 5 shows a case in which this is applied. Finally, Section 6 discusses the findings and draws conclusions.

2 Background on the constituent road-map of product design

The CRPD builds further on the design matrix of AD. The design matrix forces the designer to organise the conceptual capability of the design. This is being done by organisation of the following relationships: (i) Customer Attributes and Functional Requirements (CAs & FRs), (ii) Functional Requirements and Design Parameters (FRs & DPs), and (iii) Design Parameters and Process Variables (DPs & PVs). These relations (i, ii, & iii) must be properly substantiated during the product development process. AD provides solutions for substantiation, the CRPD provides overview of the development process.

* Corresponding author: erik.puik@hu.nl

2.1 Constituent roadmap of product design

The CRPD is a merged matrix of 7x4 cells that embeds product hierarchy on the vertical axis. The hierarchy that is applied in the CRPD is borrowed from the widely applied V-Model, and in particular its German variant; the 'V-Modell XT' [3]. The V-Modell XT defines a hierarchical division in four levels: (i) Project, (ii) Product, (iii) Systems, and (iv) Parts. This hierarchy has proven its use in industrial environments.

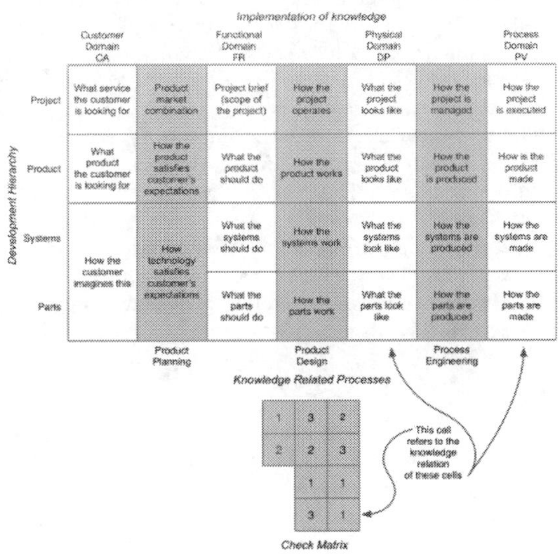

Fig. 1. The CRPD and its check matrix

The domains of AD are represented by the odd columns in Figure 1. The domains of AD contain factual descriptions of respectively: (indicates column numbers) (1) what the customer expects, (3) what the system should do, (5) how this is realised, and (7) how this can be achieved. The designer will apply his knowledge to the domains and as this happens 'the designers' knowledge' turns into 'applied knowledge'. Applied knowledge is directly related to the product design. Therefore, applied knowledge is static. It consists of lifeless descriptions of which knowledge was once the foundation. As a result, the applied knowledge in the columns will not change unless the designer executes his design activities again and updates the applied knowledge.

The even columns store 'descriptive knowledge' that was necessary for the designer to generate the static descriptions in the odd columns. As its name indicates, descriptive knowledge describes the knowledge that underlies: (again column numbers) (2) the process of product planning, (4) the product design, and (6) the process engineering processes.

2.2 The check matrix

Descriptive knowledge, as exerted by the designer, is the source of current and future understanding of the design. It is stored in the form of high-level knowledge structures like design matrices that define solid design relations. This is where the check matrix proves its value; it keeps track of descriptive knowledge that is directly related to understanding of the design. If enough descriptive knowledge is present with the designer, the design may be considered to be well-understood; it may be considered to be a 'good design' [4]. Using the check matrix, only a number of ten relations that are represented by numerical values, are sufficient to assess the total product design, including customer interactions and processes.

Two restrictions apply; the CRPD applies two general assumptions that (i) designers are idealistic people with no double agenda that simply pursue a dependable and reliable product design, and (ii) they are granted enough time and means to apply their descriptive knowledge to the design. As a result, adequate knowledge of the designer will lead to a good design and all FRs will be satisfied [1]. Under these presumptions, the only binding condition to guarantee a good design is to make sure that the knowledge of the designer, represented in the even rows, is adequate to guarantee a correct relation between the cells left and right of the even rows (lower right, Figure 1). This relation is weighted and scored with a value in the check matrix.

2.3 Three sequential development phases

The CRPD distinguishes a number of three phases in the design process [1]. The phases are respectively: (i) 'Exploration', (ii) 'Conceptual', and (iii) 'Robustness':

- The Exploration phase leads to an initial product/process definition and exposition. It creates coherence in the process of product design by definition and organisation of temporary CAs, FRs, DPs, and PVs of new and adolescent elements in the design;
- The Conceptual phase will lead to product/process specification and decomposition. Conceptualisation verifies the concept by completion and decoupling of the product and process design matrices. The result is that product and processes become completely decomposed and specified (i.e. proof of concept). A completed conceptual phase is equivalent to satisfaction of the Independence Axiom;
- Finally, the Robustness phase is applied to enforce a statistically sound relation between PVs, DPs, and FRs. A completed robustness phase is equivalent to a satisfied Information Axiom.

The statuses of the design relations in the CRPD are represented in the check matrix with a number from 0–3, directly referencing to the best-completed development phase of the particular relation, this is shown in Figure 2:

0. Status of Project, Product, System, or Part unknown;
1. Exploration phase was successfully completed;
2. Conceptual phase was successfully completed;
3. The robustness phase was successfully completed.

Using these four statuses, the check matrix can be applied as a measure to track progression of the product development process.

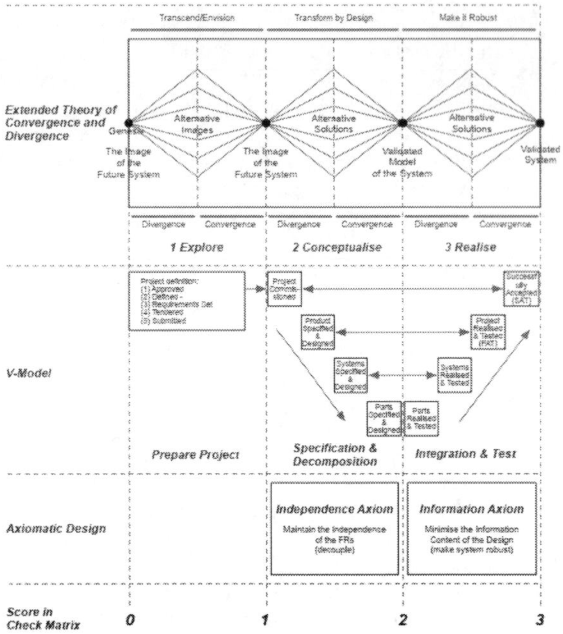

Fig. 2. The three phases of the design process that form the basis of the CRPD

3 Approach

3.1 Analysis

The representation with the check matrix was introduced late 2015 by Puik et al. [1] and its application is bound to a number of guidelines. The guidelines are the main topic of investigation in this paper.

Problem statement

Early attempts to apply the CRPD sometimes showed quite erratic check matrices with numbers 0–3 scattered all over the matrix, especially in the beginning of the project. The question is what would be good practice for application of the check matrix during the process of design:

What are the rules of conduct when rating the design relations in the check matrix of the CRPD (horizontally and vertically).

Current situation

Firstly, the CRPD is inspired by the V-Model XT. The V-Model has a preferred path in phases 2 and 3 that are also applicable and even preferred for the CRPD.

Secondly, AD uses the procedure of zigzagging to address the design relations top-down during the conceptual phase.

Thirdly, Puik et al. [5] have introduced the concept of 'reverse zigzagging' to be applied during the robustness phase. Both methods, zigzagging and reverse zigzagging are adopted as a temporary guideline for determination of the values in the check matrix.

Key limitations

At this point, there are no proven procedures for good practice to apply for the check matrix when applying the CRPD. A substantiated guideline could improve application of the CRPD from the perspective of ease as well qualitative.

3.2 Methodology

Project flow of the V-Model

The project flow of the V-Modell XT was accurately described by Höhn et al. [3]. Figure 2 shows this flow in relations to the three phases of the CRPD. The project definition corresponds with the Explorative phase. It can also be seen that the 'left leg of the V-Model' is applied for the conceptual phase and 'the right leg' is applied for the robustness phase. The transition from the conceptual to the robustness phase takes place when the product is fully decomposed and specified, which is the case at the tip of the 'V'.

The project flow in the V-Model during conceptual phase is top down, which means that higher hierarchical levels are specified first followed by the lower levels. During the robustness phase, this is reversed and the flow is bottom up.

Zigzagging

Zigzagging is standard procedure of AD that was described by Suh [4]. Zigzagging in AD adds an important aspect to the project flow in comparison to the V-Model; it connects the different domains. Analogue to the V-model, the flow is top-down but zigzagging also structurally verifies the design relations (CA)-FR-DP-PV increasing the score from 1 → 2. Zigzagging cannot be executed in the V-Model because that model does not differentiate between the customer, functional, physical, or process domains.

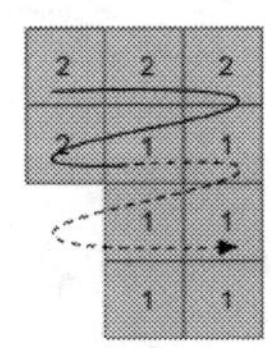

Fig. 3. Project flow through the check matrix when zigzagging

Reverse zigzagging

Reverse zigzagging is applied during the robustness phase. The basic principle is comparable to the standard zigzagging process but the hierarchical direction is reversed from top-down to bottom-up and from left-right to right-left. After succesfulhe values of the check matrix are increased from 2 → 3.

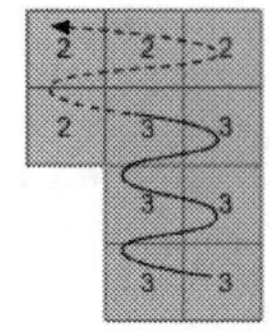

Fig. 4. Project flow through the check matrix when reverse zigzagging is applied

The project flow of the V-Model as well as basic and reversed zigzagging seem fully compatible; though the hierarchical direction during exploration is not really set, this indeed is the case during the conceptual phase (top-down) and the robustness phase (bottom-up). Zigzagging adds the project flow through the domains, where the V-Model has no capability because the domains are not applied for the V-Model.

How are the key limitations addressed?
To substantiate the procedures for application of the check matrix, the constituent roadmap will be applied to a product development case. The flow of the V-Model, zigzagging and reverse zigzagging will be applied. The project, and how the check matrix develops, will be accurately monitored during this process.

4 Case study: Development of a biglide-manipulator for 3D printers

The applied case concerns a novel manipulator for a newly developed 3D 'Fused Deposition Modelling' (FDM) printer (Figure 5). This manipulator is based on a 'Biglide' servo system [6].

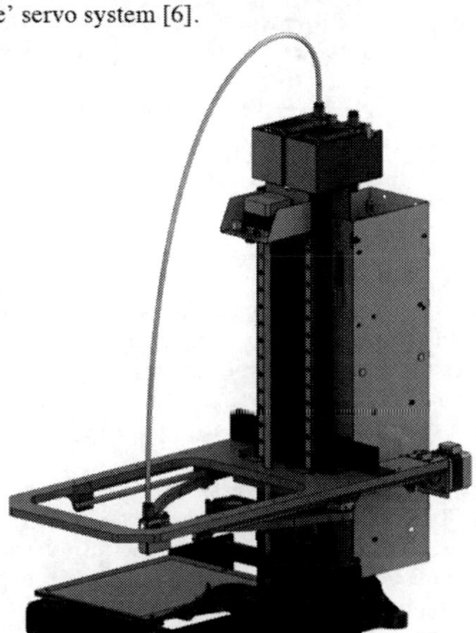

Fig. 5. Biglide-manipulator applied for 3D printing

Figure 6a shows a top-view of the manipulator, Figure 6b a schematic representation of the kinematics. The biglide-system uses a double linear guideway that is converted to an X-Y movement by a double arm. The arm uses a flexible joint near the tool centre point (TCP) to compensate for the distance variations between the slides A and B. In Z-direction, a similar linear guideway is applied for an independent perpendicular manipulation of the bi-glide system.
The accuracy of the manipulator is subject of investigation.

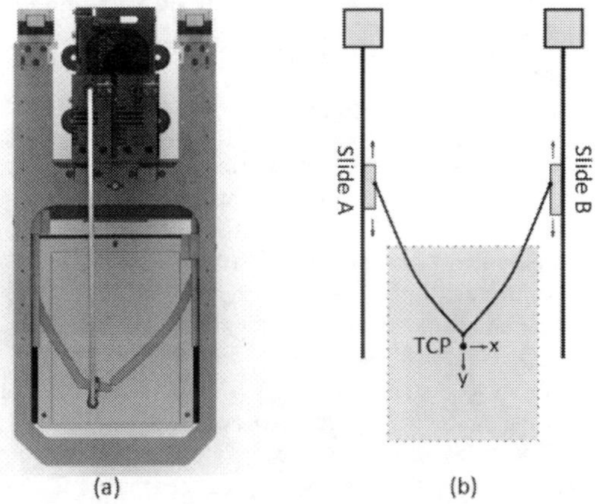

Fig. 6. (a) Top view of biglide-system, (b) kinematic model

4.1 Exploration phase

The exploration phase aims to define the 'Image of the Future System' (figure 2). It addresses a lot of uncertainties in the project, not only from a technological perspective but also from the marketing perspective. Analyses were executed for:
(i) Customer interactions (CA-FR);
(ii) Product development (FR-DP);
(iii) Process development (DP-PV).

(i) In this case, the manipulator was developed to replace an existing servo system. However, the change of manipulator was not really perceptible from the customer point of view. This left the CA-FR relation unaffected, leaving the product-market combination unaffected. The product complies when the new manipulator is able to satisfy the FRs.

(ii & iii) System engineering tools were applied to gain knowledge of the desired manipulator and its interfaces with the rest of the system design; it was functionally decomposed using QFD and IDEF-0 for respectively the product- and the process-designs.
The manipulator was realised as pre-prototype (test setup for functionality testing). Initial tests were performed and the system had the capability of producing reasonable quality 3D prints. Materials for realisation were determined from the perspective of functionality, manufacturing and cost price. Preliminary relations were determined for the mapping of FRs-DPs and DPs-PVs.
A number of alternative options were kept open and were tested in parallel (different options for spindles and motors and many options for the flexible hinge).

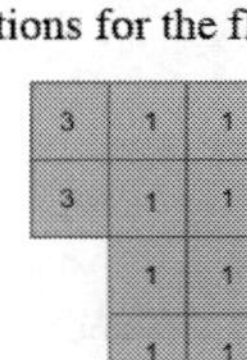

Fig. 7. Check matrix after completion of the explorative phase

Figure 7 shows the check matrix after the explorative stage. At this point, decoupling and robustness of the design relations cannot yet be guaranteed.

4.2 Conceptual phase

The design should be decoupled to acquire conceptual rigour of the design. This means that the Independence Axiom is met, guaranteeing that the FRs indeed can be satisfied with the chosen DPs (same for DPs & PVs). To enable this, the system is accurately modelled by CAD; kinematics and tolerances are simulated. The process of zigzagging got stuck due to coupling at systems level. This was caused by: (i) double-interfaces of the mechanical lay-out, and (ii) conflicts of the electrical-connections crossing the modular framework, both problems leading to coupling of the design. To address the problems, the modular capability of the manipulator was improved by extending the modular decomposition of the 3D-printer by use of an 'Entity Relationship' model, unravelling complicated interrelations in the modular structure. Mechanical and electrical components were reordered for an independent modular layout. This process was implemented in a prototype. To close the conceptual phase, zigzagging was resumed to verify the independence of the product- and process-design matrices. This time the process was successful down to the parts level of the design. The check matrix was upgraded to '2's comparably to the '1's in Figure 6.

4.3 Robustness phase

The third phase, revealed a weakness in the mode of implementation of the biglide-manipulator. Though X- and Y-positioning were fast and accurate, the system had an adverse effect on the Z-positioning. When applying the process of reversed zigzagging, it appeared that the Z-accuracy could not satisfy the aimed values of the FRs. Analysis learned that the inaccuracy of some of the parts in the slides (Figure 5) were amplified by the length of the biglide-arm. A lack of knowledge on the implementation of the biglide-mechanism, led to reduced accuracy of the realised prototype. The initial construction was gradually improved by a tuning process with a number of iterations. After this, the reverse zigzagging process was restarted and completed all the way up. The acquired knowledge on the initial prototype has enabled modification of the geometry of the biglide-mechanism. It realised a major improvement on robustness of the system. The re-engineered biglide-servo-system eliminated all the conflicts between FRs, DPs, and PVs.

5 Discussion

In this case study, the check matrix was regularly updated during the ongoing engineering process of the manipulator. It allows the engineers to keep track of the development process as it progresses. By doing so, the matrix supports the go/no-go assessments that determine if the next phase can be started.

During this exercise, the expectations for application of the check matrix were largely confirmed. Note that from elemental perspective, values at higher hierarchical levels in de check matrix cannot have higher scores in the check matrix, because errors escalate hierarchically upwards through the decomposition tree (and therefore also upwards through the check matrix). The exception is the process of zigzagging. Zigging moves top-down through the matrix, as shown in Figure 3, and increases the values in the check matrix from '1' to '2'. By doing this, it follows the same direction as the V-Model where 'Specification and Decomposition' is applied in the left leg and also moves from top to bottom. However, when the upper cells in the check matrix are advanced to '2', this is under the assumption that the lower cells will follow. If this is not the case, the process of zigzagging will stop and the higher values need to be set back to their old value ('1').

Strengths of this approach
The CRPD is based on AD and because of this it shares its rigour. The check matrix adds optimal overview of the project for the designer. This is done by tracking knowledge of the designer that is needed to complete the design.
Application of the check matrix enforces a gradual reduction of project risks as the project evolves. It prevents different risk levels in the project from drifting apart. When larger risks remain present in the project, it may lead to engineering efforts being lost; finished and well-engineered parts of the design may need to be altered to address the risks, and as a result the engineering process needs to be redone.

Weaknesses of this approach
Systems engineering methods typically cause overhead for the designer. These efforts are only valuable if it saves the designer from executing repair actions for the design. The method indeed is able to save the designer from rework as errors are found in an early stage and do not aggravate for longer times.
The decomposition tree of a product design gets a significant width at the bottom of the tree. The score in check matrix always represents the lowest value of any one of the decomposed elements. If there is only a single low scoring element it gives the same score as when there are many low scoring elements. This muddies the view of the designer.

Other Considerations
The check matrix uses a limited amount of numbers from 0 to 3. The check matrix could be tailored to focus on systems representing the sub-developments, enabling more detailed tracking.

References

[1] E. C. N. Puik and D. Ceglarek, "Axiomatic Product Design in Three Stages: A Constituent Roadmap That Visualises the Status of the Design Process by Tracking the Knowledge of the Designer," *ASME 2015 International Mechanical Engineering*

Congress and Exposition, pp. V015T19A003–V015T19A003, Nov. 2015.

[2] E. C. N. Puik and D. Ceglarek, "The Quality of a Design Will Not Exceed the Knowledge of its Designer; an Analysis Based on Axiomatic Information and the Cynefin Framework," *ICAD2015*, vol. 34, pp. 19–24, 2015.

[3] R. Höhn, S. Höppner, M. Broy, A. Rausch, R. Petrasch, S. Biffl, R. Wagner, W. Hesse, and K. Bergner, *Das V-Modell XT*, 1st ed. Heidelberg: Springer, 2008.

[4] N. P. Suh, "Axiomatic Design - Advances and Applications," in *advances and applications*, Oxford University Press, New York.Oxford, 2001, Chapter 5, pp. 239-298., 2001.

[5] E. C. N. Puik, E. Smulders, J. Gerritsen, B. V. Huijgevoort, and D. Ceglarek, "A Method for Indexing Axiomatic Independence Applied to Reconfigurable Manufacturing Systems," *ICAD2013*, vol. 7, pp. 186–194, Jun. 2013.

[6] S. D. Stan, R. Balan, and V. Maties, *Optimal design of parallel kinematics machines with 2 degrees of freedom*. 2008.

Improving Reliability of a fire-fighting pump set with Axiomatic Design

Gabriele Arcidiacono[1], *Pierpaolo* Placidoli[1,*], *Stefano* Nuzzi[2], and *Marco* Molon[3]

[1] *Department of Innovation & Information Engineering, G. Marconi University, Via Plinio 44, 00193 Rome, Italy*
[2] *Lean Six Sigma Researcher, Leanprove, Via A. La Marmora 45, 50121 Firenze, Italy*
[3] *R&D Department DAB PUMPS Spa, Via Marco Polo 14, 35035 Mestrino (PD), Italy*

Abstract. This paper introduces a case study featuring Axiomatic Design and Multi-Level Hierarchical model (MLH) applied to redesign a fire-fighting pump set. In particular, two different design concepts are presented to be applied to the supporting frame of the system to limit a vibration problem that can arise during potential malfunctioning of the fire-fighting pump. The selection of the best design has been carried out through reliability evaluation process and through the cost of failure based on the MLH model.

1 Introduction

This paper aims at demonstrating the efficient application of Axiomatic Design (AD) on a case study, where AD has been applied to improve the reliability of a fire-fighting pump set. The need for this improvement can be traced back to the fact that, in a global market where goods are easily and more available to customers, quality and reliability play a fundamental role for companies competitiveness. Innovation has become one of the most important factors for the long-term success of a company, since increased customers expectations and growing international competition call for massive product variety. Companies have had to respond to customers demand to survive on the market, and they have had to be quick in developing new products due to the shortening of product life cycle [1]. In this scenario, the design process covers a fundamental role. Engineering design is usually divided into conceptual design and detailed design [2]. Conceptual design is carried out at the earliest stage of engineering design, and the most important decisions are formulated at this stage, including the overall functional requirements and characteristics of a product. Size and shapes of components are instead determined in the detailed design stage, using numerical analyses and experiments. On the one hand, wrong decisions taken in the conceptual stage are recognized to affect subsequent decisions and processes of the product, and can lead to a major defect in the product. On the other hand, wrong decisions in the detailed design stage can impact the reliability and the overall quality of the product. Failure in one of these stages can be very hard to cope with when the product is already in production; moreover, the iterative steps required to correct mistakes can be either very expensive or, in worst case scenarios, insufficient. Therefore, a rational and methodological approach is desirable to avoid issues caused by wrong decision-making during both the above-mentioned product development stages. The process of reliability improvement is in fact traditionally carried out at subsystem/component level in the last stage of design development. Classical techniques, characterized by the cycles of build-test-evaluate-fix, thus significantly increase the product development time and life cycle cost. As it has been established by Suh in [3], it is known that AD can efficiently avoid those issues, as it suggests a systematic approach which divides a large design problem into manageable small sub-problems that make the design process less prone to decision errors.

As per reliability itself, a simplification that is often done is the independence of component failure. Some studies on reliability in the automotive industry [4], among which the fundamental work on FMEA [5], have instead shown that only a small part of the system failure is caused by the failure of the single component. On the contrary, the most frequent cause is the interaction between subsystems or bad designed interfaces. The state of a system or a component is simplified in "success" or "failure" following the binary state assumption. Although binary approach can be appropriate for reliability goal setting, it gives few clues for engineering design regarding the improvement of design parameters [6]. The Multi-Level Hierarchical (MLH) method proposed by Hubka and Eder [7] and after enhanced by Trewn and Yang [8], integrating the reliability of functions with the concept of dependent failure and cost of failure, is able to overcome the above-mentioned critical issues.

In this study, the AD methodology and the MLH analytical system are applied together to redesign the supporting structure of a fire-fighting pump set produced by DAB Pumps Spa. During the design phase, two concepts (that we have indicated in the study as Alpha and Beta) have been evaluated to find the best design in terms of reliability, lower complexity, and expected cost of failure.

*e-mail: p.placidoli@unimarconi.it

2 Methodology

Theory of the resolution of invention-related tasks (TRIZ) [9], Failure Mode and Effect Tree Analysis (FMETA) [10], and Fault Tree Analysis (FTA) [11, 12] are among several methodologies that have been developed and applied to improve system reliability in various domains. TRIZ, for instance, has been used – among several applications – to increase quality and reliability with regard to the manufacturing process of an industry that designs and builds molds and equipment to produce aluminum food containers [13]. FMETA looks for the most critical characteristics of the product from a reliability point of view, and provides the designer with a set of possible changes. FMETA has been successfully applied, for instance, to develop a reliability tree to evaluate both the RPN for the component of the product and to find the reliability relation useful for the following optimization, validated by an application to an automotive heavy-duty diesel engine [10]. FTA, namely, Comparative FTA, has proved useful to compare the reliability of an electronic braking system with its mechanical counterpart [14]. Complexity is defined by Suh [15] as the measure of uncertainty in satisfying functional requirements (FRs), caused by poor design or by lack of knowledge (or understanding) about the system under consideration. The versatility of AD has indeed been successfully tested in its application to several contexts, among which the authors have worked on virtual studios and television recording [16] within the product domain, and, within process domain, they have studied an application of AD to improve the process of airport assistance to patients with reduced mobility [17]. Due to its rate of successful applications, as already stated above, the novelty of this paper is the application of AD together with MLH, as the most suitable methodology to be applied to improve the reliability of the fire-fighting pump set. Therefore, a comparison has been established and debated among the best design solutions from the point of view of system components reliability. Ultimately, this paper aims at successfully applies AD integrated with MLH to optimize the design and improve the reliability of a machinery.

2.1 Axiomatic Design Principles

When applying AD, the design activity can be schematized by using four domains: the customer domain, the functional domain, the physical domain and the process domain [3]. The customer domain describes the Customer Attributes (CAs); the functional domain (deducted from CAs) describes the design objectives and Functional Requirements (FRs); the physical domain provides Design Parameters (DPs) for the implementation of the FRs; the process domain translates the DPs into the Process Variables (PVs). Mapping among design domains is performed according to two axioms, representing the core of the methodology. The first axiom is called the *Independence Axiom* and it states that the independence of FRs must always be maintained. The second axiom is called the *Information Axiom* and it states that among those designs that satisfy the Independence Axiom, the best design is the one that has the smallest Information Content [3]. The AD mapping process between the functional domain and the physical domain is defined as follows:

$$\{\mathrm{FR}\} = [A]\{\mathrm{DP}\}\{a_{ij} = (0,1)\} \tag{1}$$

where [A] is the design matrix that maps the DPs to the FRs; a_{ij} is the element of the matrix [A] that maps the j-th DP to the i-th FR. In this application, it is used as a design tool and the values of the matrix are assumed to be only 0 or 1.

2.2 Analytical Multi-Level Hierarchical Modeling

As an independent development in the theory of Engineering Design, Hubka and Eder [7] defined a technical system at various levels of abstraction. It is called Multi-Level Hierarchical system and, similarly to AD, it describes the design process from the highest abstract level to the lowest concrete level. However, differently from AD, in MLH, after the physical space, the Component Space is also defined, describing the concrete Component Structure (CS) of the design. To merge AD and MLH, Trewn and Yang [8] developed a theoretical 2-step framework to characterize the relationship between functional reliability and component reliability with the presence of failure dependence. The underlying concept is that two case scenarios can occur in a process design:

- Several Design Parameters can be encapsulated into a single component.
- A single Design Parameter is delivered by using several components.

Therefore, the structure of relationships among components is often different than that of DPs. From a reliability perspective, it is the subsystem/component structure that determines the reliability, hence mapping the component reliability to the function structure determines the function reliability of the system. Basically, Trewn and Yang [2000] introduce the matrix [B] that maps the Design Parameters in the design space to the component structure in the component space.

Mathematically speaking:

$$\{\mathrm{DP}\} = [\mathrm{B}]\{\mathrm{CS}\}\{b_{jk} = (0,1)\} \tag{2}$$

Where {CS} is a vector with k components that characterize the component space and b_{jk} is the element of the matrix [B] that maps the k-th component to the j-th design parameter. For the purpose of reliability analysis, the element b_{jk} is defined to be binary, where 0 = no relationship and 1 = related. By combining the equations 1 and 2:

$$\{\mathrm{FR}\} = [\mathrm{D}]\{\mathrm{CS}\} \tag{3}$$

where the matrix $[D] = [A] \circ [B]$ represents the relationship between the FRs and the components and it maps the relationship of each component of the system to the FRs that satisfies. The operator ($\circ$) is a composite relational operator for binary matrices. Finally, the reliability model is established by integrating failure probabilities of the components into this hierarchical multilevel model through the following equations:

$$R_s = \prod_{i=1}^{m} P(\mathrm{FR}_i) \tag{4}$$

where $P(FR_i)$ is the probability that FR_i is successfully delivered and:

$$P(\mathrm{FR}_i) = \prod_{k=1}^{n} (1 - p_k)^{d_{ik}} \tag{5}$$

where d_{ik} is the entry of [D] matrix in i-th row and k-th column and p_k is the failure probability of component k. Clearly, d_{ik} =1 indicates that k-th component will affect FR_i and vice versa. Hence:

$$R_s = \prod_{i=1}^{m} \prod_{k=1}^{n} (1 - p_k)^{d_{ik}} = \prod_{k=1}^{n} (1 - p_k)^{\bigcup_{i=1}^{m} d_{ik}} \tag{6}$$

This model allows to analyze the exact impact on the product of component failure, and to assess the damage of the failure with greater accuracy.

2.3 Cost of Failure

Within a system, when failure of a component occurs, it may cause a number of components to fail simultaneously. It is said that such failure is a dependent failure. In this case, these components may have to be repaired or replaced. However, the components usually affect the system in different ways. For example, they can affect either some minor functions of the product or some key functions that, in case of failure, can cause the entire system failure. Moreover, different components have different repair/replacement costs. In the MLH model discussed earlier, the following failure cost model is introduced to analyze the cost of component and function failures on system performance:

$$E[\mathrm{C_{CS_k}}] = \sum_{j=1}^{n} [p_{k|j} \times p_j] \left(\mathrm{CR_{CS_k}} + \sum_{i=1}^{m} d_{ik} \mathrm{C_{FR_i}} \right) \tag{7}$$

Where:
$E[C_{CS_k}]$ = Expected cost of failure of component k
CR_{CS_k} = Cost of replacement of component k
C_{FR_i} = Cost of loss of function i
Equation 7 states that the expected cost of failure due to component k is proportional to the component replacement cost and the cost of losing relevant product functions affected by the failure of component k.

3 Case Study

3.1 Fire-Fighting Pump Set Description

The fire-fighting pump sets are part of fire sprinkler system's water supply used in residential, public and commercial buildings, hospitals, and industrial plants. Fire-fighting pump sets are needed when the local municipal water system cannot provide sufficient pressure to meet the hydraulic design requirements of the fire sprinkler system prescribed by UNI EN 12845:2015. This usually occurs if the building is very tall, such as in high-rise buildings, or in systems that require a relatively high terminal pressure at the fire sprinkler in order to provide a large volume of water. The system is usually powered by diesel and electric motors, and typically connected to the public underground water supply piping, or a static water source (e.g., tank, reservoir, lake). The pump provides water flow at a higher pressure to the sprinkler system risers and hose standpipes. It starts and releases water when one or more fire sprinklers are exposed to a heat level which is beyond their design temperature, and the pressure in the fire sprinkler system drops below a certain set threshold. Alternatively, the fire-fighting pump set starts due to other fire hoses reels or other firefighting connections opening, causing a pressure drop in the fire fighting main.

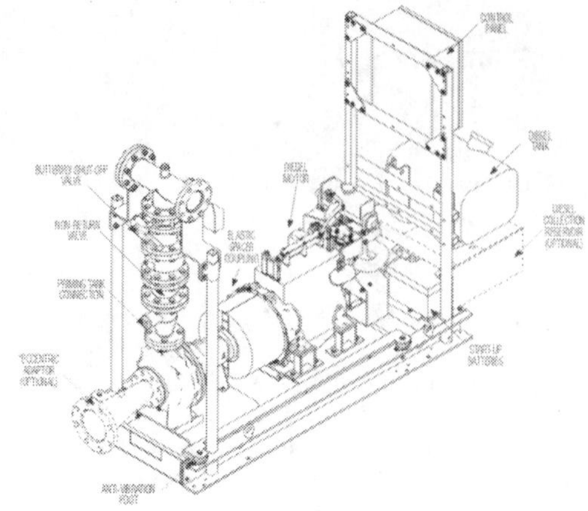

Fig. 1. Fire-fighting pump set

3.2 Fire-Fighting Pump Set Redesign Motivation

After a market investigation that involved both partners and customers, the following needs were assessed:

- Reducing components cost to be more competitive on market.
- Increasing the overall reliability of the fire-fighting set to reduce the extraordinary maintenance costs met by the customers.

To accomplish these tasks, negotiations with dealers have brought to use different components (e.g. diesel motor, control panel) instead of the old ones. Such substitution of the components is the main reason for the redesign of the existing fire-fighting pump set shown in Figure 1. Due to the partial incompatibility between the newly chosen components and the supporting structure, the redesign process has focused on the developing of a new supporting frame entirely designed and built by DAB Pumps.

DOI: 10.1051/matecconf/201712701014

Table 1. [A] Matrix

	DP_1	DP_2
FR_1	1	0
FR_2	0	1

3.3 Fire-Fighting Pump Supporting Frame Redesign

Following the AD method, the following functional requirements and design parameters are chosen for the frame:

FR_1= Support the fire-fighting pump set components

FR_2= Limit the fire-fighting pump set vibration while operating

DP_1= Fixed frame

DP_2= Anti-vibration system

The design matrix [A] is shown in Table 1. The mapping between the physical space and the component space defined by the MLH theory is performed by applying the equation 2. At this stage, the definition of components of the supporting frame (i.e the CS vector) has lead to two different design concepts called *Alpha* (Figure 2) and *Beta* (Figure 3), the CSs of which are:

Alpha concept

CS_1= Anti-vibration rubber bells

CS_2= Pump base

CS_3= Anti-vibration foot abutment

CS_4= Diesel motor base

CS_5= Longitudinal beams

CS_6= Control panel pillars

Beta concept

CS_1= Anti-vibration rubber bells

CS_2= Pump base

CS_3= Bracket support of the uprights

CS_4= Diesel motor base

CS_5= Longitudinal beams

CS_6= Control Panel pillars

The mapping between the DP and CS domain is completed by building the [B] matrix for each design concept, table 2 and 3. These matrices are built considering the structural dependence between each DP and the chosen structural component. For example regards to the *Alpha* concept (table 2), DP_1 depends on $CS_{2,4,5,6}$, since they are the components that detail the fixed frame and hence carry out the function of supporting the fire-fighting pump

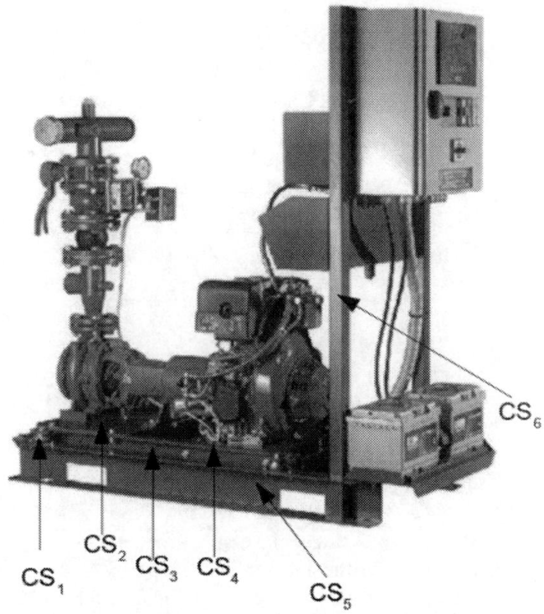

Fig. 2. Alpha design

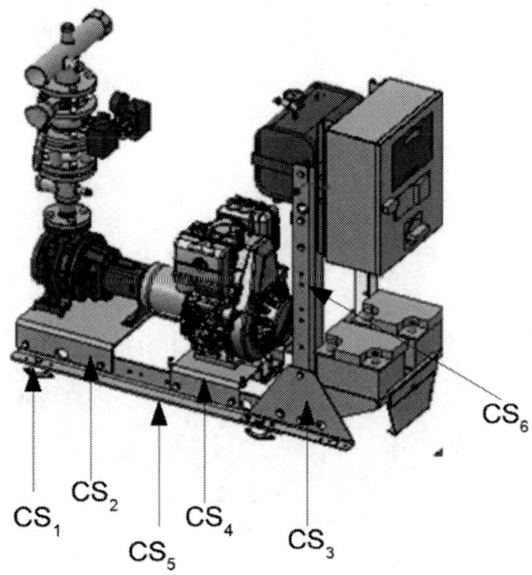

Fig. 3. Beta design

Table 2. [B] Matrix - Alpha

	CS_1	CS_2	CS_3	CS_4	CS_5	CS_6
DP_1	0	1	0	1	1	1
DP_2	1	0	1	0	1	0

Table 3. [B] Matrix - Beta

	CS_1	CS_2	CS_3	CS_4	CS_5	CS_6
DP_1	0	1	1	1	1	1
DP_2	1	0	0	0	1	0

Table 4. [D] Matrix - Alpha

	CS_1	CS_2	CS_3	CS_4	CS_5	CS_6
FR_1	0	1	0	1	1	1
FR_2	1	0	1	0	1	0

Table 5. [D] Matrix - Beta

	CS_1	CS_2	CS_3	CS_4	CS_5	CS_6
FR_1	0	1	1	1	1	1
FR_2	1	0	0	0	1	0

(FR_1). $CS_{1,3,5}$ are instead the components chosen to detail DP_2 and to fulfill the anti-vibration function (FR_2). The same metrics is used to build the [B] matrix for the *Beta* concept (table 3). In both cases DP_1 and DP_2 are coupled by the longitudinal beams (CS_5) that are structurally connected with the anti-vibration rubber bells; hence, they can be considered part of both the fixed frame and anti-vibration system. The reliability of the functional requirements for both concepts is determined by equation 6 given the failure probability p_k estimated for each component (table 6) and the related [D] matrix (Table 4 and 5):

Alpha concept

$$R_{FR_1} = (1-0.05)^0(1-0.1)^1(1-0.01)^0 (1-0.1)^1(1-0.1)^1(1-0.01)^1 = 0.7217 \quad (8)$$

$$R_{FR_2} = (1-0.05)^1(1-0.1)^0(1-0.01)^1 (1-0.1)^0(1-0.1)^1(1-0.01)^0 = 0.8465 \quad (9)$$

Beta concept

$$R_{FR_1} = (1-0.3)^0(1-0.1)^1(1-0.1)^1 (1-0.1)^1(1-0.01)^1(1-0.01)^1 = 0.7145 \quad (10)$$

$$R_{FR_2} = (1-0.3)^1(1-0.1)^0(1-0.01)^0 (1-0.1)^0(1-0.1)^1(1-0.01)^0 = 0.63 \quad (11)$$

Out of the comparison among the reliability values of the two designs, it is possible to highlight that the function with the worst reliability in the *Alpha* concept is the function of support the fire-fighting pump set components (FR_1), while the function with the worst reliability in the *Beta* concept is the function of the supporting frame of limiting the vibration of the system (FR_2). This poor reliability of FR_2 of the *Beta* concept is primarily due to the poor reliability of the anti-vibration rubber bells (CS_1) that depends on the assembly of the *Beta* concept. The pump base, the motor base and the longitudinal beams are in fact positioned on the anti-vibration rubber bells that in this scenario become more subject to wear.

Table 6. Failure probability (p) of components.

	Alpha	Beta
p_1	0.05	0.3
p_2	0.1	0.1
p_3	0.01	0.01
p_4	0.1	0.1
p_5	0.1	0.1
p_6	0.01	0.01

From a cost perspective, the cost of failure needs to be considered in order to select the best concept. To proceed with the calculation, the matrix [P] is built for each design, and it represents the dependence failure between components and, therefore, the possibility that a single failure mode may cause a number of components to fail simultaneously. In table 7 end 8 are represented the matrix entries with the cost of replacement (CR_{CS_k}) of each component structure (CS_k). Given the cost of loss of function for FR_1=300 € and for FR_2=100 €, both of them consider the cost of the damage to the client, due to the failure of the system, and the cost related to the assistance service needed for the inspection and the repairing. Considering the scenario where failure occurs of the longitudinal beams (CS_5) of the *Alpha* concept, the calculation of the expected cost of failure applying the equation 7 is the following:

$$E[C_{CS_5}] = [(p_{5|1}p_1) + (p_{5|2}p_2) + (p_{5|3}p_3) + (p_{5|4}p_4) + (p_{5|5}p_5) + (p_{5|6}p_6)] \cdot (CR_{CS_5} + \sum_{i=1}^{m} d_{i5}C_{FR_i}) = [(1\cdot 0.05) + (0\cdot 0.1) + (0\cdot 0.01) + (0\cdot 0.1) + (1\cdot 0.1) + (1\cdot 0.01)]\cdot[45 + (1\cdot 300 + 1\cdot 100)] = 71.2€ \quad (12)$$

Clearly, the introduction of dependent failure analysis allows a broader and more thorough understanding about the damage caused by the failure of component 5. Assuming the independence, the expected cost of failure of component 5 is in fact 45.00 €; however, by introducing the dependent failure model, it becomes 71.2 € due to the dependence of component 5 on the performance of components 1 and 6. Once the procedure is applied for each component, the estimated cost of failure of the design is calculated by simply adding each $E[C_{CS_k}]$. The calculation for the two concepts, which is not shown here in view of a previous confidentiality agreement, has lead to select the *Alpha* concept as the one to have the best design, due to its less expected cost of failure.

4 Conclusions

The redesign of a supporting structure of a fire-fighting pump set has been addressed using AD and a MLH model

Table 7. [P] Matrix - Alpha

CR_{CS_k}		CS_1	CS_2	CS_3	CS_4	CS_5	CS_6
10€	CS_1	1	0	1	0	0	0
50€	CS_2	0	1	1	1	0	0
42€	CS_3	1	1	1	1	1	0
45€	CS_4	0	1	1	1	0	0
45€	CS_5	1	0	0	0	1	1
65€	CS_6	0	0	0	0	1	1

Table 8. [P] Matrix - Beta

CR_{CS_k}		CS_1	CS_2	CS_3	CS_4	CS_5	CS_6
10€	CS_1	1	0	1	0	0	0
45€	CS_2	0	1	1	1	0	0
55€	CS_3	1	1	1	1	0	0
45€	CS_4	0	0	1	1	0	0
35€	CS_5	1	0	0	0	1	1
55€	CS_6	0	0	0	0	1	1

to evaluate the dependent failure of components and their related costs. The application of these procedures has allowed to carry the entire design process from the conceptual design stage to the detailed design stage. In particular, the MLH method has enabled the evaluation of two competing concepts in terms of uncertainty to functional delivery, thanks to the mapping process that has linked the functional requirements domain to the component structure domain. This systematic approach in conjunction with the dependent failure cost estimation has led to choose the best design with regard to lower complexity and improved reliability. The amount of information acquired during the design process has accelerated the decision-making process, while improving the entire design process, thus avoiding the trial-and-error approach typical of heuristic and empirical methodology.

References

[1] J. van Iwaarden, T. van der Wiele, *The effects of increasing product variety and shortening product life cycles on the use of quality management system*, International Journal of Quality & Reliability Management **29**, 470 (2012)

[2] D. Ullman, ed., *The Mechanical Design Process* (McGraw-Hill Education, New York, USA, 2015)

[3] N. Suh, ed., *Axiomatic Design advances and applications* (Oxford Univ. Press, New York, USA, 2001)

[4] G. Arcidiacono, J. Wang, *Automotive Reliability*, Quality and Reliability Engineering International **20**, 3 (2004)

[5] P. Palady, ed., *Failure Modes and Effects Analysis* (PT Publication Inc, 1995)

[6] A. Giorgetti, C. Cavallini, G. Arcidiacono, P. Citti, *A Mixed C-VIKOR Fuzzy Approach for Material Selection during Design Phase: A Case Study in Valve Seats for High Performance Engine*, International Journal of Applied Engineering Research **12**, 3117 (2017)

[7] V. Hubka, W.F. Eder, eds., *Theory of Technical System* (Springer-Verlag, 1988)

[8] J. Trewn, K. Yang, *The relationship between system functions, reliability and dependent failures*, in *The 1988 IEEE International Conference on Systems, man and Cybernetics* (San Diego, 1988)

[9] G. Altshuller, *Creativity as an Exact Science: The Theory of the Solution of Inventive Problems* (Gordon and Breach Science Publishers, New York, 1984)

[10] G. Arcidiacono, G. Campitelli, *Reliability Improvement of a Diesel Engine using FMETA Approach*, Quality and Reliability Engineering International Journal Special Issue on Automotive Reliability **20**, 143 (2004)

[11] W. Schneeweiss, *The fault tree method:(in the fields of reliability and safety technology)* (LiLoLe-Verlag, 1999)

[12] Vesely, Goldberg, Roberts, Haasl, Tech. rep., Nuclear Regulatory Commission Washington dc (1981)

[13] G. Arcidiacono, L. Bucciarelli, *TRIZ: Engineering Methodologies to Improve the Process Reliability*, Quality and Reliability Engineering International Journal **32**, 2537 (2016)

[14] G. Arcidiacono, *Development of a FTA versus Parts Count Method Model: Comparative FTA*, Quality and Reliability Engineering International Journal pp. 411–424 (2003)

[15] N. Suh, *Complexity: theory and applications* (Oxford University Press on Demand, 2005)

[16] G. Arcidiacono, P. Placidoli, *Reality and illusion in Virtual Studios: Axiomatic Design applied to television recording*, in *Proceedings of ICAD2015, 9th International Conference on Axiomatic Design* (Florence, Italy, 2015)

[17] G. Arcidiacono, A. Giorgetti, M. Pugliese, *Axiomatic Design to improve PRM airport assistance*, in *Proceedings of ICAD2015, 9th International Conference on Axiomatic Design* (Florence, Italy, 2015)

Low-cost Antenna Positioning System Designed with Axiomatic Design

Joseph Timothy Foley[1,*], *Vladimir* Omelianov[1], *Slawomir* Koziel[1], *Adrian* Bekasiewicz[1]

[1] *Reykjavik University, Engineering Department, Menntavegur 1, 101 Reykjavik, Iceland*

Abstract. The Engineering Optimization and Modeling Center at Reykjavik University has been carrying out research on antenna CAD, including the simulation-driven design of novel antenna topologies. However, simulation is not enough to validate a design: a custom RF anechoic chamber has been built to quantify antenna performance, particularly in terms of field properties such as radiation patterns. Such experiments require careful positioning of the antenna in the chamber accurately in 3-axis with a short development time, challenging material constraints, and minimal funding. Axiomatic Design Theory principles were applied to develop an automated 3-axis positioner system for a reference antenna and the antenna to be calibrated. Each axis can be individually controlled with a repeatability of 1 degree. This 3000 USD device can be fabricated using easily available components and rapid prototyping tools.

1 Introduction

For the last 50 years, ways of communicating have been evolving more progressively than ever. Every ten years there has been a breakthrough in speed and range of wireless transmissions. This progress creates new challenges in the design of antenna structures that need to satisfy stringent requirements concerning electrical performance but also geometry constraints, which is particularly important for hand-held and wearable systems, as well as short-range communications such as in Internet of things applications. Increasing complexity of antenna systems makes automated EM-simulation-driven design more and more important. The Engineering Optimization and Modeling Center (EOMC) at Reykjavik University has been involved in research concerning novel and computationally efficient techniques for design optimization of antennas, mostly in the GHz range, as well as the design of novel antennas (especially in terms of reduced-size structures). The following articles have been published concerning this area by the Center:

- Fast multi-objective surrogate-assisted design of multi-parameter antenna structures through rotational design space reduction [1]
- Compact UWB monopole antenna for internet of things applications [2]
- Suppressing sidelobes of linear phased array of microstrip antennas with simulation-based optimization [3]
- Structure and design optimization of compact UWB slot antenna [4]

The EOMC uses CST, Matlab, self-developed algorithms to automatically generate geometries and simulates the field characteristics of conceptual antennas. The current simulation efforts have matured sufficiently that the next phase, validation, is needed. In short, the antennas need to be fabricated and tested for comparison to simulation results.

In 2015, the EOMC received funds from the Icelandic Center for Research (RANNIS) to build an anechoic chamber to prove their designs. A radio frequency (RF) anechoic chamber is a shielded room whose walls have been covered with a material that scatters or absorbs so much of the incident energy that it can simulate free space.

An example of a similar chamber at CSEM is shown in Fig. 1 and described thus:

> The fully anechoic chamber with remote control offers a controlled propagation environment for antenna radiation pattern and gain measurement, e.g. for WPANs, BANs and UWB systems. The chamber consists of a metallic Faraday cage of 4.72×4.05×3.05m with absorbent materials and a rotating platform on the inside. If required, the chamber can be made semi-anechoic by removing the absorbers on the floor. The useful space inside the chamber is 3.81 × 3.14 × 2.14m, and the chamber can be used for measurements above 400 MHz. The upper limit is determined by measurement equipment. The chamber is equipped with reference antennas, a 40 GHz network analyzer, and a 26.5 GHz spectrum analyzer. It can be used for 2-D antenna radiation pattern measurements, total radiated power (TRP) measurements and EMC measurements. A human body phantom and a human hand phantom are also available [5].

* e-mail: foley@ru.is

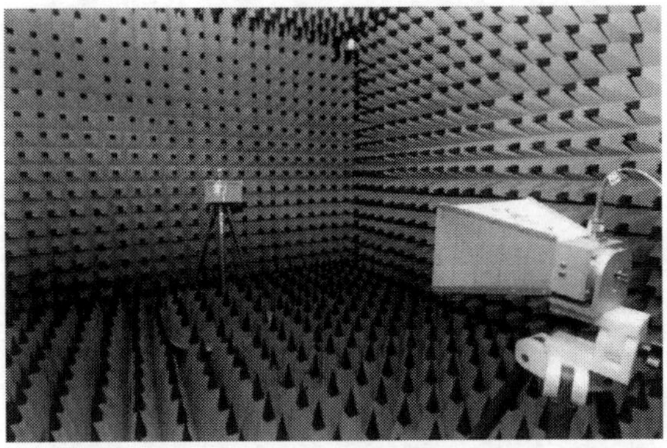

Fig. 1. Example of a fully equipped anechoic chamber at CSEM. Note the anechoic damper spikes, manual positioner, and wooden tripods [5].

As seen in the example, for a complete system, more is needed than just an RF chamber designed to eliminate interference and reflections. A mechanism is needed to position the antennas accurately and repeatably. The majority of the funds allocated were devoted to the purchase, configuration, and installation of the chamber; much smaller funds remained (3000 USD) for the positioning mechanism.

The main challenge with designing an appropriate positioner is that each anechoic chamber is used for very specific measurements: [6]:

- Radiation Pattern and Gain Measurement
- Phase Measurement
- Polarization Measurement
- Impedance Measurement
- Scale Model Measurement
- SAR (Specific Absorption Rate) Measurement

The size of the measured antennas and frequencies have a big role as well. As a result, testing many combinations of these variables requires versatile equipment.

1.1 Prior Art

Consider two commercially available positioner systems:

- TDK 3-Dimensional Manipulator, Model 3DM-01LDs (Fig. 2a)
  - Non-conductive commercial grade fiberglass and ABS plastic
  - 2 axis of rotation
  - Fiber optic interface
  - Accuracy: ± 2° standard with ± 0.5° accuracy
  - Rotation Angle: 360° continuous
  - Price: 39000 USD (does not include control unit)
- Sunol EUT positioner, Model ELA275 (Fig. 2b)
  - Continuous Rotation allowed in both Elevation & Azimuth (with optional components)
  - Low-Density EUT holder
  - Low RF Cross-Section materials above drive units
  - Portable (no permanent installation necessary)
  - Remote Azimuth Drive Option separating drive units
  - Fiber Optic connection to Controller (requires SC104V System Controller)
  - Price: 31000 USD (with a control unit)
  - Precision: ± 0.25°
- ETS-Lindgren 2120CR Multi-Axis Positioner (Fig. 2c)
  - 360° Independent Rotation in Both Theta and Phi Axes, Continuous Rotation in Phi Axis
  - Angular Positioner Accuracy Better than ± 0.025°
  - Price: 54000–80000 USD (depending on configuration and excluding controller)

As we can see all of these solutions have the following limitations, making them unsuitable for our situation:

- All of the towers do not have an axis of rotation at the same point
- Custom mounting plates required for each antenna design
- Installation requires a flat surface
- Absence of coaxial connection on the antennas mount as a default option
- The average price of the mentioned above manipulators is 40000 USD without a controller. This puts the positioners well outside the range of most small grants.

2 Design

This positioner design was developed using the Axiomatic Design methodology which focuses on the mapping between customer needs into instantiation [10]. The customer is the antenna measurement team and our top level need is:

CN_0 Measure the performance of the antenna under test.

Other needs emerge decomposing this main goal:

CN_1 Compatible with our anechoic chamber
CN_2 Reference antennas of interest are up to $260 \times 260 \times 260$ mm
CN_3 Designed antennas are $10 \times 10 \times 2$ mm to $300 \times 30 \times 2$ mm
CN_4 Do not exceed budget of 3000 USD
CN_5 Can quickly change designed antennas
CN_6 Easily reconfigured for different kinds of experiments
CN_7 Re-orient the antenna without human intervention
CN_7 Complete design to implementation in 3 months

Customer Needs are translated into Constraints (Cs) and Functional Requirements (FRs) which are fulfilled by Design Parameters (DPs). Constraints are designed envelopes that affect many elements within the system but do not define its functionality.

2.1 Constraints

C_1 Each module mass below 20 kg
C_2 Use coax cables of fixed lengths 100, 200, 400, 600, 800 mm

DOI: 10.1051/matecconf/201712701015

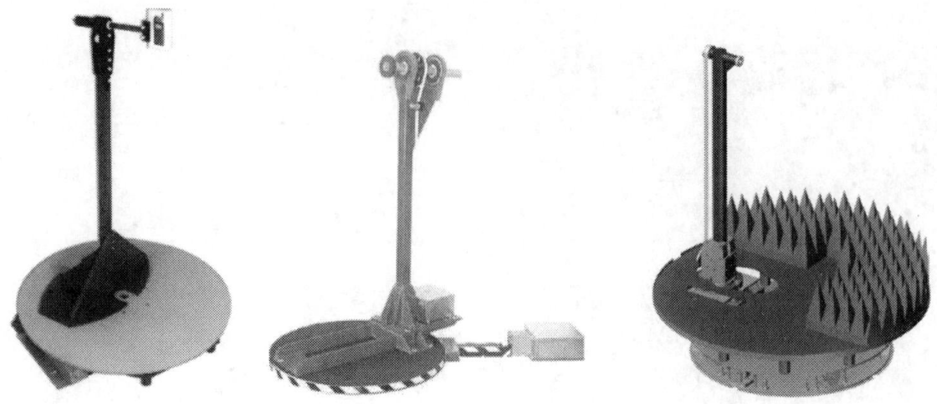

(a) TDK Model 3DM-01LDs [7]. (b) Sunol Model ELAZ75 [8]. (c) ETS-Lindgren Model 2120CR [9].

Fig. 2. Existing commercial 3D positioners for use in RF anechoic chambers.

C_3 Have time that required to install measuring antennas be at most 5 minutes
C_4 Have easy access to cables and connectors
C_5 Have high repeatability of measurements
C_6 Time constraint: 3 months
C_7 Fabrication using equipment at Reykjavik University
C_8 Support reference antennas with weight up to 3 kg
C_9 Support reference antennas with dimensions up to 260×260×260 mm
C_{10} Support dimensions of measured antennas that are 10×10×2 mm to 300×30×2 mm
C_{11} Keep cables from bending over 10 mm radius
C_{12} Do not exceed budget of 3000 USD

2.2 Functional Requirements (FRs)

Best practices for FRs are that they must start with an action or transformative verb and able to be validated. [10, 11] The CNs are considered to generate top-level Functional Requirements (FRs):

FR$_0$ Rotate measured antenna in two axes and reference antenna in polarization angle without introducing interfering elements

DP$_0$ Stepper-driven 2-axis positioner for measured antenna and 1-axis positioner for reference antenna both made primarily of plastic

For brevity, we have combined the results of zigzagging into the following FR and DP decompositions.

FR$_1$ Rotate measured antenna in two axes with 1-degree resolution.
- **FR**$_{1.1}$ Rotate measured antenna in XZ (vertical) plane by 180°.
- **FR**$_{1.2}$ Rotate measured antenna in XY (horizontal) plane by 360°.
- **FR**$_{1.3}$ Mount measured antenna with 1 mm repeatability without tools.

FR$_2$ Measure affect of reference antenna polarization angle with 1° resolution.
- **FR**$_{2.1}$ Rotate reference antenna XZ (vertical) plane by 180°.
- **FR**$_{2.2}$ Fixture multiple commercial reference antenna mounting schemes.
- **FR**$_{2.3}$ Align relative position of the measured and reference antennas.

FR$_3$ Avoid introducing additional RF interference during antenna excitation
- **FR**$_{3.1}$ De-energize motor controllers during measurement.
- **FR**$_{3.2}$ Supply signal to antennas.
- **FR**$_{3.3}$ Supply power and control signals in shielded cables to components.
- **FR**$_{3.4}$ Eliminate any material that would change antenna performance.

FR$_4$ Provide interface for user to setup and run experiment.

FR$_5$ Stand on the chamber's spiked floor.

2.3 Design Parameters

Design Parameters are the methods, elements, and quantities that allow for instantiation. To best describe such parameters, they must start with a noun and be something that can be compared or quantified [10, 11].

DP$_1$ Stepper motor and timing belt driven "receiver tower" to operate with measured (small) antennas
- **DP**$_{1.1}$ Plastic vertical rotary disk on wheels
- **DP**$_{1.2}$ Plastic horizontal rotary plate on custom nylon-ball thrust bearing
- **DP**$_{1.3}$ Plastic adjustable small antenna holder with hand-tightened clamp to SMA connector on antenna

DP$_2$ Stepper motor and timing belt driven "transmitter tower" to operate with reference (big) antennas
- **DP**$_{2.1}$ Plastic vertical rotor on horizontal shaft with ball bearings
- **DP**$_{2.2}$ Plastic antenna adapter plate with slots in most common antenna mounting configurations
- **DP**$_{2.3}$ Detachable laser inclinometer located in front of axis of rotation

DP$_3$ Interference mitigation procedures and elements including RF absorbing foam
- **DP$_{3.1}$** Smoothie Motor controller able to de-energize motors during operation (Controller device)
- **DP$_{3.2}$** Flexible coax cable and rotating couplings
- **DP$_{3.3}$** DIN9 shielded cables
- **DP$_{3.4}$** No plastic in axis of measurement, metal components 100 mm from surface of measured antenna

DP$_4$ MATLAB Software interface between network analyzer and motor controller

DP$_5$ Aluminum Tripod with 1/4" connector covered in RF absorbent foam

2.4 Design Matrix

This leads to creation of a design matrix from the Cartesian product of coupling coefficients on FR and DP vectors (Eq. 1) [10, 11]. In many cases the coupling quantitative value is unknown (or hard to quantify) so first-order effects are denoted with the variable X.

$$\begin{Bmatrix} FR_1 \\ FR_2 \\ FR_3 \\ FR_4 \\ FR_5 \end{Bmatrix} = \begin{bmatrix} X & 0 & 0 & 0 & 0 \\ 0 & X & 0 & 0 & 0 \\ X & X & X & 0 & 0 \\ 0 & 0 & 0 & X & 0 \\ 0 & 0 & 0 & 0 & X \end{bmatrix} \begin{Bmatrix} DP_1 \\ DP_2 \\ DP_3 \\ DP_4 \\ DP_5 \end{Bmatrix} \quad (1)$$

This design matrix is decoupled i.e. path-dependent, so the order in which things are designed is important. It should be not surprising that FR$_3$ is coupled to FR$_1$ and FR$_2$ due to the concern of RF interference during design. The design matrix decompositions for FR$_1$ and FR$_2$ are uncoupled (diagonal) due to the modularity of the design and are omitted. The second level design matrix in Eq. 2 is decoupled, due to the in-axis interference affecting other decisions.

$$\begin{Bmatrix} FR_{3.1} \\ FR_{3.2} \\ FR_{3.3} \\ FR_{3.4} \end{Bmatrix} = \begin{bmatrix} X & 0 & 0 & 0 \\ 0 & X & 0 & 0 \\ 0 & X & X & 0 \\ 0 & X & X & X \end{bmatrix} \begin{Bmatrix} DP_{3.1} \\ DP_{3.2} \\ DP_{3.3} \\ DP_{3.4} \end{Bmatrix} \quad (2)$$

PTC CREO Parametric 3.0 was used to develop the CAD model based upon these DPs.

2.5 Receiver tower

The biggest challenges in this design are avoiding metal elements, large variation in antennas, the routing of cables, and having no obstacles in front and behind of the antennas. This is why the circular part of the tower persisted through the stages of the design. The early version in Fig. 3 had the antenna wire wrapping around the wheel created an unacceptably large blind spot in measurements.

In the next version, the wheel was rotated at 180 degrees allowing for easier cable management. However, the weight of tower, considering it was made from 10 mm Plexiglas was at 24 kg, violating C$_1$. By "reinventing" the wheel into a socket that will hold the antenna holder, the design resulted in 10 kg device after reducing the width of Plexiglas to 6 mm as shown in Fig. 4. A cutaway is shown in Fig. 5 to show the main components.

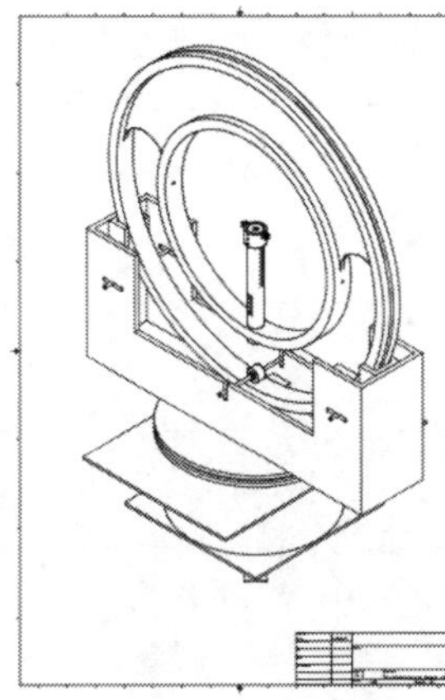

Fig. 3. Early design of the receiver tower (V4).

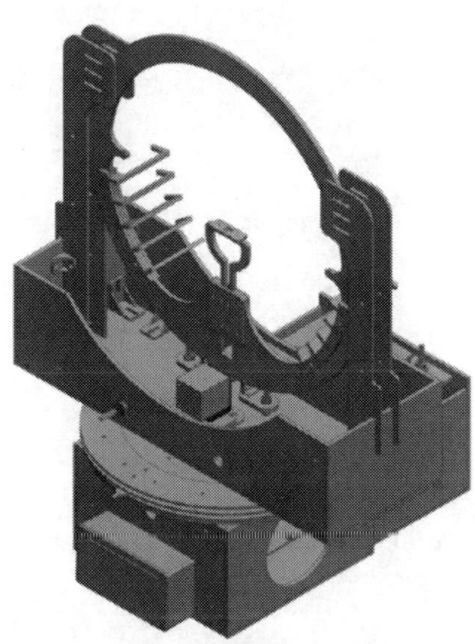

Fig. 4. Design of the receiver tower at its final stage (V5.3). Note the cable guide fingers on the side of the ring.

The mass of the tower is approximately 10 kg (including the antenna) and total material cost 1500 USD (including cables).

Rotating elements are driven by timing belt connected to a NEMA 23 bipolar hybrid stepper motor with 200 steps per revolution ($N_{\text{stepper}} = 200$). Each stepper motor has a sprocket for connecting to the belt with $N_{\text{sprocket}} = 20$ teeth. In the case of the large vertical ring, the pulley of the stepper drives an inverted timing belt adhered to the side of the ring with $N_{wheel1} = 738$ teeth. The horizontal platform rolls on a custom made plastic ball thrust bearing

DOI: 10.1051/matecconf/201712701015

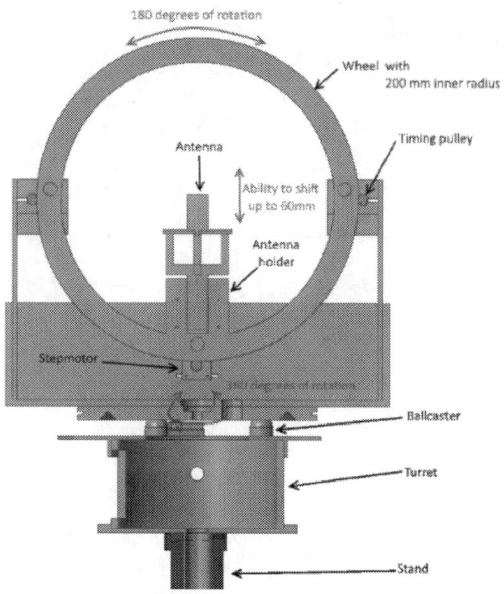

Fig. 5. Annotated cut-away drawing of the receiver tower.

Fig. 6. 3-D configuration of the receiver tower.

with a timing belt of $N_{wheel2} = 533$ teeth. To calculate the angular resolution (θ_R), the timing belt gear ratio must be taking into account.

$$\theta_{\text{step}} = \frac{360^\circ}{N_{\text{step}}} \tag{3}$$

$$R_{\text{wheel}} = \frac{N_{\text{wheel}}}{N_{\text{sprocket}}} \tag{4}$$

where

The resolution for a given step is proportional to the wheel's ratio; combining Eq. 3 & 4 results in the angular resolution (θ_R):

$$\theta_R = \frac{\theta_{\text{step}}}{R_{\text{wheel}}} = 360^\circ \frac{N_{\text{sprocket}}}{N_{\text{step}} N_{\text{wheel}}} \tag{5}$$

The vertical ring has a resolution of 0.049° per step. The horizontal rotation has a resolution of 0.068° per step. Both are well within the requested resolution of 1°.

2.6 Transmitter tower

The transmitter tower has a much simpler design due to fewer movement axis. The most challenging design problem is that reference antennas varying greatly in shape and weight. The current design is shown on Fig. 10 on page 7. This stepper motor and timing belt configuration has $N_{\text{wheel3}} = 130$ resulting in a resolution of 0.277° per step, which meets the requirements.

It is worth noting that the center of mass shifts depending on the type of antennas attached in this design. To connect the antennas an adapter plate is laser-cut for each antenna. The weight of the device is approximately 15 kg (including the antenna) and material cost 800 USD (including cables) According to customer restrictions, the proximity of metals doesn't heavily affect reference antenna performance as long as it is off axis.

2.7 Control unit

The control unit is built around a SmoothieBoard 500 USD Open Source Hardware CNC controller board based on the LPC1768 Cortex-M3 chip [12]. Interfacing with the controller is done through GCODE over a USB-serial connection. Our Matlab program commands the controller to move then de-energizes the motors after the motion to reduce the noise. In addition, Matlab 2015 added support of VISA protocol for direct control of our Anritsu MS4640A network analyzer.

3 Results and Discussion

The effect of the mechanical components and fixtures of the receiver tower (Fig. 6) on the accuracy of the measured field characteristics of the antenna at hand has been validated.

More specifically, a comparison between simulation and measurement data has been performed for several test designs. Despite utilization of low-permittivity plastic as the construction material of the tower, rotation of the ring in the vicinity of the line of sight between the transmitter and receiver tower results in strong distortions of the measured signal. Moreover, an additional set of tests has indicated that the base of the rotary tower, even though entirely covered by absorbing material, noticeably influences the characteristics of the antenna under test due to varying

 DOI: 10.1051/matecconf/201712701015

Fig. 7. Reykjavik University's RF anechoic chamber with the two towers installed. Receiver tower is in 2-D configuration.

Fig. 8. 2-D measurements in progress on monopole antenna as viewed through the test chamber CCTV system.

patterns of signal reflections from the rotating absorber tapers.

The aforementioned effects could be compensated for by appropriate post-processing of the measured signal. For example, distortions caused by rotations of the receiver tower could be simulated and then subtracted from the measured signal. However, the major problem is that accurate simulations of tower-induced distortions can be performed only using computationally expensive full-wave EM model, evaluation of which is a matter of days per simulation. At the same time, for correction of 3-D measurement data, at least a few hundred of EM simulations of the tower at different positions are required. Clearly, such a procedure is numerically prohibitive.

Notwithstanding, about 90% of antenna measurements require only horizontal rotations of the receiver antenna. From this perspective, simplification of the tower construction seems to be a reasonable solution. Due to the modular design, reconfiguration was accomplished without significant changes to the system (cf. Fig. 7).

A designed monopole antenna under test mounted on a reconfigured receiver tower is shown in Fig. 8.

The measurements in the E- and H-planes took approximately 3 minutes each (360° rotation with a step size of 5°). It should be noted that 500 frequency points in a range from 1 GHz to 20 GHz are captured at a time for each allocation of the antenna. Consequently, no extra calibration of the system is required for varying frequency ranges. Fig. 9 on page 7 shows a comparison of simulated and measured radiation pattern characteristics of the antenna at selected frequencies. Using Axiomatic design a complete RF antenna positioning system has been developed, designed and built, with an overall budget of 3000 USD.

References

[1] S. Koziel, A. Bekasiewicz, *Fast multi-objective surrogate-assisted design of multi-parameter antenna structures through rotational design space reduction*, IET Microwaves, Antennas & Propagation (2016)

[2] A. Bekasiewicz, S. Koziel, *Compact UWB monopole antenna for Internet of Things applications*, Electronics Letters (2016)

[3] S. Koziel, S. Ogurtsov, A. Bekasiewicz, *Suppressing sidelobes of linear phased array of microstrip antennas with simulation-based optimization*, Metrology and Measurement Systems (2016)

[4] A. Bekasiewicz, S. Koziel, *Structure and design optimisation of compact UWB slot antenna*, Electronics Letters (2016)

[5] G. Dash, *How RF Anechoic Chambers Work*, Glen R. Dash Charitable Foundation (2005)

[6] *Antenna measurements* (2011), `http://www.antenna-theory.com/measurements/antenna.php`

[7] *Antenna tripods, masts and positioners — EUT manipulators — horn positioners* (c2001–2016), `http://www.ramayes.com/tripods_masts_positioners.htm`

[8] *Sunol sciences corporate website* (2015), `http://www.sunolsciences.com/`

[9] *2120cr multi-axis positioner (maps) all info* (2014), `http://www.ets-lindgren.com/all/2120CR`

[10] N.P. Suh, *The Principles of Design* (Oxford University Press, 1990)

[11] N.P. Suh, D.S. Cochran, P.C. Lima, *Manufacturing System Design*, in *48th General Assembly of CIRP, Annals of the CIRP* (1998), Vol. 47, pp. 627–639

[12] *SmoothieBoard: Open Source Hardware CNC controller board* (2015), `http://smoothieware.org`

DOI: 10.1051/matecconf/201712701015

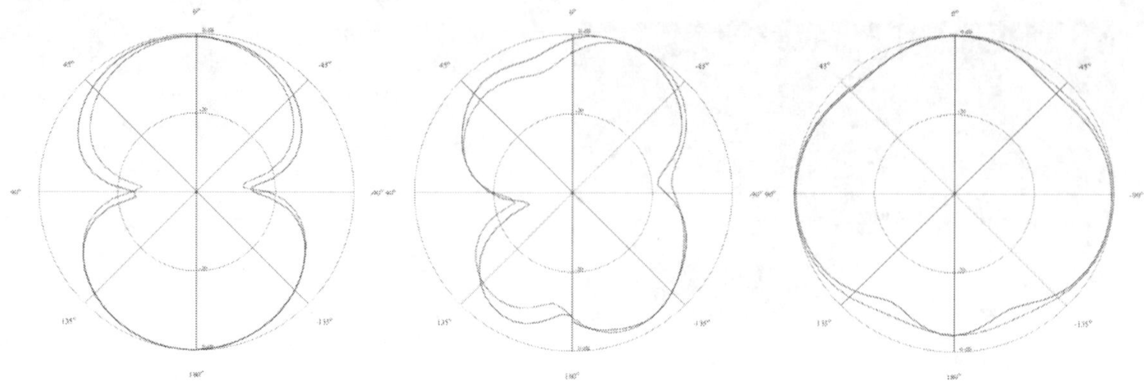

(a) 2 GHz on the E plane (b) 9 GHz on the E plane (c) 9 GHz on the H plane

Fig. 9. Simulated (dotted black) and measured (red) radiation pattern characteristics of the monopole antenna of Fig. 8.

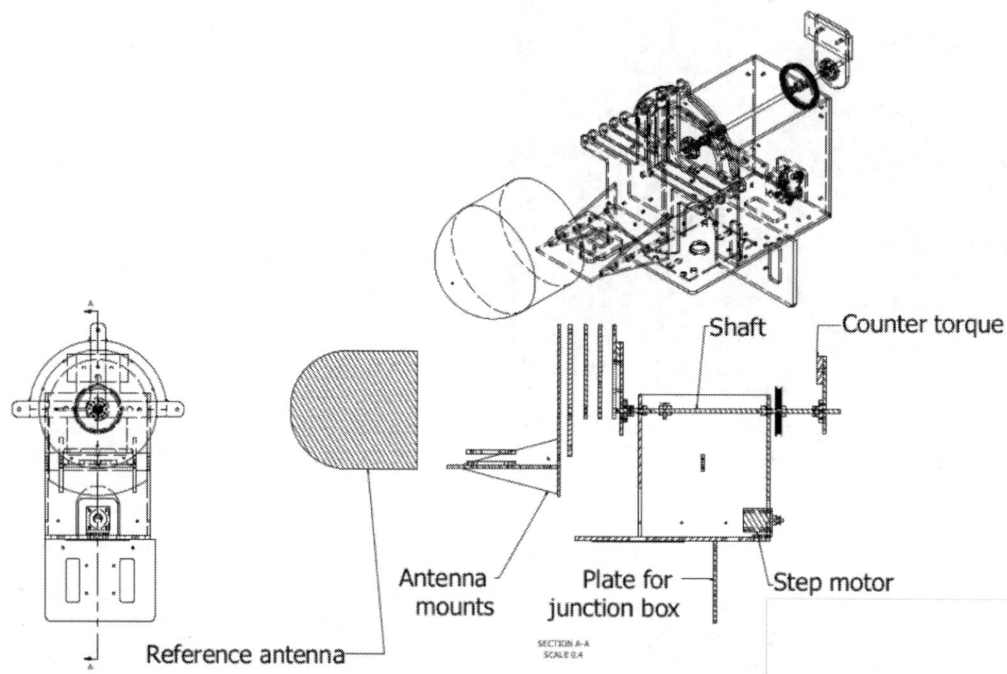

Fig. 10. The transmitter tower assembly must be able to securely mount a large variety of reference antenna geometries and masses.

(Re-)Design of a Demonstration Model for a Flexible and Decentralized Cyber-Physical Production System (CPPS)

Georg Egger[1,*], *Erwin* Rauch[2], *Dominik T.* Matt[1,2] and *Christopher A.* Brown[3]

[1] Fraunhofer Italia Research s.c.a.r.l., Innovation Engineering Center (IEC), 39100 Bolzano, Italy
[2] Faculty of Science and Technology, Free University of Bozen-Bolzano, Bolzano, 39100 Italy
[3] Dept. of Mechanical Engineering, Worcester Polytechnic Institute, Worcester, 01609, MA, USA

Abstract. Cyber-physical production systems (CPPS) enable completely new possibilities in the factory of the future through the connectivity between the digital world and the physical production system. It has so far been difficult to transfer these advantages and concepts to students as well as professionals in a clear and practical oriented manner. The Fraunhofer Italia team has built a demonstration model for a flexible and decentralized CPPS system for showcase purposes. As part of an improvement of the existing system, Axiomatic Design (AD) was applied as the scientific design theory. Starting from the identification of the Customer Attributes, Functional Requirements were derived and the Design Parameters for the new design were defined by means of the AD decomposition and mapping process. In this paper, the application of AD for product improvement is described step-by-step based on the example of the redesign of the CPPS demonstration model.

1 Introduction

Cyber-Physical Systems (CPS) and other Industry 4.0 technologies are the enablers for new business models, which have the potential to be disruptive [1]. The term "Industry 4.0" is spoken of highly as a bright vision in research and industry to revolutionize production management and the factory of the future. After mechanization, electrification and computerization of industrial production we are now at the beginning of a new epoch in production, where web technology, intelligent automation as well as digitalization supports the development of CPS [2].

Many companies in various industries have reorganized their production in the recent past, following the principles of Lean Production [3, 4] or even taking advantage of novel production strategies such as Agile Manufacturing [5] and Mass Customization [6], and thereby increasing flexibility and achieving significant progress in productivity and in readiness for delivery [7].

New Industry 4.0 technologies and CPS enable completely new opportunities for the realization of highly efficient and responsive production systems for the production of individual products on demand. Industry 4.0 technologies facilitate the fabrication of customized products and thus, the concept of mass customization [8].

The majority of enterprises is still quite sceptical regarding the vision of Industry 4.0. In addition, large enterprises tend to feel better prepared than small enterprises. In other words, SMEs still show deficits compared to large enterprises [9].

Thus, Industry 4.0 represents a special challenge for businesses, but also for education. One possibility to train employees as well as students in Industry 4.0 technologies is learning factories. Learning factories can make a substantial contribution toward the understanding of Industry 4.0. Workplace-related scenarios can be mapped providing practical learning. This process enables participants to transfer learned knowledge directly to the own workplace [10]. In recent years, a large number of learning factories have been created for the purpose of knowledge transfer [10, 11, 12]. However, it is not always possible to train and show these emerging concepts directly in a real factory environment. Therefore, demonstration models are a popular alternative and complementary solution, where the concepts and technologies can be demonstrated and explained in a miniaturized way to employees and students.

The paper shows an Axiomatic Design (AD) based redesign of demonstration model of a flexible and decentralized Cyber-Physical Production Systems (CPPS). The demonstration model created by Fraunhofer Italia is intended to facilitate the knowledge transfer of Industry 4.0 concepts to project partners, industrial firms as well as students from schools and universities. The paper is structured as follows: after this introduction, the authors summarize the theoretical background on CPPS and demonstration models. Afterwards, the current design of the demonstration model is described in detail in section 3. In section 4, the authors show an AD based approach starting with the collection of the Customer Attributes (CAs) and defining the Functional

* Corresponding author: georg.egger@fraunhofer.it

Requirements (FRs). After this, they derive the Design Parameters (DPs) of the new model through an AD decomposition and mapping process. In section 5, they illustrate the redesigned concept for the demonstration model and close the paper with a brief summary and an outlook for future research activities.

2 Theoretical background

The theory section presents a brief overview and the state of the art regarding to CPPS as well as the purpose and use of demonstration models.

2.1 Industry 4.0 and Cyber-Physical Production Systems (CPPS)

The term cyber-physical system (CPS) stands for the continuously increasing presence of computing and communication capabilities in physical objects in the real world. The decision making process of such systems may be supported or handled autonomously by computational intelligence.

The concept of CPS has already been the subject of research for over 10 years [13], although first in other than production-related contexts. When the vision of Industry 4.0 was formulated [14], direct reference to CPS for production industry was made. CPS positively affected manufacturing in form of CPPS in process automation and control [15]. Since then, the terms Industry 4.0 and CPPS are used for the impact of the macro-trend digitalization on the production industry (see Fig. 1).

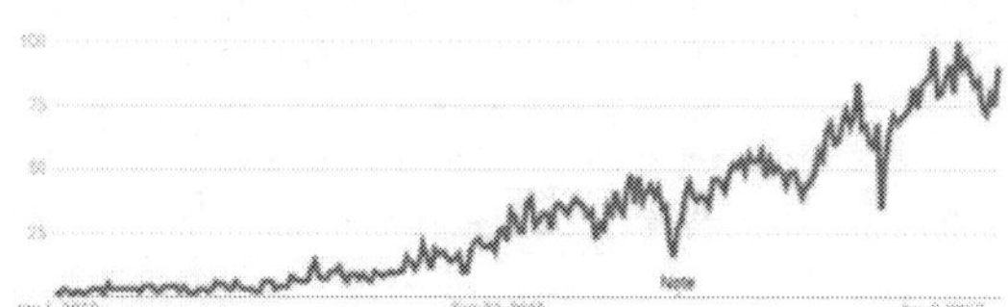

Fig. 1. Increasing (relative) popularity of the search term "Industry 4.0" on Google since 2013 (the term was particularly popular in Germany, Italy, Japan, India and the UK) [16]. The values indicate the search interest relative to the highest point in the chart in the specified period.

The vision of Industry 4.0 tries to respond to today's challenges like [14]:

- Demand for improved efficiency, especially in developed countries, in terms of productivity and energy efficiency,
- Trend towards individualisation and small batch sizes,
- Need to create horizontal value networks extending across businesses.

In order to achieve the goals, Industry 4.0 foresees 4 pillars [17]: Interconnection of humans and machines via the Internet, information transparency between the physical world and its virtual model, autonomous decisions at lowest possible level (decentralised), and finally, technical assistance in decision making and problem solving to humans to cope with the ever more complex CPPS. Across all pillars, standards, security, safety and human-machine-interfaces play a significant role.

The term Industry 4.0 is often being used by suppliers and governmental bodies, and on technical components that are sold by numerous suppliers. However, its practical use in factories is impeded by shortcomings in, for example, the lack of common standards for both horizontal and vertical integration, models for controlling complex structures, and qualified personnel [18]. Consequently, companies, especially small and medium sized enterprises (SMEs), are often forced to postpone the comprehensive adoption of the concepts of Industry 4.0.

2.2 Industry 4.0 Labs and Demonstration Models

Demonstration in a safe environment ("sandboxing") overcomes part of the obstacles in implementing Industry 4.0 concepts in production, because it does not affect the operational production. This encourages the experimental use of advanced methods for controlling productions and innovative technologies, and creates a breeding ground of regional innovation by training the involved people. If such an infrastructure is located in an independent institution like a Fraunhofer Institute, open to all interested companies, its effectiveness is maximised and a positive impact to the regional companies can be achieved.

These benefits were already recognised particularly in Germany, where application examples, laboratories and test centres are united through the network "Plattform Industrie 4.0" [19]. This platform counts almost 284 test examples for Industry 4.0. Such labs and application centres benefit from a favourable ecosystem, e.g., universities with relevant research focus, or suppliers of technologies. For example, in Kaiserslautern, where the German Research Centre for Artificial Intelligence (DFKI) partnered up with the local technical university and well-known companies such as Siemens, Bosch, SAP and several others, a supplier-independent Smart Factory lab for innovative technologies, control architectures and components, as well as a consulting services for interested companies was created [20]. The initiative fostered a successful ecosystem and soon several other companies participated in the initiative.

Demonstration is an important step towards the implementation of Industry 4.0 concepts in companies [20], where smart factory labs are an obvious step to make. The major R&D challenges for demonstration models are listed here for a summary [20]:

- Context-adaptive and (at least partially) autonomous systems,
- Cooperative production systems,
- Identification and prediction of dynamical systems,
- Robust scheduling,
- Fusion of real and virtual systems,
- Human–machine symbiosis.

 DOI: 10.1051/matecconf/201712701016

In order to enhance usefulness, the ability to demonstrate the potential of Industry 4.0 to the interested audience to perform research in one or more of the fields listed above needs to be developed.

3 Current design of the Demonstration Model

The current model was built by a team of Fraunhofer Italia researchers and students to demonstrate the potentials of a cyber-physical production system in the factory of the future. The model has been presented the first time in public during the long night of research in September 2016 in the Free University of Bolzano. Mainly the model aims to demonstrate the following concepts of typical and modern factory of the future concepts to students and SMEs:

- Flexible Transport System
- Intelligent Workpiece Carrier
- Decentralized Control
- Digital Interconnection
- Efficient Human-Machine Interface.

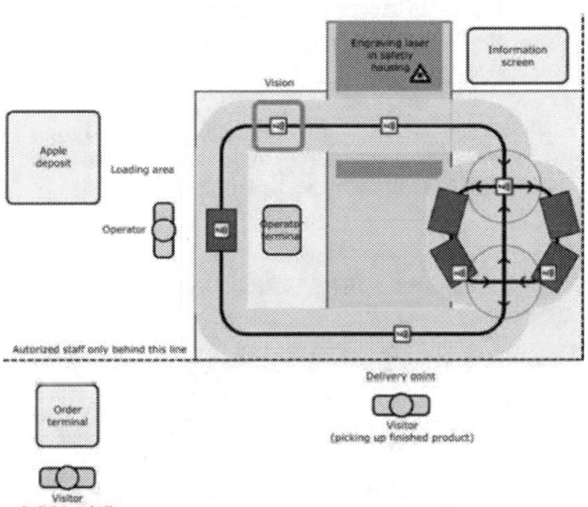

Fig. 2. System Architecture of the demonstration model. Yellow areas around the black tape indicate the boundaries of vehicle navigation; purple rectangles represent the dimensions of the vehicles; dotted circles indicate the manoeuvring area around crossings, which should be respected by the other vehicles.

Figure 2 and 3 illustrate the system architecture and the real demonstration model consisting of a:

- Laser engraving head
- Safety housing (custom design)
- Fume extraction unit
- Air compressor
- NFC (near field communication) pads
- Vehicles for product transport.

The vehicles presented in Figures 3 and 4 consist of a commercial robotic platform with 4 DC motors, an Arduino-compatible controller board, an internally developed apple-spin mechanism (apple symmetry axis aligns to spin axis), a custom built line sensor with 8 analogue sensors, an IR distance sensor for collision avoidance, an apple-eject mechanism, and a control algorithm (line follower) with routing capability and the ability to detect and take crossings. In addition, a user interface was developed to get orders from a computer terminal. Visitors may enter their name and a personal message to be engraved on the apple. After confirmation through an individual RFID card or tag. Before the order is executed, the message needs approval by a human operator. When ready, a screen informs the visitor to pick up his apple. Visitors need to present their RFID card in order to start the delivery of the apple.

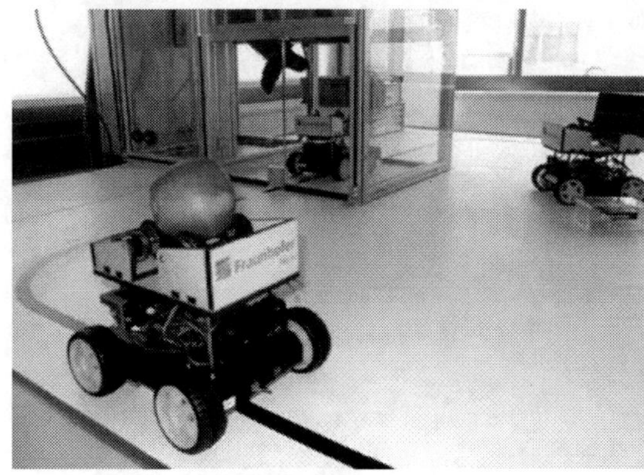

Fig. 3. CPPS demonstration model.

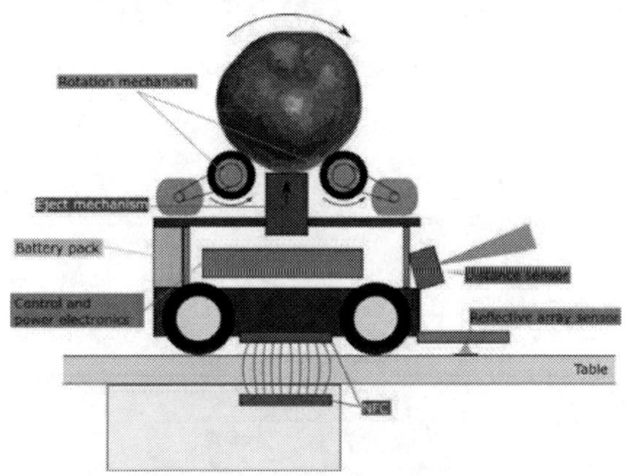

Fig. 4. Semi-autonomous vehicle - schematic view with major subsystems including (near-field communication) NFC connection between vehicle and stationary parts (pads).

4 Re-design of the CPPS Demonstration Model using Axiomatic Design (AD)

After the first successes of the demonstration model at the Long Night of Research, it should now be presented to a larger audience by planning to disassemble the model and transport it in an efficiently way and to build it up on-site at schools, SMEs, universities or other facilities or events. For this purpose, the design is revised, further functions should be integrated and at the same time analysed critically regarding design flaws and possible improvements. For this purpose, a workshop was held in the presence of an AD expert.

AD was developed by Nam P. Suh in the mid-1970s in the pursuit of developing a scientific, generalized, codified, and systematic procedure for design. The scientific theory get its name from two axioms in AD that have to be respected. The first is the Independence Axiom: Maintain the independence of the functional elements, i.e., avoid coupling in the system (e.g., avoiding dependencies between the DPs and other FRs). The second is the Information Axiom: Minimize the information content: select the solution with the least information content, i.e., that has the highest probability of success [21]. In order to apply these axioms, parallel functional and physical hierarchies are constructed, the latter containing the physical design solutions. The impact of AD is that the designer learns how to construct large design hierarchies quickly that are more structured, thus freeing more time for mastering applications [22].

In the initial workshop, requirements and so-called CAs were collected. Based on this input, FRs and Cs are defined and design parameters for a redesign were derived in an AD top-down decomposition and mapping process.

4.1 Workshop to define Customer Attributes (CAs)

In the workshop, the research team collected the requirements and needs and categorized them in the following groups [23]:

a) Constraints (Cs) are usually hard limits or values (minimum, maximum, between).
b) Functional Requirements (FRs) help the designer in the determination of the sub-levels requirements and related design solutions. They should be independent from each other to comply with axiom one, reduce complexity of the system design and are characterizing the functional needs of the artefact.
c) Non-Functional Requirements (non-FRs) focus on "how" the artefact should be (usually "should be" together with an adjective) and can influence functional requirements.

The following CAs could be identified (see Table 1):

Table 1. Customer Attributes (CAs).

Nr.	Customer Attribute	C, FR, n-FR	Existing
CA_1	Demonstrate intelligent and decentralized control of individualized production (lot size 1)	→ FR_4	Yes
CA_2	Permit rapid scaling of the capacity up and down automatically	→ FR_2	In part
CA_3	The product should have a local link and allow marketing of the region of South Tyrol	→ n-FR_1	Yes
CA_4	The model should be realized with students for training purpose	→ n-FR_2	Yes
CA_5	The demonstration model should show a complete production process	→ n-FR_3	In part
CA_6	The maximal budget for realization are 20,000 Euro	→ C_1	Yes
CA_7	Modularity in order to reuse the single components also in other educational or research settings.	→ C_3	Yes
CA_8	Maximum space for the demonstration model is 6 m²	→ C_2	Yes
CA_9	The demonstration model needs to be movable to use it in different events and facilities	→ C_4	In part
CA_{10}	Safety for user and visitors has to be guaranteed	→ FR_3	Yes
CA_{11}	Allow interaction between visitor and the CPPS demo model	→ FR_3	Yes
CA_{12}	Traceability of orders	→ FR_4	In part
CA_{13}	Quality check of the order before delivery	→ FR_3	In part
CA_{14}	Delocalisation of order entry (e.g. on mobile devices)	→ FR_3	Yes
CA_{15}	Demonstration of advanced industrial robotics in the CPPS	→ FR_1	No
CA_{16}	Experience the production from the point of view of the product	→ FR_5	No

Table 1 shows also if the requirements are fully fulfilled or only partly fulfilled (improvable) in the current demonstration model or if they are new.

4.2 Definition of high-level Functional Requirements (FRs) and Design Parameters (DPs)

The highest level of FRs and DPs are:

FR_0 Demonstrate Industry 4.0 concepts for CPPS in a practical way.

DP_0 Demonstration Model for a flexible and decentralized CPPS.

Based on the outcome of the initial workshop the following Cs for the (re)design were defined:

C_1 Maximum total budget of 20,000 Euro for new investments.
C_2 Maximum space of 6 square meters.
C_3 Modular structure with standard components.
C_4 Mobility of the demo model for flexible use.

Further the following n-FRs were defined:

n-FR_1 Products should have a local link with the region of South Tyrol.
n-FR_2 The model should be realized and run with the support of students for training purpose.
n-FR_3 The demonstration model should show a complete production process.

Finally the remaining CAs were associated to high-level Functional Requirements deriving Design Parameters:

FR_1 Apply advanced industrial robotics in the CPPS.
FR_2 Allow automatic scaling of capacity up and down.
FR_3 Ensure safety during operation of personnel, visitors and equipment.
FR_4 Event-based dynamic control and monitoring of a production line for mass customized products.
FR_5 Visualize the production from the point of view of the product.

DP_1 Lightweight robot and vision system for bin picking at the loading station.
DP_2 Buffer for waiting vehicles and automatic call.
DP_3 Safe user-interface between user/visitor and the cyber-physical system
DP_4 Intelligent and autonomous vehicles driven by a decentralized control architecture.
DP_5 Camera system on the work piece carrier.

The design matrix on the first level is decoupled and shows the dependencies between the solutions (DPs) and the functional requirements (FRs):

$$\begin{Bmatrix} FR_1 \\ FR_2 \\ FR_3 \\ FR_4 \\ FR_5 \end{Bmatrix} = \begin{bmatrix} X & 0 & 0 & 0 & 0 \\ X & X & 0 & 0 & 0 \\ 0 & 0 & X & 0 & 0 \\ X & 0 & X & X & 0 \\ 0 & 0 & 0 & X & X \end{bmatrix} \begin{Bmatrix} DP_1 \\ DP_2 \\ DP_3 \\ DP_4 \\ DP_5 \end{Bmatrix} \quad (1)$$

DP_1 has also influence on FR_2 and FR_4 and DP_3 has influence on FR_4. The same holds for DP_4 and FR_5. These off-diagonal interactions, showing a coupling of DPs and other FRs, are explained more in detail in Section 4.3.6 on the different levels. Figure 5 shows the FR-DP tree of the highest hierarchical levels.

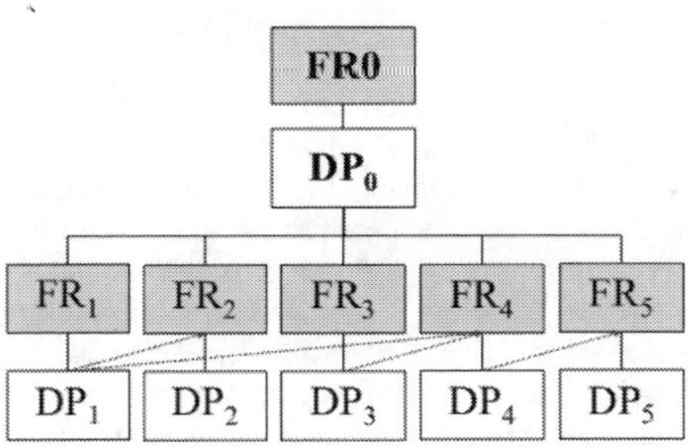

Fig. 5. Highest-level FR-DP tree.

4.3 Top-Down decomposition and mapping process

The decomposition process of top-level FRs and DPs aims to transform the abstract requirements into more concrete parameters that are close to the daily practice and therefore relevant for implementation. The FR-DP pairs on the highest hierarchical level represented in Figure 5 are a starting point for the top-down decomposition and mapping process in AD. The decomposition is performed separately for each of the FR-DP pairs shown in Figure 5 to obtain a better understanding of the process.

4.3.1 FR_1-DP_1 – Industrial Robotics

Industrial robotics can be integrated using a lightweight robot for picking apples from the container and loading them on the vehicles. Starting from FR_1, further FRs and DPs of the successive hierarchical level can be defined as follows:

$FR_{1.1}$ Localize and identify apple for flexible feeding.
$FR_{1.2}$ Grasping of sensitive products.

$DP_{1.1}$ Lightweight robot combined with vision system for bin picking of the apple.
$DP_{1.2}$ Flexible gripper for complex and sensitive products.

The design matrix shows an uncoupled design:

$$\begin{Bmatrix} FR_{1.1} \\ FR_{1.2} \end{Bmatrix} = \begin{bmatrix} X & 0 \\ 0 & X \end{bmatrix} \begin{Bmatrix} DP_{1.1} \\ DP_{1.2} \end{Bmatrix} \quad (2)$$

For flexible feeding, the research team can use existing equipment. A mobile station with a mounted UR3 lightweight robot combined with a camera system allows flexible feeding without additional investments. For grasping the apples, a flexible and sensitive gripper is required to avoid damages to the product.

4.3.2 FR_2-DP_2 – Scalability

Scalability is a major requirement of modern production systems. While in the current demonstration model the number of vehicles is fixed, a buffer should be created in the redesigned demonstration model. All other stations (laser engraving and robotized loading station) are sufficiently rapidly scalable in their performance. Vehicles not needed in periods with low demand can be parked in the buffer to reduce energy consumption in the system, while they are called automatically, when demand is rising. FR_2 can be decomposed further as follows:

$FR_{2.1}$ Provide function for rapid scaling down
$FR_{2.2}$ Provide function for rapid scaling up to guarantee capacity for higher demand.

$DP_{2.1}$ Crossing points with NFC pads to detect vehicle direction for ejection of the vehicles in a buffer line.
$DP_{2.2}$ Buffer line with sufficient length to guarantee the needed capacity.

The design matrix shows an uncoupled design:

$$\begin{Bmatrix} FR_{2.1} \\ FR_{2.2} \end{Bmatrix} = \begin{bmatrix} X & 0 \\ 0 & X \end{bmatrix} \begin{Bmatrix} DP_{2.1} \\ DP_{2.2} \end{Bmatrix} \quad (3)$$

To realize the buffer line some more NFC pads have to be made for integration in the demonstration model. In addition, the dimensions (length) of the buffer line shall be defined according to the maximum number of vehicles, in order to guarantee the expected performance of the model during visitor presentations.

4.3.3 FR_3-DP_3 – Interaction User-System

To increase the attention and know-how transfer during visitor presentations the model should allow for interaction between the visitor/user and the CPPS. In the current demonstration model, visitors may create an individual order for writing an individual text on an apple by using a desktop station or their smartphone. Any order requires approval by a supervisor (in order to avoid inappropriate texts). To avoid injuries and malfunctions of the production equipment, the visitor cannot touch the vehicles or any other stations, and the finished apple ejects to a withdrawal tray, where the visitor may grasp it without interfering with the vehicle itself. In the current system, a quality check is missing for the simulation of a complete production process. Further, in addition to the visualization on a screen, the result of the quality check as well as the availability of the apple at the delivery station should be sent to the visitor via app. Thus, this new functions should be integrated in the redesigned demonstration model. FR_3 can be decomposed in the following lower level FRs and DPs:

- $FR_{3.1}$ Prevent direct intervention by the user in unsafe areas
- $FR_{3.2}$ Create individual order in-situ or remotely.
- $FR_{3.3}$ Compliance check of incoming orders.
- $FR_{3.4}$ Quality check after processing.
- $FR_{3.5}$ Inform user/visitor about the order progress.

- $DP_{3.1}$ Separation of unsafe areas (e.g. through acrylic glass screen).
- $DP_{3.2}$ Order creation (individual text on the apple) at the order terminal or via smartphone (app).
- $DP_{3.3}$ Approval by supervisor on a monitor screen.
- $DP_{3.4}$ Camera system at laser engraving station to compare the result with the text in the order.
- $DP_{3.5}$ Notification to the visitor after laser engraving station and at delivery station.

The design matrix shows a decoupled design:

$$\begin{Bmatrix} FR_{3.1} \\ FR_{3.2} \\ FR_{3.3} \\ FR_{3.4} \\ FR_{3.5} \end{Bmatrix} = \begin{bmatrix} X & 0 & 0 & 0 & 0 \\ 0 & X & 0 & 0 & 0 \\ 0 & X & X & 0 & 0 \\ 0 & 0 & 0 & X & 0 \\ 0 & 0 & 0 & X & X \end{bmatrix} \begin{Bmatrix} DP_{3.1} \\ DP_{3.2} \\ DP_{3.3} \\ DP_{3.4} \\ DP_{3.5} \end{Bmatrix} \quad (4)$$

In addition to the diagonal interactions, $DP_{3.2}$ also influences $FR_{3.3}$. This influence occurs, because a remote order creation via smartphone in $DP_{3.2}$ allows visitors to write a text on the apple. To avoid non-suitable text writing during demonstrations the text needs to be checked manually for its compliance ($FR_{3.3}$). Furthermore also $DP_{3.4}$ shows an influence on $FR_{3.5}$. The result of the quality check at the laser engraving station ($DP_{3.4}$) determines, if information can be transmitted and visualized to the user/visitor ($FR_{3.5}$).

While $DP_{3.1}$ to $DP_{3.3}$ were already part of the original model, the other two DPs shall be implemented in the redesigned demonstration model.

4.3.4 FR_4-DP_4 – Decentralized Control

The decentralized control as well as the traceability of mass customized products in the demonstration model is currently solved by the use of intelligent (NFC technology) and autonomous vehicles. FR_4 can be decomposed in the following lower level FRs and DPs:

- $FR_{4.1}$ Vehicles shall be aware of their position and communicate with the CPPS.
- $FR_{4.2}$ Bring mass customized products decentralized to their next processing station.

- $DP_{4.1}$ NFC technology for both communication and location awareness.
- $DP_{4.2}$ Autonomously navigating vehicles with their own drive, routing capability and controller for every work piece carrier.

The design matrix shows an uncoupled design:

$$\begin{Bmatrix} FR_{4.1} \\ FR_{4.2} \end{Bmatrix} = \begin{bmatrix} X & 0 \\ 0 & X \end{bmatrix} \begin{Bmatrix} DP_{4.1} \\ DP_{4.2} \end{Bmatrix} \quad (5)$$

The choice for NFC is motivated by the fact that it provides superior robustness against electromagnetic disturbances typical for an industrial production environment and the well-defined range of operation, which allows its use not only for communication purposes but also for unambiguous position detection. Same also for the modular vehicles built with standard components and hence there are no design changes in this FR-DP pair.

4.3.5 FR_5-DP_5 – User Experience

The demonstration model should allow the visitor to follow the steps in the production process from the point of view of the product. In the current demonstration model this function was not integrated. There is no need to decompose this FR-DP pair any further, as DP_5 can be implemented through a standard camera mounted on the vehicle. The livestream of the camera shall be transmitted to the information screen and allows the visitors following the production process from loading the apple, rotating the apple in the right position, laser engraving and ejection in the delivery station.

4.3.6 Overall design matrix and summary

The decomposition and mapping process helped the research team to better structure the requirements and to derive systematically the physical design solutions (DPs) without increasing complexity of the design. In developing the final design concept the constraints identified in section 4.2 shall be respected. Figure 6 summarizes the overall design matrix at first and second level in the Axiomatic Design software Acclaro DFFS.

DOI: 10.1051/matecconf/201712701016

As shown in the decoupled first level design matrix in equation (1) some DPs influence other FRs. The overall design matrix in Figure 6 explains this influence in the lower levels. The maximum performance of the selected industrial lightweight robot in $DP_{1.1}$ determines also the maximum length of the buffer line to scale up the capacity of the system ($FR_{2.2}$). Further, $DP_{1.1}$ has influence on $FR_{4.1}$, as the industrial robot needs information on the position of vehicles in order to pick the apple and place it on the vehicles. Also $DP_{3.5}$ is affecting $FR_{4.1}$, as the status notification at the delivery station needs position data of the vehicles. The last off-diagonal interaction is between $DP_{4.1}$ as well as $DP_{4.2}$ and FR_5. Both DPs (NFC as communication technology and the use of autonomously navigating vehicles) influence the possibilities to visualize the production from the point of view of the product.

The demo model is built up in a modular way, costs less than 20 k€ and occupies less than 6 m^2. Furthermore, the n-FR are fulfilled: with bin picking and final quality control a complete production process of a local product is simulated and the demo model will be realized with the support of students at Fraunhofer Italia.

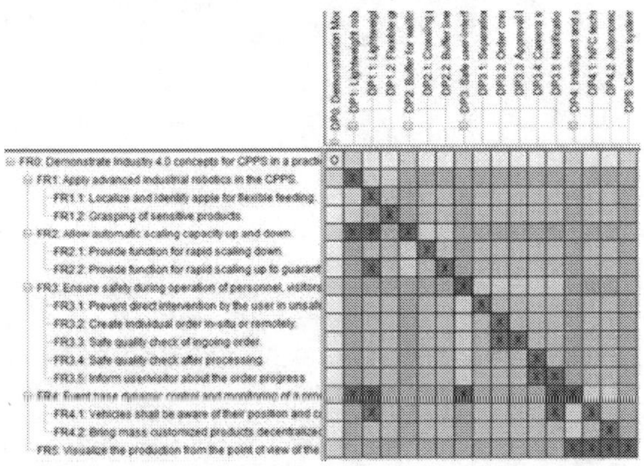

Fig. 6. Summarizing first and second level design matrix.

5 Concept of the redesigned and improved CPPS Demonstration Model

The analysis in section 4 revealed and improved a few weaknesses of the original demonstrator design, such as:

- Operation of the demonstrator required at least two people: One person is required for the actual operation in the reserved area and one for interacting with the visitors. This aspect is improved by inserting a bin-picking robotic arm in the layout, in line with $DP_{1.1}$.
- The manual placement of the apples did not require the rotation mechanism, if the operator oriented the apple correctly, as he loads the vehicle. The bin-picking gripper (result of $DP_{1.2}$) likewise disposes of such functionality, and consequently a holding cup substitutes the now obsolete rotation mechanism on the vehicles.
- Vehicles could not be automatically added to the production process for rapid scalability, i.e., immediate, decentralized adjustment of the production rate; this had to occur manually and was relying on the operator recognizing the current demand. As suggested by DP_2 a dedicated buffer line improves this situation. The required areas are obtained by re-designing the available board area. In the back, also the lateral boards now extend to the full length and the track layout considers the central area too. As a positive side effect, the overall capacity of the demonstrator was increased.
- In the waiting queues, empty and occupied vehicles were mixed in the two parking lanes. This not only violates the independence axiom, but also impedes an independent management of the vehicles required for loading area and delivery point, which resulted in unnecessarily frequent relocations of the vehicles and complex queue management.
- The table was not designed for optimal mobile use. The setup required additional structure elements to carry the tables and the cabling underneath did not allow quick and reliable setup. In line with C_3 the tables were put on their own support structure and equipped with wheels. Further, the boards are hold together with two wing nuts, which do not even require tools for mounting and dismounting. Similarly, each board is pre-wired and the electrical interconnection of all low voltage systems can be realized with RJ45 patch cables from board to board. While a field bus interconnected the NFC pads, other low-level I/O's were excluded from that system, resulting in a heterogeneous wiring and unhandy complexity. New developed devices on the field bus substituted these non-standard components. Also, on underneath the boards, the mechanical placement of the field bus devices underwent unification process. Whereas previously each device was screwed into a particular position, rails were installed accommodating the field bus components. Now a displacement along the rails is easily possible for all components.
- The vehicles and the NFC pads have been subject of continuous improvement since the public presentation of the demonstrator. The field bus system and the associated communication protocol were continuously expanded. The NFC library was completely rewritten for improved reliability and usability. Also, the precision of the line follower algorithm was improved significantly reducing lateral motion.
- As one of the major goals of the demonstrator is to reach public attention for our research, also the non-functional aspects deserves attention, such as an attractive presentation. Previously the information screen merely informed the visitors when product were ready and showed videos from a fixed camera inside the laser housing – the latter mainly due to safety concerns. It turned out that the videos attracted much attention, though vehicles rested only briefly inside the laser. As suggested by DP_5 the presentational aspect improves significantly by transmitting live video from a camera mounted on a vehicle. The resources on the vehicles previously

used for the rotational mechanism may now be conveniently used for video transmission.

Most of the improvements are reflected in the layout of the demonstrator, which is illustrated in Figure 7.

In the redesigned demonstration model there is a clear distinction between active waiting for jobs (green), active waiting for delivery (purple) and standby in the buffer line (blue) vehicles. The loading mechanism not only grips the apples and places them on the vehicles, but also aligns them so that the rotation mechanism of the vehicles becomes obsolete. Hence, the vison process is now part of the loading. The operator is relieved from repetitive loading and may assist visitors. In addition, visitor may place orders remotely.

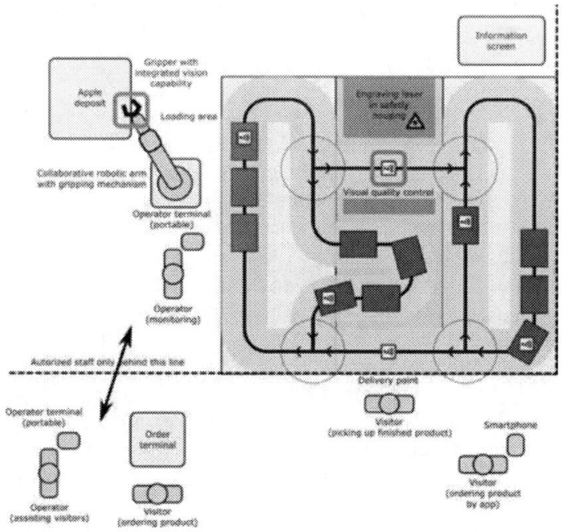

Fig. 7. System Architecture of the redesigned demonstration model.

6 Conclusion and outlook for future research

The present research activity has shown that axiomatic design is a powerful tool not only for new designs, but also for analysing and improving existing designs. It helped particularly in sharpening the focus on the original objectives, which during the implementation phase of the demonstrator got fuzzy. Furthermore, the systematic exercise of applying axiomatic design theory identified also gaps in the previous design, like e.g. the lack of quality control, missing buffer line, redundancy in functions (rotation mechanism, manual placement). Overall, the demonstrator benefits significantly from the activity: Its capacity increased just by changing the topology of the tracks, at the same time the control algorithms are simplified and the presentational quality improves by including also bin-picking robotic arm and live videos directly from the vehicles. Finally, the demonstrator gained in efficiency, as less people are required for operation and setup.

There remain some points for improvement:

- The overall weight of the demonstrator is unchanged, which hinders its portability. Particularly the laser (safety housing, fume extractor unit and compressor) is massive and in future lighter alternatives may be explored.
- The reliability of the vehicle motion control turned out to be limited without position feedback, as the wheels slip on the surface, which increases with usage. The use of inertial measurement units could improve the accuracy of movement particularly at crossings.
- When developing the updated setup, a variety of possible topologies was found. Without proper means of simulating their performance, the authors had to estimate the performance based on their experience. A quantitative confirmation of this result, as well as exploration of other possible topologies (e.g. a full mesh topology, Figure 8) is of interest to the authors and may be addressed in future work.

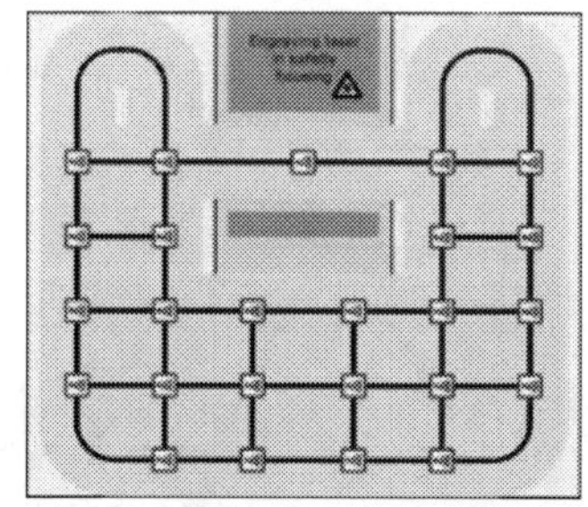

Fig. 8. Full mesh topology allowing dynamic reorganisation of the layout at the cost of several NFC pads. Its benefit and the potential reduction shall be analysed with adequate means of simulation in future.

The results of this research activity are applicable also to ongoing research projects, such as "DeConPro2, which shares many of the objectives of the demonstrator. The focus is on decentralized control, with realization of a model factory with industrial-grade components.

In the research project "SME 4.0", two work packages will develop design concepts for highly adaptable and intelligent CPPS for SME. As the working title already reveals, research focuses on the development of new concepts and the adaptation of existing approaches that are especially suitable for SME.

efre·fesr
Südtirol · Alto Adige
Europäischer Fonds für regionale Entwicklung
Fondo europeo di sviluppo regionale

This research is part of actual research activities in the project DeConPro (Decentralized control of production processes in the factory of the future) and in the project SME 4.0 (Industry 4.0 for SMEs). The first has received funding from the European Regional Development Fund ERDF 2014-2020 under the grant agreement with project code FESR1017 (CUP B56J16001730001) and the second from the European Union's Horizon 2020 research and innovation program under the Marie Skłodowska-Curie grant agreement No 734713.

References

1. E. Rauch, S. Seidenstricker, P. Dallasega, R. Hämmerl, Collaborative Cloud Manufacturing: Design of Business Model Innovations Enabled by Cyberphysical Systems in Distributed Manufacturing Systems, Journal of Engineering, Article ID 1308639, 12 pages (2016).
2. S.P.A. Datta, Dynamic socio-economic disequilibrium catalyzed by the Internet of Things. Available from http://dspace.mit.edu/bitstream/handle/1721.1/86935/Dynamic%20Socio-Economic%20Disequilibrium%20_%20Shoumen%20Datta.pdf?sequence=226 [Accessed 06th February 2016], pp. 1-9, (2014).
3. D.T. Matt, E. Rauch, Implementing Lean in Engineer-to-order manufacturing - Experiences from a ETO Manufacturer, in: Modrák, V.; Semančo, P. (Eds.), *Handbook of Research on Design and Management of Lean Production Systems*, Hershey, IGI Global, 148-172, (2014).
4. N.V.K., Jasti, R. Kodali, Lean production: literature review and trends. International Journal of Production Research, 53(3), 867-885, (2015).
5. D.T. Matt, E. Rauch, Design of a scalable modular production system for a two-stage food service franchise system, International Journal of Engineering Business Management, **32**, 4 (2012).
6. B. Stump, F. Badurdeen, Integrating lean and other strategies for mass customization manufacturing: a case study, Journal of Intelligent manufacturing, **23**, 1, 109-124, (2012).
7. M. Brettel, N. Friederichsen, M. Keller, M. Rosenberg, How Virtualization, Decentralization and Network Building Change the Manufacturing Landscape: An Industry 4.0 Perspective, International Journal of Mechanical, Aerospace, Industrial, Mechatronic and Manufacturing Engineering, **8**, 1, 37-44, (2014).
8. D.T. Matt, E. Rauch, Designing assembly lines for mass customization production systems, in V. Modrák, D. Mourtzis (Eds.), *Mass Customized Manufacturing: Theoretical Concepts and Practical Findings*, Boca Raton, CRC Press Francis & Taylor, 15-35, (2017).
9. L. Sommer, Industrial revolution-industry 4.0: Are German manufacturing SMEs the first victims of this revolution? Journal of Industrial Engineering and Management, **8**, 5, 1512-1532, (2015).
10. C. Prinz, F. Morlock, S. Freith, N. Kreggenfeld, D. Kreimeier, B. Kuhlenkötter, Learning Factory Modules for Smart Factories in Industrie 4.0, Procedia CIRP, **54**, 113-118, (2016).
11. D.T. Matt, E. Rauch, E., P. Dallasega, Mini-factory–a learning factory concept for students and small and medium sized enterprises, Procedia CIRP, **17**, 178-183, (2014).
12. C. Faller, D. Feldmüller, Industry 4.0 learning factory for regional SMEs, Procedia CIRP, **32**, 88-91, (2015).
13. R. Rajkumar, I. Lee, L. Sha, J. Stankovic, Cyber-Physical Systems: The Next Computing Revolution, Design Automation Conference, June 2010, 731-736, (2010).
14. H. Kagermann, W. Wahlster, J. Helbig, Securing the future of German manufacturing industry, Recommendations for implementing the strategic initiative INDUSTRIE 4.0 Final report of the Industrie 4.0 Working Group, acatech, (2013).
15. L. Monostori, Cyber-physical production systems: roots, expectations and R&D challenges, Procedia CIRP **17**, 9-13, (2014).
16. Industry 4.0, Available from https://trends.google.com/trends/explore?q=Industry%204.0 [Accessed 24th July 2017].
17. M. Hermann, T. Pentek, B. Otto, Design Principles for Industrie 4.0 Scenarios, 49th Hawaii International Conference on System Sciences (HICSS), 3928-3937, (2016).
18. K. Zhou, T. Liu, L. Zhou, Industry 4.0: Towards future industrial opportunities and challenges, Proceedings of 12th International Conference on Fuzzy Systems and Knowledge Discovery (FSKD), 2147-2152, IEEE, (2015).
19. Labs Network Industry 4.0, Available from http://lni40.de/ [Accessed 10th April 2017].
20. D. Zuehlke, SmartFactory—Towards a factory-of-things, Annual Reviews in Control **34**, 129–138, (2010).
21. N.P. Suh, *Axiomatic Design - Advances and Applications*. New York, Oxford University Press, (2009).
22. C.A. Brown, Teaching axiomatic design to engineers—Theory, applications, and software, Journal of Manufacturing Systems, **24**, 3, 186-195, (2005).
23. M.K. Thompson, A Classification of Procedural Errors in the Definition of Functional Requirements in Axiomatic Design Theory, Proceedings of the 7th International Conference on Axiomatic Design, Worcester, MA, 107-112, (2013).

Functional Case Test Design to Optimize the Software Development in Italian Tax Processes (Part II): the F23 Tax Payment Form

Fernando Rolli*, *Chiara* Parretti, *Paolo* Citti, and *Massimo* Rinaldi

Department of Innovation and Information Engineering, Guglielmo Marconi University, Via Plinio 44 - 00193 Rome, Italy

Abstract. In this case study, the methodology of test case preparation proposed in the first article is applied to the design of a testing plan in order to verify the compliance of the functional requirements for the compiling system of an F23 tax payment form. The objective of this approach is the definition of the functional requirements coverage matrix to associate one specific test case with each system component. This methodology's aim is to equip the software designers with an accurate testing plan that is perfectly aligned with the designing logics of the system, respectively in order to optimize the time used for software implementation, to ensure that the tax deadlines are met, and to satisfy the user requirements. This approach also allows to manage a test plan configuration for the software's future versions, while having, at the same time, an updated technical documentation always available. In fact, with the application of the reuse technique we can identify the software objects affected by the technical and regulatory annual updates. Specific test cases are designed for them, whereas the unmodified components will keep the test cases used in their previous version.

1 Introduction

This article describes the AD methodology application procedures to arrange a functional testing plan process: in this specific case, the implementation involves the compiling procedures of an F23 form using a Holistic non-conformities reduction (HNCR) model [1-3]. The objective of this approach is the definition of the functional requirements coverage matrix to associate one specific test case with each system component. AD is indeed a flexible methodology suitable to be effectively applied to several range of context and scenarios whereby processes [4-5], product [6], product development [7] and teaching approach [8] optimization is required.

1.1 F23 tax payment form

The F23 tax form is used to pay certain types of taxes, fees and penalties, as provided for by the Italian fiscal regulations. More specifically, the F23 model is used to pay taxes such as registration fees, mortgage and land registry fees, which are managed by the Revenue Agency's offices. It is also used for the payment of fees for public concessions and for the payment of penalties imposed by the judicial and administrative authorities (for example, fines and penalties). In addition, the F23 form can be used by a property owner to collect his/her tenants' rents. The form is a very efficient tool, as it monitors payment delays, arrears and cash flow. This feature is important in case of disputes between a property owner and a tenant. It also allows to meet the tax obligations established by the Italian law.

1.2 Definitions and correspondences

The Revenue Agency [9, 10] defines and publishes the technical specifics and the F23 model compilation rules, which will be used, in the present study, as customer attributes (CA). For simplicity's sake, other user requirements are not considered. Starting from this data, the study proceeds with the decomposition of the functional requirements up to the necessary level of detail needed to design the testing plan. Then, it proceeds building the test case coverage matrix (M) in accordance with the proposal described in Part I of the article. Finally, it presents an example of reuse of the test case application, in case of a functionality modification in the F23 payment model. The whole method is based on a zigzagging process between the domain of the functional requirements (FR) and the domain of the data files (DP). This decomposition is summarized by an A correlation matrix. The decomposition process of the functional requirements follows the axioms of independence and information. For the first principle, the A matrix must be a diagonal or triangular matrix, whereas for the second axiom, in

* Corresponding author: f.rolli@unimarconi.it

the presence of multiple alternative configurations, it is necessary to select the functional composition entailing the minimum level of information. In the latter case, function points are an estimation tool for the system's functional size. The various test cases are built on the relationship defined by the A matrix. For this reason, each element of the A matrix must be tested with a specific test case. The final result will be the construction of the test case matrix.

2 Test case preparation

The test case coverage matrix can be built at each decomposition level of the functional requirements. Levels with a major abstraction match with the verifications related to the highest levels of the V model [11].

2.1 Decomposition process

In this context, the most abstract level coincides with the functional system trial test. The test cases that describe the actions and the operating conditions of the program to be tested are explained and made comprehensible to non-technical users. Gradually, as the decomposition of the functional requirements reaches a major level of detail, the test cases are described using technical descriptive languages, thus making them more appropriate for the operating context concerned. The lowest level of functional requirements decomposition is represented by the logical design of the system. At this level, each test case describes the unitary test of each single elementary object. A full definition of the test cases at a higher level can only be produced when the functional decomposition process is over. Therefore, starting from the elementary test cases, coinciding with the unitary test case, we can give a full definition of the test cases at a higher level. This means that the test cases placed at a higher level contain the execution of tests at their lower level. For example, the system test cases are aimed at the execution of the interfaces among the various elementary objects, but they also include the execution of the elementary test. This process leads to the highest level, which corresponds to the procedure's formal testing. This is illustrated in the V model mentioned in Article I, on the left side of the Figure 1.

2.2 Test case formalization

The test cases represent the specifics of the tests to be executed. They are defined in a theoretical form by the following triplet: < test data input, expected result, application environment and conditions >[12-16]. The set of more test cases constitutes one suite of test cases. Often, in order to be significant, test cases must be performed according to a precise logical sequence, which can be determined by the occurrence of specific conditions. In these situations, a suite of test cases is the entire sequence of tests to be performed in order to verify a specific functional requirement. The test cases must foresee a detailed description of the tests to be executed, so that the test can be repeated by different users and reused in the future versions of the product. This means that the test case must at least contain [11]:

- Test identification code number;
- Description of the test to be executed as a sequence of elementary activities;
- Pre-existing conditions for test application;
- Input data;
- Expected results;
- Anomalies encountered at execution phase;
- Tester identification;
- Date of test execution.

3 Test case decomposition procedure

3.1 First level decomposition

The AD methodology is top-down, therefore the starting point is the highest logical level. In this case, FR = compiling the F23 form. It follows that: FR=F23()*DP, where DP is the data needed to fill in the form. Let the condition be that the F23 procedure to be tested does not consist in a simple editable data entry, but rather that it can be integrated with a more complex system at an enterprise level, where data can be retrieved: this data is available in coded form within the interchange environment with the company's information system. The F23 payment form to be implemented must be verified by running a test plan [11]. Part of the testing plan consists in the verification of the adherence of the functional requirements specified by the Revenue Agency with the application's logical design. The specific V model design of the software allows to proceed with the decomposition of the functional requirements and reach the logic implementation of the system's design that joins the test plan preparation. At this stage, the software's development process involves the encoding of the system, which is firstly associated with the execution of the test on the developed elementary objects (Unit Test), then with an interface test among the basic components (System Test), and finally with the acceptance test. The trial, instead, is a contractual verification of the adherence of the product to be released with respect to the technical specifications agreed with the supplier. In this context, the test case coverage matrix allows to associate a series of relevant tests to each functional requirement.

3.2 Second level decomposition

3.2.1 Second level decomposition of functional requirements

Proceeding with the decomposition at a lower level, as summarized in Figure 1, we can define, as second level macro functional requirements, both the compilation of the F23's header and the compilation of the data concerning the actual payment:

		DP_1	DP_2
		Header Data	Payment Data
FR_1	Header	A_{11}	
FR_2	Payment		A_{22}

Fig. 1. Second level correlation matrix A.

The form's data can be edited or pre-loaded through a specific process, upon request of the company's information system. In this case, the pre-load process is activated by a specific trigger, which consists of a periodic or an extraordinary event. For example, rent billings or condominium fees allocated to tenants are to be considered as periodic events, whereas the payment of a specific administrative sanction is to be considered as an extraordinary event. In the present analysis, many steps are simplified in order to emphasize the construction of the functional test coverage matrix.

3.2.2 Detection of second level test cases

At this level, we can already start building the test case coverage matrix. The decomposition of the functional requirements enables us to identify, within the correlation matrix, the $A_{ij}()$ methods and the DP_{ij} data files that define each functional requirement. In fact, we know that $FRi=\sum_j A_{ij}()DP_{ij}$. If we consider the $A_{11}()$ element in Figure 1, we can assume that its relative test case can be formalized in the following data sheet [11]:

Table 1. Second level test case formalization.

Test Case	
Project Name	F23
CT Id	CT1
Application Version	V1.0
Test Case Object	F23 General header compilation
Test Preparation	Preparatory conditions list for testing
Test Execution	F23 Header compilation; Payer's data compilation; Beneficiary's data compilation;
Input	F23 Header data; Payer's data; Beneficiary's data
Expected Result	The F23 general header data must be saved in the DP1 database and must be visualised in the F23 model
Tester	XXXXXXX
Execution Date	03/24/2017
Anomalies Found	Header insertion not completely insertable
Test Duration	2 minutes
State	To be executed/In progress /Successfully completed
Supervised by	YYYYYYY
Date of Closure	03/26/2017

The test cases defined at this level are very general: since they entail a very high level of abstraction, they can be considered as functional for the trial test with the client. However, the functional decomposition must be completed before they are wholly formalized. Thus, unlike the functional requirements' breakdown, which is a top-down process, the decomposition of test cases is a bidirectional process that involves two phases: firstly, a general setting phase which accompanies the functional decomposition; secondly, a phase of methodical definition of the instructions to be followed for each level of decomposition. Therefore, if the decomposition of the functional requirements and the system design are not complete, it is not possible to obtain a comprehensive definition of the testing plan.

3.3 Third level decomposition

3.3.1 Functional requirements' third level decomposition

The compilation process of the F23 form is governed by the Revenue Agency's instructions [9, 10]. Therefore, we propose to match the functional decomposition of our system with the articulation of the sections of the form. At this level, Table 2 shows the correspondence between functional requirements (FR) and data files (DP).

Table 2. Functional requirements' third level decomposition.

Functional requirements	**Data files**
FR_{11}: fill the header registry	DP_{11}: Header registry
FR_{12}: compile the payer registry	DP_{12}: Payer's registry
FR_{13}: compile the recipient registry	DP_{13}: Recipient's registry
FR_{21}: compile the reason for payment	DP_{21}: Type of payment
FR_{22}: insert the payment purpose codes	DP_{22}: Payment purpose codes
FR_{23}: compile the amount of payment	DP_{23}: Amount of payment
FR_{24}: compile the payment details	DP_{24}: Payment details

This means that, at this level, the functional decomposition of the user requirements corresponds to the following correlation matrix A:

		Header data			**Payment data**			
		DP_{11}	DP_{12}	DP_{13}	DP_{21}	DP_{22}	DP_{23}	DP_{24}
FR_1	FR_{11}	$A_{11,11}$						
	FR_{12}		$A_{12,12}$					
	FR_{13}			$A_{13,13}$				
FR_2	FR_{21}				$A_{21,21}$	$A_{21,22}$		
	FR_{22}					$A_{22,22}$		
	FR_{23}						$A_{23,23}$	
	FR_{24}							$A_{24,24}$

Fig. 2. Third level correlation matrix A.

In terms of a UML simplified diagram, we obtain the diagram illustrated in the attached Figure 6.

3.3.2 Third Level Test Case Identification

The decomposition of the functional requirements enables us to identify, within the correlation matrix, the $A_{ij}()$ methods and the DP_{ij} data files that define each functional requirement. In fact, we know that $FRi=\sum_j A_{ij}()DP_{ij}$. Considering the $A_{11}()$ element of Figure

2, its corresponding test case can be formalized by the following data sheet:

Table 3. Third level test case formalization.

Test Case	
Project Name	F23
CT Id	$CT_{11,11}$
Application version	V1.0
Test Case object	F23 Header Compilation
Test Preparation	Preparatory conditions list for testing
Test execution	Execute $A_{11,11}()$, (to fill the header registry)
Input	F23 Header data
Expected result	The F23 general header data must be saved in the DP11 database and must be visualised in the F23 model
Tester	XXXXXXX
Execution date	03/24/2017
Anomalies found	Header insertion not completely insertable
Test duration	2 minutes
State	To be executed/In progress /Successfully completed
Supervised by	YYYYYYY
Date of Closure	03/26/2017

Therefore, the $CT_{11,11}$ test case is used to verify the correctness of the $A_{11,11}()$ method related to the DP_{11} data files. The input data contained in the test case are a significant subset of DP_{11}. Likewise, the other test cases are built for a complete coverage of all the relations present in the relation matrix in Figure 1. Hence, Table 4 enlists, for each method of the matrix in Figure 3, its related associated test case.

Table 4. Matching of the third-level test cases.

Methods	**Data files (DP)**	**Related Test Case**
$A_{11,11}()$: Header Data Compilation	DP_{11}	$CT_{11,11}$
$A_{12,12}()$: Payer's Data Compilation	DP_{12}	$CT_{12,12}$
$A_{13,13}()$: Data Compilation	DP_{13}	$CT_{13,13}$
$A_{21,21}()$: Payment Data Compilation	DP_{21}	$CT_{21,21}$
$A_{21,22}()$: Tax code no. Compilation	DP_{22}	$CT_{21,22}$
$A_{22,22}()$: Tax code no. Pre-Compilation	DP_{22}	$CT_{22,22}$
$A_{23,23}()$: Payment Amount Compilation	DP_{23}	$CT_{23,23}$
$A_{24,24}()$: Payment Details Compilation	DP_{24}	$CT_{24,24}$

3.4 Building the functional tests coverage matrix

At this stage, all the elements deemed necessary to build the functional tests case coverage matrix are available. First, each element of Figure 2's A matrix must contain at least one test case. In this way, we can surely verify all the functional requirements for the system implementation. Unfortunately, a robust-type test case construction is not possible, as it is impossible to build an ideal test that excludes the presence of malfunctions. Tests can detect errors, but cannot exclude their presence [15]. Reporting the test cases in Figure 2's matrix, we obtain the test case coverage matrix, as described in Figure 3.

	CT_{11}	CT_{12}	CT_{13}	CT_{21}	CT_{22}	CT_{23}	CT_{24}
FR_{11}	$CT_{11,11}$						
FR_{12}		$CT_{12,12}$					
FR_{13}			$CT_{13,13}$				
FR_{21}				$CT_{21,21}$	$CT_{21,22}$		
FR_{22}					$CT_{22,22}$		
FR_{23}						$CT_{23,23}$	
FR_{24}							$CT_{24,24}$

Fig. 3. Test case coverage matrix.

3.5 Test case execution mode

The coverage matrix of test cases also carries useful information about the sequence of testing. Considering the test case disposition in Figure 3, we can affirm that almost all test cases can be executed autonomously. In fact, they refer to functional requisites that are logically independent. We may, however, choose a test execution mode that simulates the conventional behavior of the application's user. In this case, the axiomatic decomposition of functional requirements allowed to obtain the tests execution order, which can proceed from top to bottom, and from left to right. For this reason, the $CT_{11,11}$ case test can precede $CT_{12,12}$. However, test cases related to the functional requisite FR_{21} are mutually dependent. For the same reason, the $CT_{21,21}$ case test must precede $CT_{21,22}$. In this last case, the correlation matrix shows a relation between the two test cases. This relationship of dependence between two test cases might lead to the presumption that the second test execution ($CT_{21,22}$) is ordinated to the occurrence of a specific condition in the preceding test case ($CT_{21,21}$). On the other hand, the test cases that are logically independent in the coverage matrix can be only subordinated to the execution sequence, and no logical conditions that can alter the operation are present in the preceding cases. This consideration derives directly from the axiom of independence, because they are arranged along the diagonal of the matrix [17].

4 Test case reuse

The adoption of an axiomatic design allows to reuse not only the software components, but also its supporting documentation. In the specific case of applications designed to manage the tax processing procedures, an annual adjustment is often required in compliance with the regulatory implementations and updates introduced by the law. The object-oriented development techniques allow to easily reuse the software components that are not affected by the adjustment measures, to adapt or delete the parts to be modified, and to add new items in order to meet the new functional requirements. In this case, with an axiomatic design approach we can easily identify the test cases to be reused, and to redefine the new matrix of test cases. This implies a reduction in testing time, focusing on the components modified or introduced and their relation with any pre-existing objects. In other words, the axiomatic approach can facilitate a regression testing process on a system that has been affected by an adjustment [11, 14, 16].

4.1 Cataloguing the system's logic components for reuse

The Function Point Analysis is used to identify the logic components that are subject to regulatory changes [18-20]. The function point method allows to estimate the capacity of the software components. This estimate can be used to provide a measure of comparison according to the axiom of information among different functional requirement decompositions. Thus, in the presence of an equal coverage of functional requirements, the most robust solution would be the one with a minor function point size. This would imply less a minor information content. Taking into consideration the purposes of our article, however, the function point technique is used to provide a rational cataloguing of software interventions in terms of regulatory compliance for the years to follow. Cataloguing is a useful tool to optimize the axiomatic process for the preparation of system functional tests. Therefore, the logic components that have been modified are catalogued as follows:

- DEL. These are the data files (ILF and EIF) and the transactional functions (EI, EO and EQ) that are deleted, since they are not foreseen by the new functional specifications. The deleting process involves a certain effort, which is equal to the original value in terms of deleted items' function points, in a percentage reduction;
- CHG. These are the data files and the transactional functions that continue to be used because they are still included in the technical specifications. However, they must be adjusted according to the new taxing rules;
- ADD. These are, instead, the new data files and the transactional functions provided by the new technical specifications of the Revenue Agency. They were not present in the previous software version. They need implementing.

4.2 Software update

According to the Revenue Agency's resolution dated 17th March 2016, effective from 1st January 2017, taxes, penalties and interests due for the submission of the inheritance declarations must be paid using the "F24" form, as instructed by the Revenue Agency's resolution n.16, dated 25th March 2016. With reference to the inheritance tax, the F23 form must be used in case this method of payment is specified in the documents issued by the Revenue Agency for the payment of the amounts due mentioned above. These measures required the software vendors to update the compilation procedures. Considering the type of action required, the data contained in the data files had to be updated with the tax codes and the info on the reason of payment. The program structure has remained basically unchanged. The new simplified UML diagram is illustrated in Figure 7, at the last page of this article. This new scheme can be translated into the following test coverage matrix:

	CT_{11}	CT_{12}	CT_{13}	CT_{21}	CT_{22}	CT_{23}	CT_{24}
FR_{11}	$CT_{11,11}$						
FR_{12}		$CT_{12,12}$					
FR_{13}			$CT_{13,13}$				
FR_{21}				$CT_{21,21CHG}$	$CT_{21,22CHG}$		
FR_{22}					$CT_{22,22CHG}$		
FR_{23}						$CT_{23,23}$	
FR_{24}							$CT_{24,24}$

Fig. 4. Test case coverage matrix with reuse

This means that, with the exception of test cases affected by the change of tax code and reason for payment, the test plan is unchanged and can be reused for the checks to be performed on the F23 (year 2017 version). As for the three modified test cases, a minimal intervention on the input data file is performed. Some tax codes and reasons for payment have been disabled, and new ones have been inserted. The three test cases are updated, forcing them to follow the new instructions provided by the Revenue Agency. The structure of the coverage matrix corresponds to the decomposition correlation matrix of the functional requirements. This process ensures the complete coverage of the tests and provides useful information on the sequence and the chronological order of their execution.

5 Final considerations

The decomposition of the suite of test cases follows the decomposition of the functional requirements specified in the table above. It reaches a sufficient level of detail to define all the necessary elements for its design. This equals to defining, in the decomposition matrix of the testing domain, a suite of test cases for each functional requirement. The obtained test case decomposition matrix mirrors the functional requirements decomposition matrix. It represents the minimum coverage of the test cases that verify all the functional requirements of the system. This solution will never be robust, because, as shown by Dijkstra [15], program testings can detect the presence of malfunctions, but cannot demonstrate their absence. This means that the functional test coverage does not guarantee the absence of malfunctions in the system. In terms of fiscal management software, our advantage lies in the fact that the fiscal procedures have an annual characterization. Therefore, the observation, the cataloguing and the analysis of historical non-conformities allows to proactively identify any critical areas, as already described in part I. For this reason, any additional test cases that might be required can be entered in the CT matrix. The test case decomposition matrix would no longer respect the axiom of information because it would add test cases with a greater amount of information, but at the same time with a higher probability of detecting the malfunctions. Of course, a test case that contains multiple test trials requires more resources and more time for its preparation as well as for the following execution phase of the developed software. This leads to a trade-off instance, as to whether to release the application first -implying a high risk of non-conformities for the final customer- or to continue with the testing activities and debugging -thus jeopardizing the final delivery deadlines. For this purpose, Musa and Ackermann [11, 21] have designed the so-called fault removal curve, which is based on the following formula:

$$V(t)=V_0\,(1-e^{-(\lambda_0/V_0)t}) \quad (1)$$

where V_0 represents the number of expected errors. This figure can easily be derived if we consider the historical series of the past fiscal software versions [21-23]. λ_0 represents, however, the number of errors detected during the first day of tests. The curve can also be built manually, by recording the number of detected errors on a daily basis. Ultimately, the error removal curve tells us that, even in the presence of an ongoing program testing process, we will never be sure that all malfunctions are deleted. From a certain stage onwards, we can notice that the benefit of detecting an error is minor than the cost of the resources wasted in terms of man / days needed to locate it. For this reason, a limit to the testing activities must be established: this limit varies depending on several parameters such as the levels of service required by the software client and the maintenance costs encountered during this procedure.

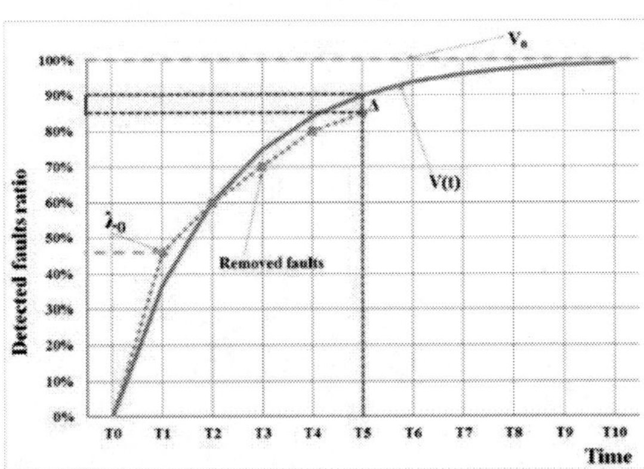

Fig. 5. Fault removal curve.

6 Conclusions

With the use of AD designing, the testing and functional verification processes are implemented, allowing the construction of a logically coherent testing plan that is integrated with the design logic of the system. This approach is even more effective in terms of taxation management processes, since it allows obtaining the following advantages:

- Meeting the regulatory deadlines set by the Revenue Agency;
- Reducing non-conformities;
- Determining the minimum set of use cases in order to ensure the full functional coverage of the user requirements. At least one test case is allocated for each functional requirement;
- Pre-arranging the system for any future interventions in terms of lower costs and implementation time, especially in case of future regulatory or organizational changes; Reusing the test cases of software's previous versions.

References

1. C. Cavallini, A. Giorgetti, P. Citti, A. Meneghin, *Sviluppo di un approccio olistico per l'analisi e la risoluzione delle non conformità,* AISS, **3,** 1 (2012);
2. A. Giorgetti, C. Cavallini, A. Ciappi, G. Arcidiacono and P. Citti, *A holistic model for the proactive reduction of non-conformities within new industrial technologies,* IJMERR, **6**, 4 (2017);
3. A. Giorgetti, G. Arcidiacono, A. Ciappi, R. Barbieri, and P. Citti, *HNCR model following robust approach*, QREI (to be published);
4. G. Arcidiacono, A. Giorgetti, M. Pugliese, *Axiomatic Design to improve PRM airport assistance*, Proc. CIRP, **34**, 106-111 (2015);
5. G. Arcidiacono, D. T. Matt, E. Rauch, *Axiomatic Design of a Framework for the Comprehensive Optimization of Patient Flows in Hospitals*, JHE, vol. **2017** (2017);
6. G. Arcidiacono, P. Placidoli, *Reality and illusion in Virtual Studios: Axiomatic Design applied to television recording*, Proc. CIRP, **34**, 137-142 (2015);
7. G. Arcidiacono, A. Giorgetti, A. Ciappi, *An Axiomatic Design framework for reliability improvement*, ACM International Conference Proceeding Series, pp. 214-217;
8. G. Arcidiacono, K. Yang, J. Trewn, L. Bucciarelli, *Application of Axiomatic Design for Project-Based Learning Methodology*, Proc. CIRP, **53**, 166-172 (2016);
9. Italian Revenue Agency, *Instructions for completion F23 payment form*, (Italian Revenue Agency, 2017);
10. Italian Revenue Agency, *F23 payment form*, (Italian Revenue Agency, 2017);
11. A. Avellone, M, Cislaghi, E. Colonese, *Collaudo e qualità del Software*, (AICQ-CI, Uni Service, 2010);

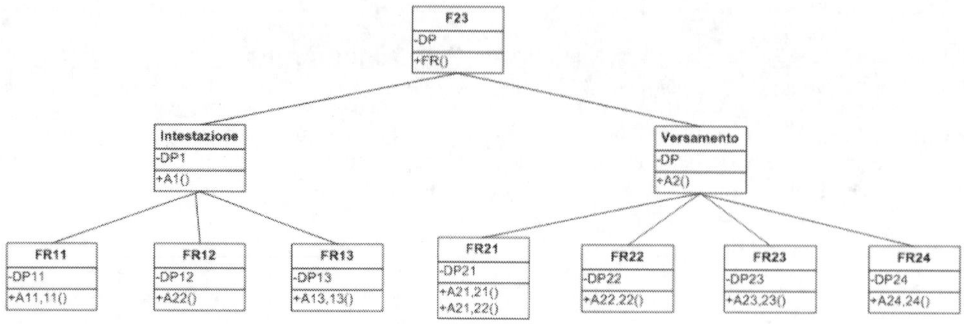

Fig. 6. Simplified UML diagram before reuse.

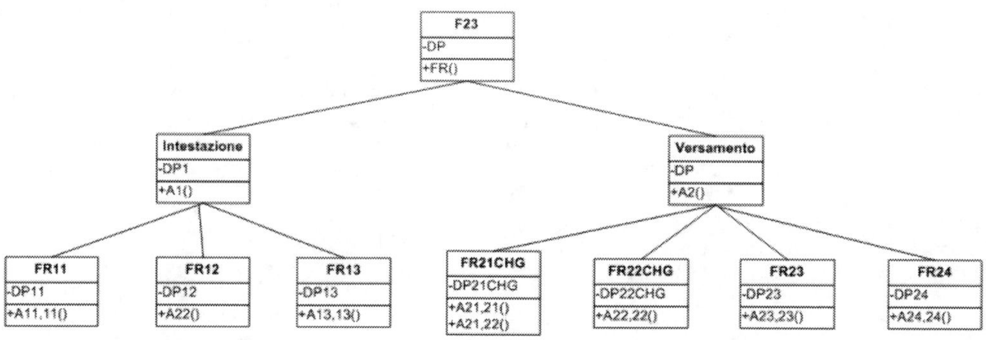

Fig. 7. Simplified UML diagram after reuse.

12. J.B. Goodenough, S.L. Gerhart, *Toward a theory of test data selection,* SIGPLAN Notices, **6**, 10 (1975);
13. L. Bougè, *A contribution to the theory of program testing*, TCS **37**, 151-181, (1985);
14. G. J. Myers, *The Art of Software Testing*, (John Wiley & Sons,, 2004);
15. E. W. Dijkstra, O. J. Dahl, and C. A. R. Hoare, *Structured Programming, London,* (Academic Press London, 1972);
16. I. Sommerville, *Software Engineering* (Addison-Wesley, 2009);
17. NP Suh, *Axiomatic Design - Advances and Applications*, (Oxford University Press, 2001);
18. IFPUG, *Function Point Counting Practices Manual*, (IFPUG, 1999);
19. F. Rolli, A. Giorgetti, P. Citti, M. Rinaldi, *Improvement of the compilation process of the Italian income certifications: a methodology based on the evaluation of the information content (Part 1),* Proc. CIRP **53**, 56-62 (2016);
20. F. Rolli, A. Giorgetti, P. Citti, M. Rinaldi, *Information content evaluation to obtain robustness of the management in Italian fiscal process (Part 2): optimization of Italian income certification process of the year 2016*, Proc. CIRP **53**, 63-69 (2016);
21. J. Musa, and A. Ackerman, *Quantifying software validation: When to stop testing,* IEEE Software, **6**, 3, 19–27 (1989);
22. F. Rolli, A. Giorgetti, P. Citti, *Integration of Holistic Non-Conformities Management and Axiomatic Design: a case study in Italian Income Tax Returns Management,* Proc. CIRP **34**, 256-262 (2015);
23. C. Jones, *Applied software measurement*, (McGraw-Hill, 2008).

* Corresponding author: f.rolli@unimarconi.it

MATEC Web of Conferences **127**, 01018 (2017) DOI: 10.1051/matecconf/201712701018
ICAD 2017

Adapt! – Agile Project Management Supported by Axiomatic Design

Jakob Weber[1,*], *David* Förster[1], *Markus* Stäbler[1] and *Kristin* Paetzold[2]

[1] Daimler AG, Process Development and Materials Department, 71059 Sindelfingen, Germany
[2] Universität der Bundeswehr, Institut für Technische Produktentwicklung, 85577 Neubiberg, Germany

Abstract. This paper presents a novel approach for the use of Axiomatic Design Theory in combination with agile project management methods like Scrum for an effective, structured and combined product design and development process. Agile project management methods give a guideline how to manage a project, but there is only minor assistance regarding the actual product development process itself. Axiomatic Design can be used to support these methods in this point. In concrete terms, the results of the decomposition process of this theory can be used to formulate and structure the work packages for the agile project managing process. The Independence Axiom of Axiomatic Design Theory has a substantial contribution by ensuring the independence of the work packages which can be assigned to different project team members and can be processed independently by them. The combination of the different methods not only helps to ensure a good design solution but also helps to work more agile within a project team. The here proposed approach is one part of a holistic product design and development process for changeable production units – called *Adapt!* – and is described within a use case in the automotive sector.

1 Introduction

Today's industries and especially the automotive industry face manifold challenges. These challenges exist since the companies are in turbulent settings caused by many different influences like globalization, the introduction of new and disruptive technologies, politics and much more (Figure 1) [1, 2].

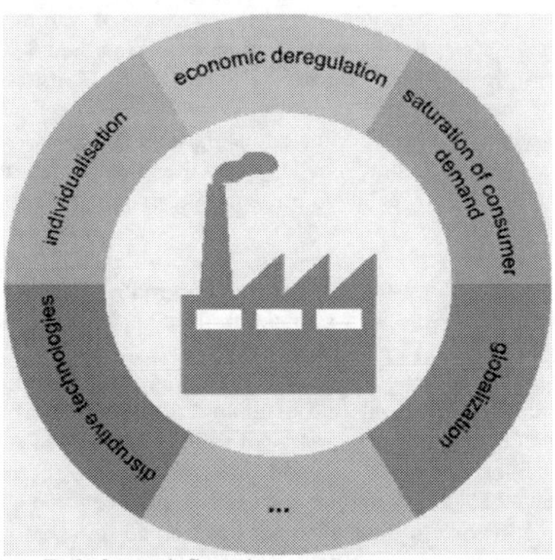

Fig. 1. Turbulences influencing a company.

The turbulences affect the production systems of the companies, which have to react by adapting and changing. This circumstance expresses itself in two different ways. Firstly, the product life cycles of the production units decrease as it is known from the products themselves. In order to be competitive this ends up in the need to accelerate the design and development process of production units.

Secondly, the design of production units gets more and more complex. Caused by new technologies and by the claim of producing an increasing number of variants with the same production unit, the complexity of their design increases.

Major work is done in research according design methods and changeability of production units. Also considerable work is done in context of project management methods in order to give full particulars to a basic concept. However, there is no easy to handle approach combining design methods with project management methods in order to guarantee a holistic design and development process. In this paper, one element of an approach – called *Adapt!* – is suggested combining the benefits of Axiomatic Design Theory with agile project management methods e.g. Scrum. The benefits of Axiomatic Design are the universal applicability on different disciplines, the focus on product functions and the optimized learnability of this theory. Combining these with the procedure of Scrum ensures a modern technology design process.

As a starting point within this paper related work regarding Axiomatic Design and Scrum is outlined. Based on this, the proposed approach combining Axiomatic Design and Scrum is explained. In the

* Corresponding author: jakob.weber@daimler.com

following an example is given, which is envisaged to be processed applying the proposed approach. A discussion on this topic is carried out followed with a conclusion and outlook on future work.

The research questions that have to be answered are the following:

- How can Axiomatic Design support the subsequent project management process after the design phase?
- In what kind of environment is the proposed approach successfully applicable?
- What are the expected benefits of this approach?

2 Related work

The following sections describe the fundamentals and the related work of the used methods. The basics of Axiomatic Design Theory are outlined, a brief summary of Scrum as one possible agile project management method is given.

2.1 Axiomatic Design

Axiomatic Design is a design theory mainly based on two axioms [3, 4]. The aim of this theory is to give a scientific and therewith a learnable foundation to design. The theory describes the design process as mapping of requirements and solutions between four domains (see Figure 2). The domains are customer, functional, physical and process domain. Within the customer domain all customer attributes (CA) are summarized. The CA are usually free of any hierarchical order. They will be transformed to functional requirements (FR) within the functional domain. These are all requirements that are demanded of the later product. Each FR will be mapped to a design parameter (DP), which is the physical solution to the specific requirement. The mapping process can be described as switching from the question "what do we want to achieve?" to "how do we achieve it?". By switching repeatedly between these two questions, the design task gets decomposed and more and more specific. This procedure is called "zigzagging". In the next step, the DP of the physical domain are mapped to the process domain by defining suitable process variables (PV). For this work, the relevant step is the mapping from functional to physical domain.

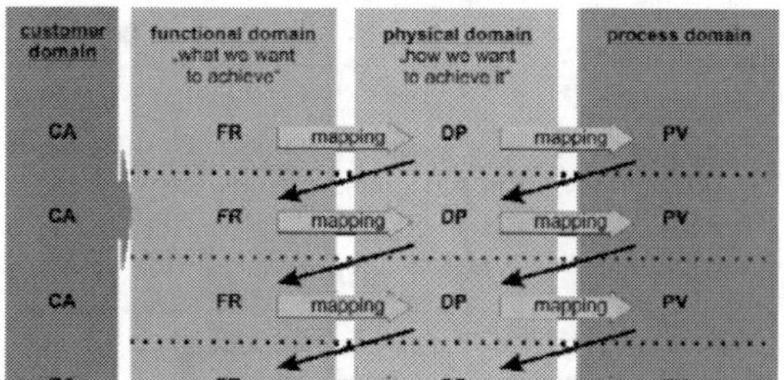

Fig. 2. Decomposition of the design task in Axiomatic Design.

To support the solution determination of the mapping process between the domains, Axiomatic Design uses the already mentioned two axioms. The first axiom – *Independence Axiom* – claims that the FR have to remain independent by finding appropriate DP. The second axiom – *Information Axiom* – advocates to minimize the information content of the design. This advice is based on the context between information content and the complexity of the proposed solution.

There is major work in the field of production system design. Naming all of them goes beyond the scope of this paper. Rauch et al. give in [5] an overview of publications using Axiomatic Design in this context. One essential conclusion of their work is that almost three-quarter of all work focus on the Independence Axiom as it is the case also for this paper. This assumption is also supported by the work of Kulak et al. in [6].

2.2 Scrum

Scrum is a framework enabling the treatment of complex projects and problem statements. Furthermore, the creative and productive development of high-graded products is supported. Scrum gives a detailed classification of a project team, strict rules and an accurate course of action. The aim of Scrum is to optimize the work within a project team and to easily control risks by an iterative step by step organization of the development process. Due to Scrum, the process will fulfil the following three characteristics: transparency, inspection and adaption [7].

The main elements of the framework are the Scrum team, the Scrum artefacts and the Scrum events. The Scrum team consists of the Scrum master, the product owner and the development team [7].

The Scrum master is in charge of the abidance of the theory, proceeding and laws of Scrum by the whole team. Furthermore, he tackles all obstacles which hinder the team to fulfil their work.

The product owner is the only person who organizes the product backlog, one of the artefacts of Scrum. This means he prioritizes the product backlog items which have to be developed by the Scrum team. The items of the product backlog are all requirements of the later product and are formulated as clear work orders, which can be fulfilled independently by the development team. Moreover, he is the representative to the stakeholders (e.g. customers).

Other Scrum artefacts are the sprint backlog and the product increment. Related to the product backlog, the sprint backlog is a choice of product backlog items, which should be finished during one sprint. The sprint backlog is being replenished by a plan for delivering the product increment and realizing the sprint goal. The increment is a summary of all accomplished sprint backlog items. At the end of a sprint the new increment must be "done", that means its sprint backlog items must fulfil the definition of done, determined ex ante by the Scrum team. The most important elements of Scrum are the Scrum events, especially the sprint. A sprint is a time box during which the elements of the sprint backlog must reach the definition of done. They contain daily meetings of the project team, the daily Scrums, the sprint reviews, termination presentations of the fulfilled tasks at the end of every sprint and the sprint planning. All these elements are a subject to tight restrictions, which must be observed by the team members. The Scrum process is depicted in Figure 3.

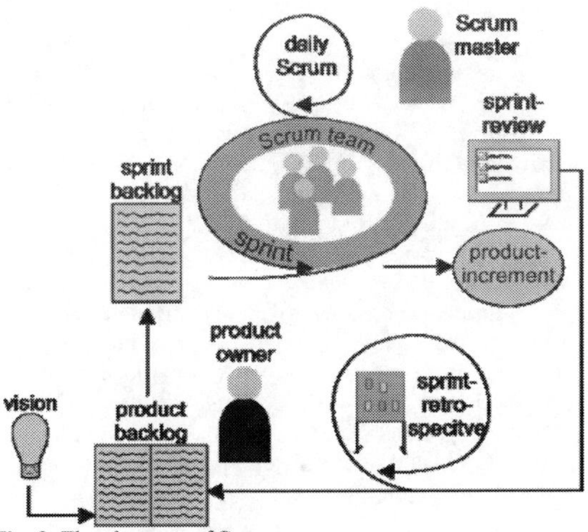

Fig. 3. The elements of Scrum.

3 Proposed approach

The development process of innovative production units and in particularly of changeable production units underlies specific challenges. In contrast to a team which develops e.g. software, the development team of changeable production units is usually cross-disciplinary. A common team composition includes engineers and practitioners of different disciplines. So, this inter-disciplinary teamwork is one challenge and has to be supported.

Another challenge lies in the nature of work which has to be carried out. The design and development process of production units normally starts with more theoretical and conceptual work and ends with a practical implementation and optimization of the production unit. Hence, there is a switch in the type of work which is depicted in Figure 4. This point makes it inevitable to use a methodology which supports both theoretical and practical work. Design as well as development cannot be treated isolated.

Using Axiomatic Design offers substantial possibilities for lean development processes especially in large organizations. Related work regarding the development of changeable production units is presented in [8, 9]. To take account of the mentioned shift of theoretical and practical work, these works have to be extended with a procedure to support the practical part of the development work. This is done in a methodology, we call *Adapt!*. The name refers to the approach itself and also to the product, which is designed and developed with it. Both, the approach and the later product is adaptable to new circumstances.

The proposed procedure is also extended by an analysis and evaluation part, which results in a holistic approach for designing and redesigning changeable production units [10]. The following sections limit on the design and development process of *Adapt!*.

The basic idea of *Adapt!* is to provide an easy to understand and learn approach to design. Therefore, the Independence Axiom of Axiomatic Design is used to decompose a design task. This is done in accordance to [9] by only decomposing the task on the highest and most abstract levels. The resulting hierarchical design tree is transformed to a design matrix. It is assumed that the customer attributes of a design task not only result from one customer within a large company, but from different departments. Therefore, it is useful to colorize the resulting functional requirements and design parameters according to the origin of the former customer attribute. So, dependencies in the design matrix are colorized and can be referred to the department which claimed the specific functional requirement. On this basis, it is possible to enter into a dialog with the customer departments and to start a discussion with the aim to overthink some of the stated requirements with the aim of simplifying the design task. After this the decomposition of the design task is done again. In case of obtaining a satisfying design solution according to the Independence Axiom, the result is a conceptual design of a changeable production unit fulfilling the design task [8].

Starting from this interim result, the shift from conceptual to practical work starts. The basic concept has to be refined and a first prototype has to be engineered. For this purpose a development team consisting of several experts of different subjects is initiated. There is also a change of roles of the project manager. From being quite on his own during the design phase, he becomes part of the Scrum team. In the case of using Scrum he becomes product owner (Figure 4).

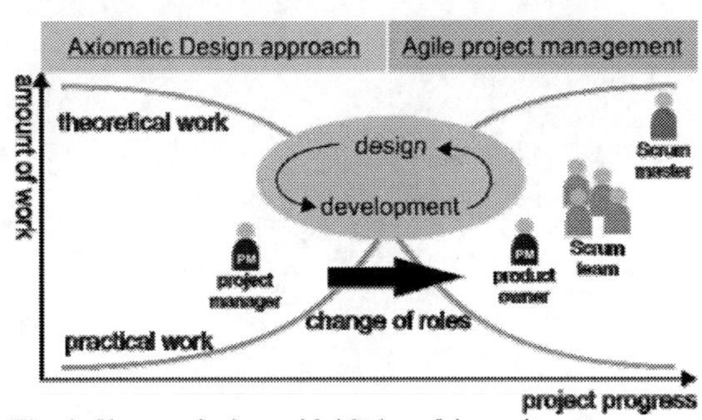

Fig. 4. Change of roles and initiation of the project team.

In order to coordinate their work and to be able to react on unforeseen circumstances, Scrum is a suitable framework as already explained in the related work section. A central aim of Scrum is to enable self-organized work which is done in sprints. In order to describe the work content of each sprint there are so called refinement and sprint meetings. In a refinement meeting the tasks are specified, so that every team member knows what to do. In a sprint meeting it is defined which task will be processed during the following sprint.

Within this context, the hierarchical tree of the conceptual design can be used to organize the refinement. This is consistent with the rules of Scrum although they deny any change or exception of the Scrum rules. "The Scrum Team decides how and when refinement is done" [7]. In accordance to this, the presented paper provides a suggestion how the Scrum team can organize the refinement.

The elements of the hierarchical tree of the conceptual design can be seen as rough formulated work tasks for the single Scrum sprints. They can be listed in the product backlog. Some of the elements can already be sufficiently defined to be further processed in a sprint. Others may be too abstract to be already processed. So, they have to be detailed in a refinement meeting. Within this refinement meeting, again, the proposed approach from [9] focusing the Independence Axiom can be used to decompose the design task. If the granularity of the branch of the hierarchical tree is fine enough, they are adequate as a single work task and can be accepted to be consigned to the sprint back log of a future sprint. This is depicted in Figure 5.

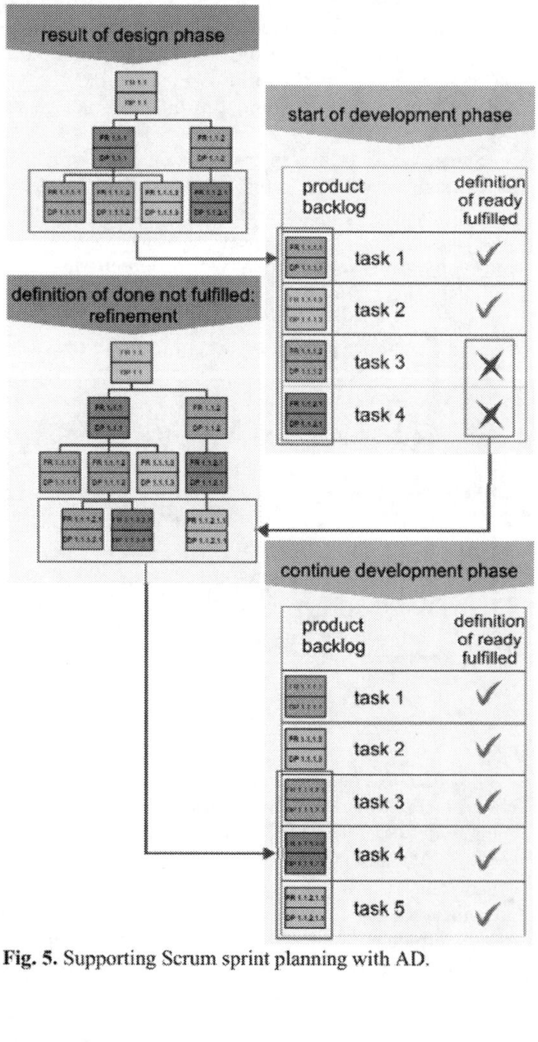

Fig. 5. Supporting Scrum sprint planning with AD.

4 Practical example

For illustrating the use of *Adapt!* hereafter the approach will be explained on a practical example. The described project is in the conceptual phase and *Adapt!* will be applied from the beginning for the first time. At first the product development process of the upper layers of the hierarchical tree will be illustrated. Subsequently, the distribution of roles by the use of Scrum in an industrial environment will be explained.

In the beginning technical concepts must be worked out. This is done by the project manager who is a development engineer. He summarizes the customer attributes and starts the decomposition of the hierarchical tree. He is doing his work mainly himself. Only in the case of needing further information he asks for bilateral support by experts of the affected department. During this process the elements of the Axiomatic Design tree are colorized according to the department where they originate from. The design parameters are selected by applying the first axiom of Axiomatic Design. The decomposition ends when it is detailed enough to formulate product backlog items out of the functional requirements and related design parameters of the lowest level of the hierarchical tree.

By this point, the Scrum team is initiated with the aim of implementing a mechanical prototype of the later product. In this particular example the team consists of the development engineer, an implementation engineer, a design engineer, a software specialist, an electrician and a mechanic. These specialists have to be deployed to the single functions of the team in a favorable way.

In the development phase the project manager of the design phase should have a leading role in order to have an overview of the project. This is done in the best way when the project manager of the design phase is assigned as product owner of the development phase. By this he keeps the overview of the whole project and can prioritize the work tasks. Furthermore, with his detailed knowledge about the project he can properly communicate with the stake holders.

Another crucial role is given by the Scrum master. For this position the implementation engineer is predestinated. His most important task is to abolish impediments which hinder the Scrum team. In his work as implementation engineer one of his tasks is already the abolishment of impediments during realization phase of a production unit. Hence, he brings the right mind-set to enable the work of the whole Scrum team. The distribution of roles within the Scrum team is illustrated in Figure 6.

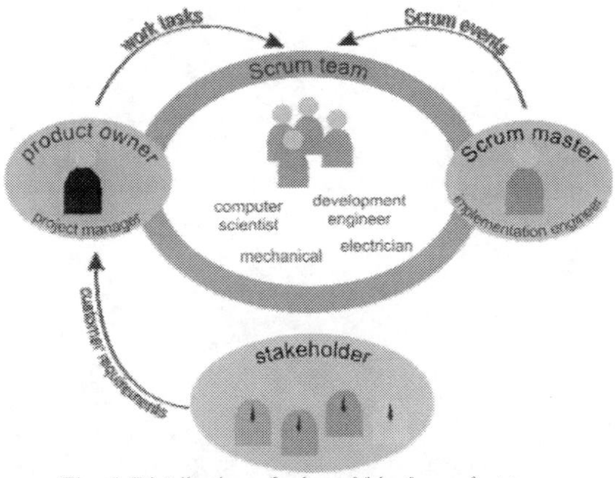

Fig. 6. Distribution of roles within the project team.

With this team composition, the development process starts. This is the current status of the launched project. For the further project's duration, the following benefits are expected:

Through the use of Axiomatic Design Theory, the extensive independence of single work tasks of the later product development process should be ensured. This will be favorable because every team member can work on his own work task independently and does not have to rely on others. This will support an agile project handling and a self-organized way of work. On this basis, a high-capacity utilization of the team members is expectable. So, waiting times are reduced and the design and development process is accelerated.

Finally, the continuous decomposition of the design task leads to an also continuous and complete documentation of the design and development process. This reduces efforts for ex post documenting.

5 Discussion

A critical assessment on the proposed approach can be done from the methodical point of view. Two existing and well-established procedures are used. By only combining them, the specific shortcomings of each of the two methodologies remain unchanged. E.g. there is no further work done in supporting creativity during the design phase, which is an often-criticized shortcoming of Axiomatic Design Theory. Furthermore, the execution of Scrum cannot be simplified. Applying Scrum makes it inevitable to have a specific mind-set within the Scrum team and also within the company especially within the management.

However, combining these two procedures helps to innovate our production technologies. To the contrary, by not predetermining every single step and by not overburdening the design process, an easy-to-use approach is achieved.

Another point of criticism might be that there is no strict specification how detailed the Axiomatic Design tree has to be, before initiating the Scrum team.

Quite the contrary, it can be argued, that this is one advantage of *Adapt!*. The procedure can always be adjusted to the specific needs of a development team.

One more big challenge is the fact, that the members of the Scrum team have different professional qualifications. This is a requirement which originates from the circumstance of developing hardware. According to Scrum every team member is called developer and there is no hierarchy. This might cause troubles due to different qualifications of team members. But the advantages of working in an agile way overtake this challenge.

In comparison to the mentioned disadvantages and challenges there exist also a lot of advantages of this approach. By using the approach, the design and development process is structured. Despite of this structuring the whole procedure is very agile and allows the development team to react on unforeseen events. Overall, it ensures the development of changeable production units.

6 Conclusion and Outlook

This paper presented an innovative approach for a consistent product design and development process using Axiomatic Design to support agile project management methods like Scrum.

The need for a consistent approach for design and development of changeable production units was revealed. Moreover, the possibility of using hierarchical trees from the decomposition of the design task with Axiomatic Design as input for the product development process with agile methods like Scrum was shown. In addition to this an example was given, where the proposed approach – a part of a method named Adapt! – is applied for the first time. A possible composition of a project team with the aim of designing and developing a changeable production unit was given. The desired benefits of the approach were presented in detail, too. Finally, a critical discussion of the proposed approach was done.

Future work involves the elaboration of the holistic evaluation, design and development process for the design of changeable production units. Furthermore the applicability of the presented approach has to be proven.

References

1. E. Westkämper, Marktorientiertes Produzieren in dynamischen Strukturen. In: H. J. Warnecke, ed. *Fabrikstrukturen im Zeitalter des Wandels – welcher Weg führt zum Erfolg?* 12-21 (Springer, 1995)
2. H.P. Wiendahl, C.L. Heger, *Justifying Changeability. A Methodical Approach to Achieving Cost Effectiveness*. Proceedings of CIRP 2nd Int. Conf. on Reconf. Manuf. (2003)
3. N.P. Suh, *The Principles of Design* (Oxford University Press, 1990)
4. N.P. Suh, *Axiomatic Design: Advances and Applications* (Oxford University Press, 2001)

5. E. Rauch, D. T. Matt, P. Dallasega, *Application of Axiomatic Design in Manufacturing System Design. A Literature Review*, Procedia CIRP **53** 1-7 (2016)
6. O. Kulak, S. Cebi, C. Kahraman, *Application of Axiomatic Design Principles. A Literature Review*. Expert Systems with Applications **37** 6705-6717 (2010)
7. K. Schwaber, J. Sutherland, *The Scrum Guide* (2016)
8. J. Weber, D. Förster, J. Kößler, K. Paetzold, *Design of changeable production units within the automotive sector with Axiomatic Design*. Procedia CIRP **34** 93-97 (2015)
9. J. Weber, J. Kößler, K. Paetzold, *An Approach for Industrial Application of Axiomatic Design*. Proceedings of ICED (2015)
10. M. Stäbler, J. Weber, K. Paetzold. *Implementing Changeability in a System with Prioritization Indicators*. Procedia CIRP **44** 50-54 (2016)

MATEC Web of Conferences **127**, 01019 (2017) DOI: 10.1051/matecconf/201712701019
ICAD 2017

Selection of a Solution When Using Axiomatic Design

Laurenţiu Slătineanu[1], *Oana* Dodun[1], *Margareta* Coteaţă[1,*], *Valeriu* Dulgheru[2], *Petru* Duşa[1], *Felicia* Banciu[3], *Irina* Beşliu[4]

[1]"Gheorghe Asachi" Technical University of Iaşi, Machine Manufacturing Technology Department, Blvd. D. Mangeron, 39A, 700050 Iaşi, Romania
[2]Technical University of Moldova, Fundamentals of Machine Design Department, 9/8, Studenţilor Street, block of study no. 6, Republic of Moldova
[3]Polytechnic University of Timisoara, Materials and Manufacturing Engineering Department, Mihai Viteazu Street 1, 300222 Timisoara, Romania
[4]"Ştefan cel Mare" University of Suceava, Department of Mechanics and Technology, Universităţii Street 13, 720229 Suceava, Romania

Abstract. Over the years, the importance of the creativity inclusively in the field of design activities was highlighted. In accordance with the opinions of certain researchers, the divergent thinking could contribute to the increase of creative processes efficiency. On the other hand, the axiomatic design method is considered as a method able to stimulate the technical creativity when the problem of designing a mechanical equipment is stated. To increase the efficiency of using the axiomatic design method, the possibility of selecting the most convenient solution among many available solutions could be discussed. The analysis revealed that there are many methods that could be applied in the process of optimum solution selection among many available solutions. In this paper, some aspects concerning the possibilities of using the method of analytic hierarchy process are analyzed, inclusively by considering a case study concerning a device for investigating the universal horizontal lathe rigidity. Afterwards, the first axiom from axiomatic design method was applied to define the selected solution for the approached device.

1 Introduction

In a short definition, *the creativity* could be defined as the ability to generate new ideas or concepts, eventually by applying methods able to help the process of new ideas generation. There is not a unique opinion concerning the person who used firstly the concept of *creativity*. Thus, in a work concerning the of *aesthetics* evolution, the Polish poet and theoretician of poetry Maciej Kazimierz Sarbiewski (1595–1640) is considered as the first person who applied the word "creation" in the field of poetry [1]. On the other hand, the English mathematician and philosopher Alfred North Whitehead is taken into consideration as the inventor of the word "creativity"; he used the concept when defining his metaphysical scheme [2].

In a book published in the Romanian language (I. Căpâlneanu, *Intelligence and creativity*, Editura Militară, Bucharest 1978), there is the opinion that the concept of *creativity* was introduced by Gordon Allport, in 1937 [3].

Over the years, various definitions for the concept of creativity were proposed by the researchers from distinct activity fields. The researchers considered also that there is a certain connection between the significances and applications of the concepts of *creativity* and *divergent thinking*. The last concept (divergent thinking) takes into consideration the generation of multiple alternatives for solving the addressed problem. The distinction between the *convergent thinking* (aiming to identify a single accepted solution) and *divergent thinking* was made by the American psychologist J.P. Guilford; in fact, he used the concepts of *convergent* and *divergent production*, the concepts of convergent and divergent thinking being adopted subsequently.

Generally speaking, *the divergent thinking* is an intellectual process of fluent and operative generation of various solutions for a certain problem. Just from this definition, one could notice the connections between creativity and divergent thinking. In solving technical and engineering problems, it is important to find many solutions in the initial stages of problem-solving, so that subsequently, applying adequate selection methods, the most convenient alternative or alternatives are established.

Such an aspect is also highlighted by a principle of management; this principle shows that when for a strategic problem, a single solution seems to exist, there is a high probability that this solution is not the best one [4]. In accordance with such a principle, the same idea of the significance of the necessity to firstly find many solutions for the addressed strategic problem is stated. Only in a subsequent stage, the selection of the best solution could be approached.

In the last decades, many techniques and methods were proposed and applied to stimulate the technical creativity and some of them take into consideration the

* Corresponding author: mcoteata@tcm.tuiasi.ro

divergent thinking as a way of finding many solutions for the problem to be solved. More than 190 techniques usable as ways of searching and identifying innovative solutions are highlighted in [5].

The axiomatic design, as a method which could be applied to solve technical problems or problems from other fields of human activity, aims also to efficiently use the specialists' creative abilities [6]. In a set of slides [6] based on the professor Nam Pyo Suh's works [7-9], the significance of the axiomatic design as a method able to stimulate the creativity is highlighted showing that "axiomatic design enhances creativity by eliminating bad ideas early and thus, helping to channel the effort of designers" [6].

In one of the stages of axiomatic design method, there is highlighted the necessity of developing the design parameters because of a zigzagging activity between functional domain and physical domain. In this stage, the designer must search and identify the design parameter for each functional requirement previously established by considering the customer needs.

In the last decades, works describing the contributions of the creativity in applying the axiomatic design were developed and published. Thus, Slocum appreciated that within axiomatic innovation, the creativity has the role of an exact science [10]. As an addition to the axioms defined and applied in the axiomatic design, he took into consideration the technical contradiction axiom, the physical contradiction axiom, and the ideal result axiom, which are used in the TRIZ method; in his opinion, a hybridization of TRIZ method and axiomatic design method could be logical and necessary step.

A possible combination of principles specific to TRIZ method and axiomatic method to enhance the efficient use of the creativity was also discussed [10-18]. Crowell and Gregson used just the concept of *creative axiomatic design*, to highlight the capacity of the axiomatic design to facilitate identification of creative solutions [19]. They proposed a general creativity matrix, in which design parameters *DPs* or process variables *PVs* could be expressed as functions of their behaviors and appreciated that in this way the functional fixation could be avoided.

The objective of this paper was to present the authors' opinions concerning some possibilities of applying firstly the divergent thinking principles in using the axiomatic design method for developing a mechanical device /equipment. Subsequently, using an adequate method of selection (analytic hierarchy process, AHP), a possible optimized solution could be identified.

2 Use of divergent thinking when applying the axiomatic design method

It is well known that the axiomatic design method was proposed by the professor Nam Pyo Suh, in the years '70 of the previous century, when he was working at the Massachusetts Institute of Technology of Boston (U.S.A.). In works published in that period, the professor Suh was referring to the axiomatic approach of manufacturing and of manufacturing systems. The use of axiomatic design method developed gradually and nowadays there are many economic, technical or other fields where applications of this method were identified. Essentially, the method supposes developing 4 stages, in which the customer needs, the functional requirements, the design parameters and the process variables are gradually established. A first advantage of applying the axiomatic design method is the clearer highlighting of the requirements supposed by the design theme and the continuous connection of the design activity to these requirements.

In applying the method of axiomatic design, one could notice that there is a stage when the designer divides functional requirements *FRs* and establish the design parameters *DPs* able to correspond to each functional requirement. The activity of successive passing from the functional domain to the physical domain is called "zigzagging" and it is expected that during this activity, new or at least improved solutions for the design parameters could be identified so that finally the desired equipment could be characterized by certain original and possible inventive aspects.

To operatively identify the adequate answer for each functional requirement, the designer could limit his searching activity to the first found solution; this means that a convergent thinking way could be preferentially accessed by the designer (Fig. 1).

To increase the weight of divergent thinking method – appreciated as a more able to generate creative solutions, one could take into consideration to search if there are techniques and methods able to increase the possibilities of applying divergent thinking way during the zigzagging process.

The analysis of this problem could lead to two possible approaches:

1) A first approach could take into consideration the applying of divergent thinking for each design parameter. This could mean to firstly search many design parameters for each functional requirement and only later to select those considered as more convenient. This way seems to need a high volume of efforts and it does not take into consideration the image of the entire desired assembly/equipment. For example, problems could

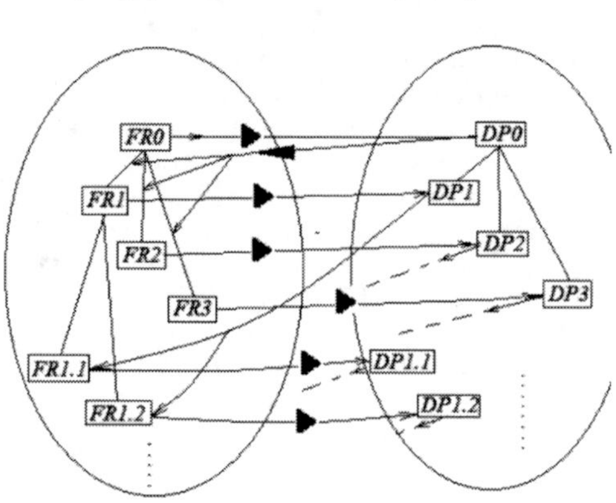

Fig. 1. Possibilities of applying convergent thinking when using functional requirements *FRs* to define each design parameter *DP* (convergent thinking process was highlighted by the symbol ►).

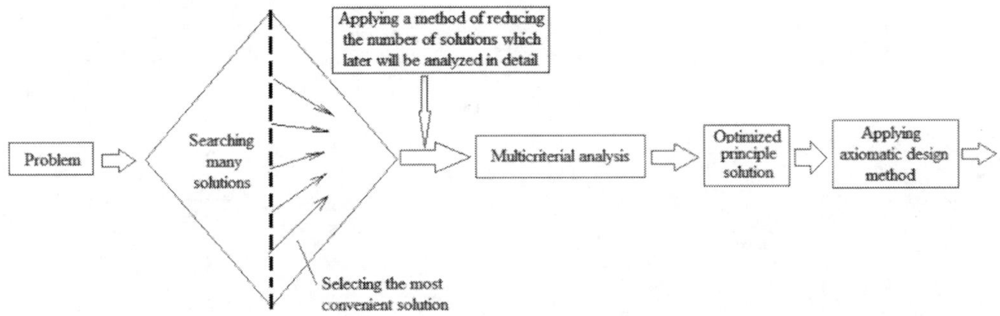

Fig. 2. Applying the divergent thinking method in association with a method of reducing the number of solutions which will be later analyzed in detail and a method of multicriterial analysis, respectively.

appear in this case in assembling the design parameters in the desired general solution;

2) Identifying a possible searching way which could be able that just from beginning to integrate all the design parameters and searching for the convenient solutions for all functional requirements. Such a way could ensure the use of divergent thinking, but it could be more operative and just from the beginning, the entire desired assembly could be considered. A possible solution corresponding to such a way of solving the design problems could be found in the so-called multicriterial analysis or optimizing the selection by means of multicriterial analysis (Fig. 2). A disadvantage of this method could be introduced by the fact that the zigzagging activity diminishes and the probability of identifying optimized solution for each design parameter decreases also.

One must mention that if the convergent thinking supposes a continuous narrowing of the investigated field, by removing the solutions considered as not or less convenient, the applying of the divergent thinking involves practically two distinct stages, a first stage in which the designer efforts are focused on searching many solutions for the addressed problem and a second stage, when practically the convergent thinking is applied.

In a paper published in 2005, Coelho et al. analyzed the use of quality function deployment by adopting the axiomatic design principles [20]. They concluded that the quality function deployment could be applied to improve the existing designs, but in association with the axiomatic design principles, and a faster design process of new solutions is possible.

In a master thesis defended in 2013, Shi showed that the combination of several basic level concepts from the detail design parameters corresponding to the axiomatic design could increase the creativity by highlighting more possible design solutions [21]. He appreciated that the selection of a certain design concept could be achieved by using the axiomatic design ontology Foley and Cochran considered that the axiomatic design is an ontology able to facilitate the representation of the manufacturing system design decomposition in a knowledge interchange by means of a web ontology language and certain software tools [22].

3 Methods of optimization

As above mentioned, to ensure the use of the most convenient solution able to be developed by using the axiomatic design method, a so-called *method of selecting optimal version* for an object, an equipment or a process could be identified and applied. Since usually the desired solution should correspond to many requirements, a method belonging to the group of *multicriterial optimization* could be preferentially applied.

Nowadays, there are some such methods of multicriterial optimization with a larger or narrower use: for example, one could take into consideration the Technique for Order of Preference by Similarity to Ideal Solution (TOPSIS), the Analytic Hierarchy Process (AHP), the Analytic Network Process (ANP), the Preference Ranking Organization Method for Enrichment Evaluation (PROMETHEE), the Multi-Objective Optimization on the basis of Ratio Analysis (MOORA), the elimination and choice expressing reality (in French, ELimination Et Choix Traduisant la REalité, ELECTRE), the method of utilities etc. [23-25].

The last decades showed an extended use of the AHP method; this method was applied in the research presented in this paper to select the most convenient version able to optimally solve a design problem.

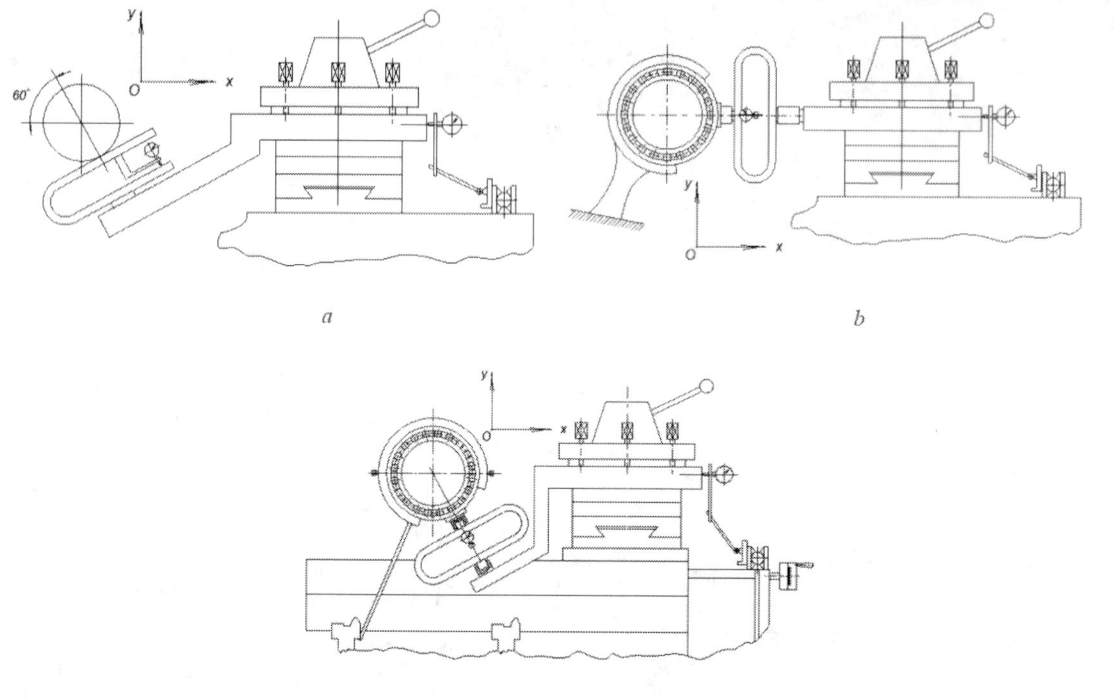

Fig. 3. Versions of a device for evaluating the universal lathe rigidity: (*a*) device for evaluation of static rigidity; (*b*) device for evaluation of the rigidity using the rotation of the lathe main shaft and a system for loading along the axis *Ox*; (*c*) device for evaluation of the rigidity using the rotation of lathe main shaft and a system for loading along two axes, *Ox* and *Oy*.

4 Use of AHP method in selecting the most convenient alternative

Let take into consideration the problem of selecting the device which could be used for the study of the rigidity that characterizes a medium size universal horizontal lathe. When trying to generate the functional requirements and the design parameters corresponding to such a device, the alternatives presented in Figure 3 should be to be taken into consideration for a more detailed analysis. The three considered versions are the following:

1. The alternative *A1*, based on the use of a device recommended in an older regulation for the study of *static rigidity* (Figure 3, *a*): essentially, this device supposes the use of a bar fixed in the universal chuck and in the live center. Using this device, a loading like those corresponding to a transversal turning process is generated. To calculate the lathe static rigidity, the loading force is measured by means of a dynamometer, while the elastic displacement of the tool holder along the *Ox* conventional axis is determined by means of a dial gauge;

2. The alternative *A2*, able to load the technological system with a force directed only along the direction *Ox*, but taking into consideration the rotation of the bar clamped in the universal chuck and in the live center. To ensure the loading just during the bar rotation process, a bearing could be placed on the bar, and the dynamometer takes contact with a bush placed on the bearing external ring (Fig. 3, *b*). The alternative is closer to the real use of the lathe, taking into consideration the bar rotation, but using only the loading along a single axis (*Ox*);

3. The third alternative, *A3*, facilitates the bar rotation, but taking into consideration a system loading along two axes, *Ox* and *Oy* (Fig. 3, *c*).

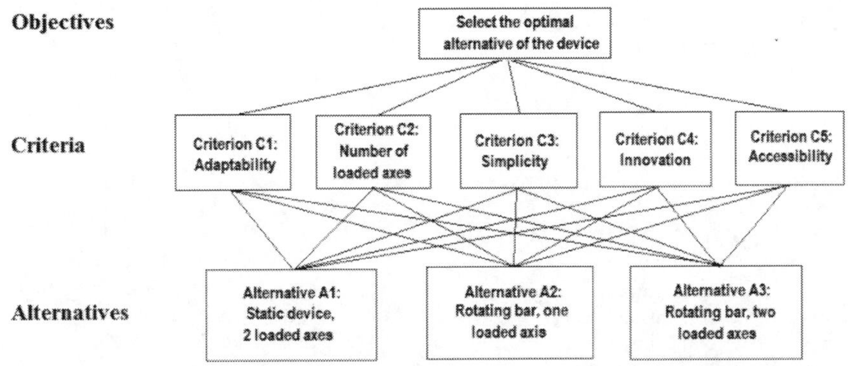

Fig. 4. Applying the AHP method to optimize the principle solution in the case of the device for investigating the lathe system rigidity (in accordance with [26]).

Table 1. Results of comparing the evaluation criteria.

A is more important than B?					**Situation of equality**	**How many times is it important?**							
A		**or**	**B**		**1**	**2**	**3**	**4**	**5**	**6**	**7**	**8**	**9**
X	Adaptability	or		Number of controlled axes		X							
X	Adaptability	or		Simplicity	X								
	Adaptability	or	X	Innovation			X						
X	Adaptability	or		Accessibility		X							
X	Number of controlled axes	or		Simplicity	X								
	Number of controlled axes	or	X	Innovation		X							
X	Number of controlled axes	or		Accessibility		X							
	Simplicity	or	X	Innovation					X				
X	Simplicity	or		Accessibility	X								
X	Innovation	or		Accessibility			X						

The selection of the most convenient solution could be based on the use AHP method. In accordance with the stages specific to this method, its main principles could be illustrated on the base of graphical representation included in Figure 4. The main components of this graphical representation are the design objective, the selection criteria and the alternative for solving the design problem.

There are many criteria that could be used in the case of selecting a device for lathe rigidity evaluation, but in the analyzed example, only 5 such criteria were retained:

- Criterion *C1*, referring to the degrees of closeness to the real turning conditions; the short name of this criterion will be *adaptability*;
- Criterion *C2*, which takes into consideration the number of axes along which the system is loaded;
- Criterion *C3*, highlighting the constructive *simplicity*;
- Criterion *C4*, which considers the level of *innovation*;
- Criterion *C5*, based on the possibility of manufacturing or acquisition of the device components (*accessibility*).

In the first stage, these criteria are compared each other by means of a scale offering 9 degrees of evaluation, among which there are: 1 when two criteria could be considered as of equal importance, 3 when compared with the other, a criterion is considered of moderate importance, 5 – of great importance, 7 - of very big importance, 9 - of extreme importance, and 2, 4, 6 and 8 are considered as intermediate evaluation, between two of the above-mentioned degrees [26].

The results obtained in applying comparison of the criteria were included in table 1.

The information from table 2 could be written as a decision matrix [*A*] having the aspect from the relation (1):

$$\text{Decision matrix } [A] = \begin{array}{c} C1 \\ C2 \\ C3 \\ C4 \\ C5 \end{array}\overset{\begin{array}{ccccc} C1 & C2 & C3 & C4 & C5 \end{array}}{\begin{bmatrix} 1 & 2.00 & 1.00 & 0.33 & 2.00 \\ 0.5 & 1 & 1.00 & 0.50 & 2.00 \\ 1.00 & 1.00 & 1 & 0.20 & 1.00 \\ 3.00 & 2.00 & 5.00 & 1 & 5.00 \\ 0.50 & 0.50 & 1.00 & 0.20 & 1 \end{bmatrix}} \quad (1)$$

The decision matrix [*A*] could also be written including the sum of the numbers corresponding to each column, as shown in relation (2).

$$\text{Decizion matrix } [A] = \begin{bmatrix} 1 & 2.00 & 1.00 & 0.33 & 2.00 \\ 0.5 & 1 & 1.00 & 0.50 & 2.00 \\ 1.00 & 1.00 & 1 & 0.20 & 1.00 \\ 3.00 & 2.00 & 5.00 & 1 & 5.00 \\ 0.50 & 0.50 & 1.00 & 0.20 & 1 \end{bmatrix} \quad (2)$$
$$\begin{array}{ccccc} 6 & 6.5 & 9 & 2.23 & 11 \end{array}$$

The normalized decision matrix [A_n] corresponding to the previous decision matrix [*A*] could be defined by dividing each matrix element from a certain column by the sum of elements (relation (3)).

$$[A]_n = \begin{bmatrix} 0.16 & 0.30 & 0.11 & 0.14 & 0.22 \\ 0.08 & 0.15 & 0.11 & 0.22 & 0.22 \\ 0.16 & 0.15 & 0.11 & 0.08 & 0.11 \\ 0.48 & 0.30 & 0.55 & 0.44 & 0.33 \\ 0.08 & 0.07 & 0.11 & 0.18 & 0.11 \end{bmatrix} \quad (3)$$

The priority vector w_c corresponding to the selected criteria could be written as a column matrix containing elements obtained as sums of the elements included in each line of the previous matrix (relation (4)).

$$w_c = \frac{1}{5}\begin{bmatrix} 0.16+0.30+0.11+0.14+0.22 \\ 0.08+0.15+0.11+0.22+0.22 \\ 0.16+0.15+0.11+0.08+0.11 \\ 0.48+0.30+0.55+0.44+0.33 \\ 0.08+0.07+0.11+0.18+0.11 \end{bmatrix} = \frac{1}{5}\begin{bmatrix} 0.93 \\ 0.75 \\ 0.61 \\ 2.10 \\ 0.45 \end{bmatrix} = \begin{bmatrix} 0.181 \\ 0.149 \\ 0.123 \\ 0.457 \\ 0.091 \end{bmatrix} \quad (4)$$

The last column matrix (the priority vector w_c) offers information about the order of the applied criteria and considering percent values: 1. Criterion *C4* (45.7 %); 2. Criterion *C1* (18.1 %); 3. Criterion *C2* (14.9 %); 4. Criterion *C3* (12.3 %); 5. Criterion *C5* (9.1 %).

On the base of the above-mentioned values, one can determine *the principal Eigen value* λ_{max} (relation (5)), the consistency index *CI* (relation (6)), and the consistency ratio *CR* (relation (7)).

$$\lambda_{\max} = 0.181\cdot 6 + 0.149\cdot 6.50 + 0.123\cdot 9 + 0.457\cdot 2.23 + 0.091\cdot 11 = 1.086 + 0.9685 + 1.107 + 1.019 + +1.001 == 5.176 \quad (5)$$

$$CI = \frac{\lambda_{\max} - n}{n-1} = \frac{5.176-5}{4} = 0.044 \quad (6)$$

$$CR = \frac{CI}{RI} = \frac{0.044}{1.12} = 0.04040 = 3.92\,\% < 10\,\% \quad (7)$$

One could notice that the consistency ratio *CR* is lower than 10 %, and this means that the inconsistency could be appreciated as acceptable [26]. In a way, like that above presented, the components of the priority vectors could be determined for each of the three alternatives *A1*, *A2* and *A3* and by means of each of the criteria *C1*, *C2*, *C3*, *C4*, and *C5*; the results are presented in Table 2. Taking into consideration the results included in the first 6 columns from Table 2, the general composite order weights for each alternative could be determined:

A1=18.1·8.23+14.9·40.5+12.3·54.0+45.7·9.5+9.1·54.0 =148.96+603.45+664.2+434.15+491.4=2342.16= =23.42 % (8)

A2=18.1·31.50+14.9·11.4+12.3·29.7+45.7·25.0+ +9.1·29.7=570.15+169.86+365.31+1142.5+270.27= =2518.09=25.18 % (9)

A3=18.1·60.26+14.9·48.1+12.3·16.3+45.7·65.5+9.1·16.3=1090.706+716.69+200.49+2993.35+148.33= =5149.566=51,49 % (10)

The values of the general composite weights were included in the penultimate column from Table 2; in the last column, the position of each alternative is

Table 2. Evaluation of each alternative by means of each criterion.

Criterion	C1	C2	C3	C4	C5	General composite weight	Order
Criterion weight	**0.181**	**0.149**	**0.123**	**0.457**	**0.091**		
Alternative							
A1	8.23 %	40.5 %	54.0 %	9.5 %	54.0 %	23.42 %	3
A2	31.5 %	11.4 %	29.7 %	25.0 %	29.7 %	25.18 %	2
A3	60.26 %	48.1 %	16.3 %	65.5 %	16.3 %	51.49 %	1
Sum	99.99 %	100 %	100 %	100 %	100 %	100.09 %	

highlighted. One could notice that if all the criteria are considered, the most convenient alternative is the alternative *A3*, followed by the alternative *A2* and *A1*, respectively, since 51.49 %>25.18 % >23.42 %.

The calculations above presented were achieved by means of the software presented in [22]; let us notice that this software allows an easy change of the numerical values proposed when comparing criteria or alternatives, up to the moment when the consistency could be considered as acceptable.

5 Developing selected alternative by means of the axiomatic design

Once established the most convenient alternative, the stages corresponding to the application of the first axiom from the axiomatic design method could be used [8, 27]. In this way, the information included in table 3 was obtained. One considered that during the process of zigzagging activity developed to define the solution for the device for investigating the lathe system rigidity, a faster selection of a certain solution was possible by using the AHP method was applied. Subsequently, the solution was finalized using the design matrix from the axiomatic design method.

One could see that even the matrix corresponding to the device is similar to an uncoupled matrix; there is a functional requirement that, in this initial stage, is materialized by means of two design parameters, namely by the dynamometer and the dynamometer nut. Of course, some improvements could be taken into consideration to finally obtain an uncoupled matrix. The analysis could be continued by trying to minimize the volume of information involved by the design of selected alternative, in accordance with the second axiom from the axiomatic design method.

6 Conclusions

Over the last decades, gradually an opinion in accordance with a certain correlation exists between the human creativity and the divergent thinking was accepted by certain researchers. On the other hand, the axiomatic design method offers a more systematic and optimized way in approaching distinct stages of the design activity. When the design parameters are established by considering the functional requirements of the distinct order, generally the designer is tempted to use preferentially the convergent thinking way. To increase the probability of finding new and improved technical solutions, before establishing the most convenient alternative, a more intense process of divergent thinking could be recommended. There are various methods applicable firstly to identify many alternatives for solving the approached design problem. When such some alternatives able to solve the design problem are found, the selection of the most convenient one could be also aided by applying a method of optimal selection of a certain alternative. Within the research presented in this paper, there was necessary to design a device for investigating the lathe system rigidity and to obtain an adequate image on the lathe system rigidity. If usually the lathe system rigidity is determined in static conditions, the hypothesis of designing a device able to be used when the lathe main shaft rotates was formulated. Taking firstly into consideration a divergent way of thinking, three distinct alternatives for studying the lathe rigidity were identified. Among the three considered alternatives, a process of selecting the most convenient alternative was applied by means of the analytic hierarchy process method. Subsequently, the axiomatic design method was applied to clearer define the functional requirements and establish some design

Table 3. Matrix that includes the functional requirements and design parameters established in the case of the device for evaluation of the horizontal universal lathe rigidity

Design parameters / Functional requirements			Design parameters								
			Design parameters of the first level								
			DP1		*DP2:*	DP3		*DP4*			
			Design parameters of the second level								
			DP1.1: Uni-versal chuck and live center	*DP1.2:* Lathe main shaft	*DP2:* Dyna-mo-meter	*DP3.1:* Dyna-mo-meter nut	*DP3.2:* Profi-led part	*DP4.2:* Ball Bea-ring	*DP4.2:* Step with higher diame-ter and nut on the control man-drel	*DP4.3:* Exter-nal ring placed on the ball bea-ring inclu-ding a sleeve	*DP4.4:* Incomplete additional Ring and lever whose rotation is limited by the longi-tudinal guide
Functional requirement of zero level	Functional requirements of the first level	Functional requirements of the second level	Highlighting the design parameters corresponding to each functional requirement								
FR0: design a device for developing a research activity concerning the rigidity of the lathe during the rotation of its main shaft	*FR1:* Ensure rotation of the lathe main shaft	*FR1.1:* Fix the control mandrel	X								
		FR1.2: Rotate the control mandrel		X							
	FR2: Measure the force generated in the machining system				X						
	FR3: Generate the system loa-ding along a certain direction	*FR3.1:* Generate the loading			X	X					
		FR3.2: Establish the loading direction					X				
	FR4: Ensure contact between dynamometer and the lathe main shaft found in rotation	*FR4.1:* Ensure a nonrotating element placed on the rotating lathe main shaft						X			
		FR4.2: Fix ball bearing on the rotating shaft							X		
		FR4.3: Ensure contact of dynamometer elements and the lathe rotating main shaft								X	
		FR4.4. Ensure rotating complete avoidance of the ring containing the ball bearing									X

parameters. In the future, there is the intention to extend the analysis and defining the components of the selected alternative by means of the axiomatic design method. A device for investigating the lathe system rigidity will be manufactured, to experimentally obtain information concerning the lathe rigidity when the lathe main shaft rotates.

References

1. W. Tatarkiewicz, *A History of Six Ideas: an Essay in Aesthetics* (Neuhoff, The Hague, 1980)
2. S. Meyer, *Introduction: Whitehead Now.* In Handbook of Whiteheadian Process Thought (eds.: M. Weber and W. Desmond, Onto Verlag, Frankfurt / Lancaster, 2008)
3. I. Căpâlneanu, *Intelligence and creativity* (in Romanian) (Editura Militară, Bucharest 1978)
4. I. Ghinea, Buletin de informare tehnico-economică (in Romanian), 2, (1973)
5. Creativity Techniques. A to Z, available: https://www.mycoted.com/Category:Creativity_Techniques, accessed: 3.04.2017
6. 2.882, System design and analysis based in AD and complexities theories (2015), available: http:// documentslide.com/documents/axiomatic-intro. html, accessed: 28.03.2017
7. N.P. Suh, *The Principles of Design* (Oxford University Press, New York, 1990)

8. N.P. Suh, *Axiomatic Design: Advances and Applications* (Oxford University Press, New York, 2001)
9. N.P. Suh, *Complexity: Theory and Applications* (Oxford University Press, New York, 2005)
10. M.S. Slocum, available: https://triz-journal.com/innovation-methods/innovation-triz-theory-inventive-problem-solving/axiomatic-innovation-creativity-exact-science/, accessed : 15.05.2017
11. M.K. Thompson, Proceedings of the 5th International Conference on Axiomatic Design, (2009)
12. D. Mann, TRIZ Journal, June (1999)
13. Y. Borgianni, D. T. Matt, Procedia CIRP, **34**, 1, (2015)
14. S.-T. Uang, C.-L. Liu, and M. Chang, In "*Design, user experience, and usability. Theory, Methods, Tools and Practice*" (ed. A. Marcus), 6770, (Springer, Berlin Heidelberg, 2011)
15. J.R. Duflou, and W. Dewulf, Procedia Engineering, 9, 633 (2006)
16. F. Banciu, I. Grozav, Buletinul AGIR (Romania), 2 (2011)
17. F.V. Banciu, CoSME'16, MATEC Web of Conferences, 94 (2017)
18. K. Yang, 4th International Conference on Axiomatic Design, 2006
19. B. Crowell, P. Gregson, Proceedings of the Canadian Engineering Education Association (2008)
20. A. M. Gonçalves-Coelho, A. J. F. Mourão, Z. L. Pereira, Concurrent Eng-Res A, **13**, 233 (2005)
21. Z. Shi, available: http://tigerprints.clemson.edu/cgi/viewcontent.cgi?article=2779&context=all_theses, (2013), accessed: 10.05.2017
22. J.T. Foley, D.S. Cochran, Procedia CIRP, **60**, 175-180 (2017)
23. I.B. Huang, J. Keisler, I. Linkov, Science of The Total Environment, **409**(19), 3578-3594 (2011)
24. C.-L. Huang, K. Kwang sun, *Multiple Attribute Decision Making. Methods and Applications. A State-of-the-Art Survey* (Springer Verlag, Berlin Heidelberg, 1981)
25. A. Mardini, A. Josh, K.M.D. Nor, Z. Khalifa, A. Val pour, Economic Research-Kenosha Australiana, 28(1), 516-571 (2015)
26. K.D. Gospel, http://bpmsg.com/academic/ahp_catchup (2011), accessed: 5.05.2017
27. C.A. Brown, *Elements of Axiomatic Design. A simple and practical approach to engineering design* (Cazenovia, New York, 2006)

Applications of Axiomatic Design Theory in Design for Human Safety in Manufacturing Systems: A Literature Review

Leyla Sadeghi[1,*], *Mahmoud* Houshmand[1], and *Omid* Fatahi Valilai[1]

[1]Sharif University of Technology, Industrial Engineering Department, Tehran, Iran

Abstract. Design for Human Safety (DfHS) is an approach to integrate knowledge of human safety in the design process. DfHS is multi-disciplinary in its nature, requiring many kinds of information and knowledge. Number of DfHS studies tried to apply Axiomatic Design (AD) to achieve their aims. The purpose of this paper is to review the literature on application of AD in DfHS in manufacturing systems and to propose a roadmap for future DfHS works. This paper examines the number and type of publications dealing with this context. The review covers papers published between 1990 (when AD was introduced first) and 2017. It is based on a range of combinations of the following keywords: "Axiomatic design" and "safety" or "accident" or "hazard" or risk". This review has identified 15 research topics that were clustered into three main research groups: (1) application of AD in ergonomic design; (2) application of AD in human-computer interaction; and (3) application of AD in integrating safety systematically in design process. The authors also tried to identify which axiom of AD has been used in these researches.
Keywords: Design for human safety; Axiomatic design; literature review

1 Introduction

During recent decades, there has been a growing awareness of human safety in the design process. The main responsibility of making a machine safe lies in the design process [1]. In this context, the term "Design for Human Safety" (DfHS) captures this effort to integrate the knowledge on human safety in the design process [2].

A large number of studies, applied design theories, methodologies, tools and/or techniques for considering safety in the design process. Nowadays, Pahl and Beitz's Systematic Approach (SA) [3] and Suh's Axiomatic Design (AD) theory [4, 5] are some of the most widely accepted design theories. Pahl and Beitz describe a product development process as a series of transformations, from problem description to requirements list, to principal solutions and working structures, to preliminary design, to detailed layouts, and to final layout, form/dimensions, and manufacturing specifications. The design activities are classified into: product planning, conceptual design, embodiment design, and detail design. Suh's AD provides the fundamental axioms for analysis and decision making.

AD theory appears to be more effective in the context of DfHS. This theory is useful in this context because of its capacity to present design requirements and associated design parameters, and including criteria for evaluating designs. In recent years, there have been attempts to apply AD principles in DfHS. The number of studies using AD principles is gradually increasing as AD's superiorities create important advantages for decision makers in solving multi-criteria decision making problems. The integration of AD with other design theories, methodologies, tools and/or techniques, such as the systematic approach, has been also appeared in the literature.

This paper focuses primarily on the area of DfHS and investigates the development and the application of AD by an analysis of the literature during the past years. The literature review attempts to answer different questions. The first question to be answered is whether AD has a rising trend in DfHS or a falling one. More precisely, in this paper, we address the following question: How AD can be used to improve human safety early in design process. It should also be investigated, which topics were focused in recent years and whether certain trends and tendencies for the future can be identified in DfHS context. The analysis should also indicate which axioms of AD are predominantly used.

The remainder of this paper is arranged as follows: Section 2 introduces the AD theory, its four fundamental concepts and actual fields of application. In Section 3, our literature review methodology review is described. Section 4 reviews the literature for available researches based on application of AD in DfHS. Section 5 provides a discussion on the chronological and thematic perspectives. This section also identifies the future works regarding AD application in DfHS. Finally, the conclusions are given in Section 6.

* Corresponding author: sadeghi.leyla.87@gmail.com

2 Axiomatic design and its application fields

This section will briefly introduce the AD theory, its four fundamental concepts and actual application fields.

2.1 Introduction to AD

The AD theory was introduced by Suh in 1990. Its goal is to "establish a scientific basis to improve design activities by providing the designer with a theoretical foundation based on logical and rational thought processes and tools" [4]. It insures an efficient approach fulfilling "what we need" by "How we are going to satisfy the requirements". This theory consists of four fundamental concepts [4, 5]:

2.1.1 Design as a mapping process

According to AD, design is made up of four domains. The customer domain is characterized by the needs that the customer is looking to satisfy in a product, process, system or materials. In the functional domain, the customer's needs are specified in terms of Functional Requirements (FRs) and Constraints (Cs). In order to satisfy the specified FRs, Design Parameters (DPs), which are the key variables, are conceived in the physical domain. Finally, to produce the product specified in terms of DPs, AD develops a procedure characterized by Process Variables (PVs) in the process domain (Figure 1).

2.1.2 Top-down hierarchical design structure

Design usually consists in decomposition with multiple abstraction levels (Figure 1). The higher levels are more abstract; where the lower ones are more detailed. The design process has to begin at the system level and continue through more detailed levels until reaching a point of sufficient clarity to represent the design object. This process is called hierarchical decomposition and its outcome is depicted by a tree-model in each of the four domains.

2.1.3 Design matrix

The relationship between FRs and DPs is represented in a matrix which allows evaluating the structure of the product. This matrix is called the 'design matrix' which links FRs to DPs and characterizes the product design. When the design matrix is diagonal, the design is called an "Uncoupled design". The design is called a "Decoupled design" when the design matrix is triangular. A coupled design occurs when the design matrix is a full one. Both uncoupled and decoupled designs satisfy the independence axiom and are considered acceptable in axiomatic design.

2.1.4 Design axioms

Suh [4] formulated two axioms for good design:
(1) The independence axiom: maintains the independency of the FRs. In an acceptable design, mapping between the FRs and the DPs is such that each FR can be satisfied without affecting the other FRs;
(2) The information axiom: minimizes the information content of the design. If a set of designs satisfy the same FRs and conforms to the independence axiom, the best is that with the minimum information content. The information axiom provides a quantitative measure of the merits of a given design.

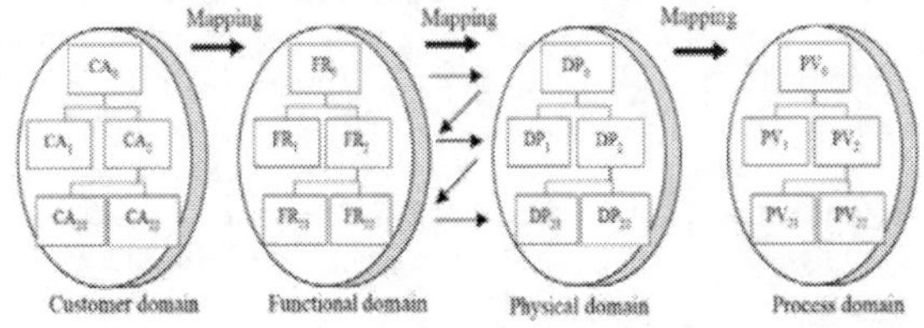

Fig. 1. Axiomatic design approach.

The reader is referred to [4, 5] for further details on AD, its concepts and architecture.

2.2 AD and DfX

AD theory is used in many different areas such as software design but also for the design of large and complex systems. Kulak et al. [6] identified the application of AD for the following areas: decision making, software design, system design, manufacturing system design, and others.

Design for X (DfX) is one of the most effective approaches to make the product better suited for its life phases, and increase the general virtues of the product in order to improve its performance [7]. According to [8, 9], X represents a specific property (e.g., quality, safety); and a life-cycle phase of the product (e.g. manufacturing and assembly).

In the past 20 years, there have been attempts to apply AD principles in DfX. Such as Application of AD in: Design for manufacturing, e.g., [10–12]; Design for cost, e.g., [13]; Design for quality, e.g., [14]; Design for recycling, e.g., [15]; Design for human safety e.g., [2]; and etc.

The purpose of this paper is to review the literature on application of AD in design for human safety (DfHS) in manufacturing systems.

3 Literature review methodology

The aim of this step is to collect enough appropriate publications related to application of AD in DfHS research. This section provides an overview and analysis of studies carried out based on (1) the author(s) name(s), (2) title of the paper, (3) the year of publication of each paper and (4) the title of the journal. This search strategy was developed by first identifying the relevant time frame, data sources and key words. Initially, this study focused on literature published between 1990 (when AD was introduced) to 2017. The preliminary search was conducted on five databases including Elsevier, Springer, Taylor & Francis, Wiley Online Library, and American Society of Mechanical Engineers (ASME). The five databases involved the main peer-referred journals on the topic of DfHS.

In the preliminary search, a search was made under the "Title" criteria in the databases, with the full search schema "Title ((Axiomatic design) and (safety))". Whereas, from preliminary search, many of papers could be found, we tried to eliminate some of them. In order to ensure the papers selected were of high quality, six journals focusing on application of AD in DfHS were chosen. Three of these journals are leading journals in the field of "engineering design". Two of them are in the field of "safety management". The remaining two are also leading journals in the field of "ergonomics". The secondary search within these six selected journals was made using the "Title/Abstract/Keyword" criteria. As none of the databases covered all the aforementioned journals, different databases had to be used. The search strategy initially identified keywords that could be associated with application of AD in DfHS. The search was based on a range of combinations of the following keywords: "Axiomatic Design" and "safety" or "accident" or "hazard" or risk". Finally, we did not limit the potential journals to cover a diverse range of publication formats including conference proceedings (specially International Conference on Axiomatic Design (ICAD) proceedings), theses and books. To ensure completeness, an Internet search was also conducted using a similar process to that used with the library databases. The search was conducted using the same keywords in the secondary search. The results of these searches were combined to provide a total of 22 documents.

3.1 Literature selection

The objective of this review was not to obtain a complete list of papers, but rather to explore the current trends, useful findings and research gaps of application of AD in DfHS. On the other hand, some of the selected papers that did not match the subject but matched the research schema were selected. It was essential to make further efforts to screen and filter the 22 papers for in-depth review. In the relevant papers selection, two filter criteria were used to further select relevant papers for in-depth review and analysis: (1) the papers were focused on application of AD in improving safety in domains other than design and manufacturing systems, for instance, construction safety; and (2) only the words in the search terms were mentioned, but not studied in depth. After applying the selection criteria, 15 relevant documents remained. Figure 2 shows relevant papers in the six journals, ICAD proceedings and other publication formats. This figure clearly shows that predominantly (40%) relevant papers are in ICAD proceedings.

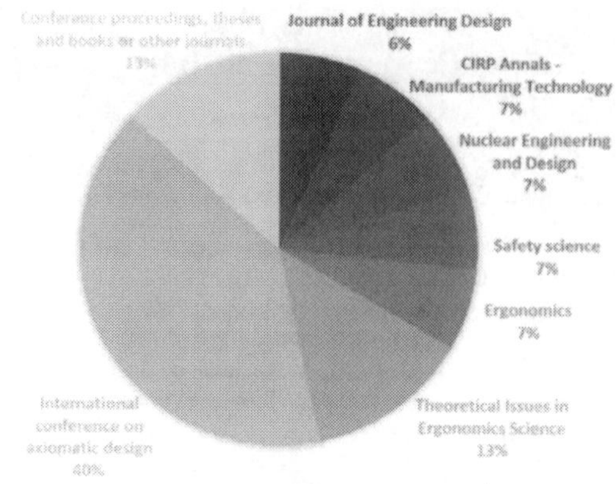

Fig. 2. The number of papers related to application of AD in DfHS.

4 Results and analysis

Initially, the search terms identified some 22 journal articles, conference proceedings, theses and books, handbooks or reports. These were then carefully filtered to establish 15 documents that were clustered into three main following research groups: (1) application of AD in ergonomic design; (2) application of AD in human-computer interaction; and (3) application of AD on integrating safety systematically in design process. In the following section, a brief description of each group is described.

4.1 AD and ergonomic design

An axiomatic approach to ergonomic design and a universal measure of system-human incompatibility was introduced by Karwowski [16]. Karwowski describes the rules of good ergonomic design which consists of human-design compatibility (Figure 3). The two axioms of axiomatic design were adapted for ergonomic design purposes. Axiom 1 stipulates the independence of the functional compatibility requirements and Axiom 2 stipulates the need to minimize the incompatibility content of the design. Ergonomic design is defined as mapping from system-human compatibility needs to relevant compatibility requirements. System-human compatibility is expressed in terms of human abilities and limitations at the beginning of the design process. Hazard prevention aspects are not taken into account.

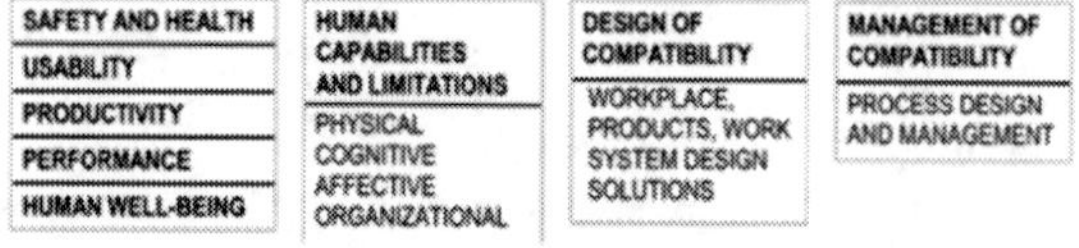

Fig. 3. Four domains of design in ergonomics [16].

Heo and Lee [17] proposed a methodology to examine the design process using AD as a measure for evaluating safety. This is particularly important for identifying vulnerabilities and creating solutions. To improve performance and safety, various design strategies such as independency and redundancy were implemented. The authors suggested an alternative viewpoint for evaluating deployment of design strategies in terms of AD. AD suggests two design principles and visualization tools for organizing the design process. The major benefit of AD is that it is capable of providing suitable priorities for deploying design strategies. AD principles were used to develop a fault tree to analyse the reliability of the design parameters used to meet the functional requirements.

4.2 AD and human–computer interaction

Helander and his colleagues illustrated the applicability of AD principles in human factors design and human–computer interaction (HCI).

Helander and Lin [18] demonstrated the use of AD for the anthropometric design of workplaces. They showed how the formulation of FRs and DPs can help in conceptualizing design principles and selecting design parameters for a seated work place. Their research suggested a new way of calculating the information contents in anthropometric design by redefining the concepts of system range and design range. The two axioms fit well with the type of design methodology that has been developed in ergonomics over the years. (1) It has been well recognized that formulations of functional requirements are essential to ergonomics design. (2) In ergonomics design, minimization of information has long been recognized as an important criteria.

Helander and Lin [19] demonstrated how AD can be used for biomechanics design of hand tools and for anthropometric design of workplaces. For this aim, they used two axioms of AD theory. The first axiom was used to demonstrate how design activity can be structured to avoid time-consuming iterative improvements of design solutions. The second axiom was used for anthropometric design of a work place.

Helander and Jiao [20] suggested that the AD framework could be used to analyse and reduce coupling in software usability heuristics. To uncouple the design a cluster analysis was performed on the original design matrix. Then, FRs were split and recombined in order to reduce the coupling.

Helander [21] and Lo & Helander [22] extended previous efforts and developed a Design Equations for Systems Analysis (DESA) methodology (Figure 4) based on the principles of AD. The aim is to identify and suggest avenues for eliminating coupling between user goals and user actions. This methodology consists of four domains, namely user goals, functional requirements, design parameters and user actions, to model the human-machine system functionally and structurally. However, this methodology describes the rules for achieving a usable design and then takes into account only the user actions to meet a specific goal. Thus, in performing a global analysis it consists of solutions from the standpoints of design and usability.

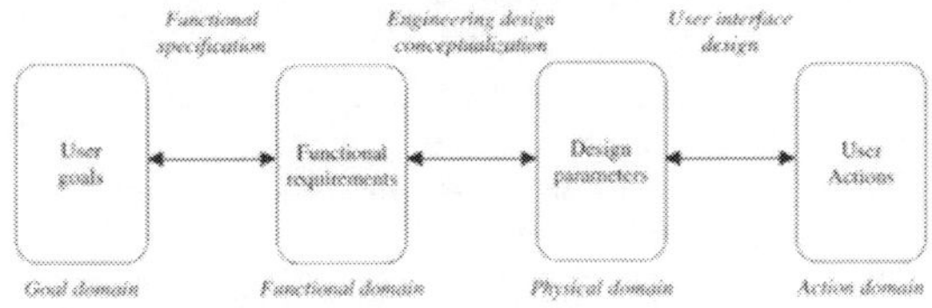

Fig. 4. DESA framework [22].

4.3 AD and integrating safety systematically in design process

To integrate safety systematically from the early design process, [23–26] first sought to formulate a systematic description of the design process. To this end, they used the "extended axiomatic design" (EAD) proposed by [27]. EAD combines the systematic approach [3] and axiomatic design [4, 5]. It consists of considering that three of the four phases of the systematic approach, i.e. conceptual, embodiment and detailed design, are divided into two domains: functional and physical (Figure 5).

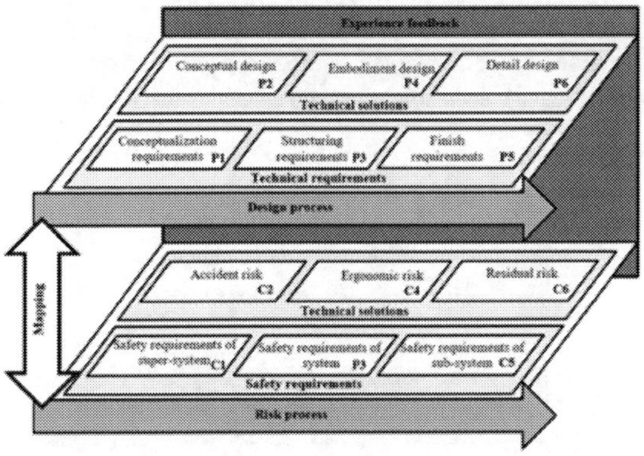

Fig. 5. IRAD framework [23].

Ghemraoui et al. used the systematic approach to formulate a typology of safety objects at each design phase [23–25]. To satisfy safety needs, they adopted a representation for the design process that links the systematic approach to AD [4, 5]. The method proposed, Innovative Risk Assessment Design (IRAD), consists of a general suggestion for systematic risk identification and human-safety integration in the early design phase. It considers design as an iterative activity between a design process and a risk process. These two processes evolve simultaneously and influence each other. The design process is divided into six phases. Similarly, the risk process is divided into six contexts. This method consists of a general suggestion for systematic risk identification and human-safety integration in the early design phase. Consequently, IRAD considers design as an iterative activity between a design process and a risk process (Figure 5). Other paper of Ghemraoui et al. [26] deals with the problem of defining safety objectives early in the product design process. They show that there are different typologies of safety objectives depending on the evolution of the product.

Sadeghi et al. attempted to operationalize the IRAD method [2, 28, 29]. To do this, they suggested a DfHS method using two sequential methods. The first method [2, 29] proposed a Functional Reverse Engineering for Safety (FRES) approach underpinned by AD to obtain design feedback from knowledge of an existing system. The aim of FRES is to acquire the original intrinsic design and safety knowledge integrated in the functional models of existing systems (Figure 6). The proposed method can distinguish the components, design parameters and function requirements of an existing system and define the hazard related to each component, the design parameter and the functional requirement. Sadeghi et al. used product breakdown structure (PBS) [30] to represent the system components by the structural decomposition. To illustrate the interaction between this system component decomposition, the functional block diagram (FBD) has been used. This diagram highlights the fluxes existing between the elements of the product (contact, energy, matter, regard), and the external environments. The second method [28, 29] proposed a Functional RE-Engineering for Safety (FR2ES) approach using AD to define a system with good mechanical safety that is reliable and robust, and with few possible human errors. They used AD and failure mode and effect analysis (FMEA) to define a system with high mechanical safety as well as reliability and robustness.

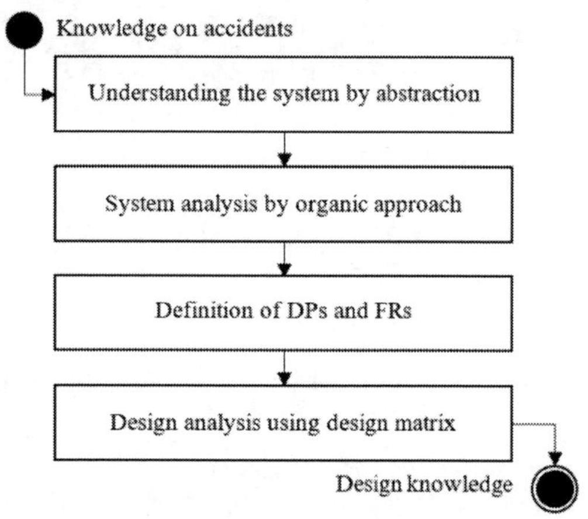

Fig. 6. Design knowledge extraction [29].

Sadeghi et al. [31] defined a safety indicator to assess the safety level. This indicator can measure safety from the conceptual design phase because, according to AD, a good design is a design with no coupling between the functional requirements. This consideration is included in the safety indicator. Reliability, which involves the life of the system, cannot be assessed in the embodiment design phase. It is also taken into account in calculating this indicator but is considered optimal in the conceptual design phase. Sadeghi et al. used two axioms of AD theory to calculate the influence of the system on hazardous event.

5 Discussion

5.1 Chronological discussion

As shown in Figure 7, the number of relevant papers published annually is not large, fewer than five before 2009. First research on application of AD in DfHS has been done ten years after introducing AD.

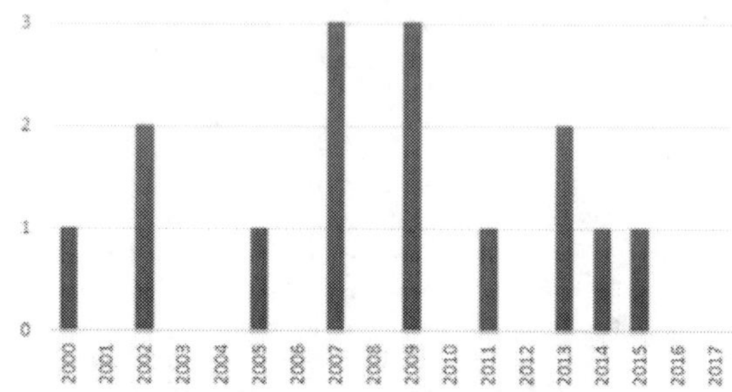

Fig. 7. Year of publications (till April 2017).

5.2 Thematic discussion

This paper summarises our findings based on our literature review of research on application of AD in DfHS. The results of this literature review are presented in Table 1.

Figure 8 shows how many of the DfHS works focus in specific the axioms of AD. The figure clearly shows that predominantly (60%) the both axioms are applied and deeper analysed. Approximately another 13% of the research papers involve first axiom of AD. Only few about 7% deepen their work also with the help of the second axiom. About 20% of researches have no focus on axioms of AD.

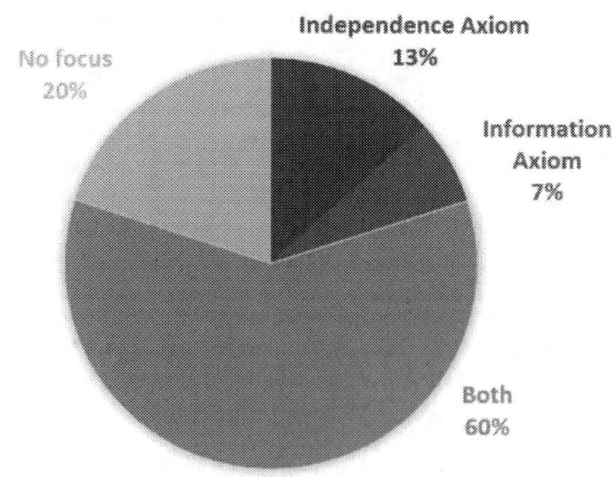

Fig. 8. Focus on axioms of AD.

DOI: 10.1051/matecconf/201712701020

Table 1. Application of AD in DfHS.

Author	Group			Focus on				Integration with others methods / tools	Application
	Ergonomic design	HCI	DfHS systematically	Independence axiom	Information axiom	Both axioms	No focus		
Helander & Lin [18]	✓					✓		-	Microscope workstation
Helander & Lin [19]	✓					✓		-	Microscope workstation
Helander & Jiao [20]	✓			✓				-	Usability testing
Karwowski [16]		✓				✓		-	Rear lighting system of an automobile
Heo & Lee [17]		✓				✓		FTA	Nuclear power plants
Helander [21]		✓				✓		-	Dual reservoir system
Lo & Helander [22]		✓				✓		-	Dual reservoir system
Ghemraoui et al. [23]			✓				✓	SA	Three-point hitch (TPH)
Ghemraoui et al. [24]			✓				✓	SA	TPH
Ghemraoui [25]			✓			✓		SA	TPH
Ghemraoui et al. [26]			✓				✓	SA	Daul knob faucet, Ski bindings
Sadeghi et al. [2]			✓	✓				SA FTA	Power take-off (PTO) drive shaft
Sadeghi et al. [28]			✓		✓			SA FMEA	PTO drive shaft
Sadeghi [29]			✓			✓		SA FTA FMEA TRIZ	PTO drive shaft & TPH
Sadeghi et al. [31]			✓			✓		SA FTA FMEA TRIZ	PTO drive shaft

5.3 Proposed roadmap for future DfHS works

The present paper aims to show how AD can contribute to human safety improvement in deisgn process. Overall, the findings of the surveys and literature reviewed indicate that AD theory is more effective in the context of DfHS. This theory is useful in DfHS because of its capacity to present FRs and associated DPs, and includes criteria for evaluating designs. This method can be implemented at the conceptual design phase; so, FRs could be considered from the most early design phases by using this theory.

Among the research works reviewed that of Ghemraoui and her colleagues [23–25] and Sadeghi et al. [2, 28, 29] should be highlighted. Their proposal consists of a general suggestion for systematic risk identification and human safety integration in the early design phase.

As mentioned previously, in [31] the safety measured in terms of dimensionless quantities parameters. The saftey measured based on hazard evaluation. But, expert opinions are often used to assess the hazards and probability of occurrence of risk in the context of DfHS. For future research directions, one path could be to investigate a method capable of taking into account uncertainties associated with expert judgements. To this, a database should store links of FR-DP-hazards. Categorization of mechanical hazards is not standardized thus, giving rise to confusion during design for human safety. The dimensions of a taxonomy for classification of hazard depend on the nature of the hazard (source of hazard) and the anatomy of accidents (consequence of hazard). To realize this link, hazards and more specificly source of hazards should be classified and standardized. To this, we can investigate on standard engineering components which use form features and support international standard for exchange of product data (STEP) formats. Therfore, to effectively integrate the hazards into the FR-DP , hazard shoud be embedded with STEP.

As a result, applying the methodology provides explicit safety knowledge related to design, as well as the relationship between this design knowledge and its corresponding design phase. This knowledge is based on the expertise and is essential for the future development of a software system that effectively provides necessary DfHS information to designers. This means providing information for each of the design phases without saturating designers with unnecessary information.

Recently, with combination of emerged technologies such as cloud computing, Internet of things, service-oriented technologies and high performance computing, a new manufacturing paradigm, named cloud manufacturing (CM), has been introduced. CM is known as a movement from production-oriented manufacturing to service-oriented manufacturing

In an ongoing research on DfHS, authors are developing an integrated, interoperable and collaborative platform to support DfHS using a service-oriented approach based on cloud computing paradigm. Considering the huge amount of different design and safety requests which should be fulfilled by this platform, a structured solution for definition, execution and management of the services is essential. This can be achieved based on the AD theory. This solution insures a feasible structure of service execution to fulfill the safety agents' request. For further researches, one objective is to demonstrate how the AD theory can be used to support our cloud-based DfHS platform.

One idea is to recommend optimization of CBDfHS platform using the second axiom of AD. Duirng DfHS, some constraints, such as lack of related information or devices, or some environmental constraints, don't allow designers to choose safer solutions. We need to consider the mapping between FRs, DPs and PVs over the time. For example, a smart vehicle is the most safe solution to prevent road traffic accidents, but a smart vehicle should be used in a smart city, and this constraint prevents to design smart vehicle. But in future, a smart city evolves and as a consequence smart vehicle could be designed and developed.

6 Conclusion

An overview and analysis of these studies were carried out based on (1) the author(s) name(s), (2) title of the paper, (3) the year of publication of each paper and (4) the title of the journal. This review identified 15 research topics that were clustered into three main research groups. The first group focused on the application of AD in ergonomic design. The second one focused on the use of AD in human computer interaction. The last group focused on integrating safety systematically in design process based on AD and systematic approach. AD is also used in safety evaluation during design process. AD appears to be more effective in the context of DfHS.

The results of this review provide a roadmap for our current research in DfHS in manufacturing systems and also vehicles. The review identified and discussed two gaps in application of AD in DfHS: A database should store links of FR-DP-hazards. In other words, the hazards should be effectively integrated with the FR-DP. For further researches, another objective is to demonstrate how the AD theory can be used to support our cloud-based DfHS platform.

The authors wish to thank to the SAIPA (Iranian Automobile Production Company) and Vice-Chancellor of Research and Technology of Sharif University of Technology who have supported the study.

Appendix: glossary

AD	Axiomatic Design
CM	Cloud Manufacturing
CBDfHS	Cloud-Based Design for Human Safety
DESA	Design Equations for Systems Analysis
DfHS	Design for Human Safety
DfX	Design for X
DPs	Design Parameters
FBD	Functional Block Diagram
FRES	Functional Reverse Engineering for Safety
FR2ES	Functional RE-Engineering for Safety
FRs	Functional Requirements
FTA	Fault Tree Analysis
FMEA	Failure Mode and Effect Analysis
HCI	Human-Computer Interaction
IRAD	Innovative Risk Assessment Design
PBS	Product Breakdown Structure
SA	Systematic Approach
TRIZ	Theory of inventive problem solving

References

1 A. C. Caputo, P. M. Pelagagge, P. Salini, *AHP-based methodology for selecting safety devices of industrial machinery*, Saf. Sci. **53**, 202–218 (2013)

2 L. Sadeghi, L. Mathieu, N. Tricot, L. Al Bassit, R. Ghemraoui, *Toward design for safety Part 1: Functional reverse engineering driven by axiomatic design*, Proceedings of the 7th International Conference on Axiomatic Design-ICAD (2013)

3 G. Pahl, W. Beitz, J. Feldhusen, and H. Grote, K, *Engineering Design A Systematic Approach*. (Springer-Verlag London Limited, 2007)

4 N. P. Suh, *The Principles of Design*. (Oxford University Press, New York, NY, 1990)

5 N. P. Suh, *Axiomatic Design: Advances and Applications*. (Oxford University Press, 2001)

6 O. Kulak, S. Cebi, and C. Kahraman, *Applications of axiomatic design principles: A literature review*, Expert Syst. Appl. **37**, 9, 6705–6717 (2010)

7 G. Q. Huang, *Design for X - concurrent engineering imperatives*. (Springer Science+Business Media, B.V., 1996)

8 C. G. van Hemel, T. Keldman, *Applying 'Design for X' Experience in Design for Environment*, in Huang GQ (ed) Design for X: concurrent engineering imperatives, 72-95 (Chapman & Hall, London, 1996)

9 R. Holt, C. Barnes, *Towards an integrated approach to 'design for X': An agenda for decision-based DFX research*, Res. Eng. Des. **21**, 123–136 (2010)

10 P. Almstroem, *Utilizing Axiomatic Design in a Manufacturing System Development Framework*, Proceedings of the 1th Int. Conf. Axiomat. Des. ICAD (2000)

11 A. M. Gonçalves-Coelho, A. J. F. Mourão, *Axiomatic design as support for decision-making in a design for manufacturing context: A case study*, Int. J. Prod. Econ. **109** 81–89 (2007)

12 I. Ferrer, J. Rios, J. Ciurana, M. L. Garcia-Romeu, *Methodology for capturing and formalizing DFM Knowledge*, Robot. Comput. Integr. Manuf. **26**, 5, 420–429 (2010)

13 T. Lee, P. Jeziorek, A*n Exploratory Study of Cost Engineering in Axiomatic Design: Creation of the Cost Model Based on an FR-DP Map*, Proceedings of the 3th International Conference on Axiomatic Design, ICAD (2004)

14 B. Nepal, L. Monplaisir, N. Singh, *A methodology for integrating design for quality in modular product design*, J. Eng. Des. **17**, 5, 387–409 (2006)

15 D. R. Wallace, N. P. Suh, *Information-Based Design for Environmental Problem Solving*, Ann. CIRP **42**, 1, 175–180 (1993)

16 W. Karwowski, *Ergonomics and human factors: the paradigms for science, engineering, design, technology and management of human-compatible systems*, Ergonomics **48**, 5, 436–463 (2005)

17 G. Heo, S. K. Lee, *Design evaluation of emergency core cooling systems using Axiomatic Design*, Nucl. Eng. Des. **237**, 38–46 (2007)

18 M. G. Helander, L. Lin, *Anthropometric Design of Workstations*, Proceedings of the 1th International Conference on Axiomatic Design, ICAD (2000)

19 M. G. Helander, L. Lin, *Axiomatc design in ergonomics and an extension of the information axiom*, J. Eng. Des. **13**, 4, 321–339 (2002)

20 M. G. Helander, J. Jiao, *Coupling in Design of Human Computer Interaction*, Proceedings of the 2th International Conference on Axiomatic Design, ICAD (2002)

21 M. G. Helander, *Using design equations to identify sources of complexity in human–machine interaction,* Theor. Issues Ergon. Sci. **8**, 2, 123–146 (2007)

22 S. Lo,M. G. Helander, *Use of axiomatic design principles for analysing the complexity of human–machine systems*, Theor. Issues Ergon. Sci. **8**, 2, 147–169 (2007)

23 R. Ghemraoui, L. Mathieu, N. Tricot, *Design method for systematic safety integration*, CIRP Ann. - Manuf. Technol. **58**, 161–164 (2009)

24 R. Ghemraoui, L. Mathieu, N. Tricot, *Systematic Human-Safety Analysis Approach Based on Axiomatic Design Principles*, Proceedings of the 5th International Conference on Axiomatic Design, ICAD (2009)

25 R. Ghemraoui, *Méthodologie de conception innovante intégrant la sécurité des utilisateurs : application aux liaisons tracteur-outils* (École Normale Supérieure de Cachan, 2009)

26 R. Ghemraoui, L. Mathieu, C. a Brown, *Defining Safety Objectives During Product Design*, Proceedings of the 6th International Conference on Axiomatic Design, ICAD (2011)

27 P. Ge, S. C.-Y. Lu, N. P. Suh, *An Axiomatic Approach for 'Target Cascading' of Parametric Design of Engineering Systems*, CIRP Ann. - Manuf. Technol. **51**, 1, 111–114 (2002)

28 L. Sadeghi, L. Mathieu, N. Tricot, L. Al Bassit, R. Ghemraoui, *Toward Design for Safety Part 2: Functional Re-Engineering Using Axiomatic Design and FMEA*, Proceedings of the 7th International Conference on Axiomatic Design, ICAD (2013)

29 L. Sadeghi, *Aide à la décision pour l'intégration de la sécurité au plus tôt en phase de conception-Approche innovante de reconception de machines agricoles*, (École Normale Supérieure de Cachan, 2014)

30 V. Ho Kon Tiat, *Aide à la décision pour la conception préliminaire de procédés d'évaporation flash*, (Université Bordeaux 1, 2006)

31 L. Sadeghi, L. Mathieu, N. Tricot, L. Al Bassit, *Developing a safety indicator to measure the safety level during design for safety*, Saf. Sci. **80**, 252–263 (2015)

Analysis of a Device for Texturing by Burnishing Using Principles from Axiomatic Design

Gheorghe Nagîț*, *Laurențiu* Slătineanu, *Vasile* Merticaru, *Marius Ionuț* Rîpanu, *Andrei Marius* Mihalache, *Lucian* Tăbăcaru, and *Mihai* Boca

"Gheorghe Asachi" Technical University of Iași, Bvd. D. Mangeron 39A, Iași, 700050, Romania

Abstract. The vibro-burnishing is a process by means a ball or a roller or other tool active surface is pressed and moved, inclusively by applying a vibratory motion, along the surface to be finished, generating a specific microrelief. A device for vibro-burnishing adapted on a universal lathe was analyzed by means of some principles corresponding to the Axiomatic Design theory. The analysis was developed by adopting some simplifying assumptions and it proved an adequate design, by considering some functional requirements and design parameters specific to the device.

1 Introduction

Frequently, within mechanical equipment, the surfaces by which a part contacts another part must have a low roughness; for example, if there is an interference fit, the recommended values for the surface roughness parameter *Ra* are of 3.2-6.4 µm, while for the clearance fit, the surface roughness parameter *Ra* has values lower than 1.6 µm. It is interesting the fact that sometimes, in the case of clearance fits, there is the recommendation that the surface has a certain microrelief, necessary in order to fulfil the condition of retaining the oil applied for diminishing the friction forces. Thus, one can meet situations when after a final machining process of grinding or another finishing process, a certain supplementary machining process must be applied, in order to generate the small cavities able to retain the oil.

There are distinct machining processes which can be used in order to generate the desired microrelief on the part surfaces for the above mentioned situations; if the main characteristics of the processes are taken into consideration, one can classify these machining processes as being based on cutting (abrasive) phenomena and on surface plastic cold deformation, respectively. In the group of machining methods based on cold plastic superficial deformation, there is a process called *texturing by burnishing*. Essentially, such a process is materialized by pressing and moving the active part of a plastic deformation tool along the pre-established trajectories on the surface of the metallic part to be machined. If a vibration is used in order to obtain the desired superficial texture and a roll or a tool similar to a roll is used, the process could be named "vibro burnishing" or "vibro-rolling".

Over the years, the texturing by burnishing constituted an objective for the researches in the field of machine manufacturing technology.

Thus, some decades ago, an ample research of this machining method was developed and promoted in the former Soviet Union by G. Schneider [1]; he proposed a set of devices for investigating the influence of distinct factors on the properties of the surface layer obtained by burnishing and vibro-burnishing processes.

Revenko et al. [2] were interested to investigate the influence of the microrelief obtained by ball vibro-burnishing of a steel part upon the corrosion resistance. They noticed that in comparison with the grinding, the vibro-burnishing ensures a better part behavior to the corrosion process in a humidity cabinet and in a salt-spray camera.

Kumar and Purohit took into consideration the possibilities of developing an improved ball burnishing tool, which could be positioned and clamped in the tool holder of a universal lathe [3]. They considered that this tool is convenient for developing a research concerning the influence exerted by some process input factors (workpiece rotation speed, feed, force, number of passes) upon the values of the parameters of technological interest.

Hadamache et al. assumed the objective to develop a device for mechanical plastic deformation by means of a ball or a roller burnishing [4]. They concluded that if the surface roughness, the hardness and the wear resistance are taken into consideration as process outputs, the roller burnishing offers a better surface roughness, while the ball burnishing is advantageous when the increase of the surface layer hardness is considered as final objective.

Korzynski and Lubas approached the problem of obtaining a certain bushing texturing by burnishing [5]. They developed a theoretical and experimental research using an oscillatory movement along the longitudinal feed in the case of finishing internal cylindrical surfaces. Distinct constructive solutions were designed in order to

* Corresponding author: nagit@tcm.tuiasi.ro

obtain a more adequate fulfilling of the machining process requirements.

Within the "Gheorghe Asachi" Technical University of Iaşi, a research developed by Nagit highlighted the possibility of using a ball vibro-burnishing process and a diamond type tool also within a vibro-burnishing process, in order to diminish the surface roughness and to improve the service properties of steel parts [6].

On the other hand, the Axiomatic Design theory takes into consideration the so-called *functional requirements* in order to adequately establish *the design parameters* and *process variables*; this design theory was used in the last years in order to design various mechanical equipment or to analyze distinct versions of solving various problems [7-10].

The objective followed by this paper was to present the results obtained by using the principles of the Axiomatic Design for analyzing a device for vibro-burnishing adapted on a universal lathe.

2 Theoretical aspects concerning the process of vibro–burnishing

As a consequence of applying distinct machining processes involving the material removal from the workpiece, asperities with various heights are generated on the machined surface. Usually, such machining methods determines also the change of some properties of the surface layer; the crystals are deformed and sometimes there is also a heat affected zone, as a result of high temperature developed, for example, when high machining speeds are used. In order to diminish the height of asperities obtained by previous applied machining process and, simultaneously, to increase the hardness of the superficial metallic layer, a burnishing process could be applied. In such a case, a ball is placed instead the cutting tool specific to a longitudinal turning process. This ball is supported by one or more rolling elements and it is pressed on the surface to be burnished. In order to increase the process efficiency, a vibratory additional movement could be achieved by the ball and, in this way, a *vibro-burnishing process* could be materialized (Figure 1).

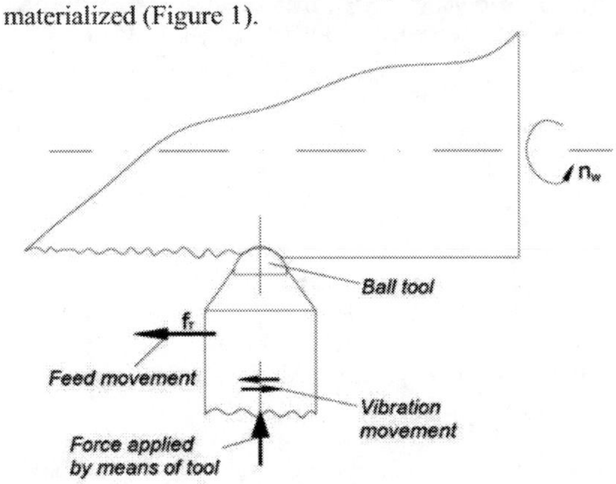

Fig. 1. Machining scheme valid in the case of vibro-burnishing on a lathe.

In the work zone, the ball presses the workpiece material found in asperities, achieving a smoothing effect; practically, as a consequence of the deformation process, the material of asperities is re-distributed, so that a decrease of the asperities height is achievable (Figure 2). A second effect of the process is the strong deformation of the crystals found in the surface layer; evidently, the crystals found near the workpiece surface are affected by a more intense plastic deformation process, while at a higher distance from the workpiece surface, crystals are practically not affected by the vibro-burnishing process.

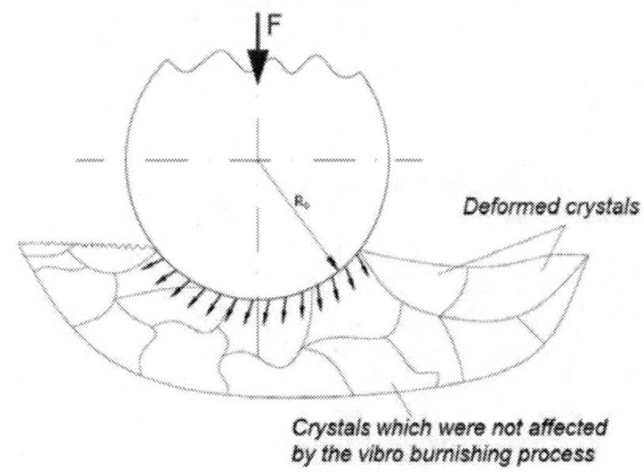

Fig. 2. Phenomena developed in the work zone in the case of vibro-burnishing.

In order to materialize the vibro-burnishing process and, in accordance with the above mentioned aspects, a device for vibro-burnishing adaptable on a universal lathe was designed and achieved [6]. The nominated device (Figure 3) includes a plate which can be placed instead of the common tool holder existing on the universal lathes. An electric motor generates a rotation movement which is transmitted by means of transmission belts to a shaft able to rotate a disk. On this disk, a cylindrical bolt could be moved along a radial direction by acting a drive screw; in this way, the bolt could be placed at distinct radial distances. The eccentric bolt is linked to a connecting rod, which determines a bar to achieve a rectilinear movement, together with the support of the burnishing tool. The bar is supported by another rod, pressed by compressing a spring able to generate a force whose value could be read due to a piece which indicates the deformation of the spring.

The tool is constituted in this case by a ball supported by a radial bearing ball, able to ensure the easy rotation of the ball found in contact with the workpiece surface.

The main work parameters are: the speed of workpiece rotation n_W [rev./min.], the speed of longitudinal feed movement f_T [mm/min.], the force/pressure *F/p* exerted by the ball on the workpiece surface, the amplitude *A* and the frequency *f* of vibratory movement achieved by the ball. In order to develop a research concerning the influence of the process input factors on the process results, it was necessary to ensure possibilities of modifying the values of the input factors between certain limits.

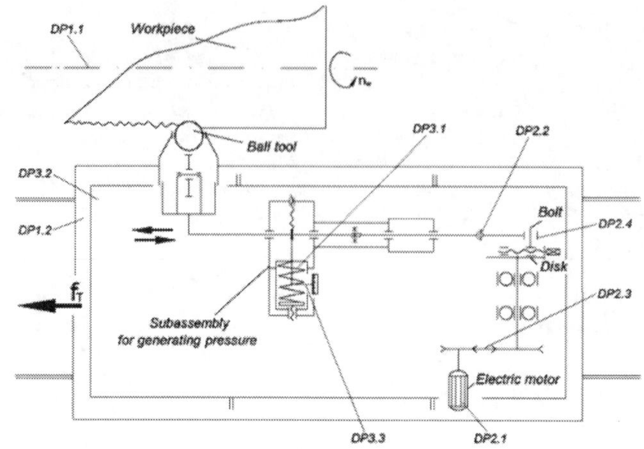

Fig. 3. Kinematic scheme of the device for vibro-burnishing on a lathe.

Thus, the rotation speed n_W of the workpiece could be achieved by means of gear box of the universal lathe. The machine tool (universal lathe) facilitates also the easy change of the speed corresponding to the longitudinal feed speed f_T.

The pressure exerted by the ball on the workpiece surface could be changed by means of the spring included in the device. A certain compression value for the spring, obtained through a screw mechanism, determines a certain small deflection and the corresponding elastic force in the ball tool's supporting shaft, which determines the force/pressure *F/p* exerted by the ball on the workpiece.

In order to change the frequency *f* of the vibratory movement achieved by the tool (ball), pulleys with distinct diameters could be used. By modifying the ratio in the belt transmission, the frequency of the vibratory movement driven by the crank mechanism is changed. The amplitude *A* of the vibratory movement could be established by positioning the bolt at a certain radial distance on the disk rotated by the electric motor. In this way, the length of the crank is modified.

3 Principles specific to the applying of axiomatic design method

There are distinct design methods able to facilitate the selecting by the designer the more adequate constructive solution among many various available solutions.

One of these design theories was proposed some decades ago by Nam Suh, who was then professor in the Massachusetts Institute of Technology (U.S.A.) [7]. Professor Suh tried to establish a more systematic and organized developing of the design activity; over the years, the method of axiomatic design became more and more known and applied, not strictly to solve design problems, but finding also applications in other various field of human activities.

The method takes into consideration two essential axioms:

1. Axiom of independence, which requests the independence of functional requirements corresponding to the equipment to be designed;
2. Axiom of information, which mentions that the quantity of information necessary in the design activity is minimum.

There are also four domains:
a) Customer domain, where the customer's requests are highlighted;
b) Functional domain, where the functional requirements are defined;
c) Physical domain, where the design parameters are established;
d) Process domain, where the process variables are determined.

4 Functional requirements and design parameters in the case of device for vibro-burnishing

As above mentioned, a device for vibro-burnishing was designed and built within a doctoral research developed by Nagit [6]. Taking into consideration the appearance of the Axiomatic Design method and in order to find if some improvements could be applied to this device, an analysis of the device by means of some principles valid in the case of Axiomatic Design was developed. One must mention that in order to ensure a reasonable length of explanations and an easier understanding the way of using the principles of Axiomatic Design, some simplifying assumptions concerning the constructive solution were applied.

Thus, one could consider that the customer (researcher) needs a device for developing a research activity concerning the vibro-burnishing of external cylindrical surfaces belonging to metallic workpieces.

As customer needs, one can mention:

CN1: the device could be achieved within a laboratory for mechanical machining, being adaptable on one of the available machine tools;

CN2: in order to ensure conditions for an experimental research, some possibilities to change the values of the vibro-burnishing process input factors must be ensured.

In accordance with the above mentioned customer needs, the main functional request is:

FR0: design a device for vibro-burnishing, adaptable on one of the machine tools available in a mechanical workshop/laboratory.

If *the functional requirements (FRs) of first order* must be formulated, these can be:

FR1: use a machine tool available in the laboratory, able to ensure a rotation movement and a longitudinal feed movement;

FR2: ensure a vibratory movement, with pre-established values of frequency f and amplitude A;

FR3: ensure pre-established values for the pressure p exerted by ball tool on the workpiece cylindrical surface;

When the problem of defining *the functional requirements of second order* is formulated, one can arrive to:

FR1.1: use the rotation movement of the machine tool main shaft;

FR1.2: use the feed movement of the machine tool table/subassembly;

FR2.1: use a supplier of rotation movement, usually easier obtained by means of electric motors;

FR2.2: transform the rotation movement in a rectilinear one;

FR2.3: ensure possibilities of changing the rotation speed;

FR2.4: ensure possibilities of changing the amplitude A of the vibratory movement;

FR3.1: include element for generating the force F;

FR3.2: ensure possibilities for changing the value of the force F;

FR3.3: ensure possibilities for highlighting the value of the force/pressure F/p exerted by the ball on the workpiece.

In accordance with the above mentioned functional requirements, the following design parameters (*DPs*) were identified:

DP1.1: main shaft of the universal lathe;

DP1.2: lathe apron;

DP2.1: electric motor;

DP2.2: crank mechanism;

DP2.3: belts transmission;

DP2.4: radial slide for moving the bolt corresponding to the connection between the crank and connecting rod;

DP3.1: spring;

DP3.2: transversal slide of the machine tool;

DP3.3: bolt which highlights the value of the spring compression, on a graduate ruler.

These functional requirements and design parameters were included in the Table 1, in order to check the validity of the independence axiom.

The correspondence between the functional requirements *FRs* and design parameters *DPs* could be written as a matrix relation:

$$\{FR\}=[A]\ \{DP\}, \qquad (1)$$

where A is the design matrix by which the transfer functions *FR* and *DP* are taken into consideration.

In the case of the identified device for vibro-burnishing, the relation (1) could be written by using Table 1, as in equation (2).

Table 1. Functional requirements and design parameters.

Design parameters (*DPs*) / Functional requirements (*FRs*)				Design parameters								
				Design parameters corresponding to the first level								
				DP1		*DP2*				*DP3*		
				Design parameters corresponding to the second level								
				DP1.1	*DP1.2*	*DP2.1*	*DP2.2*	*DP2.3*	*DP2.4*	*DP3.1*	*DP3.2*	*DP3.3*
First order *FRs*	*FR1*	Second order *FRs*	*FR1.1*	X								
			FR1.2		X							
	FR2		*FR2.1*			X						
			FR2.2				X					
			FR2.3					X				
			FR2.4						X			
	FR3		*FR3.1*							X		
			FR3.2								X	
			FR3.3									X

$$\begin{Bmatrix} FR1.1 \\ FR1.2 \\ FR2.1 \\ FR2.2 \\ FR2.3 \\ FR2.4 \\ FR3.1 \\ FR3.2 \\ FR3.3 \end{Bmatrix} = \begin{bmatrix} X & 0 & 0 & 0 & 0 & 0 & 0 & 0 & 0 \\ 0 & X & 0 & 0 & 0 & 0 & 0 & 0 & 0 \\ 0 & 0 & X & 0 & 0 & 0 & 0 & 0 & 0 \\ 0 & 0 & 0 & X & 0 & 0 & 0 & 0 & 0 \\ 0 & 0 & 0 & 0 & X & 0 & 0 & 0 & 0 \\ 0 & 0 & 0 & 0 & 0 & X & 0 & 0 & 0 \\ 0 & 0 & 0 & 0 & 0 & 0 & X & 0 & 0 \\ 0 & 0 & 0 & 0 & 0 & 0 & 0 & X & 0 \\ 0 & 0 & 0 & 0 & 0 & 0 & 0 & 0 & X \end{bmatrix} \begin{Bmatrix} DP1.1 \\ DP1.2 \\ DP2.1 \\ DP2.2 \\ DP2.3 \\ DP2.4 \\ DP3.1 \\ DP3.2 \\ DP3.3 \end{Bmatrix} \quad (2)$$

In accordance with the theory of Axiomatic Design, the matrix corresponding to the design matrix is a diagonal matrix and it is considered as *uncoupled matrix;* this could be appreciated as a result of a good design. One must mention that in an initial version considered for the design matrix, in the case of *DP1.1*, *DP1.2*, and *DP2.4*, the lathe was considered and such a version led to a coupled matrix and coupled design, which are not appreciated as adequate from the point of view of the axiomatic design. A second analysis proved the fact that the functional request *FR1.1, FR1.2, FR2.4* are really materialized by means of distinct subassemblies of the lathe and, in this way, an uncoupled matrix could be used.

In the sense of getting forward with the use of Axiomatic Design theory, distinct versions could be searched for each design parameter *DP* and subsequently changes could affect the functional requirements *FRs*.

Another possibility to develop the use of the Axiomatic Design theory could take into consideration the possibilities to split the functional requirements in order to adequately justify the distinct components of the device.

5 Conclusions

The vibro-burnishing is a machining method by which the workpiece surface layer obtained by other previously applied machining techniques is pressed by means of a ball or of other tool active surface, so that a certain relief (usually a relief characterized by a lower surface roughness) could be obtained. The pressure applied by the tool active zone determines a process of plastic deformation, accompanied by an increase of the microhardness and this effect could determine the improvement of final part service properties.

In order to develop a research concerning the influence of distinct process input factors on the values of parameters of technological interest valid in case of vibro-burnishing, a device adaptable on a universal lathe was designed and built.

Afterwards, as a result of appearance and development of the Axiomatic Design theory, the problem of analyzing the measure in which the built device corresponds to the principles of the Axiomatic Design is formulated.

In this way, a so-called uncoupled matrix is identified for a simplified application of some considerations corresponding to the Axiomatic Design theory and this could have the significance of a good design.

In the future, the analysis could be continued by taking into consideration other components and subassembly of the device for vibro-burnishing, in order to identify eventual possibilities of improving its constructive solution and, subsequently, the process variables could be established.

References

1. G. Schneider, *Properties of machine parts with regular micro-reliefs* (in Russian), (Maschinostroenie, Leningrad, 1982)
2. V.G. Revenko, G.R. Alekseeva, N.F. Stepanov, N.L. Bogdashkina, G.P. Chernova, Protection of Metals, **38**, 1 (2002)
3. P. Kumar and G.K. Purohit, International Journal of Engineering Research and Technology, **6**, 6 (2013)
4. H. Hamadache, L. Laouar, N.E. Zeghib, K. Chaoui, Journal of Materials Processing Technology, **180**, (2006)
5. M. Korzynski, J. Lubas, *Nonconventional finishing technologies* (Polish Scientific Publishers PWN, Warsaw, 2013)
6. G. Nagîţ, *Theoretical and experimental contributions concerning the machining by vibro-burnishing* (in Romanian), ("Gheorghe Asachi" Technical University of Iaşi, 1997)
7. N.P. Suh, *Axiomatic Design: Advances and Applications* (Oxford University Press, New York, 2001)
8. C.A. Brown, Journal of Manufacturing Systems, **24**, 3 (2005)
9. M.K. Thompson, *Introduction to Axiomatic Design Theory*, Tutorials of The Eight International Conference on Axiomatic Design, ICAD 2014.
10. L. Slătineanu, *Industrial property* (in Romanian), (Performantica Publishing House, Iaşi, 2015)

MATEC Web of Conferences **127**, 01022 (2017) DOI: 10.1051/matecconf/201712701022
ICAD 2017

A Road Map for Knowledge Management Systems Design Using Axiomatic Design Approach

Mahmoud Houshmand[1,*], and *Mehdi* Amani[2]

[1]Department of Industrial Engineering, Sharif University of Technology, Azadi Ave., Tehran, Iran
[2]Department of Engineering, Khatam University, Shirazi Ave., Tehran, Iran

Abstract. Successful design and implementation of knowledge management systems have been the main concern of many researchers. It has been reported that more than 50% of knowledge management systems have failed, therefore, it is required to seek for a new and comprehensive scientific approach to design and implement it. In the design and implementation of a knowledge management system, it is required to know 'what we want to achieve' and 'how and by what processes we will achieve it'. A literature review conducted and axiomatic design theory selected for this purpose. For the first time, this paper develops a conceptual design of knowledge management systems by means of a hierarchical structure, composed of 'Functional Requirements' (FRs), 'Design Parameters' (DPs), and 'Process Variables' (PVs). The intersection of several studies conducted in the field of knowledge management systems has been used to design the knowledge management model. It reveals that six essential bases of knowledge management are organizational culture, organizational structure, human resources, management and leadership, information technology, and the external environment of the organization; that are represented as top DPs in the structure of the model. These essential factors are decomposed to lower levels by means of zigzagging. The model implemented in Tehran Urban and Suburban Railway Operation Corporation (TUSROC) and the results were very promising. The most important result of this study is a roadmap to design successful and efficient knowledge management systems.

1 Introduction

Nowadays, more than ever managers and researchers realize that sustainable competitive advantage of organizations and companies stems from scarce and valuable resources such as information, knowledge and organizational procedures, which are not completely mimicked and alternated [1]. 'Knowledge management' (KM) is a series of activities, initiatives, and strategies that companies use in creation, storage, transfer and application of knowledge to improve the organizational performance [2]. Despite, the investment growth in the KM area, due to a lack of a roadmap to implement the KM activities, this investment in the mind of managers has become the fad and have additional costs [3].

Knowledge management seems very simple, but organizations that are trying to become a knowledge-based organization, facing a lot of difficulties. There are no available specific guidelines for the implementation of various methods and concepts of knowledge management [4]. Failure of 50% to 80% of knowledge management implementation projects [5, 6] is the result of (i) lack of knowledge management strategy aligned with organizational strategy; (ii) lack of an appropriate implementation procedure. Considering both lacks, the main questions are that: what knowledge is required for the organization? And how acquire it to achieve competitive advantages and sustain them?

One of the most powerful tools based on a scientific and systematic approach that can answer the above questions is the 'Axiomatic Design' (AD) Theory.

AD asks the designer to develop functional requirements in various aspects of system design systematically and defines the appropriate tools and processes to satisfy them. The separation of 'What' and 'How' in the AD results in flexibility, which is its great advantage versus other design methods [7]. On the other hand, the AD approach during the design process of a new system, based on the mapping process of one set of variables to another [8]. Hence, AD is an appropriate tool for current assessment and changes in processes.

This article uses Axiomatic Design Theory to design a 'Knowledge Management System' (KMS) based on organizational strategies. For this purpose, presents a roadmap to clarifying the objectives of knowledge management and considers the factors influencing on knowledge management system goals. This roadmap provides the appropriate Functional Requirements (FRs), Design Parameters (DPs), and Process Variables (PVs) in various stages of design and implementation to reduce the failure probability. The knowledge management system based on the Axiomatic Design approach is

* Corresponding author: hoshmand@sharif.edu

simple, fluent, comprehensive, practical, and step-by-step methodology.

2 Principle of Axiomatic Design

Suh [9] states that the ultimate goal of Axiomatic Design is to establish a science base for design and to improve design activities by providing the designer with a theoretical foundation based on logical and rational thought processes and tools. The design is an interplay between 'what we want to achieve' and 'how we will achieve it'. To systematize the thought process involved in this interplay, the concept of domains that create demarcation lines between various design activities is a foundation of axiomatic design. The world of design is made up of four domains: customer domain, functional domain, physical domain and process domain [10].

The attributes desired by customer needs (CNs) are sometimes difficult to define or vaguely defined. These needs are mapped into functional requirements (FRs). This must be defined without ever thinking about something that has been already designed or what the design solution should be. After defining the FRs in functional domain, the next step is the imagination of physical parameters in the physical domain to satisfy the functional requirements. Then, the design enters the process domain. The process variables are selected to satisfy the DPs. Design activities from customer requirements to functional requirements is named conceptual design and from functional requirements to the physical domain is called product design and eventually, from the physical domain to process domain is named process design [10].

One advantage of AD is the hierarchical structure of it, that allows for the designer to deal with design complex issues easily. In other words, by reciprocating motion (Zigzaging) between the different design domains, we create hierarchies for FRs, DPs, and PVs in each design domain (See Figure 1).

In order to mapping be satisfied between domains, two axioms must be followed:

Axiom 1: The Independence Axiom

Maintain the independence of the functional requirements (FRs).

Axiom 2: The Information Axiom

Minimize the information content of the design.

Mathematically, the set of independent FRs could be considered as a vector **FR** with m components. In the same way, the DPs may be treated as a vector **DP** with n components.

Thus the design process in which the relationships of FRs and DPs are determined may be expressed as

$$\{\mathbf{FR}\} = [A]\ \{\mathbf{DP}\} \qquad (1)$$

where A is the design matrix. Each element of design matrix, A_{ij}, may be expressed as

$$A_{ij} = \frac{\partial FR_i}{\partial DP_j}$$

So the independent design is shown by a diagonal matrix where diagonal elements are not zero, i.e:

$$A_{kk} \neq 0$$

$$A_{ij} = 0 \ , i \neq j$$

Similarly, the relationship of DPs and PVs are defined as

$$\{\mathbf{DP}\} = [B]\ \{\mathbf{PV}\} \qquad (2)$$

According to the Eqs. (1) and (2), we can deduce the relationships between FRs and PVs as

$$\{\mathbf{FR}\} = [A] * [B]\ \{\mathbf{PV}\} \qquad (3)$$

"Each component of the FR–DP–PV relationship must be uncoupled if the overall relationship is to fulfill the Independence Axiom" [8].

If the design matrix is diagonal, we have an uncoupled design. A design with triangular matrix is called a decoupled design. Independence Axiom is dissatisfied with coupled designs and in order to decouple such designs, some changes in the FRs and DPs are needed. If the DPs of a decoupled design are ordered in a special manner, the Independence Axiom is satisfied.

3 The principle of knowledge management

There is no specific definition for KM that all agree with it globally. A common problem in the definition of knowledge management is due to a wide range of knowledge. Knowledge management was initially defined as the process of applying a systematic approach to the capture, structuring, management, and dissemination of knowledge throughout an organization to work faster, reuse best practices, and reduce costly rework from project to project [12]. Dalkir [13] defines that "Knowledge management is the deliberate and systematic coordination of an organization's people, technology, processes, and organizational structure in order to add value through reuse and innovation".

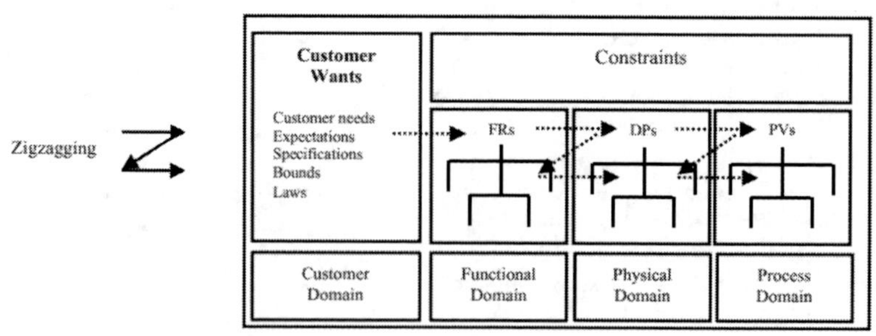

Fig. 1. Various domains of design in AD theory (enhanced from [11]).

In the traditional approach, the attractiveness of selected industry was a most important competitive advantage against competitors. But nowadays with increasing the uncertainty and dynamism in organizational environments, the new strategic researches have been focused on the 'structure - behavior - performance' model as a key competitive advantage that has led to the internal landscape called 'source-oriented'.

Knowledge is a most important strategic resource for companies in the 21st century. On the other hand, since the rate of failure of knowledge management projects is remarkable, identification of success critical factors of knowledge management can help organizations in needs assessment, planning, and implementation of knowledge management projects to reduce the failure probability. The knowledge management system is a sophisticated combine of technological infrastructure, organizational structures, organizational culture, knowledge, and people. The main objectives of a knowledge management system include:

1) Knowledge capture;
2) Improve knowledge access;
3) Enhance the knowledge environment;
4) Manage knowledge as an asset.

For knowledge management, various models has been offered by different scholars. Some of these models have focused on knowledge management activities such as the creation or transferring of knowledge, and the other models have considered a cycle of knowledge management generally and cover the various activities associated with knowledge. However, there is no knowledge management model which all agree with it.

4 A knowledge management system design using AD theory

In recent decades, extensive studies are conducted on various aspects of knowledge management systems. They cover design and implementation techniques with diverse methodologies and modeling. However, the Axiomatic Design methodology has been used by a few researchers.

Evrim Yasar et al. [14] in 2005, first began to design a knowledge management system based on the axiomatic design approach. They decomposed the main FR in three levels of functional requirements (FRs) and design parameters (DPs). This study is important because they are pioneers in applying AD theory in KMS design, however, in their study the effective factor of the knowledge management system have not been considered comprehensively.

The second study has been provided by Brown [15] in 2007. In this work, a knowledge management system has been designed based on axiomatic design principles with an overview in two levels of functional requirements (FRs) and design parameters (DPs). This study, same as the previous case, does not consider a detailed system design.

The third study, in 2013 by Hao et al. [16] entitled 'Knowledge Services In Campus: The Application Of Axiomatic Design'. In this paper, they present the knowledge services (KS) in a university setting. Hereby, they propose a tool, namely 'Knowledge Board' to achieve KS and support the knowledge sharing. This knowledge board has been designed and realized based on AD principles. Also, a case study has been conducted to exemplify the process of using AD to design knowledge services within a university environment.

As mentioned above, the previous studies have some shortcomings. Firstly, the factors affecting on knowledge management are not covered from various aspects. In other words, these factors have not been considered in functional requirements (FRs) of knowledge management system comprehensively, and secondly, for satisfying the design parameters (DPs), the process variables (PVs) have not been provided. That means the needs, how and by what processes must be satisfied have not been considered.

The advantage of the current study is that the design of the knowledge management system has been considered with the critical factors of KM comprehensively. Also, this study with respect to the objectives and strategies of the organization tries to answer the fundamental questions like: What approaches can help organization to achieve competitive advantages? How the organization can choose the route and processes to be able to apply the knowledge management system to achieve its own goals?

According to the AD fundamentals, we present the hierarchical structure to model the design processes of KMS. This structure is developed in a top-down direction, but for the implementation practices, we act based on a bottom-up pattern. The structure of the model of a knowledge management system is illustrated in Figure 2. The top level of the structure contains CNs, the ultimate goal of knowledge management systems. The next level is the conceptual notions of the knowledge management paradigm, formulated as FRs. The third level contains principles, explaining parameters that affect conceptual notions and formulated as DPs in the given model. The bottom level is methodologies,

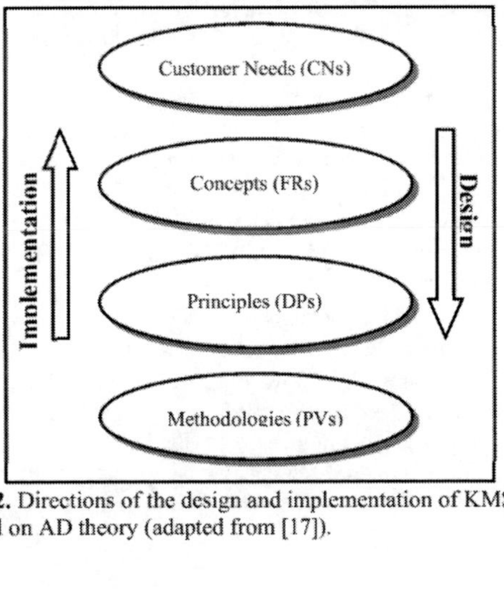

Fig. 2. Directions of the design and implementation of KMS based on AD theory (adapted from [17]).

consists of tools, resources, practices and techniques and formulated as PVs.

The abstract notions embedded in concepts (FRs) and principles (DPs) hamper their straightforward applications. But, the use of methodologies (PVs) could be helped to convert the theory into practical action.

The main purpose of this paper is to present a roadmap for the design and implementation of a knowledge management system based on the axiomatic design principles. To do it, the following steps have been taken:

1) Review of the basic concepts and principles of knowledge management;
2) Review of the basic concepts and principles of axiomatic design theory;
3) Review of a variety of models, strategies, methodologies, and cycles of knowledge management for extraction of the common factors of knowledge management systems;
4) Review of the factors of success and failure related to knowledge management systems, to evaluate the factors affecting on knowledge management systems;
5) Review of the organizational strategy document and discussion with experts to extract specific criteria for design the appropriate knowledge management system for the understudy organization (TUSROC);
6) Presenting a knowledge management system based on axiomatic design principles.

4.1 Model presentation

Now, companies and organizations persistence is to improve their outputs and performance based on the knowledge. The ability of knowledge management systems has been proven as an efficient tool to achieve this goal. This notion reflected in Figure 3. The applicability and successful implementation of this goal require a comprehensive view of all organizational factors. Hence, according to the results of extensive studies that have been conducted about the fundamental factors affecting on knowledge management systems, in this article six main factors affecting on a knowledge management system have been considered; that includes: 1. Organizational culture 2. Organizational structure 3. Human resources 4. Leadership and management 5. Information technology and 6. The external environment of the organization.

The main requirement of a knowledge management system (FR0) is 'Improving the organizational performance by knowledge based systems' which could be separated into the following six areas:

- Reduce resistance to change (FR1);
- Improve the organizational structure to adapt to change (FR2);
- Improve the human resources (FR3);
- Adoption of an excellence mentality (FR4);
- Develop the hardware and software basis (FR5);
- Use of external environment knowledge for the organization and vice versa (FR6).

To satisfy this requirement, six factors have been used as the related design parameters (DPs):

- Development and strengthening of organizational culture (DP1);
- Increasing the flexibility of the organizational structure (DP2);
- Expansion of the knowledge-based performance of personnel (DP3);
- Transformational leadership and management (DP4);
- Utilization of the IT techniques (DP5);
- Management of the external environment Knowledge (DP6).

The relationships of FRs and DPs of the first level of the model are shown in Figure 3.

Alignment of the FRs with organizational strategy was the most notable limitation of our study. Therefore, to satisfy FRs, the DPs and PVs were chosen based on the elites suggestions through extensive literature reviews and discussions with experts of the 'TUSROC'. Also, this study assumes that the chosen DPs and PVs will satisfy the FRs appropriately. For example, to satisfy FR1, it is suggested that knowledge management culture should be adopted and expanded thorough organization. However, the knowledge management culture may not be fully accepted by everyone. It is necessary to remark that in the implementation phase some of the FRs may not be adequately met; in this case, it is essential to revise DPs and PVs.

4.1.1 Organizational culture

Careful analysis of the components of a knowledge management system, displayed in Figure 3 shows that the organizational culture (DP1) is the Achilles heel of the knowledge management system, because it is associated with 'Improve the human resources' (FR3), 'Adoption of an excellence mentality' (FR4), and 'Use of external environment knowledge for the organization and vice versa' (FR6). It was predictable because when Robert Bachmann was asked to name three factors critical to knowledge management, said: "culture, culture, culture" [18]. The organizational culture is very important for the success of knowledge management system because any organizational change will be successful when the entire of the organization is committed to the processes of change [19]. Hence, the relationship of 'Development and strengthening of organizational culture' (DP1) with FR3 and FR4 is revealed. Also, each organization should commit itself to improving its stakeholders, thus DP1 will affect on FR6. For additional descriptions of these relationships refer to [20, 21].

For more explanation of the relationship between 'Reduce resistance to change' (FR1) and 'Development and strengthening of organizational culture' (DP1) and 'Creating the knowledge management culture' (PV1) we can state that "knowledge culture is a way of organizational life that enables and motivates people to create, share and utilize knowledge for the benefit and enduring success of the organization" [20]. So a knowledge management culture may be divided into three subcategories:

1) The knowledge sharing culture;

 DOI: 10.1051/matecconf/201712701022

2) The knowledge acquisition culture;
3) The knowledge creating culture.

Decomposition of the components of FR1 is shown in Figure 4.

Srivastava et al. [22] with an appropriate definition, introduce the knowledge sharing. They say "knowledge sharing is a critical team process that involves members interacting to share ideas, information, and suggestions relevant to the team's task at hand". Several studies have been done on factors influencing knowledge sharing in organizations and communities in order to facilitate the knowledge sharing. Gruber and Duxbury [23] identified several major factors in knowledge sharing culture, including openness, trust, availability, usage of different communication channels, and reward system in an organization. Another study shows the 'openness' and 'enjoy helping' have a strong relationship with knowledge sharing behavior [24]. Al-Alawi et al. [25] have investigated the role of certain factors in

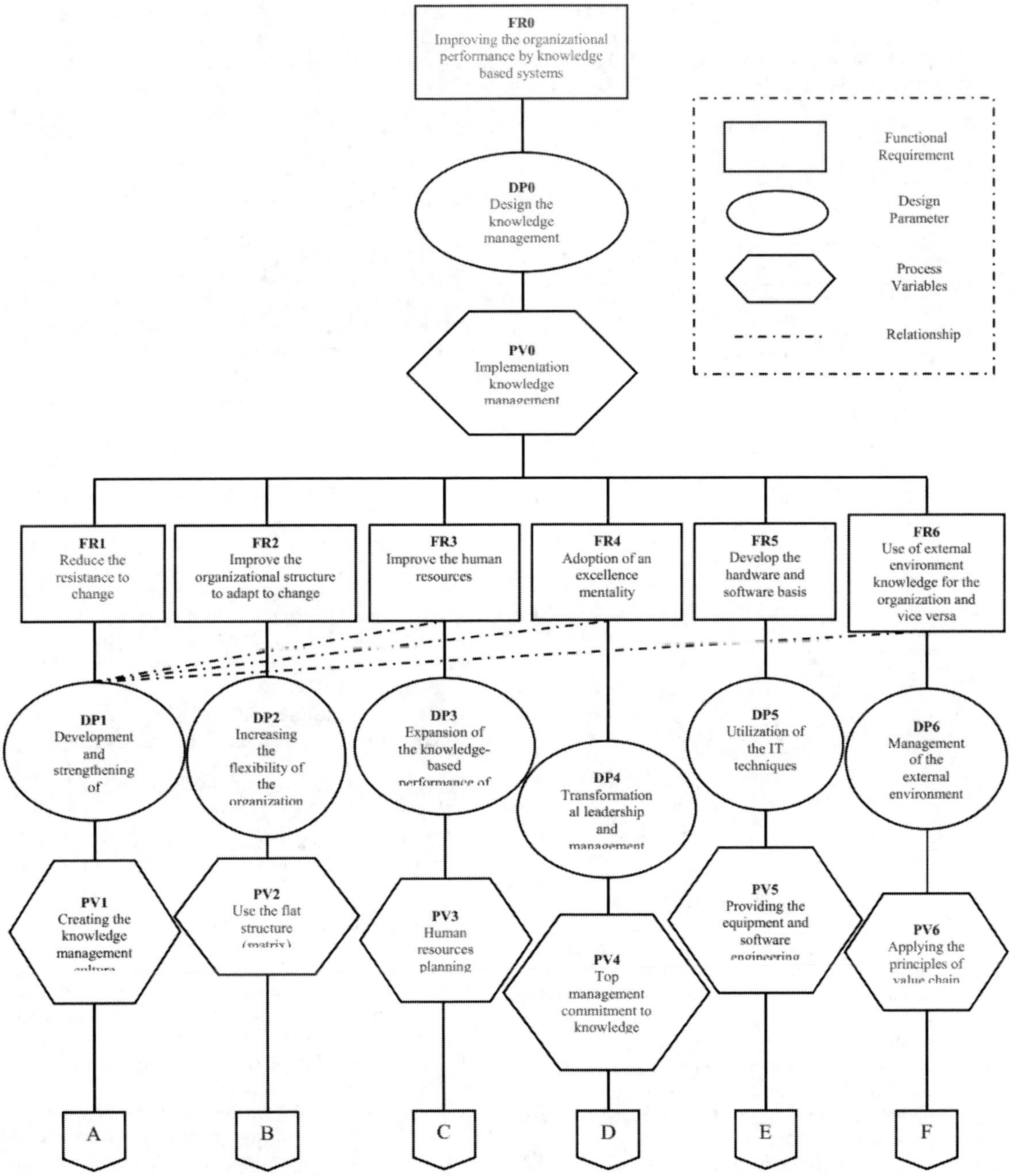

Fig. 3. First level of the knowledge management system decomposition.

organizational culture in the success of knowledge sharing using survey and a number of interviews with staff from various organizations in Bahrain from the public and private sectors. The research findings indicate that trust, communication, information systems, rewards and organization structure are positively related to knowledge sharing in organizations.

According to the most studies, 'openness' and 'trust' have the most impact on knowledge sharing in the organization, these issues are reflected in Figure 5 by the relationship of the 'Building a culture of openness' (DP112) with 'Build the trust in the organization' (FR113) and 'Use of employee suggestions' (FR114) and as well as the impact of FR114 on 'Creating a culture of trust' (DP113). Since FR113 is an abstract and intangible issue, it is decomposed further (see Figure 6 and 7).

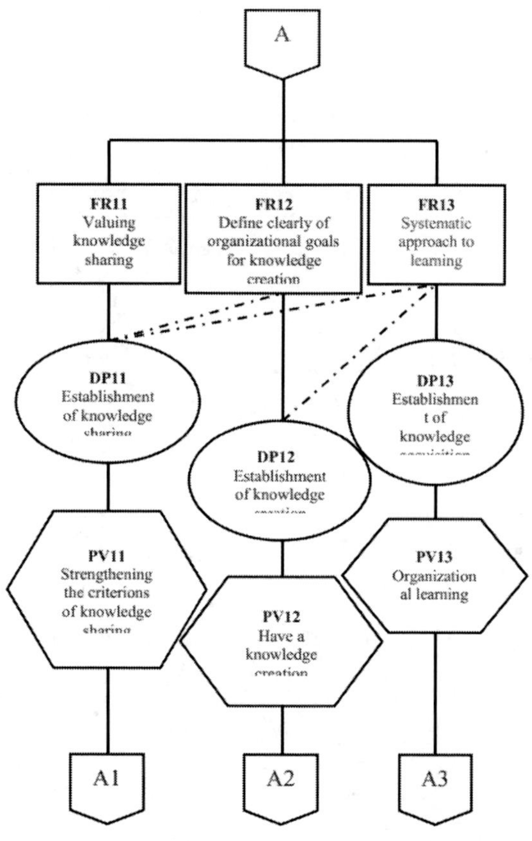

Fig. 4. Decomposition of FR1 'Reduce resistance to change'.

The knowledge creation is replacement or improvement of existing organizational knowledge through social relations and organizational cooperation [26]. By using new knowledge the organizations can improve their performance, capability and the appropriate use of existing resources. Hence the realization of concepts such as continuous improvement, organizational development, and sustainable competitive advantage depends on the continuation of the process of knowledge creation in the organization. Idea generation and opportunity exploration, enhance directly 1. Stimulating and probing employees to generate ideas (intellectual stimulation), 2. Supporting open and transparent communication processes, 3. Creating avenues for knowledge sharing and diffusion, and 4. Assigning challenging tasks to employees [27]. The studies about creativity show that employees are willing to create unusual and useful ideas. Experiences have shown that the supportive and informative assessment of employees may improve the internal motivation, which is beneficial for creativity. Organizations may be successful in exploiting knowledge in the short-term, however, in the long term, the learning and knowledge creation occurs less. Knowledge creation skills are very important and the improvement of knowledge is required to develop new processes. Success indicators of knowledge creation are the assessment of the validity of knowledge, acceptance of knowledge and preparation for using it in the organization. According to what was said, the decomposition and the relationship between components of 'Define clearly of organizational goals for knowledge creation' (FR12) are shown in Figure 8.

Another component of 'Reduce resistance to change' (FR1) is 'Systematic approach to learning' (FR13) which 'Establishment of knowledge acquisition culture' (DP13) and 'Organizational learning' (PV13) provide the tools, resources, and procedures to satisfy it. It should be noted that by improving communication and interaction among employees and relying on different knowledge structures, the organizational capacity increases to acquire new knowledge and innovating idea to achieve the objectives. Peter Senge [28] believes that "The only sustainable competitive advantage is an organization's ability to learn faster than the competitors". Organizational learning occurs when the information is collected and analyzed for the creation and development of new facts, then with communication, teaching, dialogue, and interaction of personnel is spread to all levels of the organization. The process variables that have been intended to acquire knowledge includes:

- User ID definition for access to organizational documents (PV131);
- Team-based learning (PV132);
- Provision of requirements and research grant (PV133);
- Analysis of process flow (PV134);
- Teamwork workshops (PV135);
- Database creation (PV136).

Figure 9 shows the relationship of components of FR13.

4.1.2 Organizational structure

Figure 10 presents the decomposition of 'Improve the organizational structure to adapt to change' (FR2). Since the organizational structure is the framework of organizational processes and activities of employees, it is the driving force behind organizational changes. In other words, without a suitable organizational structure, having the best employees and enormous investments on knowledge management implementation will not be useful. Organizational structure is generally described according to degree of centralization, formalization, complexity [29] .Organizational structure can enhance or impede the success of knowledge management system. The centralization and formalization are critical factors in organizational structure that impede the creation, transmission, storage and application of knowledge directly. Low centralization and formality improves organizational effectiveness by increasing the level of organizational interaction, employee motivation, and flexibility [30]. The existence of formality and centralization decreases the amount of creative solutions, while the autonomy in the organization causes self-motivation, empiricism, and freedom of expression [31].

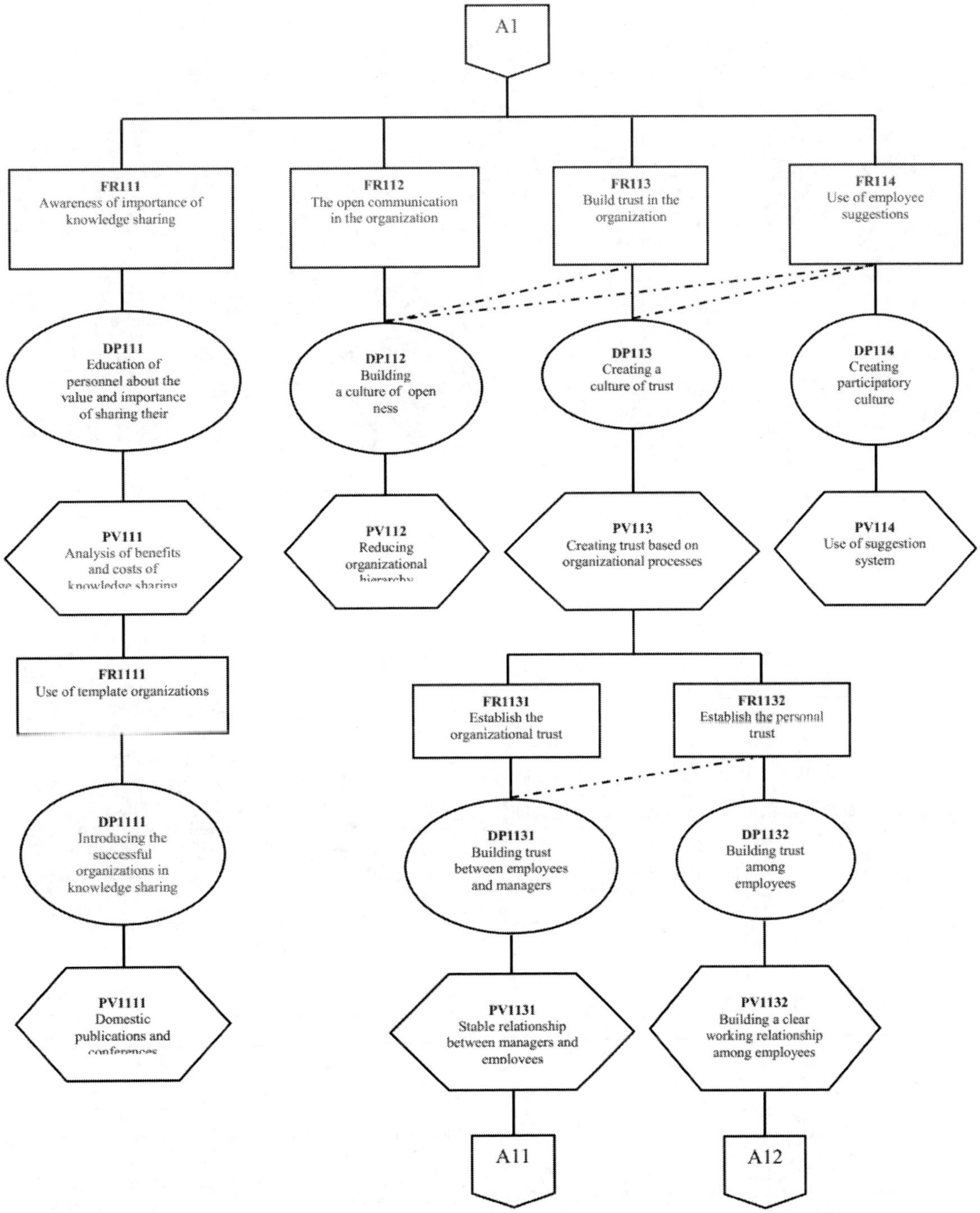

Fig. 5. Decomposition of FR11 'Valuing knowledge sharing'.

DOI: 10.1051/matecconf/201712701022

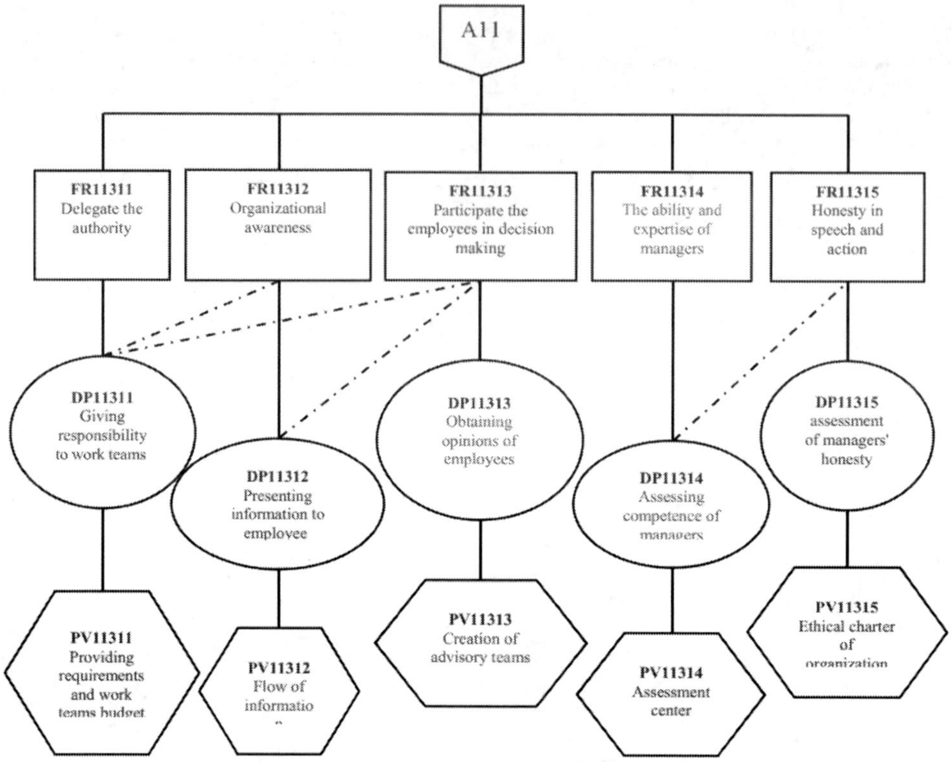

Fig. 6. Decomposition of FR1131 'Establish the organizational trust'.

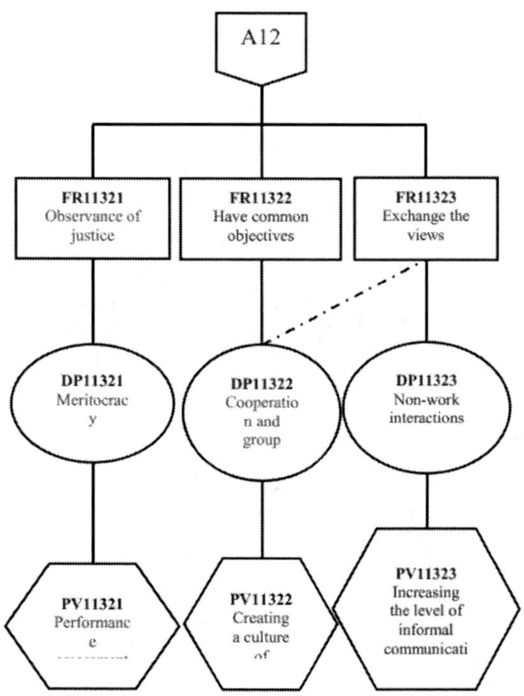

Fig. 7. Decomposition of FR1132 'Establish the personal trust'.

4.1.3 Human resources

The employees of an organization are the main source of competitive advantage because the human resources of any organization are not easily copied by competitors. Competitors can easily produce the same products, can use the same technology and can access to same capital markets. While these competitors cannot easily provide similar conditions to attract and retain human talent, these conditions are formed during a long period of time. Also, copy of social relations derived from human resources is difficult. Therefore, the capabilities of human resources has become to be one of the most fundamental sources of sustainable competitive advantage [32].

The human resources issues such as recruitment and selection, training, performance management, pay and reward system as well as creating a culture of learning are essential for knowledge management [33]. Improvement of human resources is a set of methods and measures that the organization and managers are using to improve efficiency, productivity, motivation, improvement of quality, performance assessment, job satisfaction, dynamism, and creativity of employees according to the goals of the organization. Yang Fong et al. [34] in their study concluded that recruitment and selection, teamwork, training and development, and performance appraisal, shows a positive relationship with knowledge sharing. The relationship of these items is shown in Figure 11.

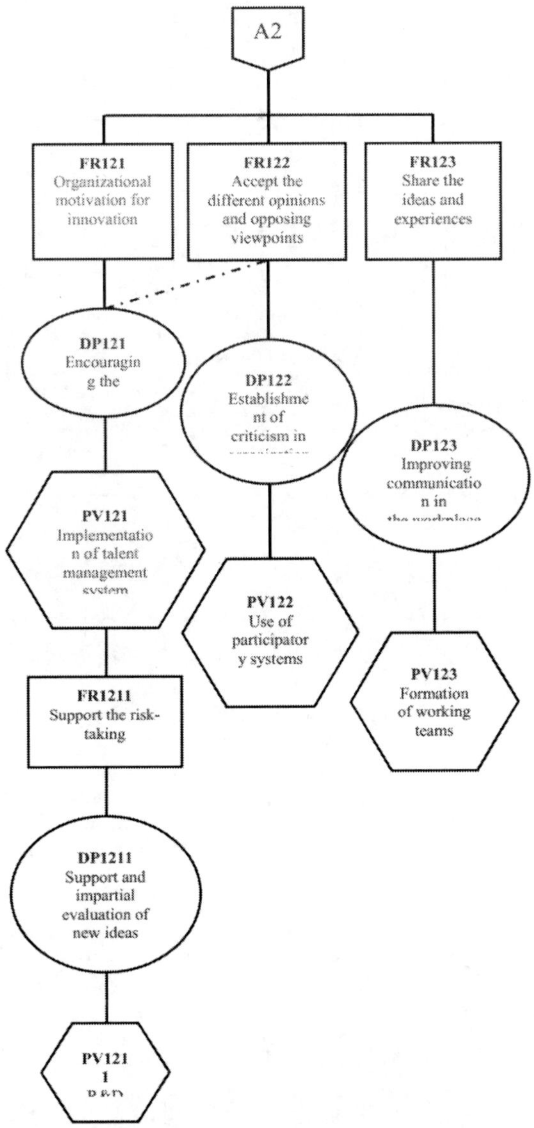

Fig. 8. Decomposition of FR12 'Define clearly of organizational goals for knowledge creation'.

4.1.4 Management and leadership

Another top-level FRs of the model is 'Adoption of an excellence mentality' (FR4), that is necessary for successful implementation of knowledge management system. 'Transformational leadership and management' (DP4) is considered to satisfy FR4. Successful implementation of knowledge management systems requires the commitment of top level of management to knowledge management efforts. In other words, a paradigm shift in the philosophy of top management is needed to be focused on defining the vision, goals, roles and responsibilities of top management. Many researchers believe that the attributes of positive leadership in different levels of management are one of the most important requirements to create a knowledge culture. The relationship of the DP1 with FR4 shows this issue. The mentioned attributes include empowering subordinates, allocation of resources, openness towards change and experimentation, developing trust, tolerance to mistakes, and building long-term perspective of the organizational goals among employees [20]. Senior managers must have the following characteristics:

- The ability to coordinate the various units involved in the implementation of knowledge management processes (FR41);
- Realistic prediction of the results of knowledge management activities (FR42);
- Persuading the employees to innovate (FR43);
- Constant communication with employees and considering their ideas (FR44).

Elenkov [35] believes that “Intellectual stimulation has been viewed as a leadership behavior that challenges followers to re-examine some of their assumptions about their work and rethink how it can be performed”. The attention to all employees is one of the new theories of leadership. This means that the leader observes the everyone’s behaviors and is aware of their activities. The leaders assess the individual situation of employees and spend the time to guide, train, and recognize their abilities and creativities. Therefore, they can plan to develop employees capabilities. These factors have a positive effect on learning, development, satisfaction, effort and commitment of employees. Decomposition of FR4 is presented in Figure 12.

4.1.5 Information technology

Organizations use IT to control and manage their knowledge assets. In other words, organizations use information technology to provide the possibility to achieve a competitive advantage through knowledge assets. In fact, IT is a phenomenon that has arisen from widespread usage of computer systems in organizations, society, and its profound transformation. Providing information systems such as the internet, intranet, extranet, groupware, etc. for storage, transfer, and exchange of knowledge, as well as providing the facilities for easy access to the hardware and software for sharing information are necessary. The employees, by aids of information systems, will help organizations to gain information technology in knowledge management system effectively. Knowledge management and information technology are strongly linked together to promote structured knowledge in organizations. The important role of information technology is supporting organizational communications, collaboration, empowerment of the cooperative learning and search of knowledge. Requirements for an effective IT system include information quality, flexible IT infrastructure, access to hardware, access to software, network, and information systems [36].The tools that can be used to meet the goals of information technology in the knowledge management system include:

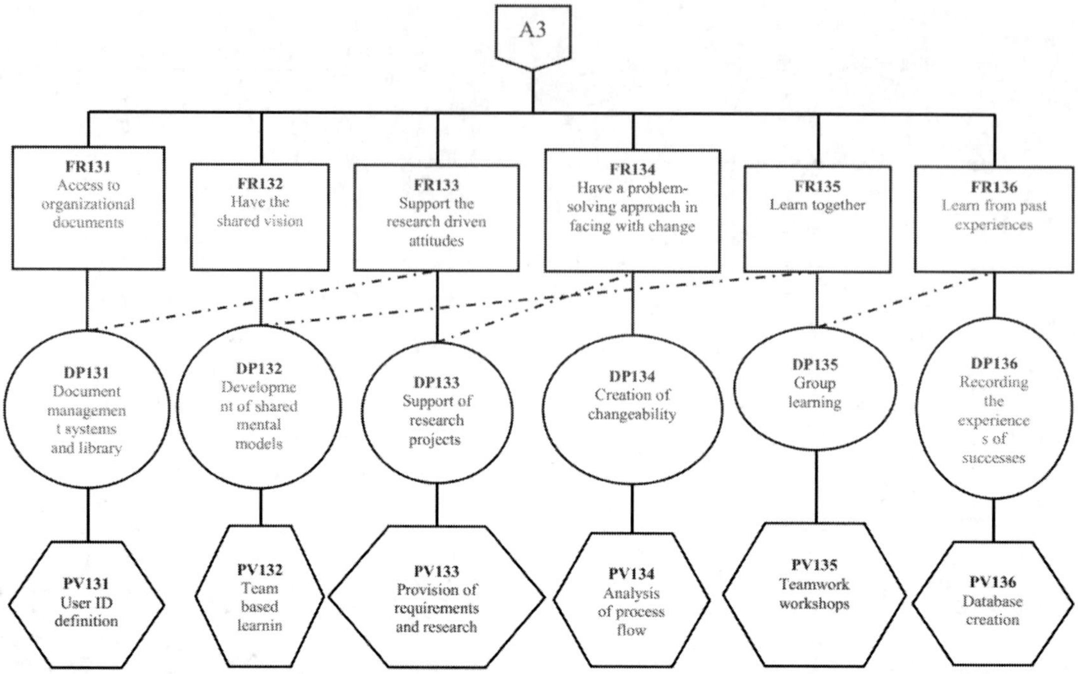

Fig. 9. Decomposition of FR13 'Systematic approach to learning'.

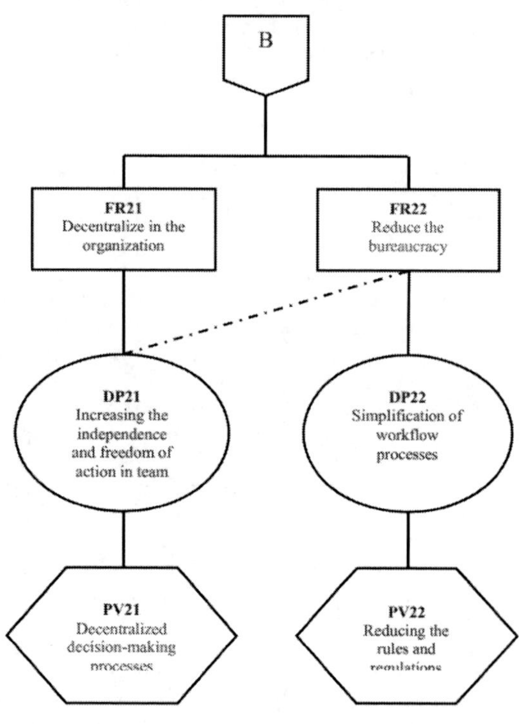

Fig. 10. Decomposition of FR2 'Improve the organizational structure to adapt to change'.

- The comprehensive software of knowledge management system (DP51): is a web-based information system that can be installed on a local and global computer network and has the capability of acquiring, creating, storing, sharing and retrieval of knowledge that created by the employees during work processes.
- Network-based tools (DP52): information networks are the suitable environment for sharing dynamic information that the hypertext structure of it facilitates the review of information and access to classified information.
- Decision support system (DP53): a decision support system (DSS) is a computer-based information system that supports business or organizational decision-making activities, typically resulting in ranking, sorting, or choosing from among alternatives. DSSs serve the management, operations, and planning levels of an organization and help people make decisions about problems that may be rapidly changing and not easily specified in advance problems. DSSs include knowledge-based systems. A properly designed DSS is an interactive software-based system intended to help decision makers compile useful information from a combination of raw data, documents, and personal knowledge, or business models to identify and solve problems and make decisions.
- Knowledge-based systems (DP54): includes a knowledge base in the limited field that provides an inference mechanism, the changing of information and entering new data.

The relationship between FRs, DPs, PVs in the field of information technology is shown in Figure 13.

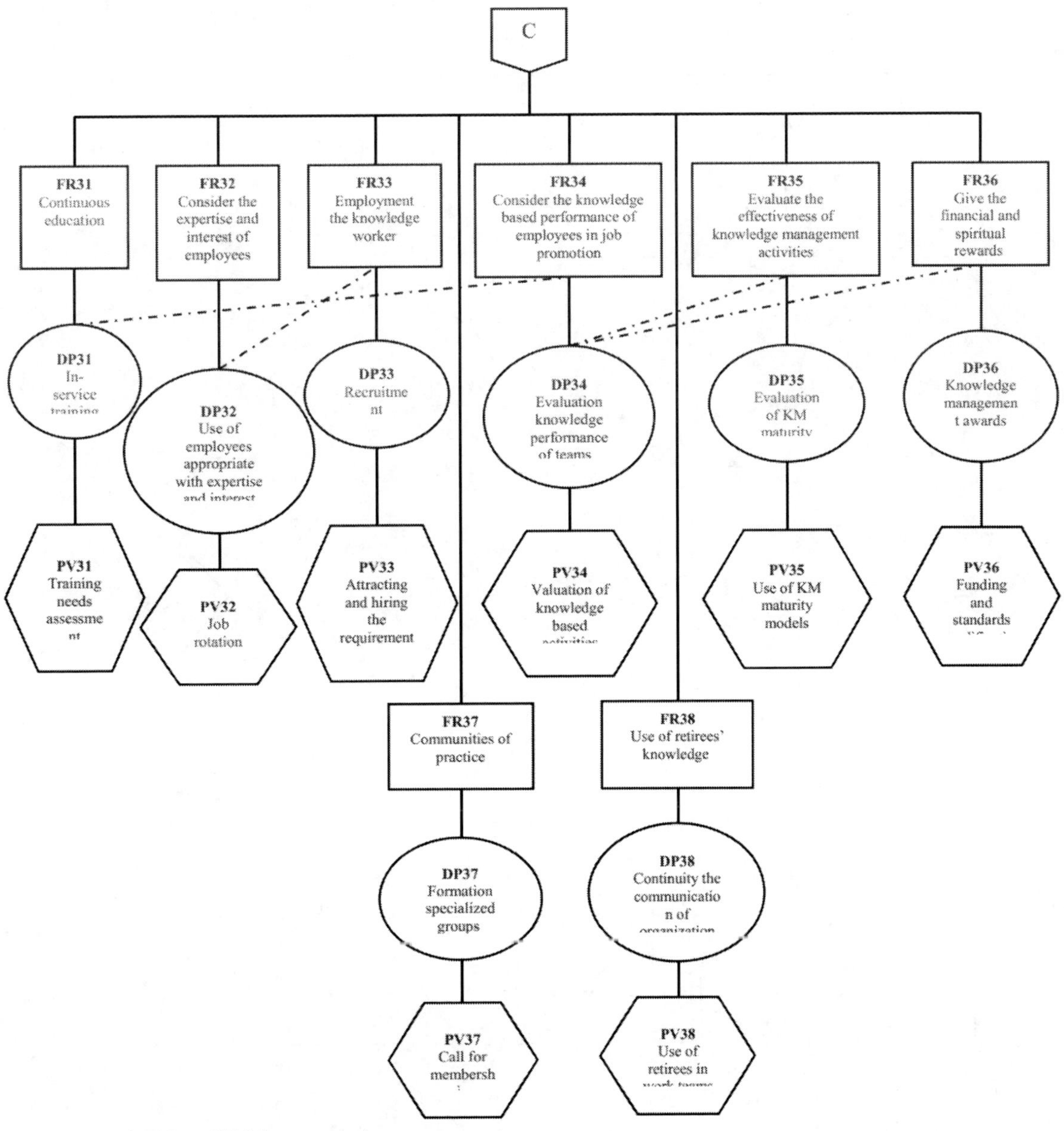

Fig. 11. Decomposition of FR3 'Improve the human resources'.

4.1.6 The external environment of organization

Since the business activities of organizations have been transferred to the supply chain level, the challenge of managers is keeping the competitive advantage by creating the stronger relationships with employees, customers, suppliers, upstream and downstream partners.

Fugate et al. [37] for acquiring knowledge in logistics systems, introduce the several factors which includes: polling customers, visiting customers' sites for better understanding of their needs, being involved in sales activities, being involved in helping to resolve customer problems, accompanying employees who deliver logistic services to observe how things work, visiting facilities of leading companies, visiting suppliers to learn more about various aspects of their business, attending events that allow networking, such as business colleges, research bodies, industry associations, trade shows, reading reports from the government and regulatory bodies. Liao & Wu [38] introduced the other indicators, including: processes for acquiring knowledge about customers and suppliers, use feedback from projects to improve subsequent projects, exchanging knowledge with business partners, acquiring knowledge about new product/services within their industry, acquiring knowledge about competitors, benchmarking performance, and formation of teams devoted to identifying best practice.

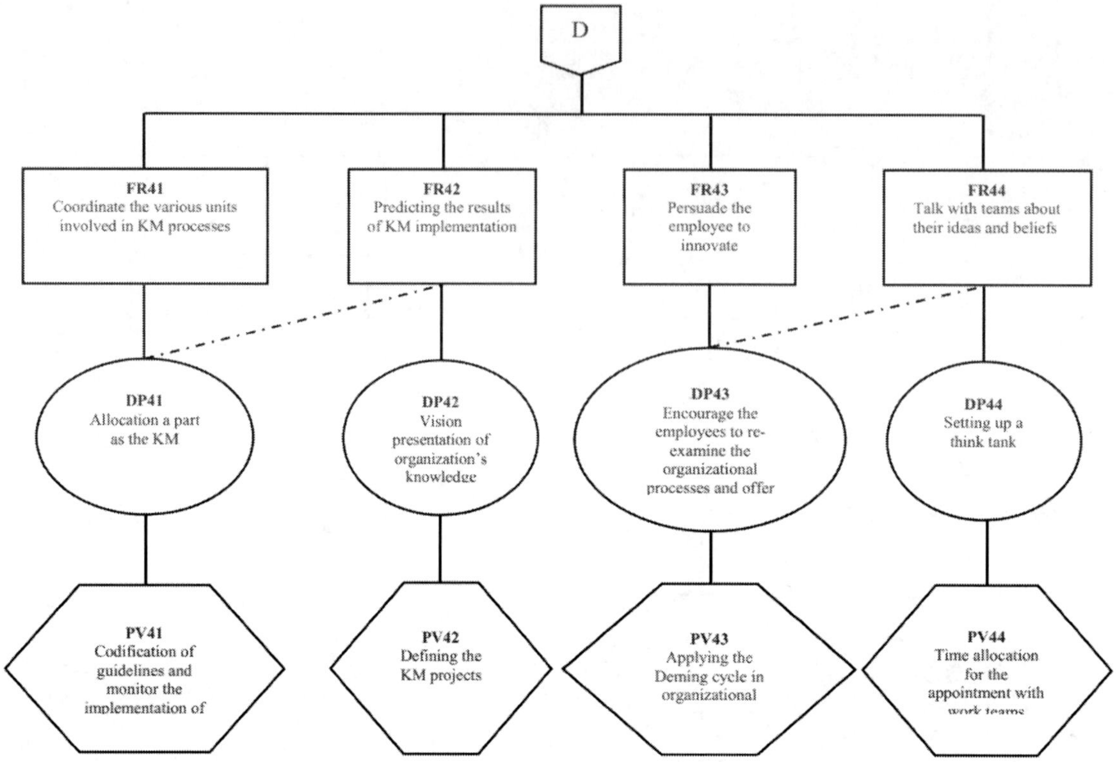

Fig. 12. Decomposition of FR4 'Adoption of an excellence mentality'.

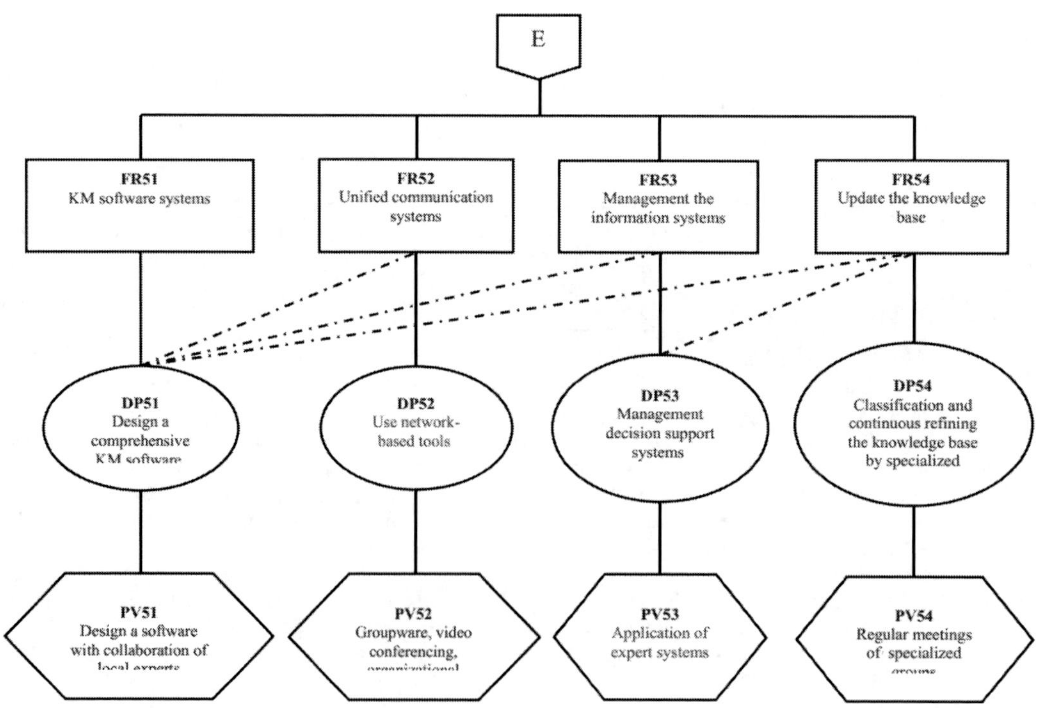

Fig. 13. Decomposition of FR5 'Develop the hardware and software basis'.

Fawcett et al. [39] have divided the process of knowledge sharing among supply chain into two key areas that are the communications and trends. They have introduced the indicators for the communications sector, such as: integration of information systems, high integrity of informational applications, systems related to customers, information systems for communications with chain members. Trends sector indicators include: regular communications with high frequency among members of the chain, sharing the information among members of the chain, the use of cross-functional groups, technical information sharing with suppliers and customers, senior level managerial interaction among supply chain members and use of supply chain teams with members from multiple firms. Hence, it seems that cloud-based solutions have the capability to provide KM services for enhancing the competitive advantage, share price, market share, productivity, response time, profitability, and decision making of the organization. Therefore, cloud-based solutions are the new tools that assist greatly in knowledge management efforts of an organization. The relationships of parameters, tools, and processes that has been considered for the management of supplier's knowledge is shown in the Figure 15.

Nowadays, with the growth of customer's role in the competition, the information and knowledge of them have become more important in knowledge acquiring from the external environment of the organization that could be an important source for innovation. Today's the customers have a valuable information about companies, products, services, markets, and competitors that are stored in the minds of customers implicitly and can be affected on innovation directly and on the efficiency of innovation indirectly. So that many organizations are looking for managing the customer knowledge along with knowledge of the organization to acquire the knowledge and ideas of customers [40]. Related knowledge of customers has different shapes and are derived from three channels. These channels are 1. The analysis of customer data, 2. Engagement with the customer, 3. Observation of the customer behavior [41]. Figure 16 shows how these factors are applied.

Another important component of the knowledge management of the external environment of an organization is 'Use of competitor's knowledge' (FR63). Figure 17 presents the decomposition of it. The knowledge of competitors is consists of the key capabilities of the competitors. In other words, competitor information contains all of the data about competitor's outputs [42]. By using this information, managers are able to make-decision with a complete notion of the current situation and future of the competition. The experts of the competitive intelligence community, state that the competitive intelligence is an ethical and systematic program for the collection, analysis, and management of the external organization's information that effecting on the programs of the organization. In other words, competitive intelligence is the improvement process of competitive ability in the market, through attention to the competitors and the competitive environment, especially for the collection and analysis of the information of capabilities, weaknesses, and intentions of business competitors by using the databases and open resources, ethically and legally. García-Murillo and Annabi [43] consider the competitor knowledge as a part of the organizational knowledge that components of it are: competitors as a partner, the knowledge of competitor's customer, the knowledge of competitor's market, the knowledge of competitor's suppliers and the knowledge of competitor's products/services. Some of the usefulnesses of competitive intelligence are:

- Increasing the confidence level of strategic decisions based on the competitive intelligence;
- Increasing market knowledge;
- Improvement of cross-functional communications in the organization;
- To help predict the market trends and fluctuations;
- Improvement of competitor's strategy prediction;
- Discovering the new customers;
- Learning lessons from success and failure of others;
- Facilitating to enter into new business;
- Increasing the productivity;
- Increasing the ability to adapt to the environmental changes.

5 Discussion

If we believe that the knowledge management is one of the requirements and competitive advantages of the organizations, we should use it carefully. The first and fundamental step to carry out a knowledge management system successfully is a right designing for it. The right design is a design that considers the needs of organizations and provides the tools, techniques, suitable and optimized processes to meet them. The main purpose of this study is the usage of the axiomatic design theory capability to design a knowledge management system for 'TUSROC' to providing suitable tools and process to satisfy the requirements of its knowledge management system that is adapting to change and moving towards innovation.

In knowledge management system based on axiomatic design, design starts with a defined framework and proceeds systematically. The creative actions are used by considering the appropriate DPs and PVs. In this work general requirements of knowledge management systems considered in the general framework of AD model, however, the specific needs, capabilities, and resources of 'TUSROC' that extracted from the strategic document and discussion with experts of 'TUSROC' have been considered as FRs, DPs, and PVs in different levels of the model. The important advantage of an AD-based model of knowledge management system is the formation of plausible relationships among different levels of design, conceptual level to practical levels. The procedure that we used in this model can be used to design a knowledge management system in any other organization.

DOI: 10.1051/matecconf/201712701022

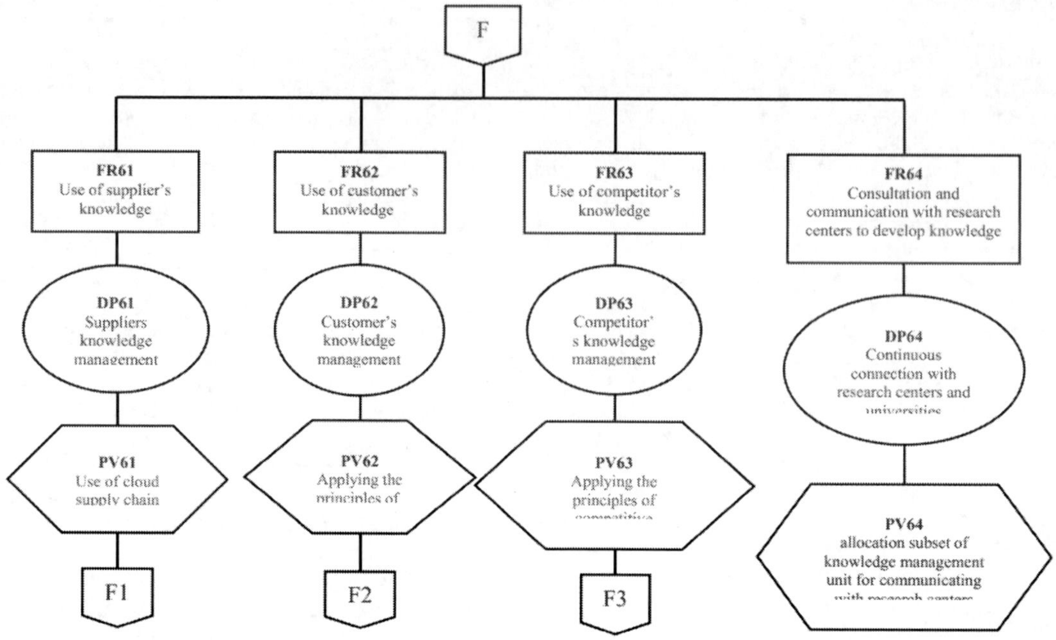

Fig. 14. Decomposition of FR6 'Use of external environment knowledge for the organization and vice versa'.

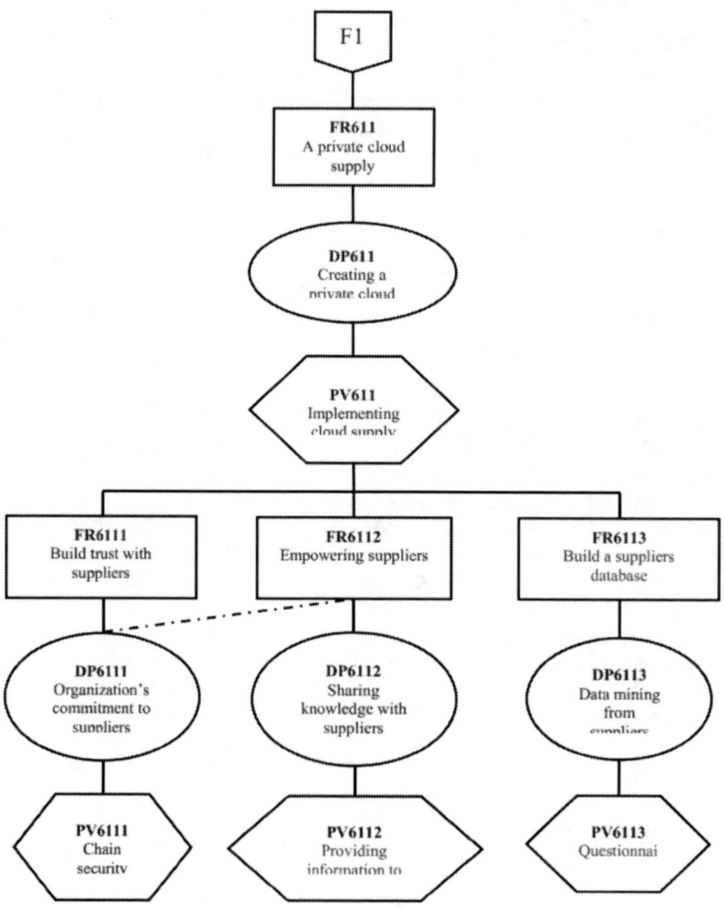

Fig. 15. Decomposition of FR61 'Use of supplier's knowledge'.

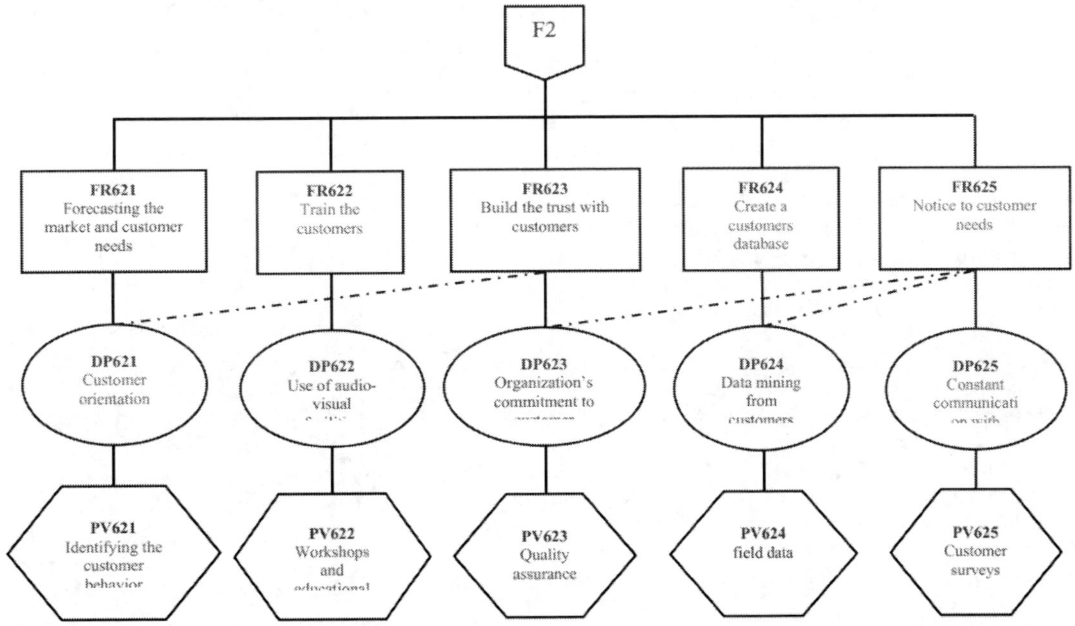

Fig. 16. Decomposition of FR62 'Use of customer's knowledge'.

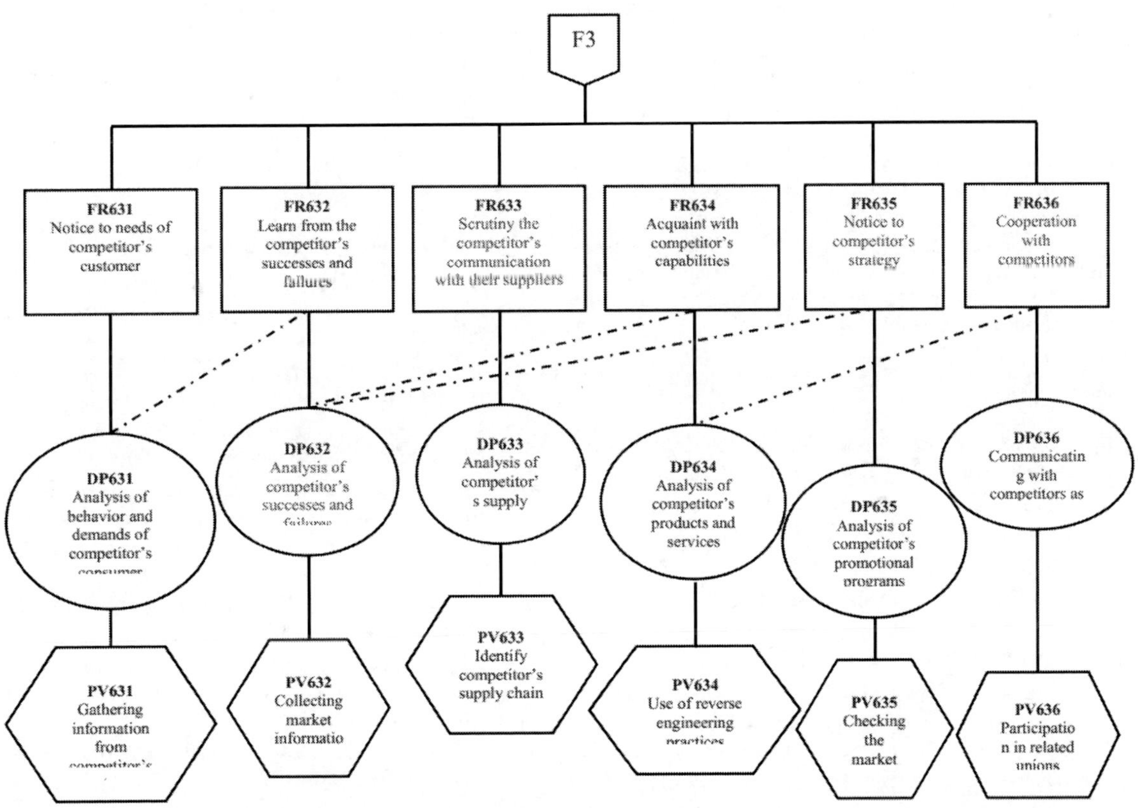

Fig. 17. Decomposition of FR63 'Use of competitor's knowledge'.

6 Conclusion

The AD based knowledge management system design for 'TUSROC' is discussed in this paper. We proposed an axiomatic model that provides a scientific base for concepts, principles, and methodologies of a knowledge management system and thereby alleviating many existing implementation shortcomings such as: lack of a scientific foundation for knowledge management and its associated transformation process, lack of precisely identified needs and reasons for change, resistance to change etc. The clear and tangible results of this work are:

1) Presenting a roadmap for design and implementation of a knowledge management system in 'TUSROC'. This model implemented in 'TUSROC' and so far the results have been very promising.
2) Learning: The developed AD model for KM can easily be transferred to novices to acquire the concepts and procedure of knowledge management system.
3) Using AD principles and relying on axioms of the subject, reduced the trial and error and the risk of failure.
4) The formation of plausible relationships among different levels of the model helps to implement issues easily.
5) By separating the functional requirements, parameters, and variables, it is possible to predict the results of activities. This helps orientation of future decision-making, control of activities, and allocation of resources where knowledge management system is implemented.
6) Providing a common and clear procedure in the framework of the design, it will help to communicate between different sectors of the system effectively.

For future research, it is suggested that the proposed model in this study to be optimized by applying the second axiom of the AD theory to consider several DP for each FR and several PV for each DP.

References

1. J. Zhao, P. Ordonez de Pablos, Z. Qi, Computers in Human Behavior **28**, 2 (2012)
2. M. Donate, J. Sanchez de Pablo, J. Business Research **68**, 2 (2015)
3. G. Natarajan, KM Review **8**, 2 (2005)
4. L.A. Kubo, J. Knowledge acquisition **3**, 3 (2006)
5. A. Rhem, KM institute, available at: http://www.kminstitute.org., 22 Sep (2015)
6. C. Lopez-Nicolas, A. Merono-Cerdan, Int. J. Information Management **31**, 6 (2011)
7. M. Houshmand, B. Jamshidnezhad, *The second international conference on axiomatic design* (MA, USA, 2002)
8. N.P. Suh, *The Principles of Design* (New York: Oxford University Press, 1990)
9. N.P. Suh, *Axiomatic Design: Advances and Applications* (New York: Oxford University Press, 1st edition, 2001)
10. D.G. Lee, N.P. Suh, *Axiomatic Design and Fabrication of Composite Structures: Applications in Robots, Machine Tools, and Automobiles* (New York: Oxford University Press, 2006)
11. V.R. Reynal, D.S. Cochran, *The Lean Aircraft Initiative Report Series* (RP96-07-28, 1996)
12. I. Nonaka, H. Takeuchi, *The Knowledge-Creating Company* (New York: Oxford University Press, 1995)
13. K. Dalkir, *Knowledge management in theory and practice* (Amsterdam, Netherlands: Elsevier, 2007)
14. A.E. Yasar, M.B. Durmusoglu, M. Dincmen, *the 35th International Conference on Computers and Industrial Engineering* (Istanbul, Turkey, 2005)
15. C.A. Brown, *SAE TECHNICAL PAPER SERIES* (World Congress, Detroit, Michigan, USA, 2007)
16. Y. Hao, J. Kantola, R.R.V. Arenas, M. Wu, *The Seventh International Conference on Axiomatic Design* (WORCESTER, MA, USA, 2013)
17. M. Houshmand, B. Jamshidnezhad, Robotics and Computer-Integrated Manufacturing **22**, 1 (2006)
18. C. O'Dell, C.J. Grayson, California Management Review **40**, 3 (1998)
19. P. Lange, B. Coltham, Performance Improvement **44**, 2 (2005)
20. Oliver, K.R. Kandadi, J. Knowledge Management **10**, 4 (2006)
21. P. Akhavan, M.E. Sanjaghi, J. Rezaeenoor, H. Ojaghi, J. Information and knowledge management systems, **44**, 2 (2014)
22. A. Srivastava, K.M. Bartol, E.A. Locke, Academy of Management Journal **49** (2006)
23. H. Gruber, L. Duxbury, available at: http://www.hc-sc.gc.ca/iacb-dgiac/km-gs/ english/ duxbury en. Pdf., (2001)
24. T. Yu, L. Lu, T. Liu, J. Computers in Human Behavior **26**, 1 (2009)
25. A. Al-Alawi, N.Y. Al-Marzooqi, F.M. Yasmeen, J. Knowledge Management **11**, 2 (2007)
26. T.H. Davenport, L. Prusak, *Working knowledge: How organizations manage what they know* (Cambridge, MA: Harvard Business School Press, 1998)
27. J.P.J.D. Jong, D.N. Den Hartog, Eur. J. Innovation Management **10**, 1 (2007)
28. P.M. Senge, *The fifth discipline: The art and practice of the learning organization* (New York: Doubleday Currency, 1990)
29. D. Miller, C. Droge, Administrative Science Quarterly **31** (1986)
30. N. Piercy, D. Cravens, Eur. J. Marketing **29**, 3 (1994)

31. F.S. Ganjavi, F. Firoozi Nia, A.R. Roohazad, T. Mahallati, Int. J. Economics, Commerce and Management **3**, 3 (2015)
32. G.L. Stewart, K.G. Brown, *Human Resource Management. Linking Strategy to Practice* (New York: John Wiley, 2009)
33. I.R. Edvardsson, Department of Human Resource Management, University of Strathclyde, Occasional Paper **14** (2003)
34. F.C. Yang, O. Keng-Boon, T. Boon-In, L. Voon-Hsien, C. AlainYee-Loong, Int. J. Manpower **32**, 5 (2011)
35. D.S. Elenkov, J. Business Research **55** (2002)
36. Y.J. Yeh, S.Q. Lai, C.T. Ho, Industrial Management & Data Systems **106**, 6 (2006)
37. S.B. Fugate, P.T. Stank, T.J. Mentzer, J. Operations Management **27**, 3 (2009)
38. S.H. Liao, C.C. Wu, Int. J. Business and Management **4**, 4 (2009)
39. S.E. Fawcett, P. Osterhaus, G.M. Magnan, J.C. Brau, M.W. McCarter, Supply Chain Management: an Int. J. **12**, 5 (2007)
40. L.D. Hollebeek, Australasian Marketing Journal **21**, 1 (2013)
41. J. Yang, Int. J. Production Economics **125**, 2 (2010)
42. S.M. Tseng, J. Retailing and Consumer Services **19** (2012)
43. M. García-Murillo, H. Annabi, J. Operational Research Society **53**, 8 (2002)

AUTHOR INDEX

EDP Sciences – Web of Conferences
17, Avenue du Hoggar
Parc d'Activité de Courtabouf
BP 112
F-91944 Les Ulis Cedex A
France

ISBN 978-1-5108-4970-9

CURRAN ASSOCIATES INC.
proceedings.com